UNIVERSALITY OF THE
SIKH RELIGION

Dr. Jaspal Singh Mayell

Mayell Publishers
Stamford, CT USA

UNIVERSALITY OF THE SIKH RELIGION

Key Words: Universality, Honesty, Equality, Sharing, Truth, Pray, Sikh History, Truthful Living, Guru Nanak, Guru Granth Sahib, Conflicts, Miracles, Education, Eating, Drinking, Punjabi Language, Propagation of the Sikh Religion.

ISBN 0-9777907-0-3

First Edition 2006

LIBRARY OF CONGRESS CONTROL NUMBER: 2006901016

Distributor
South Asia Books
2204 Nelwood Drive
Columbia, Missouri, 65203 USA
Email sabook@juno.com

Printed in India by Unistar Books, Chandigarh
This book is printed on acid free paper.

Publisher

Mayell Publishers, Stamford, Connecticut, USA

UNIVERSALITY OF THE

SIKH RELIGION

Dr. Jaspal Singh Mayell

With the help and cooperation of my wife Parkash Kaur Mayell

To my children and their spouses

Mr.	Manvin Singh Mayell	(Son)
Mrs.	Anoo Mayell	(Daughter-in-law)
Mr.	Christopher Andrew Sabo	(Son-in-law)
Mrs.	Nita Sabo	(Daughter)

And especially to my grand children

Mr. Dylan Andrew Singh Sabo
Mr. Zephan Singh Mayell
Mr. Spencer Taran Singh Sabo
Mr. Rohan Singh Mayell

Front Picture
Courtesy of www. Sacredsites.com and Martin Gray

LOGO FOR UNIVERSALITY
Designed by Dr. Jaspal Singh Mayell

UNIVERSALITY OF THE SIKH RELIGION

FORMULA FOR WORLD PEACE

RESPECT ALL RELIGIONS

FOLLOW YOUR OWN

UNIVERSALITY OF THE SIKH RELIGION
HONESTY
SHARING
EQUALITY
ੴ
ONE GOD
PRAY
TRUTH

Designed by Dr. Jaspal Singh Mayell

UNIVERSALITY OF THE SIKH RELIGION

REVIEWS

I went through the book *Universality of the Sikh Religion*. I found it to be faultless, lucid and easy to read with appropriate quotations from Guru Granth Sahib. I am glad that the contributions of Bhai Vir Singh and Bhagat Puran Singh are well documented.

Mr. Khushwant Singh
India's best-known columnist, writer and historian, New Delhi, India.

Jaspal Singh Mayell has written an informed and carefully crafted book. It is a labor of love and a beautiful volume. The arguments, synthesis and ideas are solid and progressive. The illustrations are very useful, making this an excellent book for courses and instruction relating to Sikhism. Readers will find the analysis reflecting the mainstream of thinking of Sikhs in the Diaspora living outside India.

Dr. N. Gerald Barrier
Middlebush Chair of Social Sciences and Professor Emeritus of History, University of Missouri USA

Dr. Jaspal Singh Mayell, though by profession a pharmaceutical scientist, has been studying Sikh scriptures and taking an active role in community affairs ever since he landed in New York in 1957. In fact he is one of the pioneers among the Sikh settlers who participated in the first religious gathering and later in establishing the first Gurdwara in Richmond Hills, Queens, New York.

I am delighted to know that his deep knowledge and faith in the Guru Granth Sahib along with his involvement in the community has resulted in writing *Universality of the Sikh Religion.*

In this well researched work, Dr. Mayell is at pains to stress the universal aspect of this religion, Sikhism. He has a fine analytical mind and expresses himself very well. He has discussed the issues in a way that, perhaps, have not been dealt with before. Topics are taken up in a very systematic manner.

REVIEWS (CONTINUED)

A noteworthy feature of the book is the exercise part at the end of each chapter. This will be quite helpful to students learning Sikhism. It also can serve as a textbook for a course on Sikh studies.

The most appealing message is in the last chapter of the book, "Propagation of the Sikh Religion in the Adopted Country". In it he has brought forth the very essence of the book. All hindrances to the universalism of Sikhism and their solutions are given in an orderly way. He has cited the appropriate quotations from the Guru Granth Sahib. This makes his points more convincing and forceful. That, indeed, is the main strength of all the chapters. He has made good points on language; education of the Granthis; chairs in the Gurdwaras, especially the resolution of the Dharmik Sulaakaar Committee of 1935; equality of all despite appearance and gender, distinction between rituals and procedures; hygienic conditions; definition of a Sikh supported by SD (Sikh Diaspora) poll, etc.

Dr. Mayell has worked hard on this book. I am sure it will find its place in Gurdwaras and public libraries and in private homes of the devotees of the Sikh religion.

Mr. Jagpal Singh Tiwana
Ex-Cybrarian, Nova Scotia Teachers College, Truro, Canada.

I have known Dr. Jaspal Mayell for more than 40 years. On many occasions we discussed various facets of the Sikh religion. But until I read his book, I had no real understanding of what was involved in being a Sikh.

Dr. Mayell has thoroughly researched and described the many centuries of oppression and physical mistreatment the Sikhs endured to survive and flourish. He places great emphasis on the precepts that have sustained them including a love of God and humanity, equality and diversity, prayer and truthful living.

This book is a valuable resource for anyone who wants to know more about Sikhism, be they young Indians with an interest in their heritage or lay persons who want to broaden their knowledge of one of the world's major religions.

Mr. Robert Katzeff
Editor Documents, Stamford, Connecticut, USA.

REVIEWS (CONTINUED)

Dr. Mayell, a scientist by profession, is a founding member of the first Gurdwara on East Coast: Richmond Hills, Queens, in New York City. He has continued to be concerned with the future of Sikhs, especially youth in Diaspora. In this book, he says it all with truth and compassion.

His simple straightforward approach makes it good reading for all the Sikhs, especially in Diaspora, as well as, for other people of the modern age. Dr. Mayell not only points out the problems Sikh youth face in Diaspora, but provides logical solutions. So it's a good source of information for Sikh youth abroad.

He has done commendable search to put together concepts of the Sikh religion. He uses history and scriptures, and relates them to everyday living in 21st century of science and technology. This book provides much needed information to our youngsters in Diaspora about history, scriptures, and old cultural traditions. Youths and adults can relate very well to his descriptions; he gives his eyewitness accounts where appropriate.

He takes appropriate verses from the Holy Scripture Aad Guru Granth Sahib (AGGS), and relates them to everyday life. I like his futuristic approach while sticking to the basic values. His suggestions for the future of the Sikh religion in modern society are most thoughtful and are worth consideration by Sikh intellectuals. However, he reassures again and again not to touch the basic concepts given in the AGGS; the concepts that go well with 21st century. He believes that the philosophy of Sikh gurus has no contradiction with modern, scientific discoveries. In fact that is the reason to call Sikhism a universal and modern religion.

He uses his scientific skills and logic to justify his opinions. He gives full reference, when applicable, whether the opinion is similar to his own or is different. Sikhs with an open mind will find a refreshing view of the future of the Sikh youth in this book. For the orthodox, it will take time to accept his futuristic approach, if they ever do.

The degeneration of Sikh practices in Sikh religious places is a special focus of his concern. He points out that continuation of fights in Gurdwaras and preaching of ritualism and mythical Sikhism has already alienated many young Sikhs and many more will be alienated in the near future. It's about time to change and practice: sitting on chairs, use the native language of the adopted country, educate the religious preachers, and obsere hygienic conditions in Gurdwaras.

REVIEWS (CONTINUED)

Without a futuristic approach for which Dr. Mayell has laid the foundation stone, the Sikhs as a global community are likely to alienate the younger generation in the absence of scientific approach towards Gurbani and Sikhism. Dr. Mayell`s book can help them discover the universal nature of Sikhism for the 21st century.

Dr. Sukhraj Singh Dhillon
Author of many Books, Cary, North Carolina, USA.

This book will assist to educate Sikhs especially young Sikhs about the origin and meaning of their own religion.

Mr. Howard S. Halpern
Editor Writer, Stamford, Connecticut, USA.

The book details how the principles of Sikhism as taught by the Gurus have universal applicability to the issues and concerns of people today in whatever country they may be.

Mr. Manvin Singh Mayell
Attorney, New York, USA.

The Universality of the Sikh Religion is a comprehensive, easy-to-understand guide to Sikhism. It inspires Sikhs and non-Sikhs alike to follow the universal teachings of Guru Nanak, the founder of Sikhism. Dr. Mayell has expertly articulated some very progressive and wide-ranging suggestions on how to promote the teachings of Nanak to motivate those concerned and to ensure the future of Sikhism. This book has certainly enlightened me. I find the universal principles of Sikhism to be extremely fair—sometimes that is exactly what is lacking in other religions.

Mrs. Laura G. Clark
Editor, Weston, Connecticut, USA

TABLE OF CONTENTS

TABLE OF CONTENTS (CONTINUED)

PREFACE

I wrote this book for the younger generation of Sikhs who are either born or brought up in the western societies such as the USA, Canada, UK and so on. They are very intelligent and are very knowledgeable. Since they are brought up in western culture, they have different views about the traditional culture of their parents who came from India. They are very critical about anything that is involved with religion. They are looking for very logical answers to their questions. They do not know Punjabi in Gurmukhi script but know English very well. They resent the way the Sikh religion is presented in the Gurdwara, the religious place of the Sikhs. As a result young, intelligent Sikhs are not coming to the Gurdwaras. This is my humble attempt to bring to their attention the real purpose of the Sikh Religion. Being a scientist, my style is to use logic and reasoning throughout this book. My approach is from a practical point of view, therefore, *Universality of the Sikh Religion* is written in simple English. It took me about seven years to write this book—from 1999 to 2006.

The main emphasis in this book is that everybody should earn their livelihood by honest, hard, creative work; share one's blessings with less fortunate people; treat all people as equal in all respects; pray daily to one God to obtain divine experience; and practice truthful living every day. This will be repeated many times in the book as that is the practical essence of the Sikh Religion.

In this world of very high academic achievement and technological advancement, the teachers encourage students to ask questions on anything they teach. Students are encouraged to use the word "WHY" in order to fully understand the subject under discussion. Even young children, before even they go to school, always ask their parents "WHY?". I have asked myself many times the question of why and how to understand the Universality of the Sikh Religion. Most of the answers were found in the Guru Granth Sahib and appropriate references have been given for each quotation. It is up to the individual to ponder the philosophy and teachings of the Sikh Religion as preserved in Guru Granth Sahib.

I came to USA by boat, on a one way ticket, from India in 1957 and disembarked in New York. I traveled straight in a bus from New York to Austin, Texas, to study for a Ph.D. degree in Chemistry. A gentleman sitting next to me asked me where I was from I replied that I was from India. His next question was, "What is your religion?" To that I replied, "I am a Sikh." Immediately he asked, "What is the Sikh religion?" Although I was 28 years old, had turban on my head and had a Master's degree in chemistry, I was completely perplexed by the question. I paused for many seconds that felt like eternity to me. Nobody had ever asked me such a question. It was assumed, in my mind, that everybody knows I am a Sikh.

I collected my thoughts and told him that Sikhs believe in one God. He replied that Christians do as well. The only difference is that the God of the Sikhs is not a living person while Christians claim Jesus to be the son of God [1]. I also told him that Sikhs believe in equality between all people, irrespective of their religion. Women have equal rights in all respects. As I was saying those things I was feeling bad because I realized that I really did not know the basics of my own religion. I never forgot this incident. It is one of the reasons I wrote this book and in the process I learnt more about Sikh religion.

I also wrote this book in order for my children, their spouses and grandchildren to understand the Sikh Religion. One cannot teach one's own children. One needs proper atmosphere by associating with teachers and classmates. Religious education is equally important as a professional education; it should teach you how to be a better person. It is the religious teachers and the association in the religious places that can impart that knowledge. However, at present and in the foreseeable future such teachings are not possible in the Gurdwaras. The preachers in the Gurdwaras lack education and do not know the English language. They have no involvement with the adopted country and no background on how to solve the problems the congregations face daily. This applies to preachers in India but more so to those in the USA, Canada, United Kingdom and other countries.

This book is meant for Sikhs and non-Sikhs that have an interest in Sikh Religion. It can help the students who are learning about religion in schools and universities. It can also play a great part in Sunday schools of the religious organizations. Teachers and students can discuss one chapter at a time and understand the *Universality of the Sikh Religion*. This book also will be a great help for people who come from a different religious background and are married to a Sikh person.

MY BACKGROUND

Professionally I am a retired scientist with a PhD degree in chemistry. I worked in the pharmaceutical industry for about 36 years. My approach has been to ask myself questions on every aspect of the Universality of the Sikh Religion. I have tried to produce evidence, as scientists do, to discuss and prove the hypothesis. I do not have a religious degree and am not a professional preacher. I am an ordinary person writing about the Universality of the Sikh Religion, from a historical and philosophical perspective.

I was born in 1929, Sialkot City, West Punjab, which is now part of Pakistan. In 1947, at age 18, I left Sialkot as a refugee and settled in Amritsar, East Punjab, India—the same year India received its independence from the British. During that process Punjab state was divided on the basis of religion. Muslims got West Punjab, Pakistan while Hindus and Sikhs got East Punjab, India.

My first job was in 1947, as a junior clerk in Gobind Garh Refugee Camp, Amritsar. It lasted 23 days and received Rupees 35. I was so delighted as if I have won a lottery. In 1950 I graduated from Khalsa College, Amritsar earning B.Sc (Honors) in Chemistry. In 1952 I received an M.Sc in Chemical Engineering from Delhi Polytechnic Institute, Delhi. I worked for about five years in several positions at the Irrigation Research Institute Amritsar, Bhakra Nangal Dam in Punjab and the Road Research Institute in Delhi.

In 1957, at age 28 I migrated to the United States for higher studies. I earned a Ph.D. in Chemistry in 1962. I worked for American Cyanamid, (Stamford, CT) for eight years in the fuel cell project for generation of electricity. Then I worked in the pharmaceutical research departments of DuPont (6 years) and Purdue Pharma (22 years) I became USA citizen in 1968 and I retired in 1999. Currently, I am living in Stamford, Connecticut.

It would also be very appropriate to discuss my personal appearance as a Sikh during my life. I was born into a Sikh family and had long hair and turban up to age 31. It was in the year 1960 when I was at the University of Texas, Austin,, that I cut my long hair. Obviously the next question would be, "Why?" I used to get severe headaches due to the pearcing of the thread of the net on my head. The net was used to control my long beard. My knowledge of the Sikh religion was very limited. Several other Sikhs came to that university and the first thing they did was cut their long hair. I used to go to the beach or the canal with my turban on. It was not a good experience as the weather is very hot in Texas. It is possible that if I had trimmed my beard and used cap for outdoor activities I may not have resorted to cutting my long hair. After about 19 years of not having long hair, I decided to grow my hair long in 1979. Again, people will ask why I did so. I associated with a lot of Sikhs in those days who had long hair. I also made up my mind to trim my beard and to use cap whenever necessary. I also made a firm conviction that I was not going to be fundamentalist. That meant that I was never going to hate those who did not have long hair. In fact I will treat them equal in all respects. That was my resolve for the rest of my life. Since 1979 I have had long hair and I worked for 22 years with a turban. I wear a turban whenever it is required, but I wear a cap quite often. I also trim my beard, which I find to be more comfortable. Since I am retired, I do not have to worry about a job. However, if I were very young today, I most probably would not have long hair and turban. I do believe in equality for all with or without long hair and this will be so for the rest of my life. This equality is without any reservation.

ACKNOWLEDGEMENTS

First I would like to thank my wife for going through this seven year project with me. Next I would like to thank my son, Mr. Manvin Singh Mayell, an attorney and my daughter, Mrs. Nita Sabo, for going through this manuscript and giving very valuable suggestions. Their input was very important to me, as this book is written for young people who are born or brought up in western culture.

I appreciate the advice of Mr. Khushwant Singh, the noted writer and historian, of India . He helped me significantly in improving my approach to writing this book. His review of my book lifted my siprit; I felt that my effort in writing this book was well worth it. I also am very thankful to Mr. Jagpal Singh Tiwana, the noted Librarian/Cybrarian in Canada, who wrote a review of this book. I would like to thank Dr. Harbans Lal for giving very valuable suggestions in improving the manuscript. Special thanks goes to Dr. N. Gerald Barrier, Professor Emeritus at the University of Missouri USA, for reviewing and giving considerable help in publishing and marketing the book. I would also like to thank Dr. Sukhraj Singh Dhillon, scientist and author of many books, for reviewing and making good suggestions.

Thanks to Mr. Howard S. Halpern of Stamford Connecticut for giving good ideas and writing a review. Special thanks to Mr. Robert Katzeff, a friend and neighbor for 44 years in Stamford, Connecticut, for editing several chapters of the book and giving valuable suggestions. I appreciate the help of Laura Clark for editing major portion of the book and writing a review. I would also thank Mr. Harish Jain for printing this book. Thanks also to Sikh Diaspora members and the management team who have indirectly helped me in putting forward my views in this book. I have tried to include all references after each chapter. If I have missed any, it is simply an oversight.

REFERENCE

[1] Yahoo go to "Son of God - Wikipedia, the free encyclopedia" Click "Wikipedia: Son of God". http://en.wikipedia.org/wiki/Son_of_God

Dr. Jaspal Singh Mayell
Stamford, CT USA

UNIVERSALITY OF THE SIKH RELIGION

CHAPTER 1

INTRODUCTION

The goal of this book is to show the ***Universality of the Sikh Religion based on its history, philosophy and its practical ways to enjoy life***. The Universality of the Sikh Religion as explained here applies to all types of people irrespective of religion, sex, caste, color, creed, appearance or any other way that is used to divide people.

Guru Nanak founded the Sikh religion in Punjab, India, about 500 years ago. This being one of the youngest religions in the world, it has all the characteristics required to be Universal. ***Guru Granth Sahib, the Holy Book of the Sikhs does not criticize any other religion.*** It is better to be a good person irrespective of religious affiliation. ***The major principles of the Sikh religion call for its members to be honest, to do charitable work, lead truthful lives, practice equality for everyone and above all, pray to one God.***

All of these are very practical and can be performed on a daily basis. Once one accepts the concept of Universality, the entire thinking process changes. Animosity changes to love and friendship. As there is only one God who created the whole universe, then there should be no difference from one person to another. ***God has many different names because there are many different religions but essentially, it is the same God.*** Some of the religions involved are Christianity, Islam, Hinduism, Sikhism, Judaism, Buddhism. But there are many others. When discussing religion people can become emotional. They think their interpretation is the only way religion should be taught and practiced.

This leads to fundamentalism, creates friction and even at times, fighting. To live in peace one must respect all religions. Basically, all religions believe in peace, equality and helping the less fortunate. If this is followed in practical life, the world would be a better place to live in. ***Guru Granth Sahib states very clearly that everyone must work for the good of humanity. The purpose of all religions is to bring peace of mind and tranquility***. Once a mind is at peace, the question of fighting will never arise. This also will help considerably to stop family breakdowns, reducing stress and depression. One must understand and put into practice the words written in the Holy Books of all religions. This was clearly stated by Guru Nanak and the succeeding nine Gurus, and also in Guru Granth Sahib.

As communal violence continues throughout the world, the young as well as mature people are really becoming disenchanted with religion. Religion if propagated properly can bring together people of divergent views to live in peace and harmony. This even applies to those who do not believe in God. All religions believe in God, peace and in performing good deeds. This is true as far as theory is concerned. How about in practical life? People of all religions not only fight with people of different religions, but also with people belonging to the same religion. Is fighting the fault of the religion or a misinterpretation of its religious books by its clergy?

1. WHY PEOPLE JOINED THE SIKH RELIGION

About 500 years ago mostly Hindus and Muslims lived in the northern part of India. Later, most of the Hindus, and to a lesser extent Muslims, adopted the Sikh way of life. ***The main reason was acceptance and adoption, by the public at large, of the teachings of Guru Nanak, his nine successors and the written words in the Holy Book, Guru Granth Sahib.***

Conversion was voluntary because no force, coercion or misrepresentation was ever used in conversion to the Sikh Religion. From 1499 to 1839, people in large numbers became Sikhs. ***In fact, at present there are 24 million Sikhs worldwide*** according to the 2005 World Almanac and Book of Facts 2005 [1]. This proves that people of other religions have changed to the Sikh Religion in large numbers.

If we ask individuals why they belong to a particular religion, the obvious answer is due to the affiliation of their parents. Some religions like Christianity, Islam and Buddhism are actively involved in conversions. Most of the other religions do not promote conversion.

2. GURU GRANTH SAHIB FOR ANSWERS

We all want to know the reason for whatever we do, and that also includes religion. The philosophy as well as practical aspects of the Sikh religion are contained in Guru Granth Sahib. ***My next question is how to get those answers from Guru Granth Sahib.*** I wanted to read and understand the words written in Guru Granth Sahib, but I had a serious problem. I could not read the Punjabi in Guru Granth Sahib because it is written in Gurmukhi script. I could speak and understand Punjabi but could not read it. I was born in Sialkot City, now in Pakistan, and had learned Urdu and Persian besides English in a Scotch mission school in Sialkot.

I had some understanding of the Sikh Religion that was acquired by reading books written in English. There are a few English translations, and they are very helpful. My need was to learn Punjabi. Anyway, 34 years from 1957 (when I came to U.S.) to 1991 passed by and I still could not read Punjabi. Then I came across a book called "Learn Punjabi Through English in 30 Days" written by Mr. N.S.R. Ganathe, a gentleman from the Southern part of India [2]. I began reading and learned how to write Punjabi in Gurmukhi script, as well. I then decided to read directly from Guru Granth Sahib, as that was my objective. With the help of the English translations of Guru Granth Sahib prepared by Mr. Man Mohan Singh in eight volumes [3], and also by Mr. Pritam Singh Chahil in four volumes [4], I was able to read and understood the words written in Guru Granth Sahib. For those who want to learn Punjabi by themselves, I have titled Chapter 20 in this book: "Learn Punjabi the Easy Way." This is for those who want to read Guru Granth Sahib in Punjabi and have no access to an instructor.

I then decided to read Guru Granth Sahib (1430 pages) from beginning to end with the help of English translations. It took me almost five years (1992 to 1997) to complete the reading. Now I have a little better understanding of the Universality of the Sikh Religion. ***However, it should be mentioned that to really understand and put into practice the teachings in Guru Granth Sahib takes more than one's lifetime.*** I restarted reading (January 1, 1998) Guru Granth Sahib from the beginning and it appears that this time it will take about eight years to finish.

In this book, I have tried my best to use simple day-to-day language while translating Gurmukhi into English. It is very difficult to translate literally as Guru Granth Sahib is written in poetry and the language is Gurmukhi (Punjabi). Sometimes references in Gurmukhi relate to the local customs, traditions and culture. I have tried to make it easier for English-speaking people to understand the real meaning of a quotation.

In our house, we keep Guru Granth Sahib in a separate room. It is wrapped in several sheets of cotton and silk cloth. Guru Granth Sahib is kept on a high platform, about 27 inches above the floor. We sit on a comfortable cushioned seat that is about 16 inches from the floor. Guru Granth Sahib is placed in a special palanquin made of wood and has a wooden dome above it. This is done as a mark of respect to Guru Granth Sahib and also is a tradition dating back centuries. It is not idolatry. Every day, early in the morning, I open and read Guru Granth Sahib. It is called parkash karna in Punjabi. Every evening my wife reads and closes Guru Granth Sahib. It is called sukhasan in Punjabi. ***The time for reading varies and the duration of the reading is not fixed.***

3. IMPORTANCE OF PUNJABI AND OTHER LANGUAGES

It is quite obvious that many Sikhs living in western countries do not know Punjabi and may never learn it. However, one can learn enough by reading the English translations of Guru Granth Sahib. One also can read a number of Sikh religious books written in English. They are commercially available. This book is one of them.

The literary value of the Punjabi language as written in Guru Granth Sahib is of great importance. When I was young, I heard of a very great writer, Mr. Mulkh Raj Anand from Punjab, in the northern part of India. Mr. Anand met Mr. Rabindra Nath Tagore, a 1913 Nobel Laureate in Literature, in Calcutta. Mr. Anand complained that the Bengali language (eastern part of India) had so much literature while the Punjabi language had less. Tagore listened for a while and told him that when you go back to Punjab, read Guru Granth Sahib. It is the best literature in Punjabi language. ***Tagore told Anand that he had read Guru Granth Sahib and derived great inspiration from it.***

Every year, Tagore's father used to visit the Golden Temple in Amritsar and he often accompanied him. This left a deep impression upon Tagore with respect to the Sikh Religion. Tagore has written of several memorable events in Sikh history and about Guru Gobind Singh, Banda Bahadur and Taru Singh. Tagore wrote, "that his father seated in the midst of the Sikh worshippers in the Golden Temple, would join them in songs and they would greet him with pleased cordiality" [5].

Great importance is given to other languages in Guru Granth Sahib. Although written in Gurmukhi Script, it incorporates 10 other languages. They are Sant Bhasa, Hindi, Sindhi, Lehandi, Marathi, Sanskrit, Arabic, Persian, Eastern Apabhramsa and Western Apabhramsa. It should also be mentioned that the 10th Guru Gobind Singh used Brij Bhasha (the language of Bihar province in India), Persian and Arabic, and not Punjábi, in his compositions. Maharaja Ranjit Singh also used Persian as the official language. ***Thus, the use of English or any language to spread the Universality of the Sikh Religion is perfectly justified.***

4. SUMMARY

The goal of this book is to present the Universality of the Sikh Religion based upon its history and philosophy. The main principles of the Sikh religion involve being honest, doing charitable work, leading a truthful life, practicing equality for all and above all, praying to one God. The main reason people joined the Sikh Religion was the acceptance and adoption, by the public at large, of the teachings of Guru Nanak, his nine successors and the written words in the Holy Book, Guru Granth Sahib.

Most of the answers to the questions were obtained from Guru Granth Sahib and references have been provided. Being a scientist, my style is to use logic and reasoning throughout this book. Although Guru Granth Sahib was written in Gurmukhi (Punjabi), 10 other languages also are also included. The use of English or any language to spread the Universality of the Sikh Religion is perfectly justified.

5. EXERCISES

i. Why Sikh religion does not criticize other religions?
ii. What are the five main principles of the Sikh Religion?
iii. Why people joined the Sikh Religion in large numbers?
iv. Why use of other languages is important for the propagation of the Sikh religion?
v. What is the name of the Holy Book that is used to find answers to our questions?

6. REFERENCES

[1] The World Almanac and Book of Facts, 2005, New York, NY, p. 734; Source 2004 Encyclopaedia Britannica Book of the Year.
[2] N.S.R. Ganathe, 1981, Learn Punjabi in 30 Days, Balaji Publications, Madras, India, 2nd edition.
[3] Manmohan Singh, 1981, Siri Guru Granth Sahib (Gurmukhi, English and Punjabi translations), Shiromani Gurdwara Parbandhak Committee, Amritsar, Punjab, India, 2nd edition, 8 volumes.
[4] Pritam Singh Chahil. 1993, Siri Guru Granth Sahib (Gurmukhi, Roman and English translation), Pritam Singh Chahil, New Delhi, India, 4 volumes.
[5] SikhSpectrum.com, Issue No.10, March 2003
Tagore and the Sikhs by Amalendu Bose
http://www.sikhspectrum.com/032003/tagore_sikhs.htm

UNIVERSALITY OF THE SIKH RELIGION

CHAPTER 2

INITIATION OF THE SIKH RELIGION BY GURU NANAK

UNIVERSALITY FROM 1469 to 1539

About 500 years ago, Guru Nanak (Figure 1 [1]) founded the Sikh Religion. He was born in Punjab, in the northern part of India, on April 15, 1469 [2]. His birthplace was Talwandi, now known as Nankana Sahib. It is about 48 miles from Lahore, Punjab, now in Pakistan [3]. Figure 2 [4] shows the present location of Punjab in India.

Figure 3 is a map of Punjab [5]. The solid line is the original Punjab during Guru Nanak's time. The dotted line is Punjab in 1947 when it was divided into Punjab of Pakistan (62%) and Punjab of India (38 %). Punjab of India was further divided into three portions called Punjab (13%), Himachel Pradesh (14%), and Haryana (11%). This became effective in 1966. The present percentages refer to the original Punjab before 1947.

Chandigarh is another division of Indian Punjab. Thus, as of today, the original Punjab of Guru Nanak's period, the land of the five rivers, has been divided into five parts. Punjabi is the official language and it also is spoken in the other four parts of original Punjab. Urdu is the official language of Punjab in Pakistan, while it is Hindi in Haryana and Himachel Pardesh in India.

During Guru Nanak's time, Punjab was in great turmoil. Muslims from the north were plundering India. Muslims, who had converted the entire populations of Arabia, Iraq, Turkey, Egypt, Iran, Afghanistan and several other countries, felt helpless when trying to convert Hindus. The Hindu philosophy and way of living seemed to defeat the Muslim conversion process. Except for low-caste Hindus and some others, no one seemed to accept Islam.

Guru Nanak's father was Mehta Kalu and his mother was Tripta. His sister was Nanaki and she was very devoted to her brother. Guru Nanak was married to Sulakhni and they had two sons, Sri Chand and Lakshmi Chand. As a child, Guru Nanak was friendly with both Muslim and Hindu boys. The Muslim chief of the village, Mr. Rai Bular, was so impressed by the divine knowledge of Guru Nanak, that he became his devotee.

When Guru Nanak was in his 30th year in 1499 [6], he went into deep meditation. His mind, body and soul were in perfect tune with GOD. Two things were revealed to him that laid the foundation of the Sikh Religion: the conception of God and equality among all people.

1. FIRST REVELATION

The first revelation of Guru Nanak was the conception of God. Guru Granth Sahib, the Universal Holy Book, starts with this composition. It is the basic philosophy of the Sikh Religion about God.

CONCEPTION OF GOD

PUNJABI	ROMAN	ENGLISH
੧ੴ	Ik-oNkaar	There is only one God.
ਸਤਿ ਨਾਮੁ	Sat Naam	God's Name is Truth.
ਕਰਤਾ ਪੁਰਖੁ	Kartaa Purakh	God created everything.
ਨਿਰਭਉ	Nirbha-o	God is without fear.
ਨਿਰਵੈਰੁ	Nirvair	God is not against anybody.
ਅਕਾਲ ਮੂਰਤਿ	Akaal Moorat	God's shape never changes.
ਅਜੂਨੀ	Ajoonee	God is neither born nor dies.
ਸੈਭੰ	SaibhaN	God is everywhere.
ਗੁਰ ਪ੍ਰਸਾਦਿ	Gur Parsaad	By God's grace
ਜਪੁ	Jap	Worship.

Guru Granth Sahib (p.1, line1)

FIGURE 1

GURU NANAK

(1469 to 1539)
FOUNDER OF THE SIKH RELIGION
This image is for profound respect, but not for worship.

FIGURE 2

MAP SHOWING THE LOCATION OF PUNJAB IN INDIA

FIGURE 3

MAP OF PUNJAB
BEFORE PARTITION (Solid Line)
LINE OF PARTITION IN 1947 (Dotted Line)
ORIGINAL PUNJAB IS NOW DIVIDED INTO FIVE PORTIONS

2. SECOND REVELATION

The second revelation was the equality of all people. Guru Nanak said there were no Hindu and no Mussalman [6]. It should not be taken literally because there are millions of people that belong to different religions. Guru Nanak mentioned two religions prevalent at that time but it applies to all religions. Muslims and Hindus had fought for centuries and there was no end in sight. Guru Nanak made it clear that it was not good to divide people and fight on the basis of religion. We may be diverse but we are equal in the eyes of God. The main point is: ***there should be no discrimination based on religion. We are all part of the same God and all people are equal in all respects.***

i. EQUALITY IS THE MOTTO OF THE SIKH RELIGION

The first Guru, Nanak, said:

PUNJABI AND ROMAN	ENGLISH
ਨਾਨਕ ਉਤਮੁ ਨੀਚੁ ਨ ਕੋਇ Nanak Utam Neech Na Ko-ay Guru Granth Sahib (p.7, line10)	No one is high and no one is low.

If we all are equal and there is no high and no low, then why do we discriminate? The answer is ***excessive ego***. We think only that we are important and our views are the ultimate. We are not willing to compromise and live in peace and harmony.

ii. ALL ARE EQUAL

The first Guru, Nanak, said:

PUNJABI AND ROMAN	ENGLISH
ਸਭੁ ਕੋ ਊਚਾ ਆਖੀਐ Sabh Ko Oochaa Aakhee-ai	Call everyone high
ਨੀਚੁ ਨ ਦੀਸੈ ਕੋਇ Neech Na Deesai Ko-ay Guru Granth Sahib (p. 62, line 12)	None appears to be low

iii. WHO IS A RELIGIOUS PERSON?

Guru Nanak explained very ***clearly that a truly religious person is one who treats everybody as equal.*** The purpose of religion is to unite and put people on the path of truth. Equality as Guru Nanak said is for all time to come. Guru Nanak and the succeeding nine Gurus preached equality among all people.

The first Guru, Nanak, said:

PUNJABI AND ROMAN	**ENGLISH**
ਗਲੀ ਜੋਗੁ ਨ ਹੋਈ ॥	By mere words one does not become a
Galee Jog Na Ho-ee	religious person
ਏਕ ਦ੍ਰਿਸਟਿ ਕਰਿ ਸਮਸਰਿ ਜਾਣੈ	A person who considers everybody as
Ayk Darisat Kar Samsar Jaanai	equal
ਜੋਗੀ ਕਹੀਐ ਸੋਈ ॥	truly is a religious person.
Jogee Kahee-ai So-ee	
Guru Granth Sahib (p. 730, line 13)	

Equality is the cornerstone of the Sikh Religion. There is no need to fight if all humans are equal. People fight because they have no tolerance for other religions and sometimes they fight within the same religion.

Guru Nanak's prescription is to treat all people as equal in all respects, and that will lead to peace and tranquility.

3. TRUTH AND GURU NANAK

The pursuit of Truth was Guru Nanak's permanent concern throughout his life. Truth was very important to him.

i. TRUTH FOR ALL TIMES

Guru Nanak emphasized that Truth is for all times.

The first Guru, Nanak, said:

PUNJABI and ROMAN	**ENGLISH**
ਆਦਿ ਸਚੁ	Truth was in the beginning
Aad Sach	
ਜੁਗਾਦਿ ਸਚੁ	Truth was in the endless
Jugaad Sach	centuries that followed
ਹੈ ਭੀ ਸਚੁ	Truth now prevails
Hai Bhee Sach .	
ਨਾਨਕ ਹੋਸੀ ਭੀ ਸਚੁ	Nanak Says, Truth will prevail for
Nanak Hosee Bhee Sach	all times to come.
Guru Granth Sahib (p.1, line 1)	

ii. TRUTH NEVER GETS STALE

Guru Nanak believed that Truth is always fresh.

The first Guru, Nanak, said:

PUNJABI AND ROMAN	ENGLISH
ਸਚੁ ਪੁਰਾਣਾ ਹੋਵੈ ਨਾਹੀ	***Truth never gets stale***
Sach Puraanaa Hovai Naahee	
Guru Granth Sahib (p. 956, line 1)	

iii. TRUTH IS RELIGION

Guru Nanak said ***if a religion has to have only one thing, then it must be Truth***.

The first Guru, Nanak, said:

PUNJABI AND ROMAN	ENGLISH
ਏਕੋ ਧਰਮੁ ਦ੍ਰਿੜੈ ਸਚੁ ਕੋਈ	There is one thing common
Ayko Dharam Darirhai Sach Ko-ee	among all religions:
Guru Granth Sahib (p. 1188, line 15)	everyone must practice Truth

iv. TRUTH IS THE BEST DEED

Guru Nanak further reiterated that ***Truth is the best deed*** and all others are of no avail.

The first Guru, Nanak, said:

PUNJABI and ROMAN	ENGLISH
ਹਿਰਦੈ ਸਚੁ ਏਹ ਕਰਣੀ ਸਾਰੁ	Cherishing Truth in one's heart
Hirdai Sach Ayh Karnee Saar	is the most sublime deed.
ਹੋਰੁ ਸਭੁ ਪਾਖੰਡੁ ਪੂਜ ਖੁਆਰੁ	All other pretensions and worship
Hor Sabh Pakhand Pooj Khu-aar	are of no use and are ruinous.
Guru Granth Sahib (p.1343, line 15)	

v. TRUTHFUL LIVING IS BEST

Guru Nanak also believed that one must practice Truth in everyday endeavors.

The first Guru, Nanak, said:

PUNJABI AND ROMAN	**ENGLISH**
ਸਚਹੁ ਓਰੈ ਸਭੁ ਕੋ Sachahu Orai Sabh Ko	Truth is higher than everything
ਉਪਰਿ ਸਚੁ ਆਚਾਰੁ Upar Sach Aachaar	but higher still is truthful living.

Guru Granth Sahib (p. 62, line 11)

4. MAIN CONCEPTS OF THE SIKH RELIGION

Truthful living is the essence of the Sikh Religion. The art of Truthful living is to be practiced by people of all ages. What is truthful living? In practical life, one should perform the following deeds to be a truthful person:

- *i.* ***Be honest in everyday living***
- *ii.* ***Share your blessings with the less fortunate***
- *iii.* ***Pray to one God***
- *iv.* ***Treat everybody as equal in all respects***
- *v.* ***Enjoy the diversity created by God***
- *vi.* ***To love God one must learn to love one another.***

To enjoy diversity is very important. Looking and meeting diverse people should be considered a pleasure. God created people (so far about six billion) and no two are alike, not even identical twins. Scientists are trying to clone people and it really would really be a dull place to live if there was no diversity.

It is good that there are different religions. You may call yourself Hindu, Muslim, Christian, Sikh, Jew or any other religion. The main question is not what religion you belong to, but what you do in your lifetime. Guru Nanak never criticized any religion but he spoke against the rituals and the prejudices.

5. GURU NANAK'S USE OF THE COMMON PEOPLE'S LANGUAGE

Guru Nanak's success in promoting and spreading the Universality of the Sikh Religion was due to the ***use of the common people's language.***

When Guru Nanak was in Punjab he spoke Punjabi. When he was in Iran he spoke Persian and while in Saudi Arabia he spoke Arabic and so on. It was the message that was important and it could be explained in any language.

When Guru Nanak spoke Punjabi it was a radical departure. Hindu priests used Sanskrit and Muslim religious people used Arabic or Persian. Except for the priests, others could not understand Sanskrit, Arabic or Persian. Use of Punjabi had a universal appeal to all people and they flocked to Guru Nanak. By using a common language, people clearly understood the concept of God and how to live day-to-day life as explained by Guru Nanak.

Besides Punjabi, Guru Granth Sahib has hymns from 10 other languages. This is another way to make it a Universal Holy Book. People living in adopted countries should use the language of those countries in their religious practices. Thus, the use of English in the U.S., Canada and England is perfectly acceptable for spread the Universality of the Sikh Religion.

6. GURU NANAK'S TRAVELS WITH A PERSON OF ANOTHER RELIGION

The Universality of the Sikh Religion was clearly seen by people as Guru Nanak traveled, usually with Mardana who was a Muslim and sometimes with Bala who was a Hindu. Guru Nanak sang the hymns he composed while Mardana played a musical instrument called the Rabab. Guru Nanak traveled through many countries preaching the universality of the human race: ***Tibet, Nepal, Sikkim, Bhutan, Burma, Bangladesh, Ceylon, Saudi Arabia, Iraq, Egypt, Turkey, Iran, Afghanistan, Kashmir and of course extensively throughout India and Pakistan.***

Guru Nanak's approach was universal and so people adopted his way of thinking. He preached love and associated with all human beings. Whereever Guru Nanak traveled there is a monument erected in his memory.

7. UNIVERSAL PRAYER

The Universal part of the Sikh religion as shown below applies to all people.

Let us pray to God the Almighty.

Give us happiness and peace of mind.
Give us the spirit to be humble and wise.

Forgive us for all the bad things that we have done.
Keep us into the company of those who believe in one God.

Let us be charitable and help the needy.
Help us in our endeavors and keep us in good health.

Give us the gift of Universal Religion, Sikhism, the gift of confidence, the gift of trust , the gift of faith, and the gift of remembering and believing in one God.

Help us in controlling our excessive lust, excessive anger, excessive greed, excessive ego and excessive pride.

Fulfill the desires of all those who pray earnestly.

Nanak says God's name be always on the rise.
By the grace of God let there be universal prosperity and well being.

Nanak Naam Chardee Kalla Tere Bhaane Sarbat Daa Bhalaa [7]

8. GURU NANAK LOVED BY ALL

Guru Nanak's preaching of Universality was so successful that people of all other religions respected and revered him. When he passed away in 1539, ***Hindus wanted to cremate him while Muslims wanted to bury him***.
A popular couplet [8] describes Guru Nanak as

Baba Nanak Shah Fakir Hindu Ka Guru Musalman Ka Pir
Baba Nanak, the great holy man
Guru of the Hindus and Pir of the Muslims.

It is said that when Guru Nanak died, Muslims devotees built a mausoleum and Hindu disciples a built a Samadhi on the banks of Ravi River in Punjab.

It also is known that due to a change in the river's course, both structures were washed away perhaps providentially, so as to avoid any idol worship at the Guru's last resting-place. This left behind just a fragrant of the memory of Guru Nanak who was dear to Sikhs, Muslims and Hindus [9]. Even today, besides Sikhs, Hindus and Muslims, people of all other religions revere him.

GURU NANAK THUS LAID THE FOUNDATION OF THE UNIVERSALITY OF THE SIKH RELIGION

9. SUMMARY

In 1499, when Guru Nanak went into a deep meditation, two things were revealed to him. The first: there only is one God. God's conception is explained very clearly at the beginning of Guru Granth Sahib. The second revelation was that all people are equal in all respects. Guru Nanak said there are no upper or lower classes of people.

He also emphasized that truthful living should be performed daily. Guru Nanak used a common language of the people to convey his message and traveled with people of different religions. All languages are permissible in spreading the Universality of the Sikh Religion. Universal prayer ends with words expressing that there be universal prosperity for all.

10. EXERCISES

i. What were the two revelations of Guru Nanak that formed the basis of the Sikh Religion?
ii. Why is Truthful Living higher than Truth? How can one enjoy Truthful Living on a day-to-day basis?
iii. What are the main reasons for Guru Nanak's success in spreading the Sikh Religion to ordinary people?
iv. What is the Universal prayer of the Sikhs?

11. REFERENCES

[1] Google Images, click for "Guru Nanak" select "saag8.jpg" or go to Yahoo "Sobha Singh Gallery" and select "saag8.jpg" Painting by Sobha Singh.
[2] Sandeep Singh Brar. 1998 of Website Sikhs.org http://www.sikhs.org/guru1.htm
[3] Website of Nankana Sahib http://www.nankanasahib.com/AboutNankana1.html
[4] Google Images, click on "Punjab in India," select "side_punjab_map.gif"

[5] South Asia Punjab, the Punjab and its People
http://www.cet.edu/earthinfo/sasia/punjab/PJtopic1.html
Click for 1966 map
or on Yahoo, go to "South Asia Punjab" and select "South Asia: Punjab" and click on 1966 map.

[6] Khuswant Singh. 1984 reissue, "A History of the Sikhs, Volume 1," Princeton University Press, Princeton, NJ (USA), p. 33.

[7] Dr. Harnam S. Shan, 1968, "Sayings of Guru Nanak," first edition, Shiromani Gurdwara Parbandhak Committee, Amritsar, Punjab, India. p. 265.

[8] Khuswant Singh. 1984 reissue, "A History of the Sikhs, Volume 1," Princeton University Press, Princeton, NJ (USA), p. 37.

[9] Kartar S. Duggal, 1989, Sikh Gurus, second printing, Himalayan International Institute, Honesdale, PA (USA), p. 32.

UNIVERSALITY OF THE SIKH RELIGION

CHAPTER 3

UNIVERSALITY BY THE SUCCEDING NINE GURUS

UNIVERSALITY FROM 1539 to 1708

It took about 209 years (from 1499* to 1708) to develop and nurture the Universality of the Sikh Religion as initiated by Guru Nanak*. It was a slow, time-tested process, that involved many generations. The development period associated with all 10 living Gurus is as follows:

No.	**GURU'S NAME**	**YEARS OF GURUSHIP**	**YEARS (CE)** Christian Era
1	Guru Nanak*	40	1499 to 1539
2.	Guru Angad	13	1539 to 1552
3.	Guru Amardas	22	1552 to 1574
4.	Guru Ramdas	7	1574 to 1581
5.	Guru Arjan	25	1581 to 1606
6.	Guru Hargobind	38	1606 to 1644
7.	Guru Har Rai	17	1644 to 1661
8.	Guru Har Krishan	3	1661 to 1664
9.	Guru Tegh Bahadur	11	1664 to 1675
10.	Guru Gobind Singh	33	1675 to 1708
	TOTAL	209	

*** Guru Nanak was about 30 years old in 1499 when the Sikh Religion was revealed to him.**

Gurus were selected on the basis of their devotion to the propagation of the Sikh principles as enunciated by first Guru Nanak. The selection may or may not have included close family and was decided on by the Guru before passing away. The first five and last two living Gurus were prolific writers of hymns in a poetry format and are included in Guru Granth Sahib. The sixth, seventh and eighth Gurus did not record any hymns but were extremely good in the propagation of the Sikh religion during that period.

After the passing of the 10th and the last living Guru, the Holy Book, called Guru Granth Sahib, was declared Guru for all times to come.

1. UNIVERSALITY OF THE SECOND GURU ANGAD DEV (1505-1552)

Guru Angad [1] continued the work of Guru Nanak during 13 years of Guruship (1539-1552). His special emphases were on education to illuminate the mind, and sports to maintain healthy bodies and foster a sense of discipline. Guru Angad standardized the use of Gurmukhi script for the Punjabi language. He compiled Guru Nanak's biography and continued the tradition of free kitchen (Langar). This is a shared meal that has become an important part of the Sikh way of life.

Guru Angad stressed the importance of Universality and said if ***the same God created every body whom should we call bad.***

The second Guru, Angad, said:

PUNJABI AND ROMAN	**ENGLISH**
ਆਪਿ ਉਪਾਏ ਨਾਨਕਾ Aap Upaa-ay Naankaa	God himself creates and
ਆਪੇ ਰਖੈ ਵੇਕ ॥ Aapay Rakhai Vayk	puts every one in proper place.
ਮੰਦਾ ਕਿਸ ਨੋ ਆਖੀਐ Mandaa Kis No Aakhee-ai	Whom shall we call bad
ਜਾਂ ਸਭਨਾ ਸਾਹਿਬੁ ਏਕੁ ॥ JaaN Sabhnaa Saahib Ayk	if God of all is one and the same.
ਸਭਨਾ ਸਾਹਿਬੁ ਏਕੁ ਹੈ Sabhnaa Saahib Ayk Hai	The same one God for all
ਵੇਖੈ ਧੰਧੈ ਲਾਇ ॥ Vaykhai DhanDhai Laa-ay	assigns every one a task and looks after it.
ਕਿਸੈ ਥੋੜਾ ਕਿਸੈ ਅਗਲਾ Kisai Thorhaa Kisai Aglaa	To some God gives less and some more
ਖਾਲੀ ਕੋਈ ਨਾਹਿ ॥ Khaalee Ko-ee Naahi	but none entirely empty.

Guru Granth Sahib (p1238, line 1)

2. UNIVERSALITY BY THIRD GURU AMAR DAS (1479-1574)

Amar Das, the third Guru [2] continued the Universality of Guru Nanak, during his 22 years of Guruship (1552-1574). His emphasis was on selfless service to the human race, to help the destitute and to be humble. This was required to build good character. He was a zealous preacher who gained many new followers. He vigorously campaigned against the practice of Sati (burning widows on their husband's funeral pyre).

Guru Amar Das discouraged the practice of veiling women and also prohibited the use of alcohol and intoxicants. Service to humanity, as practiced by Guru Amar Das, helped realize the ideals of Universal Brotherhood.

To propagate Universality, Guru Amar Das explained very clearly ***that God made all human beings from the same five things; thus there is no need to differentiate between any human being.***

The third Guru, Amar Das, said:

PUNJABI AND ROMAN	**ENGLISH**
ਮਾਟੀ ਏਕ ਸਗਲ ਸੰਸਾਰਾ ॥	God made the whole universe
Maatee Ek Sagal Sansaaraa	from one source.
ਬਹੁ ਬਿਧਿ ਭਾਂਡੇ ਘੜੈ ਕੁਮ੍ਹਾਰਾ ॥	but the Potter has shaped into
Bahu Budh Bhaande Gharai Kumaaraa	innumerable diverse forms.
ਪੰਚ ਤਤੁ ਮਿਲਿ ਦੇਹੀ ਕਾ ਆਕਾਰਾ ॥	All human beings are made
Panch Tat Mil Dehee Kaa Aakaaraa	from the same five things (air, water, fire, earth and soul or spirit). Today some scientists say the five are Carbon, Hydrogen, Oxygen, Nitrogen and Phosphorous, the principle constituents of DNA (deoxyribonucleic acid) [3].
ਘਟਿ ਵਧਿ ਕੋ ਕਰੈ ਬੀਚਾਰਾ ॥	Who can say which is less and
Ghat Vadh Ko Karai Beechaaraa	which is more?
Guru Granth Sahib (p1128, line 4)	

Guru Amar Das also stressed that ***service to humanity (part of the Sikh Religion) must be performed without expecting any rewards.***

The third Guru, Amar Das, said:

PUNJABI AND ROMAN	ENGLISH
ਸੇਵਾ ਕਰਤ ਹੋਇ ਨਿਹਕਾਮੀ ॥	Those who serve humanity
Sayvaa Karat Ho-ay Nihkaamee	without any reward
ਤਿਸ ਕਉ ਹੋਤ ਪਰਾਪਤਿ ਸੁਆਮੀ ॥	become closer to God.
Tis Ka-o Hot Paraapat Su-aamee	
Guru Granth Sahib (p 286, line 19)	

3. UNIVERSALITY OF THE FOURTH GURU RAM DAS (1534-1581)

Guru Ram Das, [5], maintained the Universality established by Guru Nanak during his seven years of Guruship (1574-1581). He emphasized simplicity, modesty and love for the less fortunate. He composed hymns for the simple and dignified marriage ceremony called Anand Karaj. He allowed widows to remarry. Guru Ram Das said, [5] that when a person has an important project in hand, join him or her and to make it a success. If you see that it cannot be carried out without funds, collect money from others and at the same time, contribute some thing from your own resources.

Guru Ram Das founded the Golden Temple in Amritsar, Punjab, India. It later helped tremendously to strengthen the Universality of the Sikh Religion [5]. For details on the Golden Temple see Chapter 5.

Guru, Ram Das, explained that ***people make imaginary walls between themselves and society. They live in false vanity that creates friction and leads to conflicts.***

The fourth Guru, Ram Das, said:

PUNJABI AND ROMAN	ENGLISH
ਮਿਥਿਆ ਦੂਜਾ ਭਾਉ	By giving importance to worldly things
Mithi-aa Doojaa Bhaa-o	
ਧੜੇ ਬਹਿ ਪਾਵੈ ॥	people divide into different factions
Dharhay Bahi Paavai	
ਪਰਾਇਆ ਛਿਦ੍ਰੁ ਅਟਕਲੈ	By speaking ill of other's faults
Paraa-i-aa Chhidar Atkalai	
ਆਪਣਾ ਅਹੰਕਾਰੁ ਵਧਾਵੈ ॥	it only increases their own pride.
Aapnaa AhaNkaar VaDhaavai	
ਜੈਸਾ ਬੀਜੈ ਤੈਸਾ ਖਾਵੈ ॥	As you sow so shall you reap.
Jaisaa Beejai Taisaa Khaavai	
Guru Granth Sahib (p 366, line 9)	

4. UNIVERSALITY OF THE FIFTH GURU ARJAN DEV (1563-1606)

Guru Arjan Dev, [6], continued the work of Guru Nanak during his 25 years of Guruship (1581-1606). Two of his accomplishments became pillars of the Sikh religion. First he compiled the Sikh Holy Book, Guru Granth Sahib, and second, he built the Golden Temple in Amritsar where Guru Granth Sahib was installed for the very first time. Thus Sikhs have a place to worship and Guru Granth Sahib to provide Sikh philosophy for ever.

Guru Arjan Dev's special emphasis was on Nam-Simrin (pray to God), and that it was essential to be in the company of God-loving people. He was a great composer and his 2,218 (38%) hymns out of a total of 5,894 hymns are incorporated in Guru Granth Sahib. Guru Arjan compiled not only his hymns, but also those of the preceding four Gurus, eminent Hindu saints and Sufi Muslims*, in Guru Granth Sahib. Main Mir, a Muslim, laid the foundation stone of the Golden Temple in 1589. Thus Guru Arjan Dev proved the universality of the Sikh religion.

* Sufis are not a separate sect of Islam [7], although some main stream Muslims consider them as belonging to a separate religion. Sufi Muslims observe local customs, would rather discuss than be authoritarian and care for the poor people in spreading the Muslim religion.

Guru Arjan was a great organizer and the number of people who joined the Sikh Religion increased considerably. He was a writer of intellectual vigor, a person of classical restraint, serenity of feeling and had a practical outlook on life. As the number of Sikhs increased there was a greater need for organization.

He decreed that Sikhs should set aside a certain percentage (generally 10 %) of their income for propagation of the Sikh religion. Guru Arjan also encouraged people to become involved in trade and commerce. Trading of horses especially from Kabul in Afghanistan became a popular business. Later, this helped considerably when starting an army to repulse foreign invaders.

The martyrdom of Guru Arjan Dev was carried out under orders of Jehangir, a cruel Muslim King. He considered the spread of Sikhism as a positive threat to Islam. He trumped up charges against Guru Arjan Dev and tortured him to death on May 30,1606. That began a new chapter in Sikh history and gave major impetus to advancement of the Sikh Religion.

Guru Arjan Dev propagated the Universality of the Sikh Religion by stating that ***everybody is my friend***.

The fifth Guru, Arjan Dev, said:

PUNJABI AND ROMAN	**ENGLISH**
ਨਾ ਕੋ ਮੇਰਾ ਦੁਸਮਨੁ ਰਹਿਆ	No one is my enemy
Naa Ko Mayraa Dusman Rahi-aa	
ਨ ਹਮ ਕਿਸ ਕੇ ਬੈਰਾਈ ॥	Neither am I against any one.
Naa Ham Kis Kay Bairaa-ee	
ਬ੍ਰਹਮੁ ਪਸਾਰੁ ਪਸਾਰਿਓ	God, who made this world,
Braham Pasaar Pasaario	also lives within us.
ਭੀਤਰਿ ਸਤਿਗੁਰ ਤੇ ਸੋਝੀ ਪਾਈ ॥	This wisdom I have received by
Bheeter Satgur Tay Sojhee Paa-ee	understanding the true God.
ਸਭੁ ਕੋ ਮੀਤੁ ਹਮ ਆਪਨ ਕੀਨਾ	I have befriended all and to every one
Sabh Ko Meet Ham Aapan Keenaa	
ਹਮ ਸਭਨਾ ਕੇ ਸਾਜਨ ॥	I am a friend and well wisher for all.
Ham Sabhnaa Kay Saajan	
Guru Granth Sahib (p 671, line 7)	

5. UNIVERSALITY OF THE SIXTH GURU, HAR GOBIND (1595-1644)

Guru Har Gobind, [8], carried out the work started by Guru Nanak during 38 years of Guruship (1606 –1644). His emphasis was on congregational prayer and proficiency in martial arts. This was to help protect the innocent and punish oppressors (both foreign and local).

In 1630, Guru Har Gobind carried out the universality of the Sikh religion ***by building a Muslim mosque called "GURU KI MASIT" (Guru's mosque).*** It is in Sri Hargobindpur, a city half way between Jalandhar and Amritsar, Punjab, India [9]. It was renovated in 2000 by Sikhs, Muslims and Hindus, with a generous contribution from the USA based Sikh Foundation. After restoration the mosque was handed over to the Muslims of Punjab on March 26, 2002. It was built to protect the rights of all people, and to let them pray according to their own religions.

6. UNIVERSALITY OF THE SEVENTH GURU HAR RAI (1630-1661)

Guru Har Rai, [10], continued the Universality started by Guru Nanak during 17 years of Guruship (1644-1661). He emphasized self-discipline, love of God and love for all human beings. Guru Har Rai said, " ***You can repair or build a temple or mosque but not a broken heart."*** [11].

7. UNIVERSALITY OF THE EIGHTH GURU HAR KRISHAN (1656-1664)

Guru Har Krishan, [12], maintained the Universality, during his three years of Guruship (1661-1664). He emphasized help for the needy irrespective of the recipient's' color, creed, religion or sex. He passed away at the tender age of eight.

8. UNIVERSALITY OF THE NINTH GURU TEGH BAHADUR (1621-1675)

Guru Tegh Bahadur [13] carried out the Universality, ideology and philosophy of Guru Nanak and his seven successors during his 11 years of Guruship (1664-1675). The Muslim king Aurengzeb, wanted to convert all Hindus to Muslims starting with Kashmir. Hindus from Kashmir approached Guru Tegh Bahadur to have him convince Aurengzeb to stop the conversion.

Instead Guru Tegh Bahadur was beheaded in Delhi on November 11, 1675. He sacrificed his own life to protect members of the Hindu religion. This added a new dimension to the philanthropy and Universality of the Sikh Religion. Guru Tegh Bahadur's supreme sacrifice was the first in medieval Indian history involving ***protection of fundamental human rights***. Today these human rights (including freedom for all people to worship according to their own religions) are foremost and an important rights in most of the world's constitutions.

i. GOD ABIDES IN ALL HEARTS

Guru Tegh Bahadur said if the ***same God abides in all hearts then all people are equal.***

The ninth Guru, Tegh Bahadur, said:

PUNJABI AND ROMAN	**ENGLISH**
ਘਟ ਘਟ ਮੈ ਹਰਿ ਜੂ ਬਸੈ Ghat Ghat Mai Har Joo Basai	God abides in all hearts
ਸੰਤਨ ਕਹਿਓ ਪੁਕਾਰਿ ॥ Santan Kahi-o Pukaar Guru Granth Sahib (p1427, line 2)	It is so proclaimed by God's devotees.

ii. TREAT EVERY ONE ALIKE

Guru Tegh Bahadur also said that ***an ideal person treats everyone alike***.

The ninth Guru, Tegh Bahadur, said:

PUNJABI AND ROMAN	ENGLISH
ਹਰਖੁ ਸੋਗੁ ਜਾ ਕੈ ਨਹੀ	Persons who keep their minds calm
Harkh Sog Jaa Kai Nahee	during joy or sorrow
ਬੈਰੀ ਮੀਤ ਸਮਾਨਿ ॥	and who keep friend and foe alike
Bairee Meet Samaan	are ideal persons.
Guru Granth Sahib (p 1427, line 3)	

9. UNIVERSALITY OF THE TENTH GURU GOBIND SINGH (1666-1708)

Guru Gobind Singh [14], Figure 4 [15], continued the Universality started by Guru Nanak, during his Guruship of 33 years (1675-1708). The 10th Guru Gobind Singh's contributions are far-reaching, very practical in nature and follow the Universality of the Sikh religion. For some odd reason, the tenets preached by Guru Gobind Singh either are not well presented or not well understood by people. Some of his achievements are discussed below:

i. GURU GOBIND SINGH AS AN ORIGINATOR OF HUMAN RIGHTS

Hundreds of Hindu Pundits from Kashmir came to Guru Tegh Bahadur, Gobind's father, and said that the king was going to forcefully convert them to the Muslim religion and that he was their only refuge. Gobind Rai, only about nine years old, told his father, Guru Tegh Bahadur: who could be a better person than you to convince King Aurangzeb to change this wrong policy?

Guru Tegh Bahadur went to Delhi to discuss this with Aurangzeb but instead, the King murdered him by cutting off his head in Chandni Chowk, Delhi. Guru Tegh Bahadur gave his life to protect not only his own religion but also all other religions (specifically Hindu religion, in this case). ***This sacrifice by Guru Tegh Bahadur to save the lives of innocent people marked the beginning of the human rights struggle taking place worldwide.*** It really started during the period of ninth and 10th Gurus, Tegh Bahadur and Gobind Singh, respectively [16].

FIGURE 4

GURU GOBIND SINGH
(1666 to 1708)
TENTH AND LAST LIVING GURU
Picture is for profound respect but not for worship

ii. GURU GOBIND SINGH AS A CHAMPION OF INDIA'S FREEDOM

Guru Gobind Singh said, "if those in power start killing innocent people and all peaceful means fail, then the only way to rectify this is to use force.

**" When all other means fail
it is justifiable to use the sword."**

This was not an easy decision coming from a very religious person. Thousands of years of plunder and killing by foreign invaders to forcefully convert them to another religion was the deciding factor, to use force.

Guru Gobind never used force indiscriminately. It should, however, be made clear in the present democratic society that no one person has a right to use force. One has to go through the legal process. If the law is not good, then all means should be used to change it.

However, some background is essential for this major decision to use force. The reasons are explained below.

ERA BEFORE CHRIST [17]

At first, the Aryans (about 1,500 B.C.) who were tall and fair, invaded the northern part of India and drove the dark skinned inhabitants to the south. The Persians (about 500 B.C.) came and ruled for about one hundred years. Greek armies under Alexander the Great conquered the northern part of India, 326 B.C. Later many other tribes followed and plundered India.

ERA AFTER CHRIST [17]

After a succession of Afghan invasions there came the terrible invasion of Timur from Mongolia in 1938. India did not recover from this for decades. One hundred years later, Babar, one of Taimur's descendents defeated the reigning Afghan, Abrahim Lodhi, at Panipat (Punjab) in 1526. He established the most powerful and long-lived dynasty in India's history.

Persecution of people living in India had been taking place for thousands of years before and after Christ, and no end was in sight. The Indian people were so waek they could not organize any resistance to foreign invaders.

There was no justice and killing was a daily occurrence. Most of the invaders were Muslims. They had a two-pronged approach for converting people to Islam. The Sufis converted by persuasion and the ruling Kings by force. Guru Gobind Singh tried all possible means to stress upon the Muslim rulers that they should stop their ruthless killing of innocent people. But they refused. It was under these circumstances that Guru Gobind Singh used force to bring justice and peace to the people of India.

iii. KHALSA OF GURU GOBIND SINGH

Guru Gobind Singh's main objective was to have India for the Indians, and to this end he decided that force was the only alternative left to end the tyranny. He recognized the need, at that time, for an army of saint-soldiers to effectively fight the forces of evil. Communal hatred was prevalent along with the exploitation of people based on their caste, sex and religion. Guru Gobind Singh organized an army to bring justice and peace to India.

To achieve the objective of using force to free India from all foreign invaders, Guru Gobind Singh created Khalsa. This ceremony was held in the Keshgarh Gurdwara, Figure 5 [18], Anandpur, Punjab India in1699. It coincided with the festival of Baisakhi (the time for harvesting in Punjab during April).

Khalsa was a unique person, not only a soldier but also very religious. Khalsa has five symbols that start with the letter K in the Punjabi language:

The five K's are:

i. Kachha (undergarment or short pants).
ii. Kara (steel bracelet).
iii. Kirpan (sword).
iv. Kangha (comb).
v. Kesh (uncut hair).

At the initiation ceremony of Khalsa, the following five hymns are recited [19],[20].

i. Japji of first Guru Nanak
ii. Jap of tenth Guru Gobind Singh
iii. Swayyas are ten verses of tenth Guru Gobind Singh
iv. Chaupai collection of verses of tenth Guru Gobind Singh
v. Anand Sahib ten verses of third Guru Amardas

FIGURE 5

KESHGARH GURDWARA, ANANDPUR, PUNJAB, INDIA
SITE OF THE KHALSA INITIATION IN 1699

Guru Gobind Singh's army, besides Khalsa, also had Sikhs who were not Khalsa, as well as Hindus and Muslims. It clearly shows that he accepted people other than Khalsa into the Sikh Religion, thus maintaining its Universality. This paved the way for others to join the Sikh Religion in large numbers. During those days, Sikhs, Hindus and Muslims had the same goal of freeing India from cruel foreign invaders irrespective of their religion.

This very effective force of Guru Gobind Singh's repulsed the foreign invaders. ***If Guru Gobind Singh had not used force it was just a question of time before most of India would have converted to Islam, by force or by persuasion.***

iv. SIKH GREETINGS

Sikhs greet each other with folded hands as below.

Usual greeting
Sat Siri Akal
It means "truth is eternal".

Another greeting
Waheguru Ji Ka Khalsa Waheguru Ji Ke Fateh
It means "Khalsa believes in wonderful God and the same God is supreme".

The first greeting is not controversial. The second needs explanation due to the word Khalsa.

Many Amritdhari (initiated) Sikhs believe that Khalsa is to be used only for them. Gurdwaras also consider it the same way. On the other hand many people say that the word Khalsa can be used for Hindus, Muslims and Sikhs as was done by the Sikh Gurus.

The literal meaning of the word Khalsa is pure. This means one should be pure religiously as well as in daily life dealings. Thus any body could be a Khalsa irrespective of religion and sex. The word Khalsa has been used by Kabir, the sixth Guru Hargobind and the ninth Guru Tegh Bahadur [21]. They all refer to Khalsa as pure.

Although the tenth Guru Gobind Singh used the word Khalsa for those who were initiated (baptized) in 1699 but he was very liberal in using the word Khalsa for those who were not initiated.

According to the written documents Guru Gobind Singh said the following [21]:

i. On March 12, 1699 before the initiation he said that all of the congregation (Sangat) in Machiwara, Punjab is Khalsa.
ii. On October 5, 1699 many months after the initiation he said that the congregation (Sangat) of Sarangdeo is Khlasa.
iii. Guru Gobind Singh even wrote to many Hindus and some Muslims in 1702 and 1704 that they are Khalsa.

After the death of Guru Gobind Singh in 1708, his wife Mata Sundri wrote to many Hindus, Sikhs and some Muslims as Khalsa of the Guru. These were written on October 12, 1717; October 20, 1722; June 2, 1723; October 8, 1723; and August 10, 1730 [2].

Thus it is clear that it is better to use the word Khalsa as inclusive for all Sikhs. It will help in propagating Sikh religion as universal and bring more people into the fold of the Sikh religion.

v. GURU GOBIND SINGH AS AN ORIGINATOR OF THE RED CROSS PRINCIPLE

As the fighting progressed, there were causalities on both sides. Bhai Ghanaeeya, a Sikh devote, provided water not only to his own people but also to enemies who were wounded. Several people complained about this to Guru Gobind Singh, and the Guru asked Bhai Ghanaeeya to come to him.

Bhai Ghanaeeya explained that he give water to all people, because they all looked the same to him. Guru Gobind Singh was very pleased and told Ghanaeeya that in the future, in addition to water, apply ointment to all, friend and foe alike, Figure 6 [22].

It is said that the founder of the worldwide Red Cross Organization also took inspiration from Bhai Ghanaeeya's story.

Bhai Ghanaeeya was the first person to carry out this humanitarian work. During wartime he helped the wounded medically and in other ways be they friend or enemy, [22].

vi. GURU GOBIND SINGH FOR EQUALITY AND SECULARISM

Guru Gobind Singh believed in secularism and equality for all. He had Muslims, Hindus and Sikhs in his fighting forces. He treated them alike. He was against

FIGURE 6

BHAI GHANAEEYA JI (standing) GIVING WATER
TO THE WOUNDED DURING THE WAR
INCLUDING FRIEND AND FOE ALIKE

(Note: the water is in a Mashk made out of leather.)

the regime that was forcefully converting people to Islam. Universality of the Sikh Religion was definitely continued by Guru Gobind Singh and he said very clearly as shown below [23].

Tenth Guru Gobind Singh, said

Temple and Mosque are the same.
Puja (Hindu worship) and Namaz (Muslim prayer) are the same.
All people are equal and look similar.
It is through error that they appear different.
Our eyes are the same. Our ears are the same.
We are of one body and one built.
We are a compound of earth, air, fire and water.
Allah (God of Muslims) and Abhek (God of Hindus) are the same.
Puran (Hindu Holy Book) and Quran (Muslim Holy Book) are the same.
We are all alike. We all are the creations of the same God.

vii. GURU GOBIND SINGH AND GURU GRANTH SAHIB

The greatest contribution of Guru Gobind Singh to the Universality of the Sikh Religion, was making it ***mandatory for all people to follow Guru Granth Sahib as the Guru for all time to come*** [24]. The succession of living Gurus came to an end. Guru Gobind Singh proclaimed this before passing away in 1708. This cannot be changed.

Today Guru Granth Sahib's teachings are followed by all Sikhs and people of many other religions, most noticeably, Sindhi Hindus. This will continue forever. This extraordinary achievement completely changed the way Sikhs used to follow directions from their living Gurus. Guru Granth Sahib cannot be killed, as it is not a living Guru. It should be mentioned that the Mughal Rulers at that time killed three of 10 living Gurus. They were Guru Arjan Dev (the fifth), Guru Tegh Bahadur (the ninth) and Guru Gobind Singh (the 10th).

This may be one of the reason for Guru Granth Sahib being mandated to be followed by all Sikhs.

Guru Granth Sahib is the Sikh's holy book. It is given profound respect and all Sikhs draw inspiration from it. It should, however, be made clear that Sikhs worship only one God that is not born and does not die. **The *Universality of Guru Granth Sahib easily can be established because the hymns, are composed not only by Sikhs but also by Muslims and Hindus*.** In this respect Guru Gobind Singh followed the Universal path laid out by Guru Nanak and the succeeding nine Gurus including himself.

viii. THE LAST DAYS OF GURU GOBIND SINGH

When visiting the southern part of India, Guru Gobind Singh found a picturesque spot on the banks of the river Godavari at Nanded in the central part of India. He established a beautiful Gurdwara there.

Mr. Wazir Khan, the Governer of Sirhind, Punjab, India sent two Muslim assassins to Nanded where Guru Gobind Singh was staying. They disguised themselves and eventually attacked Guru Gobind Singh. In spite of the best medical help, the wound proved fatal and he died on October 7, 1708. The assassins were caught immediately and put to death.

10. PRESENT MANAGEMENT OF THE GURDWARAS

At present Sikh Gurdwaras are run by Management Committees elected by their members. They appoint Ragis to sing hymns, and Granthis and Bhais to handle day-to-day activities and also to care for the buildings. All Gurdwaras outside of India are run independently according to their own constitutions. In Punjab, India, the historic Gurdwaras are run by one organization while others are run independently.

11. SUMMARY

The Universality of the Sikh Religion was initiated by Guru Nanak and perfected by the succeeding nine Gurus. It took 209 years to nurture and put into practice the Universality that is for all generations and for all times to come. The second Guru Angad said that same God created every body.

The third Guru Amar Das said all people are made from the same five things. He was against Sati (the burning of widows on their husband's funeral pyres), discouraged the practice of veiling women and prohibited alcohol and other intoxicants. The fourth Guru Ram Das said that imaginary walls created by people lead to friction, and as one sows so shall one reap. He allowed widows to marry. He established the Golden Temple. The fifth Guru Arjan Dev said all are my friends. He compiled Guru Granth Sahib and for the first time installed it in the Golden Temple. The sixth Guru Har Gobind emphasized congregational prayer and proficiency in martial arts. The seventh Guru Har Rai said one could repair or build a religious place but not a broken heart. The eighth Guru Har Krishan emphasized helping the needy irrespective of color, creed, religion or sex.

The ninth Guru Tegh Bahadur said God abides in all hearts. He gave his life for the protection and faith of other religions and was the first ever to propagate fundamental human rights for all people. The 10th Guru Gobind Singh said all people are equal and similar. He created Khalsa (soldiers as well as religious persons) that stopped the foreign invaders who had plundered India for centuries. He was, in fact, the originator of the Red Cross concept as he allowed those wounded in the battlefield, friend or foe, to be treated alike. Guru Gobind Singh mandated that Guru Granth Sahib be the Guru for all time to come and thus, ended the living Gurus. All 10 Gurus spread the message of the Universality of the Sikh Religion and people joined in large numbers.

12. EXERCISES

i. Explain at least one great contribution of the 2nd, 3rd, 4th, 5th and 9th Gurus as recorded in Guru Granth Sahib that contributes to the Universality of the Sikh Religion.

ii. Although the, $6^{th,}$ 7th and 8th Gurus works are not recorded in Guru Granth Sahib, what are their contributions to the Universality?

iii. What are the five great contributions of the 10th Guru Gobind Singh to the Universality of the Sikh Religion? Explain them.

13. REFERENCES

[1] Dr. Sukhbir Singh Kapoor, 1988, The Ideal Man, Khalsa College London Press. pp. 69-71.

[2] Dr. Sukhbir Singh Kapoor. 1988, The Ideal Man, Khalsa College London Press. pp. 71-74.

[3] Yahoo.com Go to "Johnson, Jerry G., World of Biology," click on "Mr. Johnson's Biology Home Page," click on Biology 11, click on "Chapter 2, "Chemical basis of Life," click on section 2.3, B, 4; Johnson is a biology teacher in Frederick, Oklahoma USA.
http://www.sirinet.net/~jgjohnso/essentialschap2.html

[4] Dr. Sukhbir Singh Kapoor, 1988, The Ideal Man, Khalsa College London Press, pp. 74-77.

[5] Teja Singh and Ganda Singh, "A Short History of the Sikhs," pp. 25-26; Macauliffe, "The Sikh Religion," Volume 2, p. 275.
Dr. Sukhbir Singh Kapoor, 1988, The Ideal Man, Khalsa College London Press, pp. 75-76.

[6] Dr. Sukhbir Singh Kapoor. 1988, The Ideal Man, Khalsa College London Press. p. 77-79.

[7] Elliot Miller, Sufis: The Mystical Muslims, Forward Magazine, 1986 (later became the Christian Research Journal).
http://www.equip.org/free/DI200-3.htm

[8] Dr. Sukhbir Singh Kapoor, 1988, The Ideal Man, Khalsa College London Press, pp. 79-82.
[9] Indian Express Newspaper, New Delhi, India, August 8, 2000 per e-mail from Professor Harbans Lal [japji@home.com].
[10] Dr. Sukhbir Singh Kapoor, 1988, The Ideal Man, Khalsa College London Press, pp. 82-84.
[11] Khuswant Singh, 1984 reissue, A History of the Sikhs, Volume 1, Princeton University Press, Princeton, NJ, USA p. 69.
[12] Dr. Sukhbir Singh Kapoor, 1988, The Ideal Man, Khalsa College London Press. pp. 84-86.
[13] Dr. Sukhbir Singh Kapoor, 1988, The Ideal Man, Khalsa College LondonPress, pp. 86-89.
[14] Kartar S. Duggal, 1989, Sikh Gurus, Second Printing, Himalayan International Institute, Honesdale, PA, USA p. 184.
[15] Yahoo Images, "Guru Gobind Singh," select "nanak10.jpg"
Painting by Sobha Singh.
http://www.singhsabha.com/guru_gobind_singh.htm
[16] Khuswant Singh, 1984 reissue, A History of the Sikhs, Volume 1, Princeton University Press, Princeton, NJ, USA p. 76.
[17] Singh, Khuswant, 1984 reissue, A History of the Sikhs, Volume 1, Princeton University Press, Princeton, NJ, USA pp.10-12.
[18] Sri Guru Singh Sabha, Glen Rock, NJ, USA 1992 Calendar of Historic Gurdwaras.
[19] Dr. Sukhbir Singh Kapoor, 1988, The Ideal Man, Khalsa College London Press, p. 114.
[20] W. Owen Cole, 1999, Number 14, Sikhism, NTC Publishing Group, Chicago, IL, USA p. 38.
[21] Dr. Virinder Singh Grewal, E-mail, Sikh-Diaspora@yahoogroups.com
April 15, 2006
Dr. Jit Singh Chandan, E-mail, Sikh-Diaspora@yahoogroups.com
January 3, 2003
[22] Nishkam Sikh Welfare Council (humanitarian organization), New Delhi, India, 1992, brochure, p. 2. (also www.nishkam.org).
[23] Iqbal Singh, 1986, The Essence of Truth: Japji and other Sikh Scriptures, Allen, McMillan and Enderson, New York, NY, USA pp.155-156; original reference is Akal Ustat, verses 16 to 86, Dasam Granth by Guru Gobind Singh.
[24] Kartar S. Duggal, 1989, Sikh Gurus, Second Printing, Himalayan International Institute, Honesdale, PA, USA p. 227.

UNIVERSALITY OF THE SIKH RELIGION

CHAPTER 4

HOW UNIVERSALITY WAS MAINTAINED DURING A POLITICALLY HISTORIC PERIOD

This chapter summarizes the history of the Sikhs starting from Guru Nanak in 1469 to the Independence of India in 1947.

While discussing the historical facts, it should be made clear that Universality of the Sikhs also was carried out during this period. Most of the invaders who came to India invariably landed first in Punjab and were Muslims. There were two types of Muslims. One was made up of ***foreign Muslims*** who invaded India for thousands of years. They used force indiscriminately, plundered the country and took away all they could lay their hands on.

I call the other type ***local Muslims***. They were recent converts from Hindus to the Muslim religion. They were of the Indian culture and more amicable and peace loving. Sikhs had no problems with the local Muslims but were against the foreign Muslim invaders**. *Finally the Sikhs were able, by force, to repulse the foreign Muslim invaders.*** The local Muslims also aligned themselves with the Sikhs as there was indiscriminate killing by the foreign Muslims.

This chapter is divided into several parts.

PART 1. HISTORY DURING THE 10 SIKH GURU'S PERIOD: 1469 to 1708

During this period, the Mughals ruled India. This reign started with Babur in 1526 and ended with Aurangzeb in 1707. Essentially, the 10 Gurus's period coincides with that of Muslim rule by the Mughals in Punjab and India.

Babur occupied India in 1526 after five initial invasions. He created havoc and tyranny in Punjab. Babur traces his ancestry on his mother's side to Genghis Khan. Genghis Khan was a Mongol Pagan [1] and not a Muslim. He was known for the death and destruction of millions of people of all religions and captured the largest empire in world history.

Babur was born in Uzbekistan [2] and was the great-grandson of Tamerlane. Tamerlane was born as Timur Lenk and was ruthless in killing people. He invaded India in 1398 and plundered Delhi, murdering 100,000 people [3]. Babur also was ruthless and his big victory in 1526 was against Muslim Sultan Lodi of Afghan who was the ruler of India at that time. Babur died soon after in 1530.

Guru Nanak describes Babur's barbarous attack and suffering of the Punjab people in the words below.

PUNJABI AND ROMAN	ENGLISH
ਖੁਰਾਸਾਨ ਖਸਮਾਨਾ ਕੀਆ	Having conquered Khuraasaan
Khuraasaan Khasmaanaa Kee-aa	(Afghanistan),
ਹਿੰਦੁਸਤਾਨੁ ਡਰਾਇਆ ॥	Baabar terrified Hindustan (India).
Hindusataan Daraa-i-aa.	
ਆਪੈ ਦੋਸੁ ਨ ਦੇਈ ਕਰਤਾ	God the Creator of all should have
Aapai Dos Na Day-ee Kartaa	felt some blame,
ਜਮੁ ਕਰਿ ਮੁਗਲੁ ਚੜਾਇਆ ॥	but instead sent Mugals as the
Jam Kar Mugal Charhaa-i-aa.	messengers of death.
ਏਤੀ ਮਾਰ ਪਈ ਕਰਲਾਣੇ	There was so much slaughter that
Aytee Maar Pa-ee Karlaanay	the people screamed,
ਤੈਂ ਕੀ ਦਰਦੁ ਨ ਆਇਆ ॥	Oh God, don't you have some
TaiN Kee Darad Na Aa-i-aa	compassion?
ਕਰਤਾ ਤੂੰ ਸਭਨਾ ਕਾ ਸੋਈ ॥	Oh God, You are the doer equally
Kartaa TooN Sabhnaa Kaa So-ee	for all.
ਜੇ ਸਕਤਾ ਸਕਤੇ ਕਉ ਮਾਰੇ	If some powerful man strikes out against
Jay Saktaa Saktay Ka-o Maaray	another man who is equally powerful,
ਤਾ ਮਨਿ ਰੋਸੁ ਨ ਹੋਈ ॥	then there is no anger in the mind.
Taa Man Ros Na Ho-ee	
ਸਕਤਾ ਸੀਹੁ ਮਾਰੇ ਪੈ ਵਗੈ	But if a powerful tiger attacks a flock
Saktaa Seehu Maaray Pai Vagai	of sheep and kills them,
ਖਸਮੈ ਸਾ ਪੁਰਸਾਈ ॥	then its Master (God) must answer for it.
Khasmai Saa Pursaa-ee.	
ਰਤਨ ਵਿਗਾੜਿ ਵਿਗੋਏ ਕੁਤੀ	This priceless country has been laid
Ratan Vigaarh Vvigo-ay KuteeN	waste and defiled by dogs,
ਮੁਇਆ ਸਾਰ ਨ ਕਾਈ ॥	and no one pays any attention
Mu-i-aa Saar Na Kaa-ee.	to the dead.
ਆਪੇ ਜੋੜਿ ਵਿਛੋੜੇ ਆਪੇ ਵੇਖੁ	God brings people together and
Aapay Jorh Vichhorhay Aapay Vaykh	also divides them but
ਤੇਰੀ ਵਡਿਆਈ ॥	this is all God's greatness.
Tayree Vadi-aa-ee	

ਜੇ ਕੋ ਨਾਉ ਧਰਾਏ ਵਡਾ Jay Ko Naa-o Dharaa-ay Vadaa	Persons may think they are very great
ਸਾਦ ਕਰੇ ਮਨਿ ਭਾਣੇ ॥ Saad Karay Man Bhaanay	and enjoy all of their heart's desires.
ਖਸਮੈ ਨਦਰੀ ਕੀੜਾ ਆਵੈ Khasmai Nadree Keerhaa Aavai	But in the eyes of the God that person is just like an insect
ਜੇਤੇ ਚੁਗੈ ਦਾਣੇ Jaytay Chugai Daanay.	nibbling on the corn.
ਮਰਿ ਮਰਿ ਜੀਵੈ ਤਾ ਕਿਛੁ ਪਾਏ Mar Mar Jeevai Taa Kichh Paa-ay	The true profit of life is learning to die
ਨਾਨਕ ਨਾਮੁ ਵਖਾਣੇ Naanak Naam Vakhaanay. ||	and chanting God's Naam, says Nanak.

Guru Granth Sahib (p. 360, line 12)

Humayun succeed his father Babur, but was defeated by Sher Shah, an Afghan King. Later, Humayun returned and managed to gain control of his father's territories before his death in 1556.

Akbar, the son of Humayun, decisively defeated the Afghans and firmly established Mughal supremacy in India. Akbar used persuasion to spread the Muslim religion and was very successful in achieving that objective. His rule lasted from 1556 to 1605.

Jehangir succeeded his father Akbar and ruled India from 1605 to 1627. ***He was a cruel king.*** Jehangir did not like the rise of the Sikh religion and an increase in their numbers. ***While passing through Punjab, he ordered fifth Sikh Guru Arjan Dev to be tortured and executed***. Guru Arjan Dev was made to sit in a cauldron of hot water, scorching sand was poured over his head and he was put on heated metallic sheets. After enduring five days of unrelenting torture, Guru Ji indicated to Sikhs that his time had come.

The executioners took him to the waters of Ravi River in Punjab [4]. Guru Ji chanted hymns known as Japji Sahib in the Guru Granth Sahib. Then, with a tranquil mind, he left for his heavenly abode on May 30,1606. Guru Ji accepted this as God's sweet will and departed with God's name on his lips. Guru Arjan Dev chanted the following hymn during his torture and to the end of his life.

The fifth Guru, Arjan Dev, said:

ROMAN AND PUNJABI	**ENGLISH**
ਤੇਰਾ ਕੀਆ ਮੀਠਾ ਲਾਗੈ Tayraa Kee-aa Meethaa Laagai	Whatever God ordains is sweet.
ਹਰਿ ਨਾਮੁ ਪਦਾਰਥੁ ਨਾਨਕੁ ਮਾਂਗੈ Har Naam Padaarath Naanak MaaNgai.	Nanak craves for the wealth of God's Naam.

Guru Granth Sahib (p. 394, line 4)

Shah Jehan, son of Jehangir, ruled India from 1628 to 1658. He will be remembered for building *the **Taj Mahal***, the massive white marble mausoleum constructed for his wife Mumtaz Mahal along the bank of the Jamuna River in Agra, India. His ruthless son, Auranbzeb, deposed his father Shah Jehan in a coup in 1658. Shah Jehan was imprisoned for eight years and buried in 1666 next to his wife in the Taj Mahal.

Aurangzeb, the last Mughal King was a ***most cruel and vicious*** person. He did not spare his own family. Aurengzeb imprisoned his father, killed his brother Dara and then showed his head to his father in prison [5]. He drove his son into exile in Persia [5]. Aurangzeb put Muslim clergy in every big city to impose Islamic Law on everyone. Hindu religious fairs were outlawed in 1668, and an edict the following year prohibited construction of Hindu temples as well as the repair of old ones. Conversion to Islam became his favorite passion [5].

Ninth Guru Tegh Bahadur assumed considerable power. People joined him in large numbers. Aurangzeb wanted to convert Guru Ji to the Muslim religion. Guru Ji, on behalf of hundred of Kashmiri Hindu priests, went to Delhi to convince him of his wrong policies. ***Instead Aurangzeb executed Guru Tegh Bahadur on November 11, 1675 in Delhi.***

Guru Tegh Bahadur used to chant the following hymn as promised to the Kashmiri pundits [6].

ROMAN	**ENGLISH**
Bah Jinahn Di Pakariye	Those whom you have undertaken to protect
Sar Dije Bah Na Chhoriye	be willing to give head but not the promise.
Tegh Bahadur Bolya	Guru Tegh Bahadur proclaimed
Dhar Payae Dharma Na Chhoriye	Sacrifice life but do not relinquish the faith.

Aurengzeb's reign lasted for 49 years from 1658 until his death in 1707. Mughal rule was finished after the death of Aurengzeb. From then on Sikhs began to assume much power.

The last living Sikh, Guru Gobind Singh, decided that when all peaceful means failed it was right to use force to get rid of foreign invaders. ***He organized an army of Khalsa Sikhs in 1699.***
They were very successful in fighting the invaders. Guru Gobind Singh went to Nanded, in the central part of India. Two Muslims assassins disguised themselves and stabbed him in 1708. When the end came on October 7, 1708, Guru Gobind Singh addressed the Sikhs as below.

ROMAN	**ENGLISH**
Sab Sikhon Ko Hukam Hai	**All Sikhs are mandated to**
Guru Manio Granth.	**believe in Guru Granth Sahib as Guru.**

It was 91 years after the death of Guru Gobind Singh that Sikhs established their kingdom under Maharaja Ranjit Singh.

PART 2. HISTORY FROM 1708 TO 1798

The period, 1708 to 1798, was a ***most traumatized time for the Sikh Religion***. It really was a period of survival. In brief, it can be said that during this period, Sikhs were persecuted and finally reorganized into a powerful army.

Muslims of Mughal, Persian and Afghan descent came to Punjab with large numbers of forces to plunder and take precious things back home. Mughals established their kingdoms, while most of the others simply destroyed and looted.

A brief summary of events is provided below. For details see Khuswant Singh's book, "History of the Sikhs, Volume 1 [7].

i. BANDA BAHADUR: 1708 to 1716

Banda Bahadur was instructed by Guru Gobind Singh to fight the Mughal and Afghan Muslim invaders. Banda won many battles but was caught by the Muslim invaders and executed in 1716. This occurred in presence of thousands of people including two Englishmen [8].

ii. THE PERSIAN INVASION: 1738-1739

Nadir Shah, King of Persia (present day Iran), created much havoc and plundered Punjab [9]. He returned home with enormous booty including the famous Koh-i-Noor diamond. He conquered Afghanistan and died in 1747.

iii. FIRST AFGHAN INVASION: 1747 to 1748

Ahmed Shah Abdali of Afghanistan was the most trusted general of Nadir Shah and thus claimed the right to conquer India. Later, he also took possession of the Koh-i-noor diamond. He invaded India with 18,000 men and clashed with the 60,000-man army of Moghuls. He was forced to retreat to Afghanistan.

During this time, Sikh Misl emerged to organize a united Sikh army. Misl describes a unit or brigade of Sikh warriors controlling their specific territory but fighting for the same cause: to be free of the Muslim invaders.

iv. SECOND AFGHAN INVASION: 1748 to 1749

Ahmad Shah Abdali again invaded in 1748. Sikhs collaborated with Kaura Mal's (follower of Guru Nanak) forces and were able to defeat the enemy. During 1749 and 1750, a great many peasants joined the Sikh fold.

v. THIRD AFGHAN INVASION: 1751 TO 1752

Ahmad Shah Abdali invaded a third time. With the death of Kaura Mal in 1751 and Mir Mannu in 1753, the country now was neglected by both Mughals and Afghans. Sikhs were the only force left and thus, several areas of Punjab came under their protection.

vi. FOURTH AFGHAN INVASION: 1756 to 1757

Ahmad Shah Abdali invaded once more and desecrated the Golden Temple in Amritsar. Later, Sikhs and Adina Beg of the Mughals defeated the Afghans. In 1758, Marathas came to Punjab and in 1759, captured Lahore, the capital of Punjab. Marathas are Hindus from the south central part of India and are known for their fighting ability. On paper, Punjab now was under control of three masters: Mughals, Afghans and Marathas. In fact, Punjab was controlled by only two masters: Sikhs and Mughal Adina Beg Khan.

vii. FIFTH AFGHAN INVASION: 1759

Ahmad Shah Abdali came with a force of 60,000 men to invade India for the fifth time. His objective was to crush the Marathas. The Marathas lost the Battle of Panipat in 1761 and left Punjab. The Afghans also left Punjab in 1761. Then the Sikhs had much of Punjab under their control.

viii. SIXTH AFGHAN INVASION: 1762

Ahmad Shah Abdali came again to destroy the Sikh's power. Abdali was very successful in defeating the Sikhs in 1762 when 30,000 Sikhs died. It is known as the great Sikh holocaust. Abdali also destroyed the Golden Temple with gunpowder. Within six months, the Sikhs again were ready and defended the Golden Temple. Abdali left and the Sikhs once more consolidated their hold on Punjab.

ix. SEVENTH AFGHAN INVASION: 1764

Ahmad Shah Abdali came from Afghanistan with a force of 18,000. Nasir Khan, of Baluchistan joined him with his 12,000 men. They captured many areas and again desecrated the Golden Temple by filling it with dead cows. Abdali and Khan left Punjab. The Sikhs retook Lahore and extended operations beyond Delhi.

x. EIGHTH AFGHAN INVASION: 1766

Ahmad Shah Abdali came again to eliminate the Sikhs. This time he was not successful. Whenever he left any city after capturing it, the residents, even the local Muslims, would turn against him. Everyone was satisfied with the Sikh administration. Abdali then left, and by the end of 1767, the Sikhs had retaken all of Punjab.

xi. NINTH AFGHAN INVASION: 1769

Ahmad Shah Abdali made his ninth and final attempt to conquer Punjab in 1769. This time, he could not do anything. He did not go beyond Jhelum, and then returned home where he died in 1772

For 22 years, from 1747 to 1769, Ahmad Shah Abdali invaded Punjab and other parts of India nine times. Every time he had to rush back to Afghanistan to put down insurrections and oversee consolidation. The Sikhs never gave up although they suffered many casualties.

Abdali was the Sikh's greatest enemy, but in the end, he turned out to be their greatest benefactor. His repeated invasions destroyed the Mughal administration in Punjab and at Panipat he dealt a crippling blow to Marathas. The power vacuum that was created helped the Sikhs. Besides being good soldiers, they also were very benevolent administrators. People of all religions including Muslims, approved their rule. People helped them in all possible ways. During the wars, peasants gave them food, tended their wounded and gave them shelter.

xii. DURING 1770 to 1798

In this period of 28 years, there was much infighting involving Sikhs with Mughals, Afghans and Marathas. ***To be free from foreign invaders, the Sikhs created an atmosphere that Punjab was for the Punjabis irrespective of their religion.*** This helped the Sikhs considerably in establishing their hold on Punjab.

However, they lacked a charismatic leader to keep them united and rule Punjab for the good of the people.

PART 3. HISTORY FROM 1799 TO 1839

UNIVERSALITY DURING MAHARAJA RANJIT SINGH 1780 to 1839

i. SECULAR GOVERNMENT OF MAHARAJA RANJIT SINGH

Finally, the Sikhs were able to find Maharaja Ranjit Singh (Figure 7) [10] as the charismatic leader they were looking for. He was the most important figure in Sikh history. At age 19, Maharaja Ranjit Singh was able to establish the first Sikh Kingdom in Punjab.

This was the second period in Sikh history when large numbers of people joined the Sikh Religion. It is said that during Maharaja Ranjit Singh's rule, the number of Sikhs increased considerably. People joined the Sikh Religion by persuasion and the teachings as enunciated by the 10 Gurus. Force was not used to convert people. However when the British took over, the number of Sikhs did not increase. Some say there were about two to three million by1881 [11].

Maharaja Ranjit Singh conquered and ruled Punjab from 1799 to 1839 (Figure 8) [12]. This occurred, about 91 years after the death of the 10th Guru, Guru Gobind Singh, in 1708. This was the first time in India's history, and after thousands of years (in the eras before and after Christ), that the country was free of foreign rulers such as the Afghans, Pathans and Mughals.

Maharaja Ranjit Singh's achievements mainly were due to the actual practice of the Universality of the Sikh Religion. ***Ranjit Singh convinced people that he wanted to establish a Punjabi state in which Sikhs, Muslims and Hindus would be equal before the law and have the same rights and duties.*** This indeed was the reason why his kingdom prospered. He paid respect to the sites of other religions and participated in their functions.

FIGURE 7

MAHARAJA RANJIT SINGH
1780 to 1839

FIGURE 8

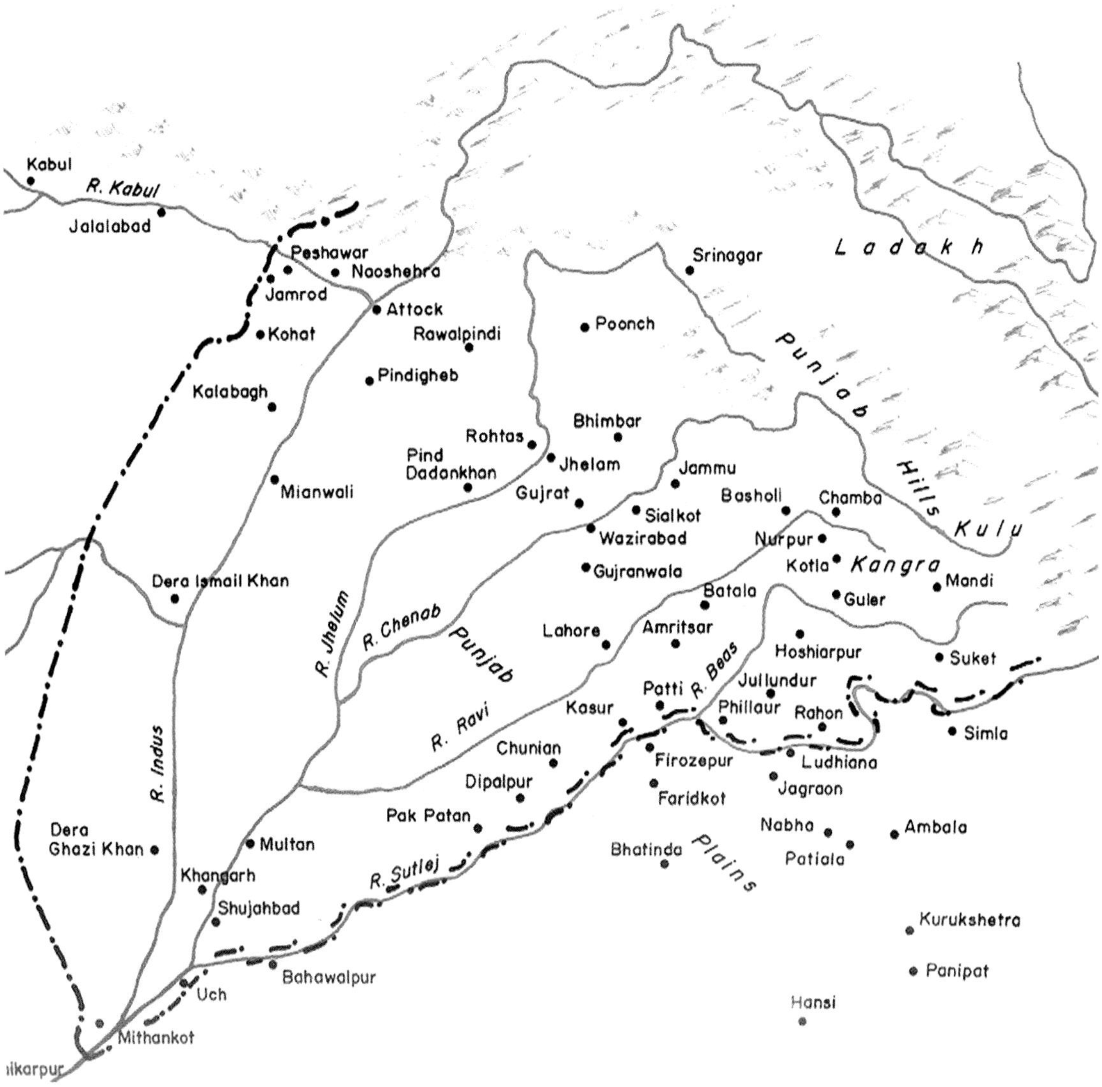

TERRITORIES DURING MAHARAJA RANJIT SINGH
ABOVE THE SUTLEJ RIVER
1799 to 1839

He recruited the best fighting men available regardless of religion or caste. His army had ***Sikhs, Gurkhas, Biharis, Oriyas, Muslims and Pathans*** [13]. Ranjit Singh employed 37 foreigners [14] to modernize his army and administration. They included, 12 ***Frenchmen***, seven ***Anglo-Indians***, four ***Italians***, four ***Germans***, three ***Englishmen***, three ***Americans***, two ***Spaniards***, one ***Russian*** and one ***Scot***. There were 40 high-ranking Muslim officers and two Muslim generals in Ranjit Singh's army [15].

His cabinet included people of all religions. It was merit alone that accounted for his appointments. Fakir Azazuddin, a Muslim, was in charge of diplomatic affairs. Raja Dina Nath, a Hindu, was in charge of revenue matters.

Ranjit Singh changed the ruling environment. It had been religious for 2,000 and now it became secular. He gave positions of trust and power in civil and military matters to Sikhs, Muslims and Hindus without any distinction. Because of his belief in the Universality of the Sikh Religion, the Sikh kingdom expanded from Punjab to Jammu and Kashmir. It also included all of the northwest frontier province right unto the Khyber Pass (Figure 8).

Ranjit Singh was stern but kind. Despite his many conquests, he did not allow wanton destruction of life or property. Many times the conquered enemies, after rehabilitation, fought alongside the Maharaja's army [16]. Throughout his life, Ranjit Singh never issued a death sentence (***no capital punishment***). Even people who tried to assassinate him were forgiven [17], [18].

ii. MAHARAJA RANJIT SINGH'S ACCOMPLISHMENTS IN HIS WORDS

Maharaja Ranjit Singh summed up his own achievements in the following words [19]:

"My kingdom is a great kingdom. It was small and it is large now. It was scattered, broken and divided and is now consolidated. It must increase in prosperity and descend undivided to my prosperity. The maxims of Taimur have guided me, what he professed and ordered I have done. By counsel and providence, combined with valor, I have conquered. ***By generosity, discipline and policy I have regulated and consolidated my government. I have rewarded the bold and encouraged merit wherever it was found.*** On the field of battle I exalted the valiant. With my troops I have shared all dangers, all fatigues.

"Both on the field and in the cabinet I shut partiality from my soul. I closed my eyes to personal comfort. With the robe of empire I put on the mantle of care. I fed faqirs and holy men and gained their prayers. The guilty as the innocent I spared and those whose hands were raised against myself have met my clemency. God (Sri Purakhji) has therefore been merciful to his servant. God increased the power so the territory now extends to the borders of China and the limits of the Afghans with all of Multan and the rich possessions beyond the Sutlej River."

The above describes Maharaja Ranjit Singh accurately and is factual.

iii. HISTORY OF THE KOH-I-NOOR DIAMOND

The Koh-i-noor is the most brilliant diamond in the world [20]. Its story goes like this. It was obtained from the famous Golconda mines in India and came into the hands of Mughal Emperors who conquered India. In 1739, the Persian King, Nadar Shah, took it, along with the Peacock Throne, from the Mughal King Mohammed Shah. When Shah was assassinated in 1747, the diamond fell into the hands of Afghan King Ahmed Shah Abdali. When Abdali died, his son Taimur Shah gained possession, and when he died in 1793 his son Shah Zaman took the diamond. When his brother, Shah Mahmud, blinded Shah Zaman the diamond was taken by his other brother King Shah Shuja and his wife Wafa Begum. ***The Koh-i-noor Diamond was given to Maharaja Ranjit Singh on June 1, 1813 by Afghan King Shah Shuja*** [21]. It was passed on to the British after the defeat of the Sikhs in 1849. Lord Dalhousie presented the Koh-i-noor diamond to Queen Victoria on June 3, 1850. This followed the British annexation of Punjab after they defeated the Sikhs. Ever since that day, the diamond has been part of the British Crown Jewel collection [22] and Figure 9 [23].

When the Moguls acquired the diamond in 1526 it was said to weigh 793 carats. Through some incredibly ham-fisted cutting and polishing by a jeweler named Borgio, it was reduced to 186 carats. The British were rather disappointed at the lack of "fire" in the diamond, and to make it more brilliant, they further reduced it from 186 carats to its present size of just about 109 carats [24].

FIGURE 9

THE KOH-I-NOOR DIAMOND IS MOUNTED AT THE TOP.
(Part of the British Crown Jewel Collection)

PART 4. HISTORY FROM 1849 TO 1947

UNIVERSALITY DURING THE BRITISH RULE

During the British rule from 1849 to 1947, Universality of the Sikh religion was maintained because the Sikhs did not criticize any other religion. Some historical facts about British rule during this period are very important to know.

i. SIKH KINGDOM LOST TO BRITISH

On March 10, 1849, the Sikh armies laid down their arms to the British. A fortnight (two weeks) later, a proclamation was read annexing the Sikh Kingdom to the British Crown. There was no charismatic leader after the death in 1839 of Maharajah Ranjit Singh. Still it took 10 years before the Sikhs surrendered. The British brought a force of 32,000 with 86 guns to fight the Sikhs. Those troops also included Biharis, Oriyas, Rajputs and Marathas to subdue the Sikhs [25]. The Sikh Kingdom was the last to fall.

ii. HONEYMOON PERIOD BETWEEN SIKHS AND BRITISH

A. HOW IT STARTED

In 1857, just eight years after the defeat of the Sikhs, the revolt against the British took place. Everybody wanted to grab power. The Marathas wanted their kingdom. ***The Muslims wanted to reestablish Mughal rule in the northern part of India, especially Punjab. The Sikhs had bitter memories of Muslim rule.*** On the other hand, the Muslims were a large majority in Punjab with about 60% to 70% of the population. The Sikhs also did not forget that Indians throughout the country were fighting on the side of the British against the Sikhs.

There was no central organization fighting for the freedom of India from British rule. Now, the Sikhs being a very small minority with no military strength, had to decide. Should they join the Muslims in Punjab for their kingdom? In this predicament, Sikhs in general had not all sided with the British. Baba Ram Singh was defiantly against the British. He had his own Sikh followers known as Namdhari Sikhs.

B. PROGRESS OF THE HONEYMOON PERIOD

Due to the fighting spirit of the Sikh soldiers, the British played a benevolent role by heavily recruiting Sikhs into the British army. They encouraged them to maintain their identity by letting them keep their long hair and turbans and follow the Sikh religion wherever they were sent to fight.

Another situation arose for the Sikhs during British rule. The Hindu Arya Samaj movement was making great strides in Punjab and claimed large numbers of adherents among the Sikhs. British missionaries were gaining converts to Christianity from the poorer sections of the community. The number of Sikhs decreased during this period.

Sikhs launched the Singh Sabha movement. Its main thrust was the publications of Sikh literature and opening of educational institutes like Khalsa College in Amritsar, Punjab in 1893. With the help of the British government, many new Sikh schools and colleges were opened. On the literary front, celebrated poet-philosopher, ***Bhai Vir Singh founded the Khalsa Tract Society and published a weekly journal, "Khalsa Samachar.*" The writings of Bhai Vir Singh uplifted the spirit of the Sikh people.

The services of **Mr. Max Arthur Macauliffe** (1841-1913), English translator of the Sikh scriptures and historian of early Sikhism were procured. ***He produced a comprehensive work consisting of his six precious volumes inscribed to the Sikh religion.***

C. ENDING OF THE HONEYMOON PERIOD BETWEEN THE SIKHS AND BRITISH

The Singh Sabha movement lost its appeal among the Sikh masses because it was too closely tied to the British government. It did not help the people gain freedom from British rule. About 4,000 Sikhs came to Canada in 1906-1907. ***The Canadian Government passed a law virtually banning Indians from entering Canada.*** Out of sheer desperation, the emigrants organized the Ghadar (mutiny) party in 1913, with the goal of freeing India from the British by any possible means. ***The Sikh-British honeymoon period came to an end during and after World War 1 (1914-1918).***

iii. SIKH VICTORIES USING NONVIOLENCE AGAINST THE BRITISH

a. 1914: KOMAGATA MARU IN CANADA

In 1914, Gurdit Singh, a well-to-do Sikh living in Hong Kong, decided to challenge the law by sending a shipload of Indians to settle in Canada as immigrants. Their legal position was that as citizens of the British Empire they could live freely anywhere in that Realm [26].

Singh chartered the Komagata Maru, a Japanese vessel. On May 23, 1914, the Komagata Maru carrying 376 people (340 Sikhs, 24 Muslims and 12 Hindus) from Punjab, India, and having British citizenship, reached Vancouver, British Columbia, Canada. There was a heated legal battle for two months between Canadian authorities and the Indians living in British Columbia. In the end, only 24 passengers were given permission to legally stay in Canada. On July 23, 1914, the Komagata Maru was forced to leave Victoria harbor with 352 passengers.

The Komagata Maru reached Calcutta on September 26, 1914. British authorities were waiting for them. ***During the scuffle, 29 passengers on the ship fell victim to the bullets of British officials and 20 died*** [27]. Here was another senseless massacre of innocent Indians at the hands of the British. This was the tragic end of the passengers of the Komagata Maru but their memory lingers on forever.

In 2000, victory came after 86 years when a Sikh born in Punjab, Mr. Ujjal Singh Dosanjh, was elected Premier of British Columbia, Canada. Dosanjh worked hard to keep the memories alive installing a plaque in honor of the 376 Indians of the Komagata Maru. The inscription reads as follows:

"On May 23, 1914, 376 British Subjects (12 Hindus, 24 Muslims and 340 Sikhs) of Indian origin arrived in Vancouver harbour aboard the Komagata Maru, seeking to enter Canada. 352 of the passengers were denied entry and forced to depart on July 23, 1914. This plaque commemorates the 75th anniversary of that unfortunate incident of racial discrimination and reminds Canadians of our commitment to an open society in which mutual respect and understanding are honoured, differences are respected, and traditions are cherished."

Plaque put at the Gateway to the Pacific, Downtown Vancouver, British Columbia, Canada.

Ironically Premier Ujjal now sees the same view of the harbor from his office in Vancouver [28] where in 1914, Canadian officials detained the Komagata Maru and its 376 Punjabi immigrants who were denied entry into Canada.

In addition to the Premier, there are many Sikhs who have been elected to the Canadian Parliament on a regular basis. It shows clearly that hard work and sacrifice do pay; it just may take long time.

STORY OF KOMAGATA MARU IN PICTURES

Figure 10 shows some of the 376 Punjabis who in 1914 came on the Komagata Maru.(http://www.sikh-history.com/sikhhist/images/portraits/passengers_of_kamagata_maru.jpg)

Figure 11 is Ujjal Singh Dosanjh, also from Punjab, who became the Premier of British Columbia in 2000. (www.punjabilok.com/news_files/dec/hot_news.y.i.s.76.y.i.s.htm)

Figure 12 is the Komagata Maru surrounded by Canadian police boats in 1914. (http://www.canadiantheatre.com/dict.pl?term=The+Komagatamaru+Incident)

Figure 13 shows the Komagata Maru when it arrived in Calcutta, India in 1914. (http://www.sikh-history.com/sikhhist/events/kamagatamaru.html)

b. 1919 JALLIAN WALA BAGH MASSACRE AND MORAL DECAY OF THE BRITISH

People (mostly Sikhs) from Punjab had organized a peaceful meeting in Jallian Wala Bagh during celebration of the Baisakhi fair in Amritsar. This event was held every year on April 13, the anniversary of the Khalsa Sikhs and also the harvesting of crops in Punjab. The Congress Party wanted to use this gathering to promote the freedom of India from the British rule.

On hearing of this meeting, General Reginald E. H. Dyer banned all meetings. Dyer brought his army and occupied the small entrance to the garden. The other exit from the area was closed with steel gates. There was no other escape. ***On April 13, 1919, General Dyer opened fire without any warning to the people to disperse. He killed 379 and wounded more than 2,000*** [29]. Figure 14 shows innocent people being killed [30].

General Dyer's superior, Sir Michael O'Dwyer, Governor of Punjab, fully approved the mass killing. All of India was aroused against British rule. The British lost their moral strength. It was the beginning of the end of British rule in India that finally became reality 28 years later in 1947. Rabindra Nath Tagore, the Nobel Prize Winner, returned his British Knighthood. General Dyer was forced to retire to Britain, but was praised by the House of Lords and given a sword studded with jewels that was purchased by public subscription. He died in 1927.

FIGURE 10

1914
Sikhs and others on the Komagata Maru
Ship, not allowed to land in Vancouver.
BC (Canada). Gurdit Singh (in white dress) was the brains behind the bold endeavor.

FIGURE 11

2000
Ujjal Singh Dosanjh, a Sikh,
Premier of British Columbia
Canada in 2000.

FIGURE 12

KOMAGATA MARU (Canada)

Arrived in Vancouver, British Columbia, Canada on May 23, 1914.
Ship in the back is surrounded by Police boats. Forced to leave on July 23,1914.

FIGURE 13

KOMAGATA MARU (India)

Arrived in Calcutta, India September 26, 1914.
British killed 20.
Thus ended the Komagata Maru story, but not its memory.

FIGURE 14

MASSACRE AT JALLIAN WALA BAGH
AMRITSAR, INDIA ON APRIL 13th, 1919

Udham Singh, a young Sikh teenager (alias Ram Mohammad Singh Azad) raised at Khalsa Orphanage, saw the massacre with his own eyes. He vowed revenge. On March 13, 1940, a meeting was being held at Caxton Hall, London. It included the East India association in conjunction with the Royal Central Asia Society. Udham Singh, at 4.30 PM, fired five to six shots from his pistol and ***killed Sir Michael O'Dwyer to avenge the massacre of April 13, 1919 in Amritsar***. On July 31,1940, Udham Singh was hanged at Pentonville jail, London [31]. Figure 15 shows General Dyer, Governor O'Dwyer and Udham Singh [32].

FIGURE 15

General Dyer

Governor O'Dwyer

Udham Singh

Jallianwala Bagh has become a place for pilgrimage. It is a hallowed spot where Indians (mostly Sikhs) shed their blood fighting for the freedom of their country. This unprovoked massacre hastened the time for India's eventual freedom from British rule.

c. 1921 NANKANA HOLOCAUST

The Sikh's final break with the British took place with the start of the Akali movement. Its objective was control all Sikh Gurdwaras. This further aroused the Sikh community against the British.

During that period people who were not Sikhs controlled Sikh religious sites. A typical case was the birthplace of Guru Nanak. It being run by Narain Das, a Hindu of shady character in cooperation with the British.

On February 20, 1921, 150 Sikhs headed by Lachman Singh Dharowalia and belonging to the Akali Party, took a vow of nonviolence and entered the Gurdwara peacefully. It was nonviolent way to gain control of the Gurdwara. Mr. Das closed the gates. His 400 thugs attacked the Sikhs. ***On that day, 130 Sikhs were killed without any provocation*** [33].

The entire Sikh community was enraged. Figure 16 shows the unprovoked killing at Nankana Sahib Gurdwara [34].

FIGURE 16

NANKANA HOLOCAUST
KILLING OF 130 SIKHS DURING A PEACEFUL PROTEST

On realizing the gravity of the situation, Mr. M.C.M. King, the Commissioner of Lahore, gave the keys of the Gurdwara to representatives of the Sikh Gurdwara Parbhandak Committee. For the murder of the 130 Sikhs, three men were sentenced to death and two, including Narain Das, were sentenced to life in prison. Later, Mahatma Gandhi visited Nankana Sahib and said: "Everything points to a second edition of Dyerism, more barbarous and more fiendish than the barbarism at Jallianwala." [34]

This was the first victory of the Sikhs in liberating their Gurdwaras.

d. 1922 GURU KA BAGH PEACEFUL PROTEST

In 1922, Sikhs belonging to the Akali movement started a nonviolent protest to gain control of the religious place called Guru Ka Bagh. ***Every day 100 Sikhs would take a vow at Akal Takht to be nonviolent*** and then proceed towards Guru Ka Bagh without uttering a word. With folded hands, they protested with God's name on their lips. British officers would beat them mercilessly with sticks covered with brass (Figure 17) [35]. They would fall down and be taken to a hospital. This went on for 19 days and there was no dearth of volunteers. Many Indian leaders and foreigners witnessed these beatings and were alarmed.

FIGURE 17

GURU KA BAGH PEACEFUL PROTEST

SIKHS BEING BEATEN BY LONG BATONS COVERED WITH BRASS

The English missionary and educator, C.F. Andrews (1871-1940), visited Guru ka Bagh [35] and wrote the following:

"Hundreds of Christs being crucified"

Andrews sent a detailed report to the press on what he witnessed on September 12, 1922 [35]. "The hands of the Akali Sikhs were placed together in prayer and it was clear that they were praying. Then, without the slightest provocation on their part, an Englishman lunged forward the head of his lathi that was bound with brass. He lunged it forward in such a way that his fist that held the staff struck the Akali Sikh, who was praying, just at the collarbone with great force. It looked like the most cowardly blow as I saw it struck. The blow which I saw was sufficient to fell the Akali Sikh and send him to the ground. He rolled over and slowly got up once more, and faced the same punishment over again. Time after time one of the four Sikhs who had gone forward, was laid prostrate by repeated blows, now from the English officer and now from the police who were under his control.

"The vow the Akali Sikhs had made to God was kept. I saw no act, no look of defiance. It was true martyrdom for them as they went forward, a true act of faith, a true deed of devotion to God."

Pundit Madan Mohan Malviya, a very well respected Hindu leader, who also was president of the Congress Party, was an eyewitness and said: [36]

"I can not resist asking every Hindu home to have at least one male child initiated into the fold of Khalsa. What I see here before my eyes is nothing short of a miracle in our whole history".

This shows how even people of other religions (Hindus) accepted the Universality of the Sikh Religion.

Finally the British gave in. By then, 936 Sikhs had been hospitalized and 5,605 had been arrested [37].

This was the second victory of Sikhs using nonviolent means to liberate their Gurdwaras.

e. 1925 SIKH GURDWARA ACT

Sikhs belonging to the ***Akali organization sustained the nonviolent agitation for five years when 30,000 men and women went to jail, nearly 400 were killed and more than 2,000 wounded*** [38]. This was done so the Sikhs could control their Gurdwaras. The movement ended in 1925 when the ***Sikh Gurdwara Act was passed.*** All Gurdwaras of historic importance in Punjab now were under control of the Sikh Society called the Shiromani Gurdwara Parbhandak Committee. In this process, the British forever lost the support and loyalty of the Sikh community. Sikhs then actively started supporting India's freedom from the British.

iv. SIKH SACRIFICES FOR THE FREEDOM OF INDIA

Sikhs were foremost in attaining India's freedom from the British. Many Sikhs were hanged, exiled for life and imprisoned for this cause. I was not able to obtain correct and reliable statistics. Some say 93 out of a total of 121 hanged were Sikhs and 2,147 out of a total of 2,708 exiled for life were Sikhs [39]. It was not possible to obtain the original reference from Maulana Abul Kalam Azad who was president of the Indian National Congress in 1923 and then from 1940 to 1946.

The Sikh contribution to the freedom of India is phenomenal. This is a fact that has been accepted by all. ***Although Sikhs are only two percent of India's population, their sacrifices for the country's freedom go far beyond their numbers.*** This indeed is a marvelous achievement.

Sikhs were the last to surrender to the British and first to fight for India's freedom. Their victories in liberating the Gurdwaras (religious places) from people who were not Sikhs by nonviolent means contributed significantly to the freedom of India. When Sikhs won the control of the Gurdwaras, Mahatma Gandhi said it was the first decisive victory in the battle for Independence [40].

The Sikh fights for freedom dates back to 1863 when Ram Singh organized the Kuka organization (Namdharis) to fight the British [41]. They boycotted all British goods and services. The British killed large numbers of Namdhari Sikhs. The leader, Ram Singh, was banished to Burma and died in 1885 pining for Punjab. ***It is a historical truth that the noncooperation movement started by Ram Singh shook the very foundations of British rule in India. Later, Mahatma Gandhi followed the noncooperation started by Ram Singh and used peaceful means to liberate India.***

v. UNIVERSALITY DURING THE 1930s AND 1940s

During 1930s and 1940s, before India's independence in 1947, ***in Punjab it was common for many Hindus to have one family member converted to the Sikh religion***. This practice showed the sacrificing spirit of the Sikhs in their effort to obtain India's freedom from the British and to protect the family in time of need. This also exhibited the Universality of the Sikh Religion. Hindus, people of another faith, accepted this in a practical way.

During the period of 1930s and 1940s, Dr. B. R. Ambedkar was leader of the Dalits. They were the lowest caste according to the Hindu religion. Dalits are untouchables or schedule caste (lowest class) people. Recently, Dalits have included people belonging to other minorities as well. Dalitism is both the ideology and nationalism of India's persecuted and suppressed masses [42].

Dr Ambedkar also wrote India's constitution. He was completely disgusted with the Hindu religion and was convinced that Dalits (untouchables) could not obtain self-respect and economic well being within Hinduism. Ambedkar spent two decades of exploring affiliations with other Indian religions. ***At one point he declared in public that Dalits should adopt the Sikh religion***. This was because the Sikh religion has no caste system and all are treated equally. ***Although Ambedkar did not become a Sikh, he did convert to Buddhism a few months before his death on October 14, 1956, along with about half-a-million Dalits*** [43].

vi. IMPORTANCE OF THE YEAR 1947

The year 1947 is very historic for India. It when ***India achieved its independence from the British.*** At the same time, Pakistan was created out of India.

The main reason for this was that Muslims wanted a separate country based on Islam. ***Thus, Punjab*** **was split into two parts**. The Muslim majority areas became part of Pakistan and non-Muslim majority areas became part of India. There was so much religious hatred and killing on both sides that large-scale migration of people occurred. It is said that about six to seven million Sikhs and Hindus came to India and about the same number of Muslims went to Pakistan. This was accomplished in just a few months, and in the process many, many people died.

According to the World Almanac [44], 12 million people (about six million on each side) crossed the India-Pakistan border and about 200,000 people died during one of the larger-scale migrations in the world's history. The 200,000 number of people killed also was confirmed by Alan Campbell Johnson, the last British Viceroy's press attaché. He was an eyewitness to history during the tumultuous months when India became free [45]. There are several historians who claim the number of people killed was between 250,000 and 500,000. However, no one knows the exact number. People who died were Muslims, Sikhs and Hindus. It was an indiscriminate killing of people and the only reason was because they belonged to different religions.

Everybody knows that killing is nothing but madness. Howeve,r there is one good result of the partition. People in two parts of Punjab now are living in peace: Muslims in West Punjab (Pakistan) and non-Muslims in East Punjab (India). Both sides paid a very high price in human life. This killing went on every day for many years before Indian independence in 1947. Religious hatred was at its peak. It may have been the best solution at that time. In the long-run it is not right to divide countries based on religion. The world is becoming smaller due to advancements in technology and greater movements of people between different countries.

5. SUMMARY

The Sikh Religion during the period of 10 Gurus (1469 to 1708) was on the rise and increased considerably in numbers. Universality was maintained throughout this period. The period from 1708 to 1798 was the most traumatized for Sikhism. Muslims of Mughal, Persian and Afghan descent plundered and killed many people. In nutshell, this can be called the era of the persecution of the Sikhs.

This led to a reorganization of the Sikh army due to the perseverance and undaunted spirit of those who were Sikhs. The Sikh Religion received a big boost from 1799 to 1839 when Maharaja Ranjit Singh established the Kingdom. Maharaja Ranjit Singh's success essentially was due to the fact that he put into practice the Universality of the Sikh religion. Ranjit Singh created a secular state rather than a religious state. Before that, religious persecution had taken place for thousands of years.

During Maharaj Ranjit Singh's reign Sikhs, Muslims and Hindus held very high positions in both the army and in the civil administration. There was no capital punishment. During this period, the Sikh population increased tremendously. This occurred by persuasion only. Punjab was the last kingdom to come under British rule.

The period from 1847 to 1947 when the British ruled Punjab and India, the Universality of the Sikh Religion was maintained. The Sikh Religion did not expand because the British were spreading the Christian religion and the Sikhs were not the rulers. The Sikhs maintained good relations with the British. However, this honeymoon period ended during World War 1.

Sikhs chartered the Komagata Maru, a Japanese vessel, in an effort to enter Canada but were sent back to India. However, in 2000 a Sikh was elected the Premier of British Columbia, the same state that disallowed Sikhs in 1914. British killed many people, mostly Sikhs, at Jallianwala Bagh in Amritsar. They were peacefully protesting British rule. This massacre hastened the departure of the British from India.

Using nonviolence, the Sikhs launched many attempts to control their Gurdwaras. The British killed a large number of Sikhs during the 1921 Nanakana Holocaust and 1922 Guru Ka Bagh nonviolent protests. Finally the Sikhs won and got control of their Gurdwaras.

The universality of the Sikhs was so popular that many Hindus began converting one male member of their family as a Khalsa Sikh. Ambedkar, leader of the Dalits (untouchable class), once thought he would convert Dalits to Sikhs. However, he ended up becoming a Buddhist.

The struggles and the victories of the Sikhs were a big boost to gaining India's freedom. Although Sikhs only are 2% of the population, their contributions and sacrifices were far beyond their numbers. India obtained freedom from the British in 1947. However, Punjab was divided into two parts: one for Pakistan and the other for India. In this process, 12 million people (about six million on each side) crossed the India-Pakistan border and about 200,000 people died.

6. EXERCISES

i. Universality of the Sikh Religion was practiced and accepted during the following three periods:

A. The 10 Sikh Gurus.

B. The rein of Maharaja Ranjit Singh

C. During British rule and before the independence of India in 1947.

Give reasons why this was so?

ii. If the Sikh Religion is universal then why are more people not joining? Give reasons and explain how this can be accomplished?

iii. What is your contribution to humanity and how can you help in spreading the Universality of the Sikh Religion?

iv. Explain the Sikh victories using nonviolence during British rule from 1914 to 1925?

v. Explain how the Komagata Maru ultimately became a factor in electing a Sikh as the Premier of British Columbia, Canada?

vi. How did the Jallianwala bagh massacre hasten the British departure from India?

vii. How many people crossed the border, and how many died in Punjab when India became independent in 1947?

7. REFERENCES

[1] Age of Kings Heaven
http://aok.heavengames.com/thegame/civs/mongols_history.shtml

[2] Babur
http://www.storyofpakistan.com/person.asp?perid=P053

[3] Encyclopedia: Timur Lenk
http://www.nationmaster.com/encyclopedia/Timur-Lenk

[4] Kartar S. Duggal, 1989, Sikh Gurus, Second printing, Himalayan International Institute, Honesdale, PA, p. 121.

[5] History and Politics, University of California Los Angeles, History of South Asia
Aurangzeb: A Political History
http://www.sscnet.ucla.edu/southasia/History/Mughals/Aurang.html

[6] The Martyrdom of Guru Tegh Bahadur
http://www.sikh-history.com/sikhhist/martyrs/nanak9martyr.html

[7] Khuswant Singh, 1984 reissue, A History of the Sikhs, Volume 1, Princeton University Press, Princeton, NJ, Chapters 6 to 9, pp. 101 to 184.

[8] Khuswant Singh, 1984 reissue, A History of the Sikhs, Volume 1, Princeton University Press, Princeton, NJ, Chapter 6, pp.116 to 117.

[9] Khuswant Singh, 1984 reissue, A History of the Sikhs, Volume 1, Princeton University Press, Princeton, NJ, Chapter 7, p. 125.

[10] Tribune, India 200 years of Maharaja Ranjit Singh's Coronation, Spectrum, a special edition, Sunday, April 8, 2001.
http://www.tribuneindia.com/2001/20010408/spectrum/gallery/pages/photo12.htm, (click on Maharaja Ranjit Singh for the picture).

[11] The Sikh Bulletin, Roseville, CA, November 2001, Vol. 3, No.11, p. 2. A paper presented at the Sikh Educational Conference, Kitchner, Ontario, Canada on September 22, 2001 as organized by the Sikh Social and Educational Society of Ontario.

[12] Patwant Singh, 1988, The Golden Temple, Time Books, India. p.94.

[13] Khuswant Singh and Rai Raghu, 1984, The Sikhs, Lustre Press Pvt Ltd., Varanasi, India. pp. 26-27.

[14] Kartar S. Duggal, 1988, Philosophy and Faith of Sikhism, Himalayan International Institute, Honesdale, PA, p. 52.

[15] Kartar S. Duggal, 1988, Philosophy and Faith of Sikhism, Himalayan International Institute, Honesdale, PA, p. 51.

[16] Khuswant Singh, 1984 reissue, A History of the Sikhs, Volume 1, Princeton University Press, Princeton, NJ, p. 293.

[17] Khuswant Singh and Rai Raghu, 1984, The Sikhs, Lustre Press Pvt Ltd., Varanasi, India. p. 28.

[18] Khuswant Singh, 1984 reissue, A History of the Sikhs, Volume 1, Princeton University Press, Princeton, NJ, USA. p. 196.

[19] Khuswant Singh. 1984 reissue. A History of the Sikhs, Volume 1. Princeton University Press, Princeton, NJ, p. 295.
Actual reference is from Lawrence, H.M.L (Major), Adventures of an Officer in the Punjab 1, pp. 64-65.

[20] Khuswant Singh, 1984 reissue, A History of the Sikhs, Volume 1. Princeton University Press, Princeton, NJ, p. 237.

[21] Khuswant Singh, 1984 reissue, A History of the Sikhs, Volume 1, Princeton University Press, Princeton, NJ, p. 241.

[22] W.S. Ward, July 1872, The Kho-i-noor Diamond, Appleton Journal of Science, Literature and Arts. (Reference Yahoo Internet).

[23] Google Images, Search for "Koh-i-noor Diamond," Click on "koh.jpg" for the picture, www.diamondtutorials.com/ famous_diamonds.html

[24] Google Web, go to http://www.bbc.co.uk/dna/getwriting/A730801
Click on BBC - h2g2 - The Koh-i-noor Diamond

[25] Khuswant Singh and Rai Raghu, 1984. The Sikhs. Lustre Press Pvt Ltd., Varanasi, India, pp. 29-30.

[26] Dr. H. Johnston, Department of History, Simon Fraser University, "The Komagata Maru Incident," Beyond Komagata Maru Race Relations, Today's Conference Proceedings, edited by Alan Dutton, The Progressive Indo-Canadian Community Services Society, 1989, pp 3-8.
http://people.lib.ucdavis.edu/tss/punjab/komagata%20maru.htm

[27] Kesar Singh, Canadian Sikhs (Part One) and Komagata Massacre. 13487-98-A Avenue, Surrey, B.C. Canada V3T 1C7, 1989.
http://people.lib.ucdavis.edu/tss/punjab/koma.html#kesar

[28] James Brooke, Sikhs in British Columbia,
http://www.sikhreview.org/march2001/dynamics.htm

[29] Khushwant Singh, A History of the Sikhs, Volume 2, pp. 161-164 Princeton University Press, Princeton, NJ
[30] Amritsar Massacre Jallian Wala Bagh http://www.amritsar.com/Jallian%20Wala%20Bagh.shtml
[31] Navjot Singh, "Challenge to Imperial Hegemony: Life Story of a Great Patriot Udham Singh, Punjab University, Patiala, India, 1998.
[32] The Jallianwala Bagh and Saheed Udham Singh http://sikh-heritage.co.uk/Martyrs/udhamsingh/b&udham.htm Also reference 30 above.
[33] Khuswant Singh. 1984 reissue, A History of the Sikhs, Volume 2, Princeton University Press, Princeton, NJ p. 199.
[34] Sikh Heritage UK www.sikh-heritage.co.uk/Martyrs/ghalugharas/ghalugharas.htm
[35] http://allaboutsikhs.com/events/gurbagh.htm Source:Encyclopaedia of Sikhism - Harbans Singh
[36] Kartar S. Duggal, 1988, Philosophy and Faith of Sikhism, Himalayan International Institute, Honesdale, PA, p. 66.
[37] Khuswant Singh, 1984 reissue, A History of the Sikhs, Volume 2, Princeton University Press, Princeton, NJ, p. 204.
[38] Khuswant Singh, 1984 reissue, A History of the Sikhs, Volume 2, Princeton University Press, Princeton, NJ, p. 213.
[39] Dr. Sarup Singh Alag, Go to Yahoo.com and search for Maulana Azad and Sikh Sacrifices; click on sikhspectrum.com, Monthly Hidden Agenda, No. 8, January 2003 by Vishavjit Singh (also quoted by Patwant Singh, Ms. Madanjit Kaur and Devinder Singh).
[40] Kartar S. Duggal, 1988, Philosophy and Faith of Sikhism. Himalayan International Institute, Honesdale, PA, p. 65.
[41] Kartar S. Duggal, 1988, Philosophy and Faith of Sikhism, Himalayan International Institute, Honesdale, PA, p. 60.
[42] V.T. Rajshekar, What Is "Dalit" And "Dalitism?" as published in DALIT VOICE (fortnightly), pp. 1 to 15, June, 1983. www.ambedkar.org/News/WhatIs.htm
[43] Encyclopedia of World Biography,. 1998 (2nd Edition), Gale Research, Detroit, MI, pp. 190-191.
[44] The World Almanac and Book of Facts 2005, A WRC Media Company, New York, NY, p. 785.
[45] Rediff On The NeT, Freedom: Alan Campbell-Johnson recalls Lord Mountbatten www.rediff.com/freedom/13allan1.htm

UNIVERSALITY OF THE SIKH RELIGION

CHAPTER 5

UNIVERSALITY OF GURU GRANTH SAHIB AND THE GOLDEN TEMPLE

GURU GRANTH SAHIB

1. COMPILATION AND INSTALLATION OF GURU GRANTH SAHIB

In 1604, the Fifth Guru, Arjan Dev, compiled the Guru Granth Sahib and installed it in the Golden Temple in Amritsar, Punjab, India. His editing standards were meticulous with regard to the content, syntax, style and rhyme. This helped the natural flow of the text. Later hymns of the ninth Guru, Tej Bahadur and one from Guru Gobind Singh were added. ***In 1708, the 10th Guru, Gobind Singh, before passing away, made it mandatory for everyone to follow the Guru Granth Sahib (Holy Book) for all time to come.*** This was the most significant development in Sikh history.

Thus, Guruship by human beings was sealed. Succession was passed on to the Guru Granth Sahib in perpetuity. These writings have been preserved without change, forever. The Guru Granth Sahib has 1,430 pages with maximum of 19 lines per page. ***It is a scripture for all nations, just as it is a lyric of divine love for all people.*** It is just one idea, one song and in praise of one God. Guru Granth Sahib not only is the Sikh Holy Book but also for the entire human race. It contains universal truth and divine love. It teaches universal brotherhood, equality for all people, spiritual beauty and Divine enlightenment.

2. WRITTEN BY PEOPLE BELONGING TO DIFFERENT RELIGIONS

A universal religion must have a universal book. To qualify, it should have hymns from people of different religions. ***The Guru Granth Sahib is the world's only holy book that incorporates and sanctifies hymns composed by Sikhs, Hindus and Muslims.*** It contains a total of 5,869 hymns. Most (4,956 or 84%) were composed by Sikh Gurus while a significant portion of the hymns, 913 (16%), were composed by 36 Hindu Bhagats, Muslim Sufis and Sikhs [1]. As a mark of respect and having complete faith in the written words, people bow low before the Guru Granth Sahib when entering the congregation. By doing this, Sikhs, Hindus and Muslims are honoring hymns written by religious people who are members of different religions. This clearly shows, and without any doubt, the universality of Guru Granth Sahib, the holy book.

3. LANGUAGES IN THE GURU GRANTH SAHIB

Guru Granth Sahib is written in the Gurmukhi (Punjabi) language. ***Hymns are composed in 11 languages but the script is Gurmukhi*** as is shown in Figure 18 of the Guru Granth Sahib. Guru Nanak wrote in the Gurmukhi script while the second Guru Angad perfected Gurmukhi. The eleven languages in the Guru Granth Sahib are [2]:

i. Punjabi	v. Lehandi	ix. Persian
ii. Sant Bhasha	vi. Marathi	x. Eastern Apabhramsa
iii. Hindi	vii. Sanskrit	xi. Western Apabhramsa
iv. Sindhi	viii. Arabic.	

4. THEME OF GURU GRANTH SAHIB

The principal message is that ***salvation can be obtained by meditation of the divine God, and this occurs through the grace of God.*** Union with God is obtained by regular, persistent and disciplined meditation. One must take into account the entire universe along with all living beings as created by God. Guru Granth Sahib also emphasizes that ***truth is very important, but truthful living still is higher.*** Equality and universal prosperity for all people are the high points of the Sikh Religion.

5. STRUCTURE OF GURU GRANTH SAHIB

The complete volume of Guru Granth Sahib is divided into the following primary categories:

Beginning Gurbani	Pages 1 to 13
Gurbani set to Classical Ragas	Pages 14 to 1,353
Other Gurbani	Pages 1,353 to 1,430

i. BEGINNING GURBANI

The first 13 pages have:

DESCRIPTION	PAGES
Japji	Pages 1 to 8
Sodar Rag	Pages 8 to 10
Rag Aasaa	Pages 10 to 12
Sohilaa Rag	Pages 12 to 13

FIGURE 18

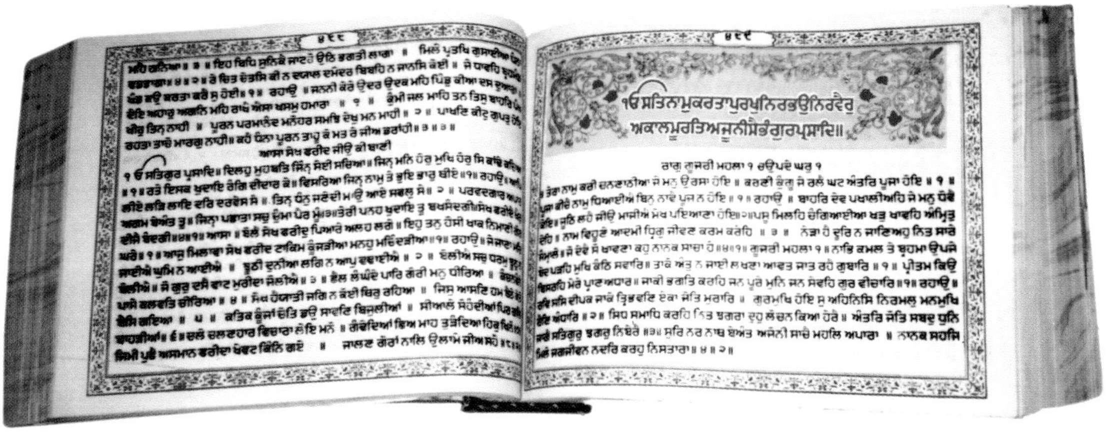

GURU GRANTH SAHIB

THE UNIVERSAL HOLY BOOK

ii. GURBANI SET TO CLASSICAL RAGAS

Guru Granth Sahib is written in poetry of the highest order and ***all hymns are sung according to classical Indian music that is comprised of 31 Ragas.*** Guru Granth Sahib ends with a Ragmala that provides a complete list of Ragas. There are six main Ragas. Each has five Raginis (like wives) and eight sons of Ragas. Thus, there are 84 Ragas (six main Ragas and 30 Raginis and 48 sons of Ragas).

Some people want to delete the list of 84 Ragas because they think it has no relevance to Guru Granth Sahib. There is absolutely nothing wrong with including a list of all the Ragas. Actually, it is a plus factor for the following reasons:

A. It does not affect the basic teachings and philosophy of Guru Granth Sahib.
B. It actually is a challenge for the musicians to incorporate these Ragas. Each main Raga is interrelated with the five wives and eight sons. Thus, there is much latitude for the musicians to improvise while singing the Shabads (hymns). This is the way a person like me, who is not a musician, interprets it.

It should however be made clear that the Raga for each Shabad (hymn), as specified in Guru Granth Sahib, must be adhered to.

No.	NAME OF RAG	PAGES	No.	NAME OF RAG	PAGES
1.	Siree	14-93	17.	Gaund	859-875
2.	Maajh	94-150	18.	Raamkalee	876-974
3.	Gaoree	151-346	19.	Nat Naaraa-in	975-983
4.	Aasaa	347-488	20.	Maalee Gaora	984-988
5.	Gujri	489-526	21.	Maaroo	989-1,106
6.	Devgandhaaree	527-536	22.	Tukhaaree	1,107-1,117
7.	Bihaagaraa	537-556	23.	Kedaaraa	1,118-1124
8.	Wad-hans	557-594	24.	Bhairao	1,125-1,167
9.	Sorath	595-659	25.	Basant	1,168-1,196
10.	Dhanaasaree	660-695	26.	Saarang	1,197-1,253
11.	Jaitsaree	696-710	27.	Malaar	1,254-1,293
12.	Todee	711-718	28.	Kaanaraa	1,294-1,318
13.	Bairaaree	719-720	29.	Kaliaan	1,319-1,326
14.	Tliang	721-727	30	Parbhaatee	1,327-1,351
15.	Soohee	728-794	31.	Jaajaawantee	1,352-1,353
16.	Bilaawal	795-858			

iii. OTHER GURBANI

There are a series of other hymns by Gurus, Muslim Sufis and Hindu Bhagats. They are as follows:

DESCRIPTION	PAGES	DESCRIPTION	PAGES
Slok Sahaskritee	1,353-1,360	Sloks of Farid	1,377-1,384
Gaathaa	1,360-1,361	Savaye	1,385-1,409
Funahe	1,361-1,363	Slok	1,410-1,428
Chaobole	1,363-1,364	Mundaawanee	1,429-1,429
Sloks of Kabir	1,364-1,377	Rag Maala	1,429-1,430

6. HYMNS AND COMPOSORS [1]

No.	Composers	Hymns, Sloks, Pauris
1.	First Guru Nanak	974
2.	Second Guru Angad	62
3.	Third Guru Amar Das	907
4.	Fourth Guru Ram Das	679
5.	Fifth Guru Arjan Dev	2,218
6.	Ninth Guru Tegh Bahadur	115
7.	Tenth Guru Gobind Singh	1
	Total by Gurus	**4,956 (84%)**

No.	Composers	Hymns, Sloks	No.	Composers	Swayyas
Hindus, Muslims and Sikhs				Bhatts (musicians)	All Hindus
1.	Kabir (Muslim)	541	20.	Kal	49
2.	Farid (Muslim)	134	21.	Mathura	10
3.	Namdev (Hindu)	60	22.	Kirat	8
4.	Ravidas (Hindu)	41	23.	Sewak	7
5.	Trilochan (Hindu)	4	24.	Nal	6
6.	Dhanna (Hindu)	4	25.	Gayand	5
7.	Beni (Hindu)	3	26.	Bal	5
8.	Mardana (Muslim)	3	27.	Kalsahar	4
9.	Bhikan (Muslim)	2	28.	Jalap	4
10.	Jaidev (Hindu)	2	29.	Sal	3
11.	Surdas (Hindu)	1	30.	Bhikha	2
12.	Parmanand (Hindu)	1	31.	Jalan	2
13.	Pipa (Hindu)	1	32.	Harbans	2
14.	Ramanand (Hindu)	1	33.	Tal	1
15.	Sadhna (Hindu)	1	34.	Jal	1
16.	Sain (Hindu)	1	35.	Bhal	1
17.	Sunder (Sikh)	1	36.	Das	1
18 &19.	Satta and Balwand (Sikhs)	1			

Total by Hindus, Muslims, Sikhs 913 (16%)

7. EMPHASIS OF GURU GRANTH SAHIB

Among the Sikhs, Guru Granth Sahib is the most revered Holy Book and is considered as a Guru. Almost all ceremonies are performed in the presence of Guru Granth Sahib. It could be the naming of a child, marriage, funeral, Amrit initiations and Gurpurbs (anniversary of the birth or death of a Guru) or any other occasion. Sikhs are mandated to follow the teachings and philosophy of their religion as mentioned in Guru Granth Sahib. They are supposed to believe and pray to one God on a daily basis. One must live a truthful life, be contented and be grateful to God who created the whole universe.

The fifth Guru, Arjan Dev, summarized Guru Granth Sahib as follows:

PUNJABI and ROMAN	**ENGLISH**
ਥਾਲ ਵਿਚਿ ਤਿੰਨਿ ਵਸਤੂ ਪਈਓ	Guru Granth Sahib is like a dish
Thaal Vich Tinn Vastoo Pa-ee-o	in which are placed three things
ਸਤੁ ਸੰਤੋਖੁ ਵੀਚਾਰੋ ॥	***TRUTH, CONTENTMENT and WISDOM.***
Sat Santokh Veechaaro	
ਅੰਮ੍ਰਿਤ ਨਾਮੁ ਠਾਕੁਰ ਕਾ ਪਇਓ	The name of the divine GOD is also
Amrit Naam Thaakur Kaa Pa-i-o	put in it
ਜਿਸ ਕਾ ਸਭਸੁ ਅਦਾਰੋ ॥	who supports us all.
Jis Kaa Sabhas ADhaaro	
ਜੇ ਕੋ ਖਾਵੈ ਜੇ ਕੋ ਭੁੰਚੈ	Those who understand and enjoy
Jay Ko Khaavai Jay Ko Bhunchai	
ਤਿਸ ਕਾ ਹੋਇ ਉਧਾਰੋ ॥	will be emancipated.
Tis Kaa Ho-ay Udhaaro	
ਏਹ ਵਸਤੁ ਤਜੀ ਨਹ ਜਾਈ	These things should never be forgotten
Ayh Vasat Tajee Nah Jaa-ee	
ਨਿਤ ਨਿਤ ਰਖੁ ਉਰਿ ਧਾਰੋ ॥	and always keep them in your mind.
Nit Nit Rakh Ur Dhaaro.	
ਤਮ ਸੰਸਾਰੁ ਚਰਨ ਲਗਿ ਤਰੀਐ ਸਭੁ	By following the above teachings we all
TamSansaar Charan LagTaree-ai Sabh	can cross over world oceans (refer to life)
ਨਾਨਕ ਬ੍ਰਹਮ ਪਸਾਰੋ ॥	Nanak proclaims that God pervades
Naanak Barahm Pasaaro.	every where.
Guru Granth Sahib (p.1429, line 9)	

It should be emphasized that religion must be enjoyed. It can be achieved by understanding the words written in Guru Granth Sahib. Finally they must be put into our daily life.

THE GOLDEN TEMPLE

8. UNIVERSALITY

For religion to be universal, it must have a place for prayer where everyone is always welcome at all times without any discriminationl. Such a place exists and it is the Golden Temple in Amritsar, Punjab, India. A view of the Golden Temple is shown in Figure 19. Its architectural beauty also is shown in the marble walkway (Figure 20)l around the Golden Temple (called Parkarma in Punjabi) [3].

The Golden Temple is built as an island in the middle of a pool. Its four doors open in all four directions to symbolize that God is present everywhere. This was a radical departure because traditional architecture provided only one entrance. ***The four doors also are a sign that they are open to all four castes (low, high, warriors and traders) and thus, everyone is equal.***

The Golden Temple is Universal place for the following reasons that will be described below.

i. FOUNDATION STONE

A Muslim, Mian Mir, a Sufi Saint (who used persuasion to spread religion) [4] laid the foundation-stone of the Golden Temple in 1589. It is unheard of in world history that foundation stone of one religion's place of worship (Sikhism), is put in place, by a religious person of another faith (Muslim). This shows the Universality of the Sikh religion in a practical way.

ii. EQUALITY

To be universal, a house of worship should have no discrimination. **The *Golden Temple is open to all, at any time of the day or night, irrespective of religion, color, race, age, sex or caste.*** This was a radical departure from the segregated way of living that went on for centuries in India. Low-caste Hindus were not allowed to enter other Hindu religious places called Mandirs. These were controlled by, high-caste Hindus called Brahmans. Women were not allowed in Muslim religious places of worship. **The *Golden Temple welcomed women by giving them dignity and equality.***

iii. SINGING OF HYMNS WITHOUT IDOL WORSHIP

Singing of hymns in the 31 classical Ragas, in praise of one God, takes place in the Golden Temple. ***Idol worship is not allowed in the Sikh religion.*** This was also a radical departure because idols depicting God are worshipped in Hindu temples and music is not allowed in Muslim mosques.

FIGURE 19

ENTRANCE TO THE GOLDEN TEMPLE
AMRITSAR, PUNJAB, INDIA

FIGURE 20

MARBLE WALKWAY (PARKARMA)
AROUND THE GOLDEN TEMPLE

iv. PROPOSED CENTER FOR WORLD RELIGIONS

The Universality of the Sikh Religion should establish the Golden Temple as the center of the world's religions. It can become a symbol for future world cultures living amicably under one roof.

The Golden Temple is like:

A. Vatican for Catholics (Rome), because it is where religious decisions are discussed and made.
B. Mecca for the Muslims (Saudi Arabia), because it is their religious center.
C. Benares for the Hindus (in India) because it is considered the holiest of the holy places.
D. Jerusalem for the Jews Muslims and Christians because it is an historical center for these faiths.

However, it should be made clear that the idea of clergy and priesthood and anything approaching a Pope is against Sikh teachings.

9. CLEANING OF THE HOLY TANK (SAROVER)

Water in the Holy Tank (Sarover) of the Golden Temple is cleaned periodically. It is called 'KAR SEVA,' the voluntary service. To a Sikh no place is holier than the Golden Temple. People from all over India and from other countries come for this occasion. It not only is considered with great pride but also a privilege to take part in Kar Seva.

The fourth Guru Ram Das started excavation of the Holy Tank (Sarover) in 1573. The Fifth Guru Arjun Dev built the Golden Temple in the middle of the tank.

The first and second Kar Seva were performed in 1923 and 1973, respectively. The third Kar Seva was performed in March 2004. ***Figure 21 shows a sea of humanity cleaning the Holy Tank. There were more than 500 thousand volunteers who cleaned the tank in 24 hours instead of the week that was anticipated.***

People covered each and every inch of the tank [5]. It was a sight to behold. This was the first time that a modern filtration system was installed. Cleaning of the tank was necessary because the water had become muddy and algae-infested. Devotees use the tank for ritual bathing. The new filtration system will make it

FIGURE 21

DEVOTEES (A SEA OF HUMANITY)
PARTICIPATING IN CLEANING
("KAR SEVA") OF THE SAROVAR (HOLY TANK) AT THE GOLDEN TEMPLE, AMRITSAR, PUNJAB, INDIA, MARCH 2004

very easy to clean the water on a regular basis. Sikhs in the United States, notably the Tut Brothers, donated money, for the filtration unit. The cost was about 5 crore Rupees or approximately a million dollars (US). An American Company carried out the installation [6] & [7].

Besides the three Kar Sevas, water in the Holy Tank (Sarover) was changed twice, once in 1984 and again in 1988 [6].

The attack on the Golden Temple in 1984 was a result of some Sikhs wanting a separate Sikh country called Khalistan. In 1984, Prime Minister Indra Gandhi, instead of using peaceful means to solve the problem, sent an army with tanks and helicopters to destroy the Golden Temple. The Indian Army called it "Operation Bluestar."

Thousands of innocent devotees gathered for a special religious ceremony were massacred. Besides blood, arms and ammunition were dumped into the Holy Tank. This desecration by the Indian army necessitated the cleaning that took place in 1984. Later, two Sikh bodyguards who had visited the Golden Temple after the attack, were so emotionally moved by the destruction that they assassinated Indra Gandhi.

In 1988, Indian Army acted again, this time as "Operation Black Thunder." Fortunately, there were no casualties. Anytime the Army enters the Golden Temple and desecrates the Holy Tank, it has to be cleaned, and so it also was done in 1988.

10. SUMMARY

Guru Granth Sahib, the Holy Book of the Sikh Religion, is the only scripture in the world where people belonging to three different religions composed the hymns. Six Sikh Gurus composed 84% of the hymns. Thirty-six Hindu Bhagats and Muslim Sufis composed about 16%. Hymns in Guru Granth Sahib are composed in 11 languages while the script is Gurmukhi (Punjabi).

Guru Granth Sahib is written in poetry of the highest order and all hymns are sung according to traditional Indian classical music comprised of 31 Ragas. The main theme of Guru Granth Sahib is that union with God is obtained by regular, persistent and disciplined meditation. To summarize Guru Granth Sahib, it is a dish where Truth, Contentment and Wisdom are placed, along with the name of God. Those who understand and enjoy this will be emancipated.

A religion to be Universal should have a place where everybody is welcome at all times. The Golden Temple is such a place. A Sufi Muslim, Mian Mir, laid its foundation stone. The Golden Temple is open to all at any time of the day or night, irrespective of religion, color, race, age, sex or caste. Idol worship is not allowed in the Golden Temple. Due to its Universality, the Golden Temple is the center of the world's religions.

Kar Seva volunteer service to clean the Holy Tank is considered by the Sikhs to be a privilege. It is a sight to watch the sea of humanity that covers every inch of the Sarovar during Kar Seva.

11. EXCERCISES

i. Why is Guru Granth Sahib considered The Universal Holy Book? Give reasons.
ii. What is the main theme of Guru Granth Sahib?
iii. What percentage of hymns, by Muslims and Hindus, are incorporated in Guru Granth Sahib?
iv. Guru Granth Sahib is sung in how many classical Ragas?
v. Why is the Golden Temple considered a Universal place for all of the world's religions?
vi. Who laid the foundation stone of the Golden Temple?
vii. Why is Kar Seva voluntary service so important for the Sikhs to clean the Holy Tank of the Golden Temple?

12. REFERENCES

[1] Dr. Sukhbir S. Kapoor, 1997, The Sikh Courier International. Volume 84. The Sikh Cultural Society of Great Britain, Middlesex, Greater London, U.K., pp. 49-50; Sandeep Singh Brar, "Sri Guru Granth Sahib Authors and Contributors," http://www.sikhs.org/granth2.htm; Singh Igbal, 1986, The Essence of Truth: Japji and other Sikh Scriptures, Allen, McMillan and Enderson, New York, NY,USA. pp.132-136.
[2] Igbal Singh, 1986, The Essence of Truth: Japji and other Sikh Scriptures, Allen, McMillan and Enderson, New York, NYUSA., pp.136-137.
[3] Contribution of Martin Gray, Arizona USA as sent to Jaspal S Mayell. Courtesy of www.sacredsites.com and martin Gray
[4] Kartar S. Duggal, 1988, Philosophy and Faith of Sikhism, Himalayan International Institute, Honesdale, PA, USA. p.112.

[5] Sea of Devotees at the Golden Temple Kar Seva,
Varinder Walia Tribune News Service, Chandigarh, India, March 26, 2004
http://www.tribuneindia.com/2004/20040326/main2.htm
"All water of holy tank to be filtered in 96 hours,"
Varinder Walia Tribune News Service, Amritsar, March 24, 2004,
http://www.tribuneindia.com/2004/20040325/punjab1.htm#8

[6] "Sea of humanity cleans Golden Temple tank in hours," by Jaideep Sarin, India News, Amritsar, March 28, 2004; "Sea of devotees at Golden Temple kar seva," posted by Shyrone K. Singh, March 28, 2004, http://www.sikhnet.com/sikhnet/discussion.nsf/0/224CC85F45CA171087256E650063E02E?OpenDocument

[7] "At Golden Temple, leap of faith is getting feet wet, hands dirty. Over 2 million people likely to show up this week to drain and desilt the sarovar so that the water flows pure" by Bajinder Pal Singh, http://www.indianexpress.com/full_story.php?content_id=43838, Indian Express, March 27 2004.

UNIVERSALITY OF THE SIKH RELIGION

CHAPTER 6

CONTRIBUTIONS BY MUSLIMS AND HINDUS

Muslims and Hindus have contributed significantly to the Universality of the Sikh Religion. Their way of thinking also was to that of the Sikh Gurus. Guru Granth Sahib, the Universal Holy Book, contains hymns composed not only by Sikhs but also by Muslims and Hindus. Sixteen percent of all the hymns in Guru Granth Sahib are attributed to 36 Hindus and Muslims [1]. They all emphasized the Universality as shown below in their compositions. They are applicable to people of all religions.

1. UNIVERSALITY OF KABIR (1380-1460)

Kabir [2] was born in Benares, Utter Pardesh, India. He was a Muslim and weaver by profession. This was considered low-caste at that time in India. In Figure 22 [3], a rare fresco shows Kabir and his wife weaving. Kabir broke away from orthodox formalism and preached Universality of the human race. Kabir's 541 hymns are incorporated in Guru Granth Sahib. Two of the hymns are shown below.

i. ALL ARE CREATED BY THE SAME GOD

Kabir proclaimed that all creation comes from the divine light of God, then ***whom should we call good and who is bad.***

Kabir, said:

PUNJABI AND ROMAN	ENGLISH
ਅਵਲਿ ਅਲਹ ਨੂਰੁ ਉਪਾਇਆ	God first created light,
Aval Alah Noor Upaa-iaa	
ਕੁਦਰਤਿ ਕੇ ਸਭ ਬੰਦੇ ॥	then by God's supreme power
Kudrat Kee Sabh Banday	made all human beings.
ਏਕ ਨੂਰ ਤੇ ਸਭੁ ਜਗੁ ਉਪਜਿਆ	From the Divine Light, God created
Ayk Noor Te Sabh Jag Upji-aa	the whole universe.
ਕਉਨ ਭਲੇ ਕੋ ਮੰਦੇ ॥	Then who is good and who is bad?
Ka-un Bhalay Ko Manday	
Guru Granth Sahib(p 1,349, line 18)	

FIGURE 22

**BHAGAT KABIR (CENTER) IS WEAVING.
HIS WIFE MAI LOI (LEFT) IS SPINNING.**

A RARE FRESCO

This picture once adorned the walls of Akal Takht in the Golden Temple Amritsar, Punjab, India. It was destroyed when the Akal Takht building was razed in January 1986.

ii. WHO IS MY FRIEND

Kabir followed Universality by explaining, "who is my friend?"

Kabir said:

PUNJABI AND ROMAN	ENGLISH
ਕਬੀਰ ਸਭ ਤੇ ਹਮ ਬੁਰੇ Kabeer Sabh Tay Ham Buray	I am worst of all
ਹਮ ਤਜਿ ਭਲੋ ਸਭੁ ਕੋਇ ॥ Ham Taj Bhalo Sabh Ko-ay	and everyone else is good.
ਜਿਨਿ ਐਸਾ ਕਰਿ ਬੁਝਿਆ Jin Aissa Kar Boojhi-aa	Those who understand this
ਮੀਤੁ ਹਮਾਰਾ ਸੋਇ ॥ Meet Hamaaraa So-ay	are my friends.

Guru Granth Sahib (p. 1,364, line 17)

2. UNIVERSALITY OF FARID (1173-1265)

Farid [4] was born 1173 in Multan, Punjab now in Pakistan. He was a Sufi Muslim preacher by profession. He died at 92. Farid's 134 hymns, in Punjabi, are incorporated in Guru Granth Sahib. ***It proves that the Punjabi language was used during Farid's time and must have been developed much earlier.***

Farid's idea of Universality was: "***If we return good for evil then nobody will fight and peace will prevail.***

Farid said:

PUNJABI AND ROMAN	ENGLISH
ਫਰੀਦਾ ਬੁਰੇ ਦਾ ਭਲਾ ਕਰਿ Freedaa Buray Daa Bhalaa Kar	Farid says return good for evil
ਗੁਸਾ ਮਨਿ ਨ ਹਢਾਇ ॥ Gusaa Man Na Hadhaa-ay	while keeping no anger in your mind.

Guru Granth Sahib p. 1382 line 1

3. UNIVERSALITY OF NAM DEV (1269-1344)

Nam Dev [5] was born in Narsi Bamni, Maharashtra, India and was a tailor by profession. He was a Hindu and lived in Punjab for 10 years. Nam Dev's 60 hymns are incorporated in Guru Granth Sahib.

Nam Dev followed Universality by saying that ***God is everywhere and pervades the whole universe.***

Nam Dev said:

PUNJABI AND ROMAN	ENGLISH
ਈਭੈ ਬੀਠਲੁ ਊਭੈ ਬੀਠਲੁ	God is with us here in this world
Eebhai Beethal Oobhai Beethal	God also is in the other world
ਬੀਠਲ ਬਿਨੁ ਸੰਸਾਰੁ ਨਹੀ II	Without God there will be no world.
Beethal Bin Sansaar Nahee	
ਥਾਨ ਥਨੰਤਰਿ ਨਾਮਾ ਪ੍ਰਣਵੈ	Nam Dev prays to an omnipresent God
Thaan Thanantar Naamaa Pranvai	
ਪੂਰਿ ਰਹਿਓ ਤੂੰ ਸਰਬ ਮਹੀ II	who also pervades the whole Universe.
Poor Rahio TooN Sarab Mahee	
Guru Granth Sahib (p 485, line 12)	

4. UNIVERSALITY OF RAVI DAS (15th century)

Ravi Das [6], a Hindu, was shoemaker by profession. His 41 hymns are incorporated in Guru Granth Sahib.

Ravi Das explained that God is very close to us and everything happens according to God's will.

Ravi Das said:

PUNJABI AND ROMAN	ENGLISH
ਕਹਿ ਰਵਿਦਾਸ ਹਾਥ ਪੈ ਨੇਰੈ	Ravi Das says God is nearer to us
Kahi Ravidas Haath Pai Nayrai	than our hands and feet.
ਸਹਜੇ ਹੋਇ ਸੁ ਹੋਈ II	As God wills so all things come to pass.
Sehjay Ho-aye So Ho-ee	
Guru Granth Sahib (p. 658, line 3)	

All the hymns composed by Muslims and Hindus in Guru Granth Sahib are universally accepted. They apply to all people irrespective of their religion. During the period of the 10 Gurus there only were three religions: Hindus, Muslims and Sikhs prevalent in the northern part of India. ***By analogy, the writings in Guru Granth Sahib and the Universality of the Sikh Religion apply to all other religions like Christianity, Buddhism, Judaism and others.***

5. SUMMARY

Guru Granth Sahib includes hymns composed by 36 Hindus and Muslims. The Muslim Kabir said all people come from the same God, then who is good and who is bad. Farid, a Sufi Muslim, said, return good for evil while keeping no anger in your mind. Nam Dev a Hindu, said God is everywhere and pervades the whole universe. Ravi Das, a Hindu, said God is nearer to us and everything happens according to God's will.

6. EXCERCISES

i. Give reasons why 16% of the hymns by 36 Hindus and Muslims are incorporated in Guru Granth Sahib?
ii. Explain the contributions of Kabir, Farid, Namdev and Ravi Das to the Universality of the Sikh Religion.

7. REFERENCES

[1] Igbal Singh, 1986, The Essence of Truth: Japji and other Sikh Scriptures, Allen, McMillan and Enderson, New York, NYUSA., pp. 132-135.
[2] Dr. Trilochan Singh, et al, 1973, The Sacred Writings of the Sikhs, Samuel Weiser, New York, NYUSA, p. 211.
[3] The Tribune, Chandigarh, India, October 9, 2002, "Original drawings offered Akal Takht restoration," by Varinder Walia. http://www.tribuneindia.com/2002/20021009/main8.htm
[4] Dr. Trilochan Singh, et al, 1973, The Sacred Writings of the Sikhs, Samuel Weiser, New York, USA, p. 219.
[5] Dr. Trilochan Singh, et al, 1973, The Sacred Writings of the Sikhs, Samuel Weiser, New York, USA, p. 223.
[6] Dr. Trilochan Singh, et al, 1973, The Sacred Writings of the Sikhs, Samuel Weiser, New York, USA, p. 229.

UNIVERSALITY OF THE SIKH RELIGION

CHAPTER 7

FIRST PRINCIPLE - HONESTY

Honesty is universal and there is no doubt about it.

In just two words, in Punjabi, the first principle is made absolutely clear.

ROMAN	ENGLISH
KIRAT KIRNEE	***Earn your livelihood by honest, hard and creative work ethics.***

Honesty is for everybody. Honesty, to be effective, must be practiced by all on a daily basis.

1. WHAT IS HONESTY?

Honesty is the best policy. How many of us follow it? People can describe honesty in many different ways according to what suits them. There are no laws relating to honesty as it focuses on one's day-to-day living. It is left for our conscience to decide. In life there is a great temptation to make money by dishonest means. It is up to the individual to make that decision.

As we all know, only the good acts will be remembered, while in the end, everything will be left behind. If your work habits are good, be they in business or service or in any profession, it will provide great satisfaction. Every day is a challenge in life. ***When all dealings are performed honestly then one's mind will be at peace.***

2. BELIEFS OF AN HONEST PERSON

One who believes in Universality of the Sikh Religion strives for the best. This world is highly competitive and stressful no matter what profession he or she may pursue. There are no compromises in achieving success. Aggressiveness shown by a believer in the Sikh Religion is borne out by the desire that, if there is anything anyone else can do, I can do it better.

One has to be progressive, assertive and steadfast in what one sincerely believes and then strive for the best to accomplish it. ***Going to work must be a fulfilling experience and not a chore.*** Every day, one must enjoy accomplishing something worthwhile and not worry about whether it is small or big.

3. EXAMPLE OF HONESTY

Let me give you an example of honesty that I saw in my local newspaper, the Stamford Advocate (Stamford, Connecticut), USA. A woman who was born 35 years ago said that, at the time, her mother could not pay her obstetrician's bills. She made an arrangement to pay $10 per month. In the meantime, the doctor closed his practice and left Stamford.

The mother had no idea where the doctor went, but she still owed him $60. Money was very tight. She had to care for three children while working in a factory, as well as taking care of a disabled husband and a 90-year-old mother. Finally, she was able to locate the doctor, and sent him a check for $60 along with an apology. The doctor was so impressed with her honesty and integrity that he wrote her a letter of appreciation. This act is an excellent and very practical example of honesty and character that will be remembered by future generations.

4. GOOD CHARACTER AND HONESTY

When J.P. Morgan (a famous American banker) was asked about the best bank collateral, he paused for a second and replied, ***"Good character."*** Being honest develops character, respect for and service to others, good citizenship, sound use of time and talent and good work ethics.

There are no set rules and regulations to prove that one has good character. It is the overall perception by society and the good deeds performed in an honest way that are the requisite for good character.

5. MONEY EARNED BY HONEST MEANS

To earn money by honest means is the right way. People who use dishonest ways to accumulate wealth are not following any religion at all, no matter what they call themselves. It is said that money is the root of all evils. That is not correct. ***It is the love of money that is the root of all evil.*** The third Guru Amar Das made it very clear that love of money leads to a life full of falsehood.

The third Guru, Amar Das, said:

PUNJABI AND ROMAN	ENGLISH
ਮਨਮੁਖ ਮਾਇਆ ਮੋਹੁ ਹੈ Manmukh Maa-i-aa Moh Hai	A self-centered person loves money
ਨਾਮਿ ਨ ਲਗੋ ਪਿਆਰੁ II Naam Na Lago Pi-aar	and has no love for God.
ਕੂੜੁ ਕਮਾਵੈ ਕੂੜੁ ਸੰਗ੍ਰਹੈ Koorh Kamaavai Koorh Sangrahai	That person also practices and spreads falsehoods,
ਕੂੜੁ ਕਰੇ ਆਹਾਰੁ II Koorh Karay Aahaar. Guru Granth Sahib (p.552, line 1)	and makes falsehoods a way of life.

Money actually is a blessing. Sikhs offer money when bowing before Guru Granth Sahib. It could be one dollar or a million dollars. Sikhs also spend much money to build Gurdwaras, their religious temples. It is an acceptance of worldly things. As such, worldly things pose no problems unless we use dishonest means to acquire them. Without money it is not possible to perform any charitable work for the benefit of society. Money earned by honest means should be used for the right causes like:

i. ***educating people.***
ii. ***eradicating disease.***
iii. ***protecting the environment.***
iv. ***elevating the standard of living of those who are less fortunate.***

Honesty does pay while living in this world. It is my observation that if a king or high elected official of any country deliberately kills numbers of their own people, they invariably end up being assassinated. The primary and foremost duty of the head of any country is to ensure the welfare of all people irrespective of caste, color, creed, religion, sex or any other orientation. How many countries practice this?

Let us consider people in general. They make money by all possible means and feel they have accomplished something in their lives. Think of how many laws of the land they may have broken and without any regard to their inner conscience. Outwardly they may look splendid, but inwardly they are full of stress.

Guru Granth Sahib has stressed the importance of honesty in day-to-day living many times. Honesty pays, not only in this world, but also in the next.

6. HOMES AND BUSINESSES

To live in this world, we have to be involved in day-to-day life and earn a living for our family, our country and the world. Guru Arjan said that ***to accumulate wealth is alright provided it is by honest means*** and God's name is heard in those possessions.

Fifth Guru Arjan said:

PUNJABI and ROMAN

ਘਰ ਮੰਦਰ ਹਟਨਾਲੇ ਸੋਹੇ
Ghar Mandar Hatnaalay Sohay
ਜਿਸੁ ਵਿਚਿ ਨਾਮੁ ਨਿਵਾਸੀ ਰਾਮ ॥
Jis Vich Naam Nivassee Raam
Guru Granth Sahib (p. 783, line 4)

ENGLISH

Homes, mansions and businesses
are all lovely provided
God's name is heard in them.

Honesty comes from the heart. There is no set of written rules. Whenever in doubt about honesty, ask your conscience and you will get the right answer. ***If a person use dishonest means to make money, that person will receive no respect.*** People may praise them while meeting face-to-face, but in their hearts they will not like them.

7. BUSINESS AND PROFIT

In any business, there has to be profit but it must be fair, as is written in Guru Granth Sahib.

First Guru, Nanak, said:

PUNJABI AND ROMAN

ਵਣਜਾਰਿਆ ਸਿਉ ਵਣਜੁ ਕਰਿ
Vanjaari-aa Si-o Vanaj Kar
ਲੈ ਲਾਹਾ ਮਨ ਹਸੁ ॥
Lai Laahaa Man Has
Guru Granth Sahib (p. 595, line 13)

ENGLISH

Do business with those who
believe in truth and
make a fair profit that brings
peace of mind.

8. HONESTY AND PEACE OF MIND

When one is not honest, he or she is apt to tell a lie which leads to another lie and on and on. If honesty is practiced, the question of lying does not arise. Honesty leads to peace of mind and satisfaction in life.

Fifth Guru, Arjan said:

PUNJABI AND ROMAN	ENGLISH
ਉਦਮੁ ਕਰੇਦਿਆ ਜੀਉ ਤੂੰ	If one makes an honest effort.
Udam Karaydi-aa Jee-o TooN	in earning and living then he or she
ਕਮਾਵਦਿਆ ਸੁਖ ਭੁੰਚੁ II	
Kamaavdi-aa Sukh Bhunch	will enjoy peace of mind.
Guru Granth Sahib, p. 522 line 15	

9. WORK AND GOD

Work is the essence of life. It keeps one away from bad ideas. As they say, an idle person's brain is the devil's workshop. ***Working while keeping God in your mind goes hand-in-hand.***

Kabir said:

PUNJABI AND ROMAN	ENGLISH
ਹਾਥ ਪਾਉ ਕਰਿ ਕਾਮੁ	With your hand and feet perform honest work
Haath Paa-o Kar Kaam	
ਸਭੁ ਚੀਤੁ ਨਿਰੰਜਨੁ ਨਾਲਿ II	but always keep God in your mind.
Sabh Cheet Niranjan Naal	
Guru Granth Sahib (p. 1,376, line 1)	

10. TRUE WAY OF LIFE AND HONESTY

If a person is dishonest, it leads to distrust by other people in day-to-day dealings. A dishonest person loses confidence in society.

First Guru Nanak said:

PUNJABI AND ROMAN	ENGLISH
ਗੁਰੁ ਪੀਰੁ ਸਦਾਏ ਮੰਗਣ ਜਾਇII	Persons who call themselves spiritual
Gur Peer Sadaa-ay Mangan Jaa-ay	leaders, who beg, and do no useful
ਤਾ ਕੈ ਮੂਲਿ ਨ ਲਗੀਐ ਪਾਇII	work do not deserve respect.
Taa Kai Mool Na Lagee-ai Paa-ay	
ਘਾਲਿ ਖਾਇ ਕਿਛੁ ਹਥਹੁ ਦੇਇII	A person who earns through honest
Ghaal Khaa-ay Kichh Hathahu Day-ay	work and gives to charity,
ਨਾਨਕ ਰਾਹੁ ਪਛਾਣਹਿ ਸੇਇII	Nanak says that person achieves a
Naanak Raahu Pachhaaneh Say-aye-e	true way of life.
Guru Granth Sahib (p. 1245, line 17)	

11. HONESTY AND THE NEXT WORLD

Honest earning in this world is carried into the next world. ***Honesty is contagious and comes naturally to a person who has a clear conscience.***

First Guru Nanak said:

PUNJABI and ROMAN	**ENGLISH**
ਨਾਨਕ ਅਗੈ ਸੋ ਮਿਲੈ	Nanak says one's rewards in the next
Nanak Agai So Milai	world are
ਜਿ ਖਟੇ ਘਾਲੇ ਦੇਇ ॥	what one gives to the needy from one's
Je Khatay Ghaalay Day-aye-e	honest earnings in this world.
Guru Granth Sahib (p. 472, line 8)	

12. HONEST LIVING AND GURU NANAK

Guru Nanak was a perfect example of a truly religious person who traveled far and wide to spread the Universality of the Sikh Religion. ***He severely criticized exploitation by the rich and advocated the cause of the downtrodden, depressed and underprivileged.*** He lived with ordinary people, shared their sorrows and joys and encouraged the role of labor and hard work.

During one of his religious tours, [1], [2], in Saidpur (now Eminabad, Pubjab, Pakistan), Guru Nanak stayed in the house of Bhai Lalo, a low-caste carpenter. Lalo was content with his poverty and loved God. Guru Nanak was extremely happy to stay with Lalo who was honest and worked hard for his livelihood. The news spread like wildfire through the town. Guru Nanak of Khatri descent and Mardana, a low-caste Muslim minstrel accompanying him, were staying and eating food in the home of Bhai Lalo, a low-caste person.

Malik Bhago (a protégé of the Muslim governor) arranged a big feast at his mansion. He also invited Guru Nanak, but Guru Nanak declined with all humility. This became an opportunity for the high-caste persons to speak ill of Guru Nanak. They told Malik Bhago that Guru Nanak insulted him. Malik Bhago's pride and ego were hurt. To convey his message of honesty, Guru Nanak agreed and went to Malik Bhago's mansion. Malik Bhago asked him why he was eating in the house of a low-caste person and bringing shame to Brahmins and Khatris (both high castes).

Guru Nanak replied that his (Malik Bhago's) money was obtained from poor and helpless people through corrupt and unfair means. The food thus prepared was stained with the blood of poor and innocent people. The food made by a pious person, Lalo, was earned by the sweat of his brow and thus, was pure.

First Guru, Nanak, then sang the following hymn:

PUNJABI & ROMAN	**ENGLISH**
ਹਕੁ ਪਰਾਇਆ ਨਾਨਕਾ	Nanak says to take what rightfully
Hak Paraa-i-aa Naankaa	belongs to another
ਉਸੁ ਸੂਅਰ ਉਸੁ ਗਾਇ II	is like eating pork for a Muslim
Us Soo-ar Us Gaa-ay	or eating cow for a Hindu.
ਗੁਰੁ ਪੀਰੁ ਹਾਮਾ ਤਾ ਭਰੇ	The Guru and the Pir will grace you
Gur Peer Haamaa Taa Bharay	
ਜਾ ਮੁਰਦਾਰੁ ਨ ਖਾਇ II	provided you refrain from eating food
Jaa Murdaar Na Khaa-ay	obtained by dishonest means.
ਗਲੀ ਭਿਸਤਿ ਨ ਜਾਈਐ	By mere talking one can not get salvation.
Galee Bhisat Na Jaa-ee-ai	
ਛੁਟੈ ਸਚੁ ਕਮਾਇ II	Salvation is obtained by truthful living.
Chhutai Sach Kamaa-ay	
ਮਾਰਣ ਪਾਹਿ ਹਰਾਮ ਮਹਿ	Putting spices into food obtained by
Maaran Paahi Haraam Meh	ill-gotten means
ਹੋਇ ਹਲਾਲੁ ਨ ਜਾਇ II	does not make that food pure.
Ho-ay Halaal Na Jaa-ay	
ਨਾਨਕ ਗਲੀ ਕੂੜੀਈ	Nanak says from false talk
Naanak Galee Koorhee-ee	
ਕੂੜੋ ਪਲੈ ਪਾਇ II	one gathers only falsehood.
Koorho Palai Paa-ay	
Guru Granth Sahib (p. 141, line 1)	

Malik Bhago and all others present listened to Guru Nanak very attentively. Malik Bhago was touched by the guilt of his conscience. He repented and sought forgiveness and mercy. He distributed his ill-gotten wealth to the poor and needy and devoted himself to the service of humanity.

Soon, word spread that a holy man, Guru Nanak, had challenged the caste system and praised the people who worked hard and lived honest lives. People flocked to him and listened to his Universal message for equality and love for God.

Guru Nanak thus clarified, only that persons ares holy who love God and earn their livelihoods by honest means.

13. SUMMARY

Above all, one must have complete faith in one God, should love God and perform good deeds. Money and worldly things are not bad, as such, provided they are earned by honest and hard work.

Real respect has to be earned. You may inherit wealth but you cannot inherit or buy respect. Honesty in thinking, in dealing and in day-to-day life is very important for a person to be really successful in this world. Good deeds will be remembered even after departing for the next world.

14. EXERCISES

i. List reasons why people should be honest with themselves, to their families and to the communities in which they live.
ii. Explain why people who earn their livelihoods by dishonest means and have worldly things still are under much stress.
iii. Discuss how Guru Nanak convinced Malik Bhago to live an honest life and perform good deeds?
iv. Discuss how money becomes a blessing and how it should be used to help humanity.

15. REFERENCES

[1] Surinder S. Johar, 1988, The Sikh Religion, National Book Shop, Delhi, India, pp. 106-108.
[2] Kartar S. Duggal, 1989, Sikh Gurus, Second printing, Himalayan International Institute, Honesdale, PA, p. 16.

UNIVERSALITY OF THE SIKH RELIGION

CHAPTER 8

SECOND PRINCIPLE—SHARING

GIVING IS BETTER THAN RECEIVING AND WE ALL CAN DO IT

In just two words, in Punjabi, the second principle is made incredibly clear.

ROMAN	ENGLISH
Wandh Chhakanna	**Share your blessings with less fortunate**

People who give for charity are lucky. One does not know when one might change to receiving from giving. It is all in God's power. It reminds people that nothing is permanent in this world. ***It is best to serve humanity while the going is good.***

1. THREE TYPES OF PEOPLE

People can be classified into three categories: 1. Those who are God oriented or people loving. 2. Those who are self-centered. 3. Those who are materialistic. You can figure out the category in which you belong.

i. PEOPLE WHO LOVE PEOPLE—FIRST CATEGORY

People who love people have a great purpose in mind and they perform it thoughout their lifespan. They also believe in loving God. According to the Sikh Religion they are called Gurmukh. Gurmukh (God- and people-loving person) consider rendering selfless service to others as the cornerstone of their life. One must be personally committed to this belief. ***It is through service to others that love is obtained.*** Service to others is part of the Sikh daily prayer. It is not always easy to give to those who are less fortunate, but if one decides that everyday I will do a little good, then that person will have great peace of mind and mental satisfaction.

ii. SELF-CENTERED PEOPLE—SECOND CATEGORY

Self-centered people always ask "What's in for me?", for anything they perform. Instead of helping they say, "I have enough of my own problems." Self-centered people become insecure, suspicious and cynical. They never build self-respect. They are never happy, as they have no love for other people. They are called Manmukh in Punjabi.

iii. MATERIALISTIC PEOPLE—THIRD CATEGORY

Materialistic people find emotional attachment to material things. Even people are things to them?to be used only for their advantage. The more things they have, the more they need. There is no end to the worldly things and their sole purpose in life is associated with acquiring more of these worldly things.. Because they lead such shallow lives, they are also called Manmukh in Punjabi.

2. WHY TO SHARE

According to the Sikh Religion, the self-centered and materialistic people are known as Manmukh. The first question that comes to a Manmukh (self-loving person) is "Why should I give to others?" I do not make enough money. Let some one else do it. It is not my job. The next question is, "Why should I care for others?" I that see people who have power sometimes abuse it. They make money in unsavory ways. One should ask the question, "Should I reduce myself to the level of the crooked people?" I must believe in my own character and must not reduce to the level of dishonest people, in spite of all the adversities. ***If people do not care for others, then this world will really be a miserable place to live.*** There will be chaos in our society and we will return to a barbaric state.

3. INVESTIGATE BEFORE GIVING

First and foremost, one must evaluate an organization to one's satisfaction before donating hard-earned money. One must be sure that the money donated is being used for the purpose promoted by the organization. Guru Nanak made it clear that reading alone is not enough; one must understand and put into practice. Similarly ***one must investigate the organization before giving money to charities.***

The first Guru, Nanak, said:

PUNJABI AND ROMAN	ENGLISH
ਅਕਲੀ ਪੜ੍ਹਿ ਕੈ ਬੁਝੀਐ Aklee ParhH Kai Bujhee-ai	While reading understand intellectually
ਅਕਲੀ ਕੀਚੈ ਦਾਨੁ ॥ Aaklee Keechai Daan.	While giving for charity investigate intelligently.

Guru Granth Sahib (p. 1245, line 4)

The following three criteria must be evaluated before giving any money or time for the charitable organization.

i. ACCOUNTS

Accounts are the most critical part of investigating a charitable organization. The best way is ***to ask for their latest annual report and a concise financial summary for the last few years.*** If they fail to provide that information, then money should not be given to them. Instead investigate and find those organizations that give clear-cut information about their accounts.

Find out from the accounts how much of the money collected is actually used for the charity and how much for administrative purposes. This is very fundamental and is very easy to get, at least in the USA. The following organization's information was obtained from Forbes Magazine [1] for the year 2000. One can also get information from Internet under different headings like charities, etc.

#	NAME OF THE ORGANIZATION	Total Revenue US $ Millions	% for Charity
A.	Gifts in Kind International, Alexandria, VA	292	100%
B.	America's Second Harvest, Chicago, Ill	475	99%
C.	Americares, Stamford, CT.	268	98%
D.	CARE, USA, Atlanta, GA	420	91%
E.	American National Red Cross, Washington, DC	2405	90%
F.	Doctors Without Borders, New York, NY	17	88%
G.	Good Will Industries, Bethedsa, MD	1650	87%
H.	Salvation Army, Arlington, VA	1707	83%
I.	American Cancer Society, Atlanta, GA	672	71%
J.	Disabled American Veterans, Cincinnati, Ohio	122	64%

The above information may not be available so easily from the organizations outside the USA.

ii. PURPOSE OF THE ORGANIZATION

This information for the well-known organizations is very easy to get, either by writing directly, calling, or through the Internet. For the lesser-known organizations, information may not be as easy to obtain especially if they are outside the USA. ***Get the mission statement, which will outline the purpose and objectives of the organization.*** Even for religious organizations, this information is available. One must know the requirements for becoming a member of the management team. The organization must state that they treat all people equally, in all respects.

iii. BACKGROUND OF THE KEY ORGANIZERS

It is very important to know the ***names and the background of the key management personnel*** who run day-to-day activities of the charitable organization. Their reputation and character are very important for one's assurance that the money will be used for the particular cause.

4. WHAT TYPE OF PEOPLE NEED HELP

People who need help may be medically handicapped, others may not have a head start in life due to adverse circumstances, and some are victims of natural disasters or wars. The reasons are innumerable. In any society not all people are lucky enough to receive their fair share in life.

5. HOW CAN WE HELP

There are two ways people can help: ***one by giving money and by giving time***. Both money and time perform the same thing. Helping others is the most difficult thing to do. We can do everything for the immediate family, but to help others is considered to be someone else's responsibility.

6. THE SIKH RELIGION AND SERVICE TO HUMANITY

The Sikh Religion does not separate God from human beings or religious worship from material things as long as God dwells in their heart and mind. The religious places are not only for worship but also a place to serve humanity. Service to humanity may include the following:

Feeding the hungry
Lodging the travelers
Educating the less fortunate
Helping the sick
Sheltering the destitute
Helping the disabled and handicapped
Providing a meeting place for social activities

People who believe in the Universality of the Sikh Religion enjoy supreme bliss in helping others.

7. GURU GRANTH SAHIB AND SHARING

The Guru Granth Sahib states that to serve people is to serve God. By sharing, one feels exaltation in the body and mind, which brings contentment. Very heavy emphasis is put on service to humanity in the Sikh Religion.

i. HUMANITY AND GOD

What is the easiest way to see God? It is not through one's eyes that one sees God; it is through the power of the mind, body and soul to perceive God.

The third Guru, Amar Das, said:

PUNJABI AND ROMAN	ENGLISH
ਗੁਰਿ ਪੂਰੈ ਵੇਖਾਲਿਆ	***Perfect God is perceived by***
Gur Poorai Vaykhaali-aa	
ਗੁਰ ਸੇਵਾ ਪਾਈਐ ॥	***serving humanity.***
Gur Sayvaa Paa-ee-ai	
Guru Granth Sahib (p. 644, line 9)	

ii. LESS SERVICE MORE DEMANDS

We always think that we will get more by giving to charity. Some people want recognition in society when donating money for some worthwhile cause. Others are just deeply interested in doing something tangible in improving conditions for downtrodden people.

The fifth Guru, Arjan, said:

PUNJABI AND ROMAN	ENGLISH
ਸੇਵਾ ਥੋਰੀ	***Paltry is my service***
Sayvaa Thoree	
ਮਾਗਨੁ ਬਹੁਤਾ ॥	***great are my demands.***
Maagan Bahutaa	
Guru Granth Sahib (p. 738, line 9)	

iii. NO HONOR WITHOUT SERVICE

Everyone wants distinction and honor in the society we live in. Honor is achieved by getting involved in the project of one's choice to serve humanity. By mere talking or doing nothing no productive results can be achieved.

The first Guru, Nanak, said:

PUNJABI AND ROMAN	ENGLISH
ਜੇਤੇ ਜੀਅ ਤੇਤੇ ਸਭਿ ਤੇਰੇ	All living beings are your creation.
Jaytay Jee-a Taytay Sabh Tayray	
ਵਿਣੁ ਸੇਵਾ ਫਲੁ ਕਿਸੈ ਨਾਹੀ II	without service to humanity
Vin Sayvaa Fal Kisai Naahee	no one receives any honor.
Guru Granth Sahib (p. 354, line 18)	

iv. DESTINED BY GOD TO PERFORM SERVICE

Theoretically it is possible that all people can perform service to humanity but in practice it doe not occur. ***Some people are destined by God to perform humanitarian service.*** They are the luckiest people and they are always contented.

The fifth Guru, Arjan, said:

PUNJABI AND ROMAN	ENGLISH
ਜਾ ਕੈ ਮਸਤਕਿ ਭਾਗ	Those who are destined by God
Jaa Kai Mastak Bhaag	
ਸਿ ਸੇਵਾ ਲਾਇਆ II	perform Service to humanity.
Se Sayvaa laa-i-aa	
Guru Granth Sahib (p. 457, line 12)	

v. THOSE WHO DO NOT THINK PROPERLY

The reason why some people do not perform humanitarian service is that their thinking is not in the right direction. They believe that it is some body else's job.

The first Guru, Nanak, said:

PUNJABI AND ROMAN	ENGLISH
ਮਤਿ ਥੋੜੀ	Because of our meager intellect
Mat Thorhee	
ਸੇਵ ਗਵਾਈਐ II	we lose the value of service.
Sayv Gavaa-ee-ai	
Guru Granth Sahib (p. 468, line 15)	

vi. SERVICE AND PEACE OF MIND

One gets peace of mind and feels happy if, everyday, a good act is performed, no matter how small it may be. We all have to go, someday, from this world. By performing good deeds one is remembered even after death. ***Helping others is the way to perceive God.***

The first Guru, Nanak, said:

PUNJABI AND ROMAN	ENGLISH
ਸੁਖੁ ਹੋਵੈ Sukh Hovai	One gets happiness and peace of mind
ਸੇਵ ਕਮਾਣੀਆ II Sayv Kamaanee-aa	by service to humanity.
ਸਭ ਦੁਨੀਆ Sabh Dunee-aa	All human beings in this world
ਆਵਣ ਜਾਣੀਆ II Aavan Jaanee-aa	continue the cycle of coming and going.
ਵਿਚਿ ਦੁਨੀਆ Vich Dunee-aa	In this world
ਸੇਵ ਕਮਾਈਐ II Sayv Kamaa-ee-ai	if you perform service to humanity
ਤਾ ਦਰਗਹ Taa Dargeh	then in the next world also
ਬੈਸਣੁ ਪਾਈਐ II Baisan Paa-ee-ai	one gets honor.

Guru Granth Sahib (p. 26, line 1)

8. GOOD DEEDS AND DESTINY

It is true whatever happens, God destines it. However, it is possible to change your day-to-day living by performing good deeds.

During one of Guru Nanak's journeys [2], he camped in a town. Due to heavy rains he had to stay in the town longer than anticipated. Several devotees came to Guru Nanak regularly. Amongst them were two friends who used to live on the same street. On their way to see Guru Nanak, one of them came across a prostitute and was allured by her charm. Thereafter, he left his home along with the friend on the pretext of going to the Guru, but instead visited her. A few days later one who came to pay his homage was picked by a thorn, while his neighbor, who visited the prostitute, found a gold coin in the street. This incident bewildered the Guru's devotee who came every day religiously. He mentioned that in the prayer meeting that morning. Guru Nanak heard it and told the devotee.

"Your friend was destined to come across a treasure but due to his evil ways, it was reduced to a single coin. While on account of your past karma you were to be impaled with a stake. Due to your good deeds, you have been left with a mere pick of a thorn."

Thus one cannot drastically change what is destined, but with good deeds one can improve considerably.

The first Guru, Nanak, said:

PUNJABI AND ROMAN		**ENGLISH**
ਸੇਵਕ	ਸੇਵਹਿ	God's devotees who perform good deeds
Sayvak	Sayveh	
ਕਰਮਿ	ਚੜਾਉ ॥	their destiny is awakened.
Karam	Charhaa-o	

Guru Granth Sahib (p. 465, line 10)

9. PRACTICAL WAYS TO HELP

Now taking into account the present competitive and stressful world, how can one person help to alleviate the suffering? Sharing is part of Universality of the Sikh Religion. It is also anticipated that you share 10% of your earnings for the charity of your choice. It could be money or your time for worthy causes to serve humanity.

Let us consider certain examples where it has made difference in people's lives. ***It is left to the imagination of anyone how to perform a meaningful service.*** There are innumerable things that need to be done. It all depends upon what you think is important to help. Some of the suggestions are:

i. Help in a Soup kitchen to alleviate hunger..
ii. Join a human rights organization in order to help innocent people from being killed all over the world.
iii. Join the Red Cross to help the needy friend or foe alike.
iv. Help to educate the deserving and poor people.
v. Help those who need medical help and cannot afford to do so.
vi. Volunteer for or donate to the American Cancer Society to alleviate suffering and pain.
vii. Volunteer for or donate to the Salvation Army to help the needy.
viii. Help third world countries to improve their standard of living.
ix. Volunteer your service in hospitals for the sick and needy.
x. Help any other organization you deem truly charitable.

10. CHARITABLE CONTRIBUTIONS

American Association of Fundraising Counsel (AFRC) Trust [3] reported that for the year 2004, Americans contributed $248 billion to various charities. There are about 1.4 million charities including religious organizations in the United States. About 70% of all households donate in any given year. There are some tax benefits for the people who give money to organizations approved by the Internal Revenue Service of USA.

Individuals contributed $188 billion (76%), foundations $29 billion (11%), bequest (given by wills) $20 billion (8%), and corporations $12 billion (5%). This is an extremely large amount; it helps a considerable number of people in their time of need and also builds the country.

President John F. Kennedy of USA said, ***"Ask not what your country can do for you—ask what you can do for your country".***

Guru Nanak explained what people aspire to when they give for charity: generous people are contented while others want honor and more money in return.

The first Guru, Nanak, said:

PUNJABI AND ROMAN	**ENGLISH**
ਸਤੀਆ ਮਨਿ ਸੰਤੋਖੁ ਉਪਜੈ Satee-aa Man Santokh Upjai ਦੇਣੈ ਕੈ ਵੀਚਾਰਿ Daynai Kai Veechaar	The mind of a generous person feels contented when they think of giving charity.
ਦੇ ਦੇ ਮੰਗਹਿ ਸਹਸਾ ਗੂਣਾ Day Day Mangeh Sahsaa Goonaa ਸੋਭ ਕਰੇ ਸੰਸਾਰੁ Sobh Karay Sansaar	Others ask thousand times more money what they donate and also want the world to honor them.

Guru Granth Sahib (p. 466, line 1)

11. HOW ONE PERSON MAKES A BIG DIFFERENCE

Many times we say what one person, like me, can do when there is so much misery and suffering in this world. If we all thought that way then it would be a miserable world in which to live. One person can make a difference, although cannot solve all the problems afflicting society. ***One person can act as a catalyst along with others to do some useful work for the humanity.*** There is a popular saying: If there is one job to be done and six people are told to do it, chances are the job will not be done.

i. BHAGAT PURAN SINGH

Let me give one example of how one person made a tremendous difference. He is Bhagat Puran Singh, Figure 23 [4], of Punjab India. ***He devoted all his life to mentally and terminally sick people.*** This was done for all types of sick people irrespective of religion, color, sex or race. He started helping the sick and destitute people under a Pipal tree in 1947 in Punjab. It grew into a full-fledged institution housing 250 patients and has now become the All India Pingalwara Charitable Society, Amritsar, Punjab, India. Bhagat Puran Singh was nominated for the Nobel Peace Prize in 1991 but he passed away in 1992 when he was 88 years old. He was also a writer, publisher, as well as an environmentalist [5].

Bhagat Puran Singh carried on his back an abandoned, mute, mentally disabled, crippled boy, named Piara Singh for 14 years. For this reason he was nicknamed the "Man with a Garland Around His Neck". His work will go on as people have recognized the needs of the poor and the sick because of the dedication of one person. **Puran Singh was to Sikhism, what Mother Teresa was to Catholicism [5].**

ii. MOTHER TERESA

Another example of what one person can do is that of Mother Teresa, Figure 24 [6]. She was born 1910 in Skopje, Yugoslavia (what is now Macedonia). ***She came to India in 1929 and spent all of her life in the slums of Calcutta, India.*** After teaching for some time in 1952 she established a Home for the Dying and Destitute in Calcutta. In 1965 it became an International Society. By 1997 Mother Teresa's Sisters numbered nearly 4000 members and 610 foundations were established in 123 countries around the world. Mother Teresa was awarded the Nobel Peace Prize in 1979. She accepted the award "for the glory of God and in the name of the poor." She was known as the Saint of the Gutters of Calcutta. She passed away at the age of 87 in 1997 in India.

Mother Teresa said
By blood I am an Albanian
By citizenship I am Indian
By faith I am a Catholic nun.

FIGURE 23

BHAGHAT PURAN SINGH 1904 - 1992
In the service of suffering humanity

FIGURE 24

MOTHER TERESA 1910 - 1997
Worked for the Unwanted, Unloved and Uncared people

iii. MR. TARLOCHAN SINGH

Let me give one example how one person made a tremendous difference in feeding hungry people. Sixty-seven-year-old Mr. Tarlochan Singh of India [7] started his mission to feed the hungry many years ago. He was inspired by the late Mother Teresa of Calcutta (Noble Peace Prize in 1979) when he met her. He looked upon Mother Teresa as his own mother and wanted to follow her example. The food is prepared overnight and taken by trucks, in the morning, to different parts of Delhi as well as the railway station. The lines outside Sis Gung Gurdwara in Delhi extend half a mile in either direction. ***To the question "Where does the money comes from?" Tarlochan raises his both hands and answers "God gives all I ask for".*** He refuses to take money from anyone but accepts gladly wheat flour, rice, daal and medicines. ***Popularly known as "the daal-roti and rice Langar," the basic staple food of India is served free of charge to anyone regardless of religion, sex, caste, color or age.*** His clinic is on the pavement where medicines are dispensed. Many other places in India are following his system to feed the hungry.

Tarlochan often quotes Guru Nanak who said

"God fills the pitchers that are empty and empties pitchers that are filled".

iv. MR. PAUL NEWMAN

Another example is of Mr. Paul Newman [8] a famous actor in the USA, who in 1980 made salad dressing as a hobby in a tub. In 1982, Newman's Own began with Mr. Newman's famous Oil & Vinegar Salad Dressing. He decided to donate all the profits to charitable causes. Over $150 million has been donated since 1982. His company now makes salad dressing, spaghetti, popcorn, and lemonade at factories in the USA, Britain and Australia. Thousands of charities have received donations from Paul Newman as a result of the sale of Newman's Own products worldwide. He has sponsored 8 camps for children who have life-threatening diseases. It is amazing how one person makes a difference in helping other less fortunate people.

Paul Newman once quipped, ***"From salad dressings all blessings flow."***

v. MR. KEN BEHRING

Mr. Ken Behring 75 years old, a businessman in the USA [9] has donated 225,000 wheelchairs in 121 countries. He says it is just the beginning. He travels in his own jet and many times delivers wheelchairs personally to the needy. It all started in 1999 when a religious organization called Church of Jesus Christ of Latter-day-Saints?the Mormons?asked Ken to deliver 12 wheelchairs to

Romania. That incident changed his whole life. ***Now it is his mission to give wheelchairs to as many people as possible.*** He said there are some 150 million people in this world who need wheelchairs. The wheelchairs are made in four factories in China to his specifications. Behring gave one wheelchair to a Chinese man named Mr. Xie Yanhong; he became the first disabled Chinese to swim the English Channel. A young man in India got a wheelchair and his father told Behring that it was the first time in his son's life that he could sit in the sun. A young man in Guatemala had gangrene in his leg wanted to borrow against the wheelchair to pay his medical expenses for an operation. The doctor wanted $100 to amputate his leg and another $25 for anesthesia. Behring gave him the $125. The young man finally accepted the money after some convincing.

Thus, it clearly shows that one person can make a big difference if one is dedicated to serve humanity.

vi. OTHER EXAMPLES

Let me give some examples [10] of how one person can make an enormous impact on our daily lives. Although these are not charities, they still have helped society at large.

Henry Ford.	Invented the assembly line technique to mass-produce cars.
Waterman.	Invented the ink cartridge for fountain pens rather than dipping.
Westinghouse.	Invented how to stop a train.
Otis.	Invented the elevator, which facilitated the construction of Skyscrapes.

This short list exemplifies that the contributions of one person can make a huge difference.

One can accomplish whatever goal is set, provided one is persistent, honest, hard working and dedicated for the cause. If each one of us does something good everyday, this world would be a wonderful place to live. Ultimately it is the combined effort of all to accomplish worthwhile results for the good of the society.

There is a famous Chinese proverb

If one wants happiness for an hour, take a nap.
If one wants happiness for a day, go fishing.
If one wants happiness for a year, inherit a fortune.
If one wants happiness for a lifetime, help some one else.

12. SUMMARY

Next to Godliness is service to humanity. Charity begins at home. Giving is better than receiving. There are three types of people, ones who love people others who are self-centered and those who only love material goods. Investigate before giving money or time to any charitable organization. There are two ways to help: monetarily or by volunteering time. Guru Granth Sahib and the Sikh Religion give top priority to service for humanity. Guru Nanak was clear when he said that to serve people is to love God.

Not all people are ready to perform humanitarian work. There are those who do not value the importance of service to the needy. Service brings peace of mind. There are many practical ways suggested to perform service.

Individuals can make a big difference by performing good deeds for humanity at large. Bhagat Puran Singh worked to help the crippled and often terminally sick people. Mother Teresa cared for the unwanted, unloved and uncared-for people. Mr. Tarlochan Singh is happy to feed the hungry. Paul Newman is helping the terminally sick children and many charitable organizations. Ken Behring is giving wheelchairs free all over the world. One person can make a difference.

13. EXERCISES

i. Write an essay about what will happen to the world if no one gives any money to charitable cause?
ii. How many organizations have you contributed money to and/or volunteered your time to and why have you done so?
iii. Are you thankful to God that you are in a position to give rather than receive? Explain what satisfaction you get.
iv. Give examples how one person can make a big difference in helping the needy.
v. Give some quotations from the Guru Granth Sahib about the importance of service to humanity?

14. REFERENCES

[1] Forbes Magazine, Give Wisely, December 11, 2000, page 298.
[2] Kartar S. Duggal. 1989. *Sikh Gurus*. Second printing, Himalayan International Institute, Honesdale, PA, USA. p. 17.

[3] Google Images Click for "aafrc.org"
Click under Chart "2004 Giving by Source of Contributions"
[4] www.pingalwaraonline.org
Pingalwara, Bhagat Puran Singh's home for the crippled.
[5] Internet Yahoo, click "Bhagat Puran Singh"
click "Read Biography of Bhagat Puran Singh"
http://www.sikh-history.com/sikhhist/personalities/sewadars/puransingh.html
[6] Yahoo. Click "Mother Teresa". Click "Beatification Mother Teresa of Calcutta" Click "Biography"
http://www.vatican.va/news_services/liturgy/saints/ns_lit_doc_20031019_madre-teresa_en.html
[7] Khuswant Singh, "No One Will Go Hungry" *The Tribune*, Chandigarh, India, September 7, 2002.
[8] *New York Times*, November 18, 1998, p 2, Special Section of GIVING.
Also http://www.newmansown.com/3a history.html
http://www.newmansown.com/5_good.html
[9] *AARP* (American Association of Retired People) The Magazine, September & October, 2004, page 74, Washington DC USA.
[10] *Reader's Digest*, January 1992, pages 79-80.

UNIVERSALITY OF THE SIKH RELIGION

CHAPTER 9

THIRD PRINCIPLE-EQUALITY FOR ALL

NO ONE IS HIGH OR LOW AND ALL ARE EQUAL IN ALL RESPECTS

1. ALL ARE EQUAL

All people are equal. As explained in Chapter 2 by Guru Nanak, equality is the cornerstone of Sikh Religion. ***There is no high or low***. This applies to all people irrespective of their religion, caste, color, creed, sex, appearance or any other way that is used to divide people. Religions try to classify people into different categories. This occurs both within a particular religion as well as between religions.. Guru Nanak said God has created everyone alike and there is no need to differentiate among people .

Sikhism is a religion of equality. It stresses equality not only between men and women but also universal equality among all human beings. ***The Sikh religion does not consider people of other religions to be inferior or non-believers***. According to the Sikh religion, God judges people by their actions. It makes no difference what religion one practices or the religion that is carried over from one's parents. The Sikh religion allows any person to visit any of their religious places (Gurdwaras) regardless of their religion, race, sex, caste and creed.

i. Guru Nanak made it clear that no one is high or low. All are equal.

The first Guru, Nanak, said:

PUNJABI AND ROMAN	ENGLISH
ਸਭੁ ਕੋ ਊਚਾ ਆਖੀਐ Sabh Ko Oochaa Aakhee-ai	Call everyone high
ਨੀਚੁ ਨ ਦੀਸੈ ਕੋਇ ॥ Neech Na Deesai Ko-ay.	no one seems low.
ਇਕਨੈ ਭਾਂਡੇ ਸਾਜਿਐ Iknai BhaaNday Saaji-ai	One God has fashioned all alike and
ਇਕੁ ਚਾਨਣੁ ਤਿਹੁ ਲੋਇ ॥ Ik Chaanan Tihu Lo-ay.	God's light pervades the three worlds.

Guru Granth Sahib (p. 62, line 12)

ii. ***God lives in every heart and God also treats everybody as equal.*** There is no need to differentiate among people.

The fourth Guru, Ram Das, said:

PUNJABI AND ROMAN	**ENGLISH**
ਘਟ ਘਟ ਅੰਤਰਿ ਤੂੰਹੈ ਵੁਠਾ ॥ Ghat Ghat Antar TooNhai Vuthaa.	God dwells deep within every heart.
ਸਭੇ ਸਾਝੀਵਾਲ ਸਦਾਇਨਿ ਤੂੰ Sabhay Saajheevaal Sadaa-in TooN	God's grace is bestowed to all
ਕਿਸੈ ਨ ਦਿਸਹਿ ਬਾਹਰਾ ਜੀਉ ॥ Kisai Na Diseh Baahraa Jee-o. Guru Granth Sahib (p. 97, line 7)	All are equal according to God's vision.

iii. We can say that all people are equal. However, there are very few who really believe that in their hearts and minds. Such is the way of life.

Ravi Das said:

PUNJABI AND ROMAN	**ENGLISH**
ਰਵਿਦਾਸ ਸਮ ਦਲ ਸਮਝਾਵੈ ਕੋਊ ॥ Ravi Das Sam Dal Samjhaavai Ko-oo. Guru Granth Sahib (p. 93, line 18)	A rare one understands that God is present equally in all.

iv. Ravi Das made it very clear that in this world there is ***no need to classify people as second or third class,*** as all are equal in all respects.

Ravi Das said:

PUNJABI AND ROMAN	**ENGLISH**
ਦੋਮ ਨ ਸੇਮ ਏਕ ਸੋ ਆਹੀ ॥ Dom Na Saym Ayk So Aahee Guru Granth Sahib (p. 345, line 14)	All are equal, there is no second or third status.

v. As the same light of God is present in each and every heart then one must treat everyone as equal in all respects.

The first Guru, Nanak, said:

PUNJABI AND ROMAN	**ENGLISH**
ਗੁਰਮੁਖਿ ਏਕ ਦ੍ਰਿਸਟਿ ਕਰਿ ਦੇਖਹੁ	A God oriented person should perceive
Gurmukh Ayk Darisat Kar Daykhhu	everyone equal
ਘਟਿ ਘਟਿ ਜੋਤਿ ਸਮੋਈ ਜੀਉ ॥	as God's divine light is present
Ghat Ghat Jot Samo-ee Jee-o.	in each and every heart
Guru Granth Sahib (p. 599, line 2)	

2. EQUALITY FOR WOMEN

In this chapter more emphasis will be put on the equality of women and their status in the Sikh Religion. Women are approximately half of the world population. How can people consider that large number as inferior in any way? ***Equality for women is a must in all spheres of our life***. We cannot deprive women of their rights when **Guru Nanak said, "Why should women be considered inferior who give birth to kings."**

According to Darwin theory [1], women were considered inferior to men mainly due to their role in reproduction. This theory is not correct. The very fact that women can reproduce should be considered an asset for which women must be honored. Scientists produced many theories to prove the inferiority of woman. They were all contradicted. It has been proved that women who performed hard labor were still able to reproduce.

Voting right is another issue. Originally women were not allowed to vote in the USA. It was only in 1920 when women received the right to vote due to the ratification of the 19th Amendment. Women waged a long struggle to receive this right.

Man's hopes and aspirations revolve around woman. ***Next to food, the physical need of man is the love for woman*** [2]. As a wife, woman takes care of the whole family by carrying out the day-to-day activities, inside and outside the house. Then as a mother she takes care of the children. In motherhood divine sovereignty is conferred upon a woman. The woman's spirit of self-sacrifice is real. Woman is revealed to man in her acts of faith, love and noble self-sacrifice. Woman deserves great honor for the work she performs.

i. MY PROPOSITION TO ACCOMPLISH EQUALITY OF WOMEN

Equality of women must begin in each and every home. My proposition is ***"If all parents throughout the world treat their sons and daughters as equals in all respects, then the question of inequality for women will vanish from this world"***. The families can start this without asking anybody's permission.

ii. EQUALITY AND THE SIKH RELIGION

Equality of women is of utmost importance for the Universality of the Sikh Religion. Ever since Guru Nanak started this religion, ***the equality of women has not only been said but also practiced for the last five hundred years***. Sometimes it may not appear so due to the influence of the local customs and the old habits. For example the proportion of women in the management of Gurdwaras (religious places) is very small. The proportion of women in all Gurdwaras all over the world must increase in significant numbers at all levels of management. That includes the president, secretary, the Ragis and Granthis (preachers). Theoretically they should be 50%, but at least they must be in proportion to the congregation. This change need not alter the constitution of any Gurdwara. Both men and women have to work together to remove this inequality. Women also have the responsibility to come forward and be willing to be elected or appointed .

iii. EQUAL STATUS OF WOMEN

Guru Nanak made it very clear that women must be treated equal.

The first Guru, Nanak, said about the status of women.

PUNJABI AND ROMAN	ENGLISH
ਭੰਡਿ ਜੰਮੀਐ Bhand Jammee-ai	From a woman we are all born,
ਭੰਡਿ ਨਿੰਮੀਐ Bhand Nimmee-ai	within a woman we were first conceived,
ਭੰਡਿ ਮੰਗਣੁ ਵੀਆਹੁ II Bhand Mangan Vee-aahu	with a woman, man is engaged and married.
ਭੰਡਹੁ ਹੋਵੈ ਦੋਸਤੀ Bhandahu Hovai Dostee	With a woman, man makes life-long friendship
ਭੰਡਹੁ ਚਲੈ ਰਾਹੁ II Bhandahu Chalai Raahu	and it is the woman who keeps the race going.
ਭੰਡੁ ਮੁਆ ਭੰਡੁ ਭਾਲੀਐ Bhand Mu-aa Bhand Bhaalee-ai	When wife dies, man looks for another woman,
ਭੰਡਿ ਹੋਵੈ ਬੰਧਾਨੁ II Bhande Hovai BanDhaan	and it is through woman that man is restrained.
ਸੋ ਕਿਉ ਮੰਦਾ ਆਖੀਐ So Ki-o Mandaa Aakhee-ai	Why should women be considered inferior

ਜਿਤੁ ਜੰਮਹਿ ਰਾਜਾਨ ॥ — who give birth to kings.

Jit Jameh Raajaan

ਭੰਡਹੁ ਹੀ ਭੰਡੁ ਊਪਜੈ — From woman is born woman

Bhandahu Hee Bhand Oopjai

ਭੰਡੈ ਬਾਝੁ ਨ ਕੋਇ ॥ — without woman there will be no human race.

Bhandai Baajh Na Ko-ay

ਨਾਨਕ ਭੰਡੈ ਬਾਹਰਾ — Nanak says without woman

Naanak Bhandai Baaharaa

ਏਕੋ ਸਚਾ ਸੋਇ ॥ — there is only one True God who exists.

Ayko Sachaa So-ay

Guru Granth Sahib (p. 473, line 8)

The above statements leave no doubt as regards the equality or may even be the superiority of women in the Sikh Religion.

3. CONDITION OF WOMEN DURING TEN GURUS (1469 TO 1708)

Let us go back to the year 1469, when Guru Nanak was born, and discuss the condition of women in those days. The status of women had sunk to the lowest level when Guru Nanak was born. As a girl she was under the watchful eyes of her parents, as an adult of her husband, and as a widow of her sons.

In general there were four types of practices that made women inferior. First was the practice of ***Sati*** (burning alive the widow with her dead husband), second ***Infanticide*** (killing of girls at the time of birth), third ***widows*** could not marry again, and fourth the ***veiling*** of women. The Sikh religion not only condemned those practices but also did very tangible things to solve them. At first the Gurus found the root cause of these bad practices. Then the Gurus devised practical measures for the equality of women in the social, economic and religious spheres of life. All four practices are described below.

3-1. SATI—BURNING ALIVE OF THE WIDOW WITH HER DEAD HUSBAND

Sati was the practice of burning alive the widow on the pyre of her dead husband, during cremation. Such a draconian practice was very common during that period.

Let us investigate why this custom was practiced. There were several reasons that are explained below.

A. REASONS FOR PERFORMING SATI

a. TO PRESERVE THE CASTE SYSTEM

Sati was performed to prevent the widow of an upper caste from marrying men of lower castes and vice versa.

b. TO MAINTAIN SUPERIORITY OF MEN

Sati was another way to prove the superiority of men over women, even after their death.

c. TO SAVE WOMEN'S HONOR

Sati was carried out to save a Hindu women's honor from abduction as the Muslim invaders used to forcibly carry women back to their country.

d. NO INDIVIDUALITY OF WIDOWS

Widows had no respect. They were considered a burden on the in-laws. Their social life was deplorable. Their presence was considered a bad omen.

B. HOW GURUS ERADICATED SATI

People really believed in the reasons described above and so were in favor of Sati. Gurus declared that Sati is absolutely wrong and must stop. There is no reason that can justify that widow should burn herself alive with her dead husband. As far as abduction by the Muslim rulers is concerned, if the women were equal, they could fight side by side with their husband and this could lead to victory instead of defeat. The Gurus vehemently condemned the practice of Sati. ***Gurus made it very clear that the barbarous act of Sati must stop.*** Third Guru Amar Das made it very clear that real Sati is one who bears the shock of her husband's death, remains humble, serves humanity, and prays daily.

The third Guru, Amar Das, said:

PUNJABI AND ROMAN	ENGLISH
ਸਤੀਆ ਏਹਿ ਨ ਆਖੀਅਨਿ Satee-aa Ayhi Na Aakhee-an	She is not called Sati
ਜੋ ਮੜਿਆ ਲਗਿ ਜਲੰਨ੍ਹਿ II Jo Marhi-aa Lag JalaNniH	who burns herself with the dead husband.
ਨਾਨਕ ਸਤੀਆ ਜਾਣੀਅਨ੍ਹਿ Naanak Satee-aa Jaanee-aniH	Nanak says real Satis are those women
ਜਿ ਬਿਰਹੇ ਚੋਟ ਮਰੰਨ੍ਹਿ II Je Birhay Chot MaraNnih	who bear the shock of separation.
ਭੀ ਸੋ ਸਤੀਆ ਜਾਣੀਅਨਿ Bhee So Satee-aa Jaanee-an	Real Satis are woman who

ਸੀਲ ਸੰਤੋਖਿ ਰਹੰਨਿ੍ ॥ Seel Santokh RahaNnih	live humble and contented lives.
ਸੇਵਨਿ ਸਾਈ ਆਪਣਾ Sayan Saa-ee Aapnaa	Real Sati serve their own God by
ਨਿਤ ਉਠਿ ਸੰਮ੍ਹਾਲੰਨਿ੍ ॥ Nit Uth SamHaalaNniH Guru Granth Sahib (p. 787, line 8)	praying early morning.

C. PRESENT STATUS OF SATI

Sati has no place in the Sikh Religion. At present people belonging to the Sikh Religion, no matter where in the world they live, do not perform Sati. In fact in India it is illegal to practice Sati although in some remote areas, among Hindus, a few cases still take place. It is due to the influence of the old customs. These, however, are very rare cases.

3-2. FEMALE KILLING

The technical terms for killing females are Feticide or Foeticide (killing at fetus stage) and Infanticide (killing after birth). The net affect is the same that girls are killed in both cases. The word female killing will be used as it aptly conveys the meaning.

Sikh Gurus vehemently denounced female killing. Today, due to advancements in medical technology female fetus killing is practiced quite often. The reasons for it were carefully studied and are given below.

A. CAUSES AND CURE OF FEMALE KILLING

a. DOWRY

Dowry is money (in the form of cash and goods of all kinds) to be paid by the bride's parents to the family of the bridegroom at the time of marriage. In addition the bride's parents also pay for all the expenses of the marriage. This tradition has been practiced in India for centuries. The amount to be paid depends upon the demands of the bridegroom's parents and the ability of the bride's parents to pay. Quite often the bride's parents borrow money and that leads to all sorts of problems including bankruptcy. That is one of the reasons why the birth of a daughter meant disgrace, anxiety and heavy expenditure. On the other hand a son increases the wealth, dignity of the family, and perpetuates the family name. Also, years ago, only men had property rights.

This dichotomy between wealth and poverty led people to female killing. The Gurus knew that dowries were one of the reasons why parents kill their daughters. This practice was definitely immoral. Gurus preached and said very clearly that both offering and accepting of dowry by the parents at the time of marriage of their daughters and sons was against the teachings of the Sikh Religion. The Sikh Religious Code called Raht Maryada [3] states very clearly that "**one who gives son or daughter in matrimony for a price or reward" must be boycotted automatically**. Assistance can be given to the newly wed couple by the parents from either side to help them establish their livelihood. There should never be a case where the dowry is demanded before the marriage can be performed. The dowry system leads to many evil results, including bankrupting many families.

Guru Ram Das made it clear, the type of dowry a daughter should ask from her father.

The fourth Guru, Ram Das, said:

PUNJABI AND ROMAN	**ENGLISH**
ਹਰਿ ਪ੍ਰਭੁ ਮੇਰੇ ਬਾਬੁਲਾ Har Parabh Mayray Babulaa	O my father, give me the name of God
ਹਰਿ ਦੇਵਹੁ ਦਾਨੁ ਮੈ ਦਾਜੋ ॥ Har Dayvhu Daan Mai Daajo	as my wedding gift and dowry.
ਹਰਿ ਕਪੜੋ ਹਰਿ ਸੋਭਾ ਦੇਵਹੁ Har Kaprho Har Sobhaa Dayvhu	My clothes should emanate God's glory
ਜਿਤੁ ਸਵਰੈ ਮੇਰਾ ਕਾਜੋ ॥ Jit Savrai Mayraa Kaajo Guru Granth Sahib (p. 78, line 18)	and with God's help I be successful in my endeavors.

It is also said that "***first, to give a dowry is bad and then to display it as a showpiece is an outrage.***"

The fourth Guru, Ram Das, said:

PUNJABI AND ROMAN	**ENGLISH**
ਹੋਰਿ ਮਨਮੁਖ ਦਾਜੁ ਜਿ ਰਖਿ ਦਿਖਾਲਹਿ Hor Manmukh Daaj Je Rakh Dikhaaleh	Materialistic people who display dowry as a show piece
ਸੁ ਕੂੜੁ ਅਹੰਕਾਰੁ ਕਚੁ ਪਾਜੋ ॥ So Koorh AhaNkaar Kach Paajo Guru Granth Sahib (p. 79, line 3)	"exhibit" nothing but false pride and worthless showmanship.

b. PREFERENCE FOR SONS AS CAUSE OF FEMALE KILLING

Sons in the family are preferred, as they:
i. Are productive members for the family.
ii. Are helpful to the parents in their old age (a sort of insurance).
iii. Carry on the family name.
iv. Bring in dowry.
All of the above are not true in today's society.

Daughters are getting the same type of education as sons and thus are as productive as sons. Now-a-days even sons, after marriage, live separately and are thus no help to the parents in their old age. Sons also are involved in their own children. It has been observed in many cases that daughters help the parents more than the sons in their time of need. ***By law sons and daughters are considered equal in all respects even with regard to the rights of inheritance. Dowry is forbidden in the Sikh Religion.***

c. LOW STATUS OF WOMEN CAUSES FEMALE KILLING

When Guru Nanak started the Sikh Religion, the status of women was extremely low. It was so bad that the birth of a girl was considered a bad omen. The girls were killed at the time of birth. This was true both with the Hindus and Muslims, the prevalent religions at that time. Muslims used to confine women indoors. They could go out only under surveillance and wrapped up in heavy veils. Female killing, though forbidden by the Holy Quran, was common among Muslims at that time [4].

B. PRESENT DAY STATUS OF FEMALE KILLING

It is very sad to report that female killing is on the increase. This is much more prevalent in countries that are not economically advanced. There is a great deal of misuse of medical technologies. Ultrasound is being widely used to determine the sex of the baby before birth. This leads to female fetuses being aborted. ***It is said that women are not safe even in their mother's womb.***

Let us take the case of India.

Punjab and Haryana High Court banned the misuse of modern techniques for sex scans and subsequent abortion of female fetus. The laws are not being enforced and thus not a single case has been registered [5].

The sex ratio for some states in India compared to Europe are shown below [5],[6]:

India	927	Females vs.	1000 males
Punjab (India)	874	Females vs.	1000 males
Haryana (India)	861	Females vs.	1000 males
Europe	1063	Females vs.	1000 males

Female killing is an inhumane attack on women. This could lead to horrendous implications [6] as below:

- i. More crime against women.
- ii. Breakdown of traditional family system.
- iii. Prostitution.
- iv. Perversions.
- v. AIDS

Although no religion allows female killing, it is still carried out on a large scale. Akal Takht, the highest spiritual body of the Sikhs has confronted this issue in a very positive way. On April 18, 2001, Akal Takht [5] used its moral authority to ban female infanticide or feticide (or foeticide). It said the ***"inhumane, immoral and irreligious practice" was in violation of the Sikh religion. The Sikh Religious Code, Raht Maryada, called for excommunication [5] of those who indulged in female killing.*** They quoted Article 16(I) of the Sikh Religious Code, Raht Maryada [5]: "A Sikh should not kill his/her daughter, nor should he/she maintain any relationship with the killer of a daughter." Although it is a very powerful, no one has been excommunicated based upon this edict.

At present laws and the religious persuasion is not working. This is a social problem and people have to be educated regarding the eradication of female killing. A survey was conducted in Punjab, India [6] on female killing and the results are as follows:

30% is due to the direct consent of the women.
45% is due to the pressure from husband.
25% is due to the family pressure.

The above data does not take in consideration religion, caste or economic status. ***Education is the key to remove this menace.*** In the state of Kerala in the southern part of India, The education rate is almost 100% and the females outnumber males there.

Those who indulge in female killing must be boycotted socially and discouraged morally.

C. POSITIVE APPROACH TO SOLVE FEMALE KILLING

In order to solve female killing women have to take the future into their own hands. ***Women have to be economically and emotionally empowered to stop female killing, dowry deaths and other atrocities.*** Keeping this in mind the Dairy Development Department of Punjab, India and Ms. Nandita Bakhshi, a former employee of Indian Revenue Service [7] started a grassroots movement in the villages (where 70% of the population of India lives). They went door to door explaining how women could make more money without leaving the security of their homes.

They selected Punjab as one of the areas worst affected by female killing. There are as few as 760 women per 1000 men there. Since Punjab is rich in milk, they concentrated on making paneer (cheese).

They organized meetings about the procedures to collectively prepare and market paneer (cheese). They formed a self-help group and by working together they started earning Rs (Rupees) 3000 to Rs 4000 per month.

This is the best way not only to solve problems facing women but also to give them an opportunity to have equal status with men. It is anticipated that this approach will spread to other villages as success breeds success.

3-3. WIDOW MARRIAGE

A. WIDOW MARRIAGE

Widows were forbidden to remarry when Guru Nanak was born in 1469. At that time according to Hindus only a widower could remarry. Widows were looked upon with contempt and were regarded as symbol of ill fate. Fourth Guru Ram Das allowed widows to remarry [8]. ***The Sikh Religion has made it clear that the widows could marry if they so desire*** but should not be forced to marry. The widow has the right to exercise her option for marriage when she wants it. Widow marriage was given moral sanctity. In the Sikh Religion the right to remarry was given to both the widow and widower, as they are both equal.

B. PRESENT STATUS OF WIDOW MARRIAGE

Remarriage for widows is being accepted socially, religiously and legally.

3-4. VEILING OF WOMEN

Veiling was prevalent in India since ancient Aryan times [9]. Aryan women had to wear a face-veil when going out. Large numbers of Muslim women wear veils even today. Some Muslim women consider veiling as liberating because it releases them from male scrutiny and the standards of attractiveness. They find that a woman's inner character, not her outward appearance, is more valued when she wears the veil. However, most of the world considers veiling as an oppression of women rights.

A. ERADICATION OF VEILING OF WOMEN

Veiling of women was quite common when Guru Nanak was born. It contributed to the perception that women were inferior. ***Guru Nanak explained that women are being suppressed when they are veiled.***

The first Guru, Nanak, Said:

PUNJABI AND ROMAN	ENGLISH
ਲਾਜ ਮਰੰਤੀ ਮਰਿ ਗਈ	My shyness and hesitation are all gone (dead)
Laaj Marantee Mar Ga-ee	
ਘੂਘਟੁ ਖੋਲਿ ਚਲੀ ॥	when I walk with my face unveiled.
Ghooghat Khol Chalee	

Guru Granth Sahib (p. 931, line 6)

Third Guru Amar Das had forbidden women to attend religious assembly in veil (Purdah) [8].

B. PRESENT STATUS OF VEILING

The veiling of women does not exist among the people who belong to the the Sikh Religion. However, it should not be confused with covering of the head that is mark of respect in eastern culture. Covering of the head both for men and women is required in the Gurdwaras.

4. DESCRIPTION OF A BEAUTIFUL WOMEN

Real beauty is what you do in your life. Evaluation of one's physical appearance is very subjective?what is beautiful to one may not be so to another.

The first Guru, Nanak, described the beautiful woman as below:

PUNJABI AND ROMAN	ENGLISH
ਨਾਰੀ ਅੰਦਰਿ ਸੋਹਣੀ Naaree Andar Sohnee	That women, among others, is beautiful
ਮਸਤਕਿ ਮਣੀ ਪਿਆਰੁ ॥ Mastak Manee Piaar	whose face radiates love like a jewel.
ਸੋਭਾ ਸੁਰਤਿ ਸੁਹਾਵਣੀ Sobhaa Surat Suhaavanee	Reputation and wisdom makes her beautiful
ਸਾਚੈ ਪ੍ਰੇਮਿ ਅਪਾਰ ॥ Saachai Paraym Apaar	and such a woman truly loves the Infinite God.

Guru Granth Sahib (p. 54, line 9)

Women are very much revered in the Sikh Religion. Woman is the one who keeps the family and the human race going.

5. DUTIES AND QUALITIES OF A WOMAN

Fifth Guru Arjan Dev spoke very clearly about the qualities and the duties of a woman in order to live a peaceful life and be respected by all.

The fifth Guru, Arjan Dev, said:

PUNJABI AND ROMAN	ENGLISH
ਨਿਜ ਭਗਤੀ ਸੀਲਵੰਤੀ ਨਾਰਿ ॥ Nij Bhagatee Seelvantee Naar	A wife is devoted to her husband and has an amicable nature.
ਰੂਪਿ ਅਨੂਪ ਪੂਰੀ ਆਚਾਰਿ ॥ Roop Anoop Pooree Aachaar	She is unequal in beauty and posses perfect good character.
ਜਿਤੁ ਗ੍ਰਿਹਿ ਵਸੈ Jit Garihi Vasai	The house where such woman lives,
ਸੋ ਗ੍ਰਿਹੁ ਸੋਭਾਵੰਤਾ ॥ So Garihu Sobhaavantaa	that house becomes praiseworthy.
ਗੁਰਮੁਖਿ ਪਾਈ Gurmukh Paaee	A rare one, who loves God,
ਕਿਨੈ ਵਿਰਲੈ ਜੰਤਾ ॥ Kinai Virlai Jantaa	finds such a bride.
ਸੁਕਰਣੀ ਕਾਮਣਿ Sukarnee Kaaman	I have obtained such a bride of good deeds,

ਗੁਰ ਮਿਲਿ ਹਮ ਪਾਈ ॥ Gur Mil Ham Paa-ee	through God's grace.
ਜਜਿ ਕਾਜਿ Jaj Kaaj	In worship, marriage,
ਪਰਥਾਇ ਸੁਹਾਈ ॥ Parthaa-ay Suhaa-ee	and everywhere she looks beautiful.
ਜਿਚਰੁ ਵਸੀ ਪਿਤਾ ਕੈ ਸਾਥਿ ॥ Jichar Vasee Pitaa Kai Saath	Whenever she goes to live in her parent's house,
ਤਿਚਰੁ ਕੰਤੁ ਬਹੁ ਫਿਰੈ ਉਦਾਸਿ ॥ Tichar Kant Bahu Firai Udaas	her husband is sad whereever he may be.
ਕਰਿ ਸੇਵਾ ਸਤ ਪੁਰਖੁ ਮਨਾਇਆ ॥ Kar Sayvaa Sat Purakh Manaa-i-aa	Serving humanity pleases True God.
ਗੁਰਿ ਆਣੀ ਘਰ ਮਹਿ Gur Aanee Ghar Meh	With God's grace the bride came to my house,
ਤਾ ਸਰਬ ਸੁਖ ਪਾਇਆ ॥ Taa Sarab Sukh Paa-i-aa	and brought happiness.
ਬਤੀਹ ਸੁਲਖਣੀ Bateeh Sulakh-nee	She is blessed with 32 merits*,
ਸਚੁ ਸੰਤਤਿ ਪੂਤ ॥ Sach Santat Poot	She is truthful and unblemished and so are all the offspring's (Children).
ਆਗਿਆਕਾਰੀ ਸੁਘੜ ਸਰੂਪ ॥ Aagi-aakaaree Sugharh Saroop	She is obedient, wise and beautiful.
ਇਛ ਪੂਰੇ ਮਨ ਕੰਤ ਸੁਆਮੀ ॥ Ichh Pooray Man Kant Su-aamee	Her husband fulfills her heart's desires.
ਸਗਲ ਸੰਤੋਖੀ ਦੇਰ ਜੇਠਾਨੀ ॥ Sagal Santokhee Dayr Jaythaanee	She is liked by her husband's elder brother's wife as well as younger brother's wife.
ਸਭ ਪਰਵਾਰੈ ਮਾਹਿ ਸਰੇਸਟ ॥ Sabh Parvaarai Maahi Saraysat	In all of the family she is the most knowledgeable.
ਮਤੀ ਦੇਵੀ ਦੇਵਰ ਜੇਸਟ ॥ Matee Dayvee Dayvar Jaysat	Her husband's younger and elder brother consult her.
ਧੰਨੁ ਸੁ ਗ੍ਰਿਹੁ ਜਿਤੁ ਪ੍ਰਗਟੀ ਆਇ ॥ Dhan So Garihu Jit Pragatee Aa-ay	Blessed is the home where she lives.
ਜਨ ਨਾਨਕ ਸੁਖੇ ਸੁਖਿ ਵਿਹਾਇ ॥ Jan Naanak Sukhay Sukh Vihaa-ay	Nanak says such a woman lives in perfect peace of mind.

Guru Granth Sahib (p. 370, line 18)

* 32 merits of a woman are:

1	Beauty	2	Modesty
3	Intellect	4	Sticking to a good cause
5	Faith in God	6	Truthful
7	Brave, Courageous	8	Pious, devoted to religion
9	Firm in conviction	10	Learned person
11	Liberal mindedness	12	Full of virtues
13	Deep conviction	14	Strong Effort to Achieve
15	Clear and pure thinking	16	Complete Faith in one God
17	Forgiveness	18	Divine knowledge
19	Self-discipline	20	Good intentions
21	Alms-giving	22	Courage in facing trouble
23	Humility	24	Emits grandeur
25	Divine love for God	26	Helping others in time of need
27	No greedy desire for money	28	No undue attachment to worldly things
29	Non-killing type	30	Not selfish
31	Not deceitful	32	Not self-centered person

6. IMPORTANCE OF WOMEN

A. DURING THE PERIOD OF TEN GURUS

Equality of women was started by Guru Nanak and was carried out by the succeeding nine Gurus in the Sikh Religion. From the beginning of the Sikh Religion, women have contributed immensely for the welfare of the community. ***Women during the period of ten Gurus played a very important role in spreading the Universality of the Sikh Religion and took an active part in social, spiritual and political fields.*** Although there were many women involved in the spread of the Universality of the Sikh Religion, the contributions of some of them are given below. For details see the article "Women in Sikhism " [10].

i. BEBE NANAKI—A UNIQUE BROTHER-SISTER RELATIONSHIP

Guru Nanak's elder sister, Bebe Nanaki [10], played a very important role in taking care of her sister-in-law while her brother, Guru Nanak, was on extended tours, preaching the Universality of the Sikh Religion. Bebe is used as a mark of respect for elder ladies. Bebe Nanaki encouraged her brother to use musical instruments—she provided him with a beautiful musical instrument called "Rebab"—to recite the hymns. She mentally prepared Mr. Mardana, a Muslim, to stay with Guru Nanak. This way Bebe Nanaki helped her brother directly and indirectly in spreading the equality and the universality of the religion to which Guru Nanak was dedicated.

The brother-sister relationship was so intense that even up to today the following three values are deeply ingrained in day-to-day living between brother and sister.

a. ***To help each other***
b. ***To respect each other's feelings***
c. ***To sacrifice for each other***

ii. MATA KHIVI—A PILLAR OF COMMUNITY SERVICE

Mata Khivi, wife of second Guru Angad Dev was in-charge of the community kitchen (Langar). The food was served everyday and it was open to all. This was a practical way to end discrimination based upon caste, sex, creed or religion. This devotion of serving Langar is being continued even today in all Gurdwaras of the Sikh Religion. ***The Langar, besides providing food, also establishes a bond of equality and cooperation with each other.*** It also helps in feeding the poor and destitute. If all religions started a Langar service then hunger problem will be considerably diminished in this world. In the USA there are soup kitchens and many other places where food is served to the needy. This does help quite a bit.

iii. BIBI BHANI—A UNIQUE PERSONALITY

Bibi Bhani has a very distinct place in Sikh history. Bibi is a word that is used to give respect to a daughter. ***Bibi Bhani had a direct relationship with eight of the ten Gurus of the Sikh Religion.*** Bibi Bhani was

a. Daughter of third Guru Amar Das
b. Wife of fourth Guru Ram Das
c. Mother of fifth Guru Arjan Dev
d. Grandmother of sixth Guru Har Gobind
e. Great-great grandmother of seventh Guru Har Rai
f. Great-great great grandmother of 8th Guru Har Krishan
g. Great-grandmother of ninth Guru Teg Bahadur
h. Great-great grandmother of tenth Guru Gobind Singh

God must have given her such a great personality in order to carry out such lineage, honor, and responsibility. At one point Bibi Bhani has asked her father, Guru Amar Das, if next Guru should have been a member of their family. Guru Amar Das decided to make Ram Das, who was not related, the next Guru. It so happened that Bibi Bhani married Guru Ram Das who became son-in-law of Guru Amar Das.

BIBI BHANI'S TWO GREAT CONTRIBUTIONS TO HUMANITY

a. ABOLITION OF DIFFERENCE BETWEEN SON AND DAUGHTER

Bibi Bhani used to take care of her father and proved the point that there is no difference between a son and a daughter. There is a myth in Indian culture that the father does not get any service from a daughter, especially after marriage. Bibi Bhani proved that both sons and daughters could serve equally well. This is a great lesson for all of us. ***If we treat sons and daughters as equals there will be no more gender discrimination in the the world.***

b. COMPOSURE DURING ADVERSITY

When her son, the fifth Guru, Arjan Dev, was arrested by the Mughal King Jahangir (king during that period) and was tortured to death, Bibi Bhani maintained her composure and did not let her daughter-in-law lose her heart. The martyrdom of her son prepared her to teach her seven-year-old grandson, Har Gobind, to abide by God's will.

Bibi Bhani was an embodiment of service, truth and modesty. She was a mark of respect, endurance and unique character.

iv. MAI BHAGO—A BRAVE WOMAN

During Guru Gobind Singh's period, women took a more active part in fighting against the atrocities being committed by the foreign Muslim rulers. Mai Bhago, a very forceful lady, brought all 40 Sikhs (believers of the Sikh Religion), who had deserted Guru Gobind Singh, under her control. She was bringing them for a pardon from Guru Gobind Singh. On the way the Mugul army attacked them and they all died while fighting. On hearing this, Guru Gobind Singh rushed to the battlefield, pardoned all of them, and tore the disclaimer written earlier on their desertion [11].

v. MATA SUNDRI—A GREAT ORGANIZER

Mata Sundri wife of tenth Guru Gobind Singh was a most significant personality. She lived 39 years after the death of Guru Gobind Singh (who passed away in 1708). She lived 80 years and died in 1747.

She was the only woman who led all Sikhs (believers of the Sikh Religion) immediately after the death of Guru Gobind Singh. ***Mata Sundri very amicably resolved disputes between the different factions of Sikhs.*** For example when soldiers of the Banda Bahadur and the Sikhs of Punjab were going to destroy each other, she resolved the dispute peacefully.

Mata Sundri led the Sikhs in the spiritual field as well. She convinced Bhai Mani Singh to establish a school in Amritsar for interpreting the teachings of the Gurus. Under her direction many copies of the Guru Granth Sahib were made. Mata Sundri's role as an organizer was crucial in the lives of the Sikh community.

Mata Sundri was a very wise, far-sighted, bold and patient woman who kept Sikhs united for the spread of the Universality of the Sikh Religion.

vi. ROOP KAUR—FIRST WOMAN EDITOR

The first woman editor in the Guru's family was Roop Kaur, daughter of seventh Guru Har Rai. She compiled 32 books for the spread of the Universality of the Sikh Religion and was thus the first woman to hold such a position.

vii. NOOR SHAH—PREACHER OF THE SIKH RELIGION

Guru Nanak met Noor Shah, a Muslim woman, and convinced her to leave the evil ways and perform good deeds. She accepted the teachings of Guru Nanak. She was so devoted that Guru Nanak, made her the main preacher in Assam, India. She carried out the duties as prescribed by Guru Nanak for the rest of her life.

viii. WOMEN AS RELIGIOUS PREACHERS

To spread the missionary work of the Sikh Religion, the third Guru, Amar Das, established 22 Manjis (sacred seats used for preaching the Sikh Religion). Out of those, two Manjis were granted to women: Matho Murari and wife of Sachan Sach [10]. The same rights and responsibilities were given to women and men for spreading the teachings and philosophy of the Universality of the Sikh Religion.

B. IMPORTANCE OF WOMEN DURING MAHARAJA RANJIT SINGH

SADA KAUR—A FORCEFUL WOMAN

Sada Kaur, mother-in-law of Maharaja Ranjit Singh was a very forceful woman. After her husband's death she organized the Sikh forces under her command.

Sada Kaur was a very smart lady and she made her son-in-law, Maharaja Ranjit Singh in-charge of all forces. This was a very big step in uniting all Sikh factions. The power, humanitarian nature and the popularity of Maharaja Ranjit Singh was so great that he captured the most important city of Lahore without firing a shot [12].

C. STATUS OF WOMEN AT PRESENT

Women enjoy great respect in the Sikh Religion and have a status of which they should be proud. They can compete for any position—religious, political or social. At present women have contributed significantly to human knowledge and skill in every field, from the arts and humanities to aviation, education, sports, science, medicine and government. In general and all over the world, the future for the equality of women looks very promising. ***Women have equal rights in almost every field.*** A woman was elected to the highest position in the Sikh religious organization (Shiromani Gurudwara Parbhandhak Committee) in Amritsar, Punjab, India in 2000. Sikh women are in every field and have contributed significantly toward human progress. There are some countries that are still behind, but progress is being made through the United Nations and many other organizations. ***Some of the issues that still need attention for the equality of women are rape, domestic violence, reproductive rights, trafficking of women, female genital mutilation, and equal access to economic opportunities and political participation.***

7. SUMMARY

All human beings are equal in all respects. Equality exists regardless of religion, caste, color, sex or any other way people want to divide them.

If all parents throughout the world, consider sons and daughters as equals in all respects, then the question of inequality for women will vanish from this world. Guru Nanak made it very clear: "How can we consider women inferior who give birth to kings?" Without women there will be no human race.

During the period of ten Gurus 1469 to 1708 the four types of practices that made women inferior were eradicated. They were the practice of Sati (burning alive of widow with her dead husband), female killing (fetus stage or afterwards), not allowing widows to remarry, and the veiling of women.

Women took a very active role in the period of ten Gurus. Bebe Nanaki showed unique brother-sister relationship. Mata Khivi was a model for her commitment to community service.

Bibi Bhani had a unique personality. She had direct relationship with 8 Gurus and proved that sons and daughters have equal rights. Mai Bhago was a brave woman.

Mata Sundri was a great organizer. She solved all problems facing the Sikh community amicably and peacefully. Roop Kaur was the first woman editor. Noorshah was the Muslim woman who spent her life in the spreading of the Universality of the Sikh Religion. Women were also preachers during the period of the Gurus. During Maharaja Ranjit Singh's rule, Sada Kaur mother-in-law of Ranjit Singh played a pivotal role in unifying all Sikh factions.

Some of the issues that still need attention for the equality of women are rape, domestic violence, reproductive rights, trafficking of women, female genital mutilation and equal access to economic opportunit and political participation through out the world.

8. EXERCISES

- **i.** Why are all human beings equal in all respects?
- **ii.** Give reasons why women should have equal rights with men with special reference to what Guru Nanak wrote in section 2, subsection iii, reference to page 473 of the Guru Granth Sahib.
- **iii.** Identify the four bad practices against women and how the Gurus resolved them.
- **iv.** What is the description and what are the merits of a beautiful woman?
- **v.** Describe the contributions of at least five women during the period of ten Gurus and Maharaja Ranjit Singh.
- **vi.** What are several areas that women still need help for equality?

9. REFERENCES

[1] Yahoo Search for "19th Century Science & The Woman Question"
Click for "19th Century Science & The Woman Question"
Click for "Introduction"

[2] Puran Singh. 1970. *The Spirit Born People*, Director Languages Department, Punjab, India. p.35.

[3] Sikh Reht Maryada, Section Six, Chapter XIII, Article XXII, sub section q, no 4, Shiromani Gurdwara Parbandhak Committee, Amritsar, Punjab, India 1945.

[4] Surinder Singh Johar 1988. *The Sikh Religion*, National Book Shop, Delhi, India p.120.

[5] http://www.the-week.com/21may06/events5.htm. Find "Noble Edict" Akal Takht bans female infanticide. Obtained from India Statescan May 6, 2001 The week.
Sikh Reht Maryada, Section Four, Chapter X, Article XVI, sub section l, Shiromani Gurdwara Parbandhak Committee, Amritsar, Punjab, India 1945.

[6] *Tribune Newspaper*, India dated January 25, 2002. "Alarming Decline in Sex Ratio."
http://www.tribuneindia.com/2002/20020126/punjab1.htm

[7] *The Tribune*, Chandigarh India Nov 20, 2004
"Women Entrepreneurs Honoured and Empowering Women is her Aim."
http://www.tribuneindia.com/2004/20041120/punjab1.htm

[8] Dr. Sukhbir Singh Kapoor, 1988, "The Ideal Man," Khalsa College London Press. p. 75. Referred to O. Cole and P.S. Sambhi *The Sikhs* p.23

[9] Yahoo search for Thanabalu Kalimuthu, Dalitstan Journal, Volume 2, Issue 6, Dec. 2000 "Veiling of Women in The Brahmanic Religion"
http://www.dalitstan.org/journal/hindutwa/htv000/veil_br.html

[10] Dr. M. K. Gill. 1998. "Women in Sikhism," *The Sikh Courier International*, Middlesex, UK. Vol 38, No 86, p. 3 to 11.

[11] K. S. Duggal. 1989. *Sikh Gurus*, Second Printing, Himalayan International Institute. Honesdale, PA, USA. p. 219.

[12] Khuswant Singh. 1984 reissue. *A History of the Sikhs*, Volume 1. Princeton University Press, Princeton, NJ. USA, p. 196.

UNIVERSALITY OF THE SIKH RELIGION

CHAPTER 10

FOURTH PRINCIPLE—PRAY DAILY TO GOD

PRAYING IS UNIVERSAL IRRESPECTIVE OF GOD'S NAME.

In just two words, in Punjabi, the third principle is made absolutely clear.

ROMAN	ENGLISH
NAAM JAPANAA	**Pray to God**

1. WHY PRAY DAILY

We are so busy in our worldly affairs, why do we need to spend time in praying? Isn't a one time remembrance of God enough?

Let me give you an example that we all face every day. It is the effect of marketing on our day-to-day lives. Let us evaluate the effect of a commercial that is broadcasted every day on the television, newspapers, radio and other media. Why do the companies repeat the same commercial many times? They are trying not only to change your way of thinking but also to get into your subconscious mind. When one sees ten different brands of the same item displayed in a supermarket, one buys the brand that was mentioned many times during the commercials.

Similarly, ***we have to pray daily in order to purify our mind and keep us away from day-to-day temptations.*** We have to perform good deeds every day. Reading and comprehending the words every day from Guru Granth Sahib is a very good reminder.

Guru Nanak gave us the prescription for how to clean our mind. We should pray as described below.

A. FOR PEACE OF MIND BY CONTEMPLATING ON GOD

It is essential that we ***must have faith in one God***. When we go to see a doctor we have faith that the doctor will cure our ailment. When we go to school we believe that the teacher will impart knowledge. Similarly we must have complete faith and believe in one God who is always there to help all of humanity. ***We must pray ourselves as well as exhort others to pray also.***

The first Guru, Nanak, said:

PUNJABI AND ROMAN	ENGLISH
ਸਿਮਰਿ ਸਿਮਰਿ ਸਿਮਰਿ	By contemplating on God again and again
Simar Simar Simar	
ਸੁਖ ਪਾਵਹੁ ॥	one obtains peace of mind.
Sukh Paavhu	
ਆਪਿ ਜਪਹੁ	Not only one should pray for one self
Aap Japahu	
ਅਵਰਹ ਨਾਮੁ ਜਪਾਵਹੁ ॥	but also should persuade others to do the
Avrah Naam Japaavhu	same.

Guru Granth Sahib (p. 290, line 4)

B. TO CLEAN OUR MIND

Guru Nanak explained very clearly that just as our clothes get dirty every day and need washing, ***our mind gets polluted and needs daily meditation to purify it.***

The first Guru, Nanak, said:

PUNJABI AND ROMAN	ENGLISH
ਭਰੀਐ ਹਥੁ ਪੈਰੁ ਤਨੁ ਦੇਹ ॥	When hand, feet and body get
Bharee-ai Hath Pair Tan Dayh	dirty
ਪਾਣੀ ਧੋਤੈ ਉਤਰਸੁ ਖੇਹ ॥	washing with water cleans them.
Paanee Dhotai Utras Khayh	
ਮੂਤ ਪਲੀਤੀ ਕਪੜੁ ਹੋਇ ॥	When the clothes are soiled
Moot Paleetee Kaparh Ho-ay	
ਦੇ ਸਾਬੂਣੁ ਲਈਐ ਓਹੁ ਧੋਇ ॥	they are rinsed clean with soap.
Day Saaboon La-ee-ai Oh Dho-ay	
ਭਰੀਐ ਮਤਿ ਪਾਪਾ ਕੈ ਸੰਗਿ ॥	When the mind is defiled with
Bharee-ai Mat Paapaa Kai Sang	sins
ਓਹੁ ਧੋਪੈ ਨਾਵੈ ਕੈ ਰੰਗਿ ॥	those are cleansed by
Oh Dhopai Naavai Kai Rang	remembering God's name.

Guru Granth Sahib (p. 4, line 11)

C. AS GOD IS THE CREATOR OF ALL

Guru Nanak explained we should keep God in our mind as ***God creates every thing and also takes care of it.***

The first Guru, Nanak, said:

PUNJABI AND ROMAN	ENGLISH
ਇਕੁ ਸੰਸਾਰੀ ਇਕੁ ਭੰਡਾਰੀ	God not only created the universe but
Ik Sansaaree Ik Bhandaaree	also sustains it
ਇਕੁ ਲਾਏ ਦੀਬਾਣੁ II	and finally absorbs it (through death).
Ik Laa-ay Deebaan	
Guru Granth Sahib (p. 7, line 2)	

D TO ENJOY THE DIVERSITY CREATED BY GOD

Guru Nanak said that ***one should enjoy the whole creation*** as God created innumerable things for us.

The first Guru, Nanak, said:

PUNJABI AND ROMAN	ENGLISH
ਰਾਤੀ ਰੁਤੀ ਥਿਤੀ ਵਾਰ II	God made day and night, seasons, days
Raatee Rutee Thittee Vaar	of the week and months.
ਪਵਣ ਪਾਣੀ ਅਗਨੀ ਪਾਤਾਲ II	God made winds to blow, water to run,
Pavan Paanee Agnee Paataal	made fire, lower and upper regions.
ਤਿਸੁ ਵਿਚਿ ਧਰਤੀ ਥਾਪਿ	In the midst of all God put
Tis Vich Dhartee Thaap	
ਰਖੀ ਧਰਮਸਾਲ II	earth as Temple.
Rakhee Dharamsaal	
ਤਿਸੁ ਵਿਚਿ ਜੀਅ ਜੁਗਤਿ	God made creatures of
Tis Vich Jee-a Jugat	
ਕੇ ਰੰਗ II	various kinds and colors.
Kay Rang	
ਤਿਨ ਕੇ ਨਾਮ ਅਨੇਕ ਅਨੰਤ II	They have endless variety and names.
Tin Ke Naam Anayk Anant	
Guru Granth Sahib (p. 7, line 11)	

E. FOR PEACE OF MIND BY SINGING HYMNS

If we pray with complete conviction in God then our mind, body and soul will be in tune and will result in complete mental satisfaction. The ordinary day-to-day problems will take back seat and one's worries, although present, will not disturb one's peace of mind.

The first Guru, Nanak, said:

PUNJABI AND ROMAN	**ENGLISH**
ਗਾਵੀਐ ਸੁਣੀਐ Gaavee-ai Sunee-ai	By singing and hearing God's hymns
ਮਨਿ ਰਖੀਐ ਭਾਉ ॥ Man Rakhee-ai Bhaa-o	piece of mind is achieved.
ਦੁਖੁ ਪਰਹਰਿ ਸੁਖੁ Dukh Parhar Sukh	Sorrows are then gone
ਘਰਿ ਲੈ ਜਾਇ ॥ Ghar Lai Jaa-ay	and happiness abides in the heart.

Guru Granth Sahib (p. 2, line 7)

2. HOW TO CLEAN OUR MIND

We have established that we have to pray daily to clean our mind. But how do we clean our mind?

Everyday when we get up and generally perform two things

i. We wash and clean ourselves.
ii. We put on clean clothes.
We should then ask ourselves the following question.
Have I cleaned my mind?

The answer is to pray God daily.

3. HOW TO PRAY GOD ON A DAILY BASIS

The first and foremost requirement is that one must have belief and complete faith in one God. There is not one set way to pray to God. In fact there are innumerable ways. ***Every person is at a different stage of spiritual level.*** There are many ways to clean the mind—it varies with the spiritual knowledge of each individual.

Let us discuss several ways people can pray to God on a daily basis.

A. BY RECITING THE NAME OF GOD

Although God has many different names, every religion has one name that it uses routinely. Repeat the name of God as practiced in one's particular religion. According to the Sikh Religion it is:

WAHE GURU (the Wonderful God)

Repeat the word with full faith every day. In the beginning the mind will wander away from the word Wahe Guru. Later with continued effort, we will obtain peace of mind and a feeling of security and stability. Our mind and body once tuned to Wahe Guru will prepare the smooth way to finally merge with the primeval source, the God.

Recite WAHEGURU (The Wonderful God) as many times as you can.

B. RECITING CONCEPTION OF GOD

Recite the Conception of God, which is given in Chapter 2 page 2.

This is very short and can be done anytime and anywhere and for any reason. Some people say it before taking meals as a form of grace from God.

C. COMPREHENDING BY READING FROM GURU GRANTH SAHIB

Some people pray daily by reading certain prescribed sections like Japji by Guru Nanak (pages 1 to 8 of Guru Granth Sahib), Sukhmani by Fifth Guru Arjan Dev (pages 262 to 296 of Guru Granth Sahib), and other parts from Guru Granth Sahib.

Others like ***to read and comprehend a small portion, daily, from Guru Granth Sahib.*** The time of prayer and the duration varies from person to person. If someone does not know Punjabi they can get help from the English or Hindi translations. Free translations are easily available on the Internet using www.srigranth.org.

D. ATTENDING GURDWARA A RELIGIOUS PLACE

It is important to go to the religious place for to listen and sing hymns with the congregation. Some join the congregation at the Gurdwara (religious place of the Sikhs).

A typical prayer is being conducted inside a Gurdwara (see Figure 25) in Mid Hudson, New York [1]. People generally gather every Sunday to pray. Some people go daily to their Gurdwara. Ladies sit on one side and men on the other side. Ragis are singing Shabads (Hymns) using Harmonium and Tabla. Guru Granth Sahib is in the center under an ornate canopy and is given very great respect.

E. MEDITATE EVERY DAY

Meditation is another way to pray to God. Meditation is also relaxation. There are many ways to meditate. There have been discussions that meditation can cure lot of ailments and diseases. At present, however, very little is known of meditation and its effect on the body. Here is an opportunity where meditation and science can work together to arrive at the same goal.

Scientifically we know that exercise and proper food allows people live better and more productive lives. The body is a wonderful chemical factory. It can produce good chemicals as well as bad chemicals. ***The bad chemicals are toxic and destroy our organs.*** The brain controls the production of these chemicals. ***If we are happy and relaxed the brain produces endorphins and other chemicals that keep the body healthy.*** A lot of research is required to characterize those chemicals. Sometimes they are in very small quantity and are not easy to identify. The level of these chemicals may explain why some people that have cancer and other such diseases can survive and go into remission.

We can judge for ourselves the type of chemicals we are producing. When we are happy, contented, and our mind is at peace then we are producing good chemicals. When we are full of anxiety, frustrated, angry, critical of other people's judgment, and have violent moods then the chemicals produced are bad. If this condition persists it can lead to diseases for which there is no cure at present.

Kundalini is meditation by chanting "Sat Nam" (God is Truth) while inhaling and "Wahe Guru" (God is wonderful) while exhaling for any length of time. Scientific technique of Magnetic Resonance Imaging (MRI) was used to study the effect of Kundalini meditation, (see Figure 26 [2]).. This study shows how science and religion can complement each other. This study was carried out, in 2000, at Harvard Medical School, Massachusetts General Hospital, Boston, USA [2].

FIGURE 25

**PRAYER CEREMONY INSIDE A GURDWARA
MIDHUDSON, NEW YORK**

Guru Granth Sahib is kept under an ornate wooden canopy. The Ragis (musicians) are singing hymns from Guru Granth Sahib using the Harmonium and Tabla, musical instruments. People are sitting on the floor, women on one side and men on the other side. Some of the men are not wearing turbans; however, everyone's head is covered.

FIGURE 26

MRI SCANS DURING CONTROL AND UNDER MEDITATION

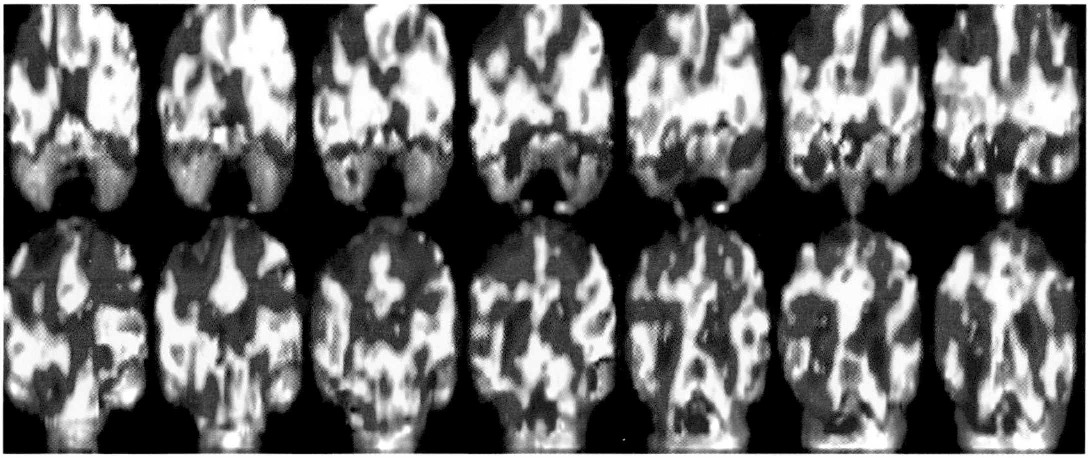

Note
Yellow is significant change
Red is low change
Grey is no change

Five people, four male and one female participated in this study. Each had practiced Kundalini meditation (referring to Yogi Harbhajan Singh's procedure) daily for at least four years. All five people during meditation repeated the words "Sat Nam" (meaning God is Truth) during inhalations and "Wahe Guru" (God is wonderful) during exhalations. These words are used every day to praise God in the Sikh Religion. During the control part of the study, no meditation was carried out. The duration of each study per person was 42 minutes: 6 control + 12 meditation + 6 control+ 12 meditation + 6 control.

This study demonstrated that MRI is useful for studying the changes in the brain activity during the practice of meditation. The scan showed that the subjects during the meditation period displayed a large, global signal decrease. The decrease was as high as to the order of p <10 raised to the power -30. This is shown in Figure 25. As previously mentioned, deep inhalation and exhalation was performed during meditation. As per the private e-mail of Dr Sara Lazar, the meditation imaging expert at Harvard Medical School, it is not clear how much effect was due to neural activity and how much was due to changes in breathing rate, as breathing also can cause changes in blood flow.

The biological effects of meditation will shed new light on the cognitive and emotional brain processing system, including the relaxation response. Relaxation through meditation decreases metabolism, heart rate, blood pressure, breathing rate and slows brain waves. It is said that people who meditate display strong emotional responses and brain activity, which lead to better and healthier lifestyles. **The Buddhist Vipassana meditation technique has shown some positive results and benefits for the overall health of human beings.** However, more work is required in using MRI as a tool for the quantitative effect of meditation. Better scientific techniques also need to be developed to further explore the meditation/body link.

The laws of science are always evolving and new discoveries are made on a daily basis. In fact, the Human Genome Project was completed in recent years,, therefore it will be just a matter of time before DNA-based medicine will be marketed to the general public for curing diseases like cancer, AIDS, Alzheimer's, diabetes, etc. However, science will never be able to achieve the power of God for all times to come.

F. PRAYING TO GOD

There are a few ways to clean one's mind on a daily basis. Work honestly, perform good deeds, treat every body as an equal, and above all pray to God every day.

Having discussed why to pray and how to pray, our inquisitive mind wants to answer the following questions: 1. "What is God?" 2. "Where does God live?" and 3. "Why can't we see God?" The answers are discussed below.

4. CONCEPT OF GOD

When Guru Nanak started the Sikh Religion he began be explaining what God was. Guru Nanak said: ***There is only one God, God's name is truth, God is creator of all, God is without fear, God is not against anybody, God's shape never changes, God was neither born nor dies, God is self-existent, selfless and every where.*** This is also clearly explained in Chapter 2 page 2.

Guru Nanak faced the same question about the conception of God many times and answered in a very clear and concise way.

The first Guru, Nanak, said:

PUNJABI AND ROMAN	ENGLISH
ਥਾਪਿਆ ਨ ਜਾਇ Thaapi-aa Na Jaa-ay	God cannot be installed or visualized (as idol)
ਕੀਤਾ ਨ ਹੋਇ ॥ Keetaa Na Ho-ay	God can not be proved, as God is not created.
ਆਪੇ ਆਪਿ ਨਿਰੰਜਨੁ ਸੋਇ ॥ Aapay Aap Niranjan So-ay	God has made Himself and maintains Himself.

Guru Granth Sahib (p. 2, line 6)

God is without matter. Science deals with matter only. Thus no scientific theory can describe God. To comprehend God one's mind, body and soul should have much higher level of thinking than one's eyes can perceive.

5. WHERE GOD LIVES

God is everywhere and even abides within all of us. This has been addressed in a very convincing way below.

The ninth Guru, Tegh Bahadur, said:

PUNJABI AND ROMAN	ENGLISH
ਕਾਹੇ ਰੇ ਬਨ ਖੋਜਨ ਜਾਈ ॥	Why do you go to search for God in
Kaahay Ray Ban Khojan Jaa-ee	the forest and remote places?
ਸਰਬ ਨਿਵਾਸੀ ਸਦਾ ਅਲੇਪਾ	God, though detached,
Sarab Nivaasee Sadaa Alaypaa	is every where
ਤੋਹੀ ਸੰਗਿ ਸਮਾਈ ॥	and lives even in all of us.
Tohee Sang Samaa-ee	
ਪੁਹਪ ਮਧਿ ਜਿਉ ਬਾਸੁ ਬਸਤੁ ਹੈ	Just as fragrance is part
Puhap MaDh Ji-o Baas Basat Hai	of the flower
ਮੁਕਰ ਮਾਹਿ ਜੈਸੇ ਛਾਈ ॥	Just as you see your reflection
Mukar Maahi Jaisay Chhaa-ee	in the mirror.
ਤੈਸੇ ਹੀ ਹਰਿ ਬਸੇ ਨਿਰੰਤਰਿ	So does God live within all of us
Taisay Hee Har Basay Nirantar	
ਘਟ ਹੀ ਖੋਜਹੁ ਭਾਈ ॥	O' people search for God
Ghat Hee Khojahu Bhaa-ee	within your heart.
ਬਾਹਰਿ ਭੀਤਰਿ ਏਕੋ ਜਾਨਹੁ	There is one God who lives within
Baahar Bheetar Ayko Jaanahu	and without us and
ਇਹੁ ਗੁਰ ਗਿਆਨੁ ਬਤਾਈ ॥	this realization has been taught
Ih Gur Gi-aan Bataa-ee	to us by our Gurus.
ਜਨ ਨਾਨਕ ਬਿਨੁ ਆਪਾ ਚੀਨੈ	Says Guru Nanak if one does not
Jan Naanak Bin Aapaa Cheenai	understand the presence of God In our body
ਮਿਟੈ ਨ ਭ੍ਰਮ ਕੀ ਕਾਈ ॥	then doubts in one's life shall
Mitai Na Bharam Kee Kaa-ee	never go away.
Guru Granth Sahib (p. 684, line 15)	

6. WHY WE CAN NOT SEE GOD

Guru Nanak was asked the question why our eyes cannot see God? Guru Nanak replied that ***God permeates the whole universe and has to be perceived by everything and thus cannot be seen by our eyes.***

The first Guru, Nanak, said:

PUNJABI AND ROMAN	**ENGLISH**
ਘਟਿ ਘਟਿ ਗੁਪਤਾ	God is permeated in the whole universe
Ghat Ghat Guptaa	and in every heart
ਗੁਰਮੁਖਿ ਮੁਕਤਾ ll	and God-loving people are liberated.
Gurmukh Muktaa	

Guru Granth Sahib (p. 939, line 11)

Why should God be present only on earth? God permeates in the whole universe and beyond. Thus, God is everywhere.

Let us discuss scientifically why we cannot see God with our eyes. Scientists have so far been able to discover the electromagnetic spectrum, which consists of wavelengths from the longest radio waves to the shortest gamma waves. They have also discovered cosmic rays, which are actually high energy, charged particles but are not part of the electromagnetic spectrum. This is as far as science goes today, however, there may be more discoveries in the future. The electromagnetic spectrum is shown graphically in Figure 27.

The human eye can detect and see only a very narrow range of the electromagnetic spectrum—wavelengths from 400 nanometers (violet) to 700 nanometers (red) (see Figure 27). ***Why should God reside in this tiny range and deprive the rest of the Universe of its existence.*** God is permeated in the whole Universe. God is beyond our reach. God has never been seen, cannot be seen now and will not be seen for all time to come.

Let us discuss more scientifically, why we cannot see God. There are many phenomena in science that cannot be seen by our eyes but we believe they exist. Some of the examples are:

A. Science can measure heat but not cold. Cold is only a word we use to describe the absence of heat. We can have more heat, super heat, or low heat. We cannot measure below -273 degrees Centigrade, which represents no heat

B. Another example is light. Light can be low, normal, or bright. Light can be measured but darkness cannot.

C. Science has found electricity and magnetism but nobody has seen with their eyes.

D. Science says that human beings were evolved from apes but nobody has seen this as a fact with their eyes. Nobody has ever observed the process of evolution at work and cannot even prove that this is an ongoing process.

E. The famous scientist Newton observed a force on earth called gravity that attracts everything towards itself. We cannot verify gravity's existence by our physical senses of sight, sound, smell, taste, or touch—we all presume it exists.

We accept that cold, darkness, electricity, magnetism, gravity, and the evolution of human beings exist, but we cannot verify their existence. Thus science,which is still in its infancy, is just a faith. Science will never be able to take the place of God no matter how hard we all try.

Let us presume that there is a spiritual force. We cannot see or feel it, but it exists. This force creates every thing, sustains it and finally absorbs it (for human beings it is in the form of death). This is the force of God. This force is essential to maintain social, ethical, moral discipline in our society. We have faith that God exists, but God cannot be seen or measured.

The real question is how can we realize God? This realization can be achieved by tuning our mind, body and soul towards one God. Then we must practice this faith by meditation and prayer.

7. GURU NANAK AS A SPIRITUAL SCIENTIST

Scientists believe in work that can be proved and repeated by other scientists. There are theories proposed and later proved to be correct or incorrect depending upon the experimental work. Let us take the case of Albert Einstein, the world famous scientist. In 1905, as part of his Special Theory of Relativity, he made the intriguing point that a large amount of energy could be released from a small amount of matter. This was expressed by Energy "E" is equal to Mass "M" times the Speed of Light "C" squared.
The above theory resulted in the creation of atomic energy (Figure 28). The first example was the use of two bombs at Nagasaki and Hiroshima in Japan that ended the World War II. The above figure shows the power of atomic bomb. The same energy is used for peaceful purposes as in the generation of electricity and in medicine.

Einstein, although not a worshipper of God, wrote about religion and science: ***"Science without religion is lame; religion without science is blind."*** [5]

FIGURE 27

ELECTROMAGNETIC SPECTRUM

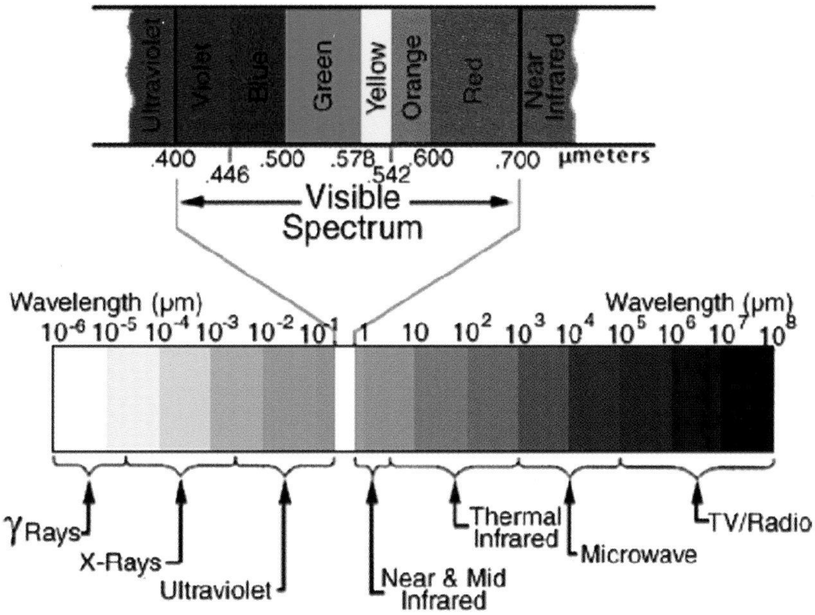

FIGURE 28

ATOMIC ENERGY

Guru Nanak also was a scientist, not in the sense that is normally observed in today's society. ***Guru Nanak said there is one God that is neither born nor dies and is present everywhere. Guru Nanak also said that all human beings are created equal and peace of mind is obtained by loving humanity and meditation on God.***

Guru Nanak's theories have been proven on human beings for hundreds of years and will be good for all times to come. ***Thus Guru Nanak was a spiritual scientist.***

8. GURU NANAK AS A SPIRITUAL DOCTOR

A medical doctor generally prescribes a medicine after diagnosis. That medicine has been tested on many patients before it is given to the general public. Similarly ***Guru Nanak studied human beings before prescribing the medicine of Naam—praying to God. The results have stood for centuries and will be true for all times to come.***

Guru Nanak studied the human mind. The whole world is suffering from problems of one sort or another. These problems relate to the mind, which controls all functions in our body. Guru Nanak said if we can control our mind then peace and tranquility will prevail. Generally we pray when afflicted with some disease or some hardship. When sickness is gone we revert to our usual routines. Guru Nanak said we have to pray everyday. Guru Nanak's prescription is given in just four words in Gurmukhi, as shown below:

The first Guru Nanak, said:

PUNJABI AND ROMAN	**ENGLISH**
ਸੰਸਾਰੁ ਰੋਗੀ ਨਾਮੁ ਦਾਰੂ ॥	The whole world is sick and
Sansaar Rogee Naam Daaroo Guru Granth Sahib (p. 687, line 17)	God's name is the cure for all that.

There is a practical way to pray God besides reading or singing hymns (shabads).

Guru Nanak explained that truthful living should be practiced on a daily basis. This will lead to peace of mind. If one wants peace everyday then one should pray daily. It is that simple.

One achieves the following by praying daily:

A. ***Peace of mind.***
B. ***One gets knowledge about Truth.***
C. ***Evils do not bother and gives the courage to bear them.***
D. ***Finally one prepares oneself to merge with the supreme God.***

9. GURU NANAK ON THE CREATION OF THE UNIVERSE

Scientists have been trying to ascertain for a very long time when was this whole universe created? No one has any clear answer. ***Guru Nanak said in a very simple and convincing way that only God knows that.*** God, who cannot be seen, not only created the whole universe but also maintains it.

The first Guru, Nanak, said:

PUNJABI AND ROMAN	**ENGLISH**
ਕਵਣੁ ਸੁ ਵੇਲਾ ਵਖਤੁ ਕਵਣੁ	What was the moment? What was
Kavan So Vaylaa Vakhat Kavan	the time?
ਕਵਣ ਥਿਤਿ ਕਵਣੁ ਵਾਰੁ ॥	What was the lunar/solar day?
Kavan Thit Kavan Vaar	What was the weekday?
ਕਵਣਿ ਸਿ ਰੁਤੀ ਮਾਹੁ	What was the season? What was
Kavan Se Rutee Maahu	the month?
ਕਵਣੁ ਜਿਤੁ ਹੋਆ ਆਕਾਰੁ ॥	When was the world created?
Kavan Jit Ho-aa Aakaar	
ਵੇਲ ਨ ਪਾਈਆ ਪੰਡਤੀ	The Pundits (Hindu religious
Vayl Na Paa-ee-aa Pandatee	preachers) do not know the time
ਜਿ ਹੋਵੈ ਲੇਖੁ ਪੁਰਾਣੁ ॥	even going through the Puranas
Je Hovai Laykh Puraan	(Hindu religious books).
ਵਖਤੁ ਨ ਪਾਇਓ ਕਾਦੀਆ	The Qazis (Muslim religious
Vakhat Na Paa-i-o Kaadee-aa	preachers) do not know the time
ਜਿ ਲਿਖਨਿ ਲੇਖੁ ਕੁਰਾਣੁ ॥	who wrote the Quran (Muslim
Je Likhan Laykh Kuraan	religious book).
ਥਿਤਿ ਵਾਰੁ ਨਾ ਜੋਗੀ ਜਾਣੈ	The Yogis do not know the
Thit Vaar Naa Jogee Jaanai	lunar/solar day or week day.
ਰੁਤਿ ਮਾਹੁ ਨਾ ਕੋਈ ॥	No body else knows season or
Rut Maahu Naa Ko-ee	the month of creation.

ਜਾ ਕਰਤਾ ਸਿਰਠੀ ਕਉ ਸਾਜੇ
Jaa Kartaa Sirthee Ka-o Saajay
ਆਪੇ ਜਾਣੈ ਸੋਈ ॥
Aapay Jaanai So-ee
Guru Granth Sahib (p. 4, line 16)

God who created and maintained
the whole universe
is the only one who knows when
the universe was created.

10. THE SIKH PRAYER (ARDAS)

Anyone, man or woman, old or young can recite the Sikh Prayer. It is not necessary that priest should perform it. Even a boy or girl can lead in the prayer in a big congregation consisting of learned and old people. This is encouraged so every one can shoulder their responsibility without the help of the priest.

No ceremony, whether religious or otherwise, is complete without prayer. Before going on a journey, opening a shop, buying a new house or any other occasion Sikhs ask God's blessings by reading from Guru Granth Sahib and offering a prayer.

The prayer varies in size and contents. Some times only a few words will do. Sometimes just saying Wahe Guru (God is great) will do. At times it could be a short prayer or a regular prayer, depending upon the occasion.

The Sikh Prayer (Ardas) is not the work of one person. It evolved over a period of centuries. It was actually during the 6th Guru Har Gobind that the Sikh Prayer became an established procedure of praying in the congregations.

When the prayer is offered, every one stands up with folded hands. All people face towards Guru Granth Sahib or towards the person who is praying if Guru Granth Sahib is not present. As a mark of respect people cover their head.

The Sikh Prayer has several sections. ***The first section (mandatory) starts with praise of God.*** Then it shows the ***history starting with Guru Nanak,*** followed by nine succeeding Gurus. Then it explains that one should ***follow Guru Granth Sahib*** for all times to come. Middle section explains ***the sacrifices made by the community*** for centuries to preserve the religion. There is no bitterness or revenge against the enemy. Only the atrocities are mentioned. This section talks of ***preserving all religious places*** especially the five important historical places at Amritsar, Patna Sahib, Anandpur Sahib, Damdama Sahib, and Nander Sahib. This section allows ***lot of latitude*** depending upon the occasion and the person who is performing the prayer. The last section is mandatory and is for the ***praise of God and for universal prosperity.***

Teja Singh [6] wrote a very good article in English in 1968 about The Sikh Prayer (Ardas). It was very helpful for understanding the background of the Sikh Prayer (Ardas). I have written a very simple Sikh Prayer in English. It is a very short and to the point. It will be very helpful for those who do not know Punjabi.

THE SIKH PRAYER (ARDAS)

The following is a Sikh community prayer in English. The first and the last part are mandatory. Changes can be made in the middle section, depending upon the circumstances.

FIRST PART (Must for all)
First remember, God the Almighty, then think of Guru Nanak.
Then of Guru Angad , Guru Amar Das and Guru Ram Das.
Remember Guru Arjan Dev, Guru Hargobind and Guru Har Rai.
Think of Guru Har Krishan whose sight dispels all sorrows.
Remember Guru Tegh Bahadur and Guru Gobind Singh.
May they help and assist us everywhere.
After ten Gurus believe in Guru Granth Sahib for all times to come.
Say Wahe Guru.

MIDDLE PART (VARIATIONS ALLOWED)

SECTION 1 SACRIFICES
We pray earnestly and with folded hands
For all those who sacrificed their lives.
The first five Sikhs, four sons of Guru Gobind Singh
And the forty brave Sikhs.
Say Wahe Guru.

SECTION 2 RELIGIOUS PLACES
Give us the strength to take care of the religious places especially the five historic Gurdwaras at, Amritsar, Patna Sahib, Anandpur Sahib, Damdama Sahib and Nander Sahib
Say Wahe Guru

SECTION 3 MAIN PART

Give us happiness and peace of mind
Give us the spirit to be humble and wise.

Forgive us for all the bad things that we have done.
Keep us into the company of those who believe in one God.

Let us be charitable and helper of the needy
Help us in our endeavors and keep us in good health.

Give us the gift of Universal Religion, Sikhism, the gift of confidence, the gift of trust, the gift of faith and the gift of remembering and believing in one God.

Help us in controlling our excessive lust, excessive anger, excessive greed, excessive ego and excessive pride.

Fulfill the desires of all those who pray earnestly.

LAST PART (MUST FOR ALL)

Nanak says God's Name be always on the rise.
By the grace of God let there be universal prosperity and well being.

Nanak Naam Chardee Kalla **Tere Bhaane Sarbat Daa Bhalaa**

11. SUMMARY

To achieve peace of mind it is very essential to pray daily. Just as cleaning of the body is important, so is cleaning of the mind—everyday. There are many ways to pray to God and one can select the procedure appropriate for oneself. Meditation as a relaxation is very beneficial for the human body. MRIs show changes in the brain due to meditation. More scientific experiments using different techniques are required to study the effects of meditation. Mind, body and soul can only perceive God. God cannot be seen, as God is present in the whole Universe and not restricted to earth and human beings alone. God lives within and without us. God who created and maintains the whole Universe is the only one who knows when the Universe was created. Guru Nanak said that the cure for all diseases of the mind is to contemplate on God in order to get peace of mind. Guru Nanak was a scientist, a spiritual doctor and explained how the universe was created. Guru Nanak's theories were spiritual and stood the practical test for centuries and will be good for all times to come. A Sikh community Prayer (Ardas) in English is presented.

12. EXERCISES

i. Why is daily prayer so important even though I work honestly and perform good deeds?
ii. Why can't we see God with our eyes?
iii. Where is God and when was the Universe created?
iv. Describe at least four ways for praying to God.
v. How has science complemented the meditation process?
vi. Explain how Guru Nanak was a spiritual scientist and a spiritual doctor.
vii. Remember by heart the Sikh community prayer (Ardas) in English.

13. REFERENCES

[1] Yahoo. Search for "Gurdwara Inside" Click "Photos" Select "No 5 Inside Gurdwara" or
www.gurdwaramidhudson.org/photos/index1.html
[2] Sara W. Lazar, George Bush, Randy L. Gollub, Gregory L. Fricchione, Gurucharan Khalsa and Herbert Benson. Harvard Medical School Massachusetts General Hospital-East, Charlestown with
A. Department of Psychiatry B. NMR center C. Department of Psychiatry, Brigham and Women's Hospital D. Department of Medicine, Beth Israel Deaconess Medical Center; Mind/Body Medical Institute, Boston, MA. http://www.mgh.harvard.edu/depts/neuroimaging/gollublab/SaraNeuroreport.pdf
[3] Google Images. Search for "Index of /nasa/education/reference/reflect" Click "egg.jpg"
[4] Google web search for " Albert Einstein and the Bomb by Doug Long"
www.doug-long.com/einstein.htm
[5] Google web. Search for "Science and Religion II, Science, Philosophy and Religion, A Symposium 1941" Click for "Albert Einstein: On Religion and Science" Click on "Religion and Science II" end of fourth paragraph is the quotation.
http://www.sacred-texts.com/aor/einstein/einsci.htm
[6] Teja Singh. 1968 A Pamphlet on "The Sikh Prayer" Publisher Shiromani Gurdwara Parbhandhak Committee, Amritsar, Punjab, India.

UNIVERSALITY OF THE SIKH RELIGION

CHAPTER 11

FIFTH PRINCIPLE—TRUTHFUL LIVING

TRUTH IS UNIVERSAL.

Guru Nanak summarized the importance of living a Truthful life in the following words.

TRUTH IS HIGHER THAN EVERYTHING
BUT HIGHER STILL IS TRUTHFUL LIVING
Guru Granth Sahib page 62 line 11

Truthful living in a practical way can be considered as the sum of the four principles as honesty (Chapter 7), sharing with less fortunate people (Chapter 8), treating everyone as an equal (Chapter 9) and praying daily to God (Chapter 10).

The Sikh religion has a very simple philosophy: ***lead an honest, Truthful life.*** The Sikh religion regards the world as a meaningful creation of God where Truthful Living and selfless actions can bring a person closer to God. This world is not considered a place of suffering but a place where one can lead a joyful family life through truthful living, equality for all, and sharing with less fortunate people. One can spend their whole life hearing about Truth, reading lot of books about Truth, contemplating day and night about Truth, preaching Truth, writing volumes about Truth, following various religions and cults [1]. However, none of these is of any help unless ***one leads a Truthful life on a day-to-day basis***.

1. TRUE, TRUTH AND TRUTHFUL

These three words are interrelated but should be examined individually.

True is agreeing with the facts, just as 6+4=10. True is correct, exact and accurate.

Truth is established principle, law, verified hypothesis and a basic scientific Truth. It is in accordance with the facts.

Truthful is being disposed to tell the Truth. It is also being factual, accurate and confirming of the Truth.

A person is living a Truthful Life when they are always truthful in their daily lives. It is not easy to practice, but once this lifestyle is adopted, the mind and body attain peace. Such a person sets a good example in society and is remembered even after the death. When a thirsty person drinks water, he receives fullness and comfort from the water, but the water, itself, does not receive fulfillment. Similarly, a Truthful person is satisfied and comforted, but it has no affect on the Truth itself.

Thus according to Guru Nanak it is very important to live a Truthful life rather than just having faith in Truth.

The first Guru, Nanak, said:

PUNJABI AND ROMAN	**ENGLISH**
ਤਬ ਲਗੁ ਮਹਲੁ ਨ ਪਾਈਐ	One cannot enter God's place
Tab Lag Mahal Na Paa-ee-ai	
ਜਬ ਲਗੁ ਸਾਚੁ ਨ ਚੀਤਿ ॥	unless Truth is permeated in the mind
Jab Lag Saach Na Cheet.	and body.
Guru Granth Sahib (p. 58, line 5)	

2. TRUTHFUL LIVING AND FALSEHOOD

Truthful living is righteous living. It is life of peace, harmony, love, knowledge, forgiveness, and spiritual beauty. It is also God oriented, selfless, fearless, honest, and, charitable. One living a Truthful life performs good deeds and prays to God.

Falsehood is irreligious. It is self-oriented. When one leads a life of falsehood one believes in the "I, me, mine," hatred, revenge, fanaticism, conflicts, prejudices, divisiveness, corruption, crookedness, sins and telling lies.

The fifth Guru, Arjan Dev, said:

PUNJABI AND ROMAN	**ENGLISH**
ਕੂੜਹੁ ਕਰੇ ਵਿਣਾਸੁ	Through falsehood one is destroyed spiritually
Koorhahu Karay Vinaas	
ਧਰਮੇ ਤਗੀਐ ॥	through righteousness one prospers.
Dharmay Tagee-ai.	
Guru Granth Sahib (p. 518, line 9)	

It is made very clear that there should be no delay in performing good deeds, but that one should steer clear of bad habits.

The fifth Guru, Arjan Dev, said:

PUNJABI AND ROMAN	ENGLISH
ਨਹ ਬਿਲੰਬ ਧਰਮੰ	Do not delay in practicing righteousness
Nah Bilamb DharmaN	
ਬਿਲੰਬ ਪਾਪੰ ॥	but delay in committing sins.
Bilamb PaapaN	
Guru Granth Sahib (p.1354, line 17)	

Truth and falsehood cannot stay together [1].
Truth is pure love and understanding. Falsehood is due to excessive ego.
Truth promotes courage and sacrifice. Falsehood breeds fear and hatred.
Truth is forgiveness and compassion. Falsehood is hurt.
Truth is wisdom. Falsehood is ignorance.
Truth is power. Falsehood is weakness.
Truth leads to objectiveness. Falsehood clouds our judgment.
Truth cautions other people about bad habits. Falsehood pampers them.
Truth is Divine. Falsehood is evil.
Truth keeps the mind in equilibrium. Falsehood creates restlessness.
Truth is giving. Falsehood is taking.
Truth is going forward. Falsehood is going backward.

The first Guru, Nanak, said:

PUNJABI AND ROMAN	ENGLISH
ਅਮਲੁ ਕਰਿ ਧਰਤੀ	Good deeds be like the earth
Amal Kar Dhartee	
ਬੀਜੁ ਸਬਦੋ ਕਰਿ	God's Name (Shabad) is like the seed
Beej Sabdo Kar	
ਸਚ ਕੀ ਆਬ ਨਿਤ ਦੇਹਿ ਪਾਣੀ ॥	Always irrigate with the Truth as one
Sach Kee Aab Nit Deh Paanee	irrigates with water.
Guru Granth Sahib (p. 24, line 1)	

The third Guru, Amar Das, said:

PUNJABI AND ROMAN	ENGLISH
ਗੁਣਵੰਤੀ ਸਚੁ ਪਾਇਆ	The virtuous person is Truthful
Gunvantee Sach Paa-i-aa	
ਤ੍ਰਿਸਨਾ ਤਜਿ ਵਿਕਾਰ ॥	They give up desire for evil and
Tarisnaa Taj Vikaar.	corruption.
Guru Granth Sahib (p. 36, line 19)	

The first Guru, Nanak, said:

PUNJABI AND ROMAN	ENGLISH
ਮਨਹੁ ਛੋਡਿ ਵਿਕਾਰ Manhu Chhod Vikaar	Banish corruption from one's mind
ਸਚਾ ਸਚੁ ਦੇਇ ॥ Sachaa Sach Day-ay. Guru Granth Sahib (p. 422, line 5)	The True God will grant one Truthful life.

3. TRUTHFUL LIVING AND SIMPLICITY

God made things in a very simple way. ***Truth and Truthful Living are very simple.*** However, the human mind does not appreciate simplicity. People with deluded minds seek out complexity and are not content with simplicity. That is why so many religions and sects have come into existence with their own complex rituals. There is no tolerance for other religions. Thus, the world is converted into a battleground.

The third Guru, Amar Das, said:

PUNJABI AND ROMAN	ENGLISH
ਤਿਸਨਾ ਅਗਨਿ ਜਲੈ ਸੰਸਾਰਾ ॥ Tisnaa Agan Jalai Sansaaraa.	The world is burning in the fire of excessive desire
ਲੋਭੁ ਅਭਿਮਾਨੁ Lobh Abhimaan	excessive greed, excessive arrogance
ਬਹੁਤੁ ਅਹੰਕਾਰਾ ॥ Bahut AhaNkaaraa Guru Granth Sahib (p.120, Line 13)	and excessive pride.

4. TRUTH AND RELIGIONS

All religions teach compassion. The problem arises when they are interpreted differently. When some begin to believe that their religion is the one true way and start finding fault with other religion, it leads to conflict. Everyone should learn that ***by sowing seeds of dissention only hatred and conflicts are reaped.***

All religions must recognize that world peace and harmony are of utmost importance. It is possible to have world peace if every individual develops love and compassion within and then shares it with everyone else. The religious leaders of their respective religion must first look within themselves and practice Truthful living. This will lead to Truthful Living throughout the world.

All religions believe in Truth, righteousness and goodness. This is the underlying unity of all religions. Prophets from all religions preach Truth. This is very simple. However, all organized religions are dogmatic and sectarian [1]. They believe that their way of believing in God is the only way. Thus they create segregation that leads to conflict and fighting. ***There is nothing wrong with having different religions*** in this world. If all people would promote peace and would live with love and harmony with people of all other religions, then this world will be a better place in which to live.

The first Guru, Nanak, said:

PUNJABI AND ROMAN	**ENGLISH**
ਮਨ ਹਠ ਬੁਧੀ ਕੇਤੀਆ	There are so many people of
Man Hath BuDhee Kaytee-aa	stubborn-minded intelligence
ਕੇਤੇ ਬੇਦ ਬੀਚਾਰ ॥	and so many who contemplate
Kaytay Bayd Beechaar.	the scriptures.
ਕੇਤੇ ਬੰਧਨ ਜੀਅ ਕੇ	There are so many entanglements
Kaytay BanDhan Jee-a Kay	in this life
ਗੁਰਮੁਖਿ ਮੋਖ ਦੁਆਰ ॥	Only a God oriented person will find
Gurmukh Mokh Du-aar.	salvation.
Guru Granth Sahib (p. 62, line 11)	

5. TRUTHFUL LIVING AS MEDICINE

Truthful or righteous living is only good when put into practice daily. As there are different medicines for different illnesses, so there are different religions for different types of people in this world. However, the basics of all religions are the same—they are focused on Truth. Truthful living is like medicine for the mind. ***In order to remove the root of mental illness caused by stress and other factors one must apply the medicine of Truthful living.***

The fifth Guru, Arjan Dev, said:

PUNJABI AND ROMAN	ENGLISH
ਸਤੁ ਸੰਤੋਖੁ ਦਇਆ ਕਮਾਵੈ Sat Santokh Da-i-aa Kamaavai	Practice Truth, contentment and kindness
ਏਹ ਕਰਣੀ ਸਾਰ ॥ Ayh Karnee Saar.	This is an excellent way to live.

Guru Granth Sahib (p. 51, line 10)

The first Guru, Nanak, said:

PUNJABI AND ROMAN	ENGLISH
ਸਾਚਿ ਸੰਤੋਖੇ Saach Santokhay	Through Truth and contentment
ਭਰਮੁ ਚੁਕਾਇਆ ॥ Bharam Chukaa-i-aa.	doubt is dispelled.

Guru Granth Sahib (p. 228, line 2)

6. TRUTHFUL LIVING STARTS WITHIN SELF

It is one's own effort that produces righteousness. ***Sincere willingness is very rare. Earnestness is very rare. True faith is very rare. Sincerity is very rare. People should live a Truthful life, but in practice, it is also very rare.*** This lack of Truthful living leads to hate. Even countries are not immune to this, which can lead to war. In order to have world peace one must have peace within oneself. The essence of religions is to create conditions for love with all human beings, be humble, help the needy and be honest in daily life.

7. TRUTHFUL LIVING AND WORLD PROSPERITY

Truthful living, having righteous thoughts as well as humility in speech and actions are the source of true peace, harmony and universal prosperity.

The third Guru, Amar Das, said:

PUNJABI AND ROMAN	ENGLISH
ਅੰਤਰਿ ਸਾਚੁ Antar Saach	One who has Truth pervading within
ਬਾਹਰਿ ਸਾਚੁ ਵਰਤਾਏ ॥ Baahar Saach Vartaa-ay.	radiates Truth outwardly also.

Guru Granth Sahib (p. 232, line 4)

The third Guru, Amar Das, said:

PUNJABI AND ROMAN	ENGLISH
ਸਾਚੁ ਨ ਛਪੈ Saach Na Chhapai	Truth cannot be hidden
ਜੇ ਕੋ ਰਖੈ ਛਪਾਏ ॥ Jay Ko Rakhai Chhapaa-ay. Guru Granth Sahib (p. 232, line 4)	even though one may try to hide it.

8. SUMMARY

Truthful living in a practical way can be considered as the sum of honesty, sharing with less fortunate people, treating everyone as an equal, and praying daily to God.

This world is not considered a place of suffering but a place where one can lead a joyful family life through truthful living, equality for all, and sharing with less fortunate people. Simply put, Truthful living is religious and the right way to live; falsehood is irreligious and the wrong way to live. The unifying force of all religions is their belief in Truth, righteousness, goodness and compassion. However, all organized religions are dogmatic and sectarian in practice. Truthful living is like medicine for the mind that brings peace and tranquility. In order for the world to live Truthfully the individual has to begin first with living a Truthful life. Truthful living will lead to true peace, harmony and universal prosperity.

9. EXERCISES

i. What should one do in practice to live a Truthful life?
ii. When all religions believe in Truth, goodness and compassion, why do they fight with each other?
iii. Why is Truthful Living like medicine?

10. REFERENCES

[1] T. Singh. "Religious Fanaticism, Part 14: It's Cure: Live Truthfully" From www.gurbani.org/webart137.htm

UNIVERSALITY OF THE SIKH RELIGION

CHAPTER 12

ENJOY THE UNIVERSALITY OF THE SIKH RELIGION

Religion should be enjoyed. But, is it really possible? Generally, people do not think of religion in terms of enjoyment. We must integrate this **enjoyment (peace of mind) into our daily lives**. The question is, How does one enjoy it? Does the Sikh Religion allow for happiness (Anand in Pujabi [Gurmukhi])? The answer is yes. **One must enjoy the diversity created by God.** At present there are about 6 billion people on this earth and all are different. No two people are exactly alike, not even the identical twins. Enjoy when meeting people. Keep the five principles of honesty, sharing with less privileged people, equality for all, praying daily to God and Truthful living as part of one's daily life. This will create peace of mind, and, ultimately, enjoyment.

1. WORD ENJOY IN THE GURU GRANTH SAHIB

The word Anand (enjoyment, peace of mind) is mentioned at least 209 times in the Guru Granth Sahib. It is found in five different spellings, ਅਨਦ (88 times), ਅਨਦੁ (56 times), ਅਨੰਦੁ (34 times), ਆਨਦ (23 times), ਆਨਦੁ (7 times) and ਅਨਦੋ (1 time). Guru Nanak used the word Anand 7 times, 1 time by the second Guru Angad, 22 times by the third Guru Amar Das, 22 times by the fourth Guru Ram Das, 151 times by the fifth Guru Arjan Dev, 3 times by Kabir, 2 times by Nam Dev and 1 time by Sur Das. Thus word Anand (enjoyment, peace of mind) has been widely used throughout the Guru Granth Sahib.

It should be mentioned that it is not an easy task to find the correct number of times the word Anand is used in the Guru Granth Sahib. This is due to the many different spellings of the word in Punjabi. Also, the computer search for the word(s) may not be perfect. This information was obtained using **www.srigranth.org.**

2. CEREMONIES FOR ENJOYMENT

There are two very important official ceremonies in Sikh Religion that start with the heading of Anand (enjoyment).

i. ANAND SAHIB (ENJOY WITH PEACE OF MIND)

After every religious ceremony the hymn Anand Sahib is sung before the final prayer (Ardas). It means to enjoy or obtain peace of mind.

Anand Sahib is composed of several verses.
The first five and the last verse are from the third 3 Guru Amar Das (Guru Granth Sahib Page 917 line 1 and Page 922 line 16)
One verse from the first Guru Nanak (Guru Granth Sahib Page 8 line 10)

Some of the salient points of Anand Sahib are:

A. I am full of joy, O' my mother, as I have obtained True God.
B. My mind now resounds with the blissful music.
C. By tuning my mind, body and soul to True God all my sufferings are gone.
D. One cannot forget God who is present everywhere. Everything happens according to God's will.
E. God has created everything and only by the grace of God we receive them.
F. Abiding God in my mind, I am blessed with peace and pleasures and all my desires are fulfilled.
G. I now profess love for God's hymns (Shabads).
H. Only the very fortunate ones comprehend God's hymns (Shabads) and all their desires are fulfilled.
I. Everyone feels happy on hearing hymns (God's Naam, Shabads).
J. Air is Guru, water is father and great earth the mother. Day and night are two nurses, male and female. The whole world plays around them. In True God's court one's merits and demerits shall be read. ***According to the deeds rendered by each person, some will remain with God while others will be separated.*** For those who contemplate God's word, their journey is completed successfully. Nanak says their faces will glow and they will be emancipated along with many others.

The above Anand Sahib gives enjoyment and peace of mind. All it requires is to keep God in your mind and perform good deeds.

ii. ANAND KARAJ (MARRIAGE TO ENJOY)

The marriage ceremony is a happy occasion and therefore it is called Anand Karaj (Marriage for enjoyment).
It was composed by the fourth Guru Ramdas (Guru Granth Sahib p. 773 line 14).

Some of the salient points of Anand Karaj, in an abbreviated form, are:

A. In a Sikh marriage the bride and bridegroom walk around the Guru Granth Sahib four times while hymns (Shabads) are being recited and sung. These are called ***four Lavaans.***

B. In the first Lavaan, one's duties in married life have begun. Emphasis is placed upon ***righteousness and good character.***

C. In the second Lavaan, one is to control excessive ego. One must realize that ***the same God is present within all of us and in the whole universe. We all are equal in all respects*** irrespective of caste, color, religion, appearance and sex.

D. In the third Laavan, the main **emphasis is on destiny.** Everything happens with the grace of God and so the marriage was destined. Love has now sprung in my heart and I am joyful.

E. In the fourth and last Lavaan, the emphasis is on the mind being steadfast. Sweetness has now permeated in my body and mind. ***I have received my heartfelt desire and now I am going to be congratulated.*** All this has occurred due to the grace of God.

Thus the marriage ceremony is an event for pleasure and should be celebrated with joy and happiness. In fact in the Sikh Religion life should be lived within a normal family. There is no need to live a secluded life.

3. TYPES OF ENJOYMENT

There are many different types of enjoyment. According to most religions, the love for God is of prime importance for enjoyment as it gives one peace of mind. However, there are many other types of love that produce enjoyment. There is love for parents, love for children, love for the spouse, love for relatives, love for friends, love for nature, etc.. They all give enjoyment. ***In order to live a normal life, love is an essential part of our living.*** Love should be normal part of ourt day-to-day lives. There is no need to be guilty about it, however, the Sikh Religion cautions us against the misuse of the excessive use of love for worldly things.

i. LOVE FOR GOD'S NAAM

One who recites and comprehends the words written in the hymns (Shabads) becomes humble, becomes tolerant of others' opinion and obtains peace of mind.

The fifth Guru, Arjan Dev, said:

PUNJABI AND ROMAN	ENGLISH
ਖਿਮਾ ਗਰੀਬੀ Khimaa Gareebee	One obtains tolerance, humility,
ਅਨਦ ਸਹਜ Anad Sahj	enjoyment and peace of mind
ਜਪਤ ਰਹਹਿ ਗੁਣਤਾਸ II Japat Raheh Guntaas	when one recites hymns (God's Naam, Shabads). God is also a treasure house of all virtues.

Guru Granth Sahib (p. 253, line 17)

ii. LOVE FOR GOD

As God is very much involved in one's happiness, it is necessary to enjoy while remembering God.

The fifth Guru, Arjan Dev, said:

PUNJABI AND ROMAN	ENGLISH
ਅਨਦ ਬਿਨੋਦ ਚੋਜ ਤਮਾਸੇ Anad Binod Choj Tamaasay	Enjoyment, happiness, playful things and entertainment
ਤੁਧੁ ਭਾਵੈ ਸੋ ਹੋਣਾ ਜੀਉ II TuDh Bhaavai So Honaa Jee-o	it all happens only by the will of God.

Guru Granth Sahib (p.100, line 4)

iii. LOVE FOR SPOUSE

In the hymn below it is stated that one should enjoy loving one's spouse. Yet, just as one enjoys loving a spouse, so one should enjoy loving God.

The fifth Guru, Arjan Dev, said:

PUNJABI AND ROMAN	ENGLISH
ਅਨਦ ਬਿਨੋਦ ਤਿਤੈ ਘਰਿ ਸੋਹਹਿ Anad Binod Titai Ghar Soheh	That house has joy and celebration where
ਜੋ ਧਨ ਕੰਤਿ ਸਿਗਾਰੀ ਜੀਉ II Jo Dhan Kant Sigaaree Jee-o.	husband and wife adore each other.

Guru Granth Sahib (p.97, line 16)

iv. LOVE FOR SPORTS

In the example below is given the example of playing sports. Just as one enjoys playing sports, one should enjoy and be happy while remembering God.

The fifth Guru, Arjan Dev, said:

PUNJABI AND ROMAN	**ENGLISH**
ਅਨਦ ਬਿਨੋਦ ਕਰੇ ਦਿਨ ਰਾਤੀ	One enjoys and rejoices day and night
Anad Binod Karay Din Raatee	
ਸਦਾ ਸਦਾ ਹਰਿ ਕੇਲਾ ਜੀਉ ॥	by keeping God forever in the mind
Sadaa Sadaa Har Kaylaa Jee-o	just as one enjoys playing sports.
Guru Granth Sahib (p. 102, line 5)	

v. LOVE FOR FAMILY

There are many types of enjoyment. Life has to be enjoyed with the family. Both father and mother should enjoy the blessings of a child. It all happens with the grace of God.

The fifth Guru, Arjan Dev, said:

PUNJABI AND ROMAN	**ENGLISH**
ਅਨਦ ਕਰਹੁ ਪਿਤ ਮਾਤਾ ॥	Father and mother enjoy and celebrate
Anad Karahu Pit Maataa	with the family (refers to childbirth).
Guru Granth Sahib (p. 627, line 11)	

vi. LOVE FOR NATURE

There is another type of love. God created nature and we all must enjoy it. As chakvi duck enjoys seeing the light of dawn, so we must enjoy nature.

God created all this diversity in nature and in the whole universe, we all must appreciate and enjoy it.

The fifth Guru, Arjan Dev, said:

PUNJABI AND ROMAN	ENGLISH
ਅਨਿਕ ਸੁਖ ਚਕਵੀ	The chakvi duck does not
Anik Sookh Chakvee	
ਨਹੀ ਚਾਹਤ	desire many comforts
Nahee Chaahat	
ਅਨਦ ਪੂਰਨ ਪੇਖਿ ਦੇਂਹ ॥	but completely enjoys
Anad Pooran Paykh DayNh	seeing the dawn.
Guru Granth Sahib (p. 702, line 2)	

vii. LOVE BY GETTING RID OF EVIL THOUGHTS

Another type of enjoyment is to get rid of evil ideas. This is in everyone's control. Though it may not be easy, ridding oneself of evil thoughts must be attempted.

The fifth Guru, Arjan Dev, said:

PUNJABI AND ROMAN	ENGLISH
ਅਨਦ ਕਰਹੁ ਤਜਿ	One should celebrate and be happy when
Anad Karahu Taj	
ਸਗਲ ਬਿਕਾਰ ॥	one abandons bad things (sins, corruption etc).
Sagal Bikaar	
Guru Granth Sahib (p. 899, line 19)	

viii. LOVE FOR COMPANY OF PEOPLE

Meeting other people is also an enjoyment. God teaches us to honor and respect one another.

The fifth Guru, Arjan Dev, said:

PUNJABI AND ROMAN	ENGLISH
ਅਨਦੁ ਕਰਹੁ ਮਿਲਿ	Enjoy meeting each other
Anad Karahu Mil	
ਸੁੰਦਰ ਨਾਰੀ ॥	O' beautiful women.
Sundar Naaree	
Guru Granth Sahib (p. 806, line 13)	

ix. LOVE FOR RECITING GOD'S PRAISES

Happiness, enjoyment and peace of mind come from the singing (reciting) of Hymns, in praise of God.

The fifth Guru, Arjan Dev, said:

PUNJABI AND ROMAN

ਸੁਖ ਸਹਜ ਆਨਦੁ ਘਣਾ
Sookh Sahj Aanad Ghanaa
ਹਰਿ ਕੀਰਤਨੁ ਗਾਉ ॥
Har Keertan Gaa-o

Guru Granth Sahib (p. 400, line 19)

ENGLISH

In order to obtain happiness, peace of mind and great enjoyment one should sing (recite) and comprehend hymns (God's Naam, Shabads).

4. HOW TO ENJOY UNIVERSALITY OF THE SIKH RELIGION

There are several things one can do in one's day-to-day life to enjoy the Universality of the Sikh Religion. They are five principles of Sikh Religion and are summarized below.

i. ***Lead honest work ethic. For details see chapter 7.***
ii. ***Share your blessings with less fortunate. For details see chapter 8.***
iii. ***Believe and put into practice equality for all. For details see chapter 9.***
iv. ***Pray to God daily. For details see chapter 10.***
v. ***Live a Truthful life. For details see Chapter 11.***

5. SUMMARY

If one enjoys doing something, chances are they will do it more often. Enjoy the diversity created by God. Enjoy loving people. The two ceremonies of Anand Sahib and Anand Karaj start with the heading of enjoyment. When one's mind, body and soul are in tune with God, one obtains peace of mind. God is present everywhere and everything happens according to God's will. The marriage ceremony is for enjoyment. The Four Lavaans (the walking of bride and bridegroom four times around the Guru Granth Sahib) lead one to righteousness, good character and happiness. God is present within all and everyone is equal in all respects. God's grace is the most important factor in life, including marriage.

The word enjoy is mentioned at least 209 times in Guru Granth Sahib and has been used by five Gurus and three Bhagats. There are many different types of enjoyment. They include love for God, love for spouse, love for sports, love for family, love for nature, love for people, and love for reciting God's praises. There are many ways to enjoy. Some of them are living an honest life, sharing your blessings, believing in and practicing equality for all, praying to God daily, and living a Truthful life.

6. EXERCISES

I. Why is the enjoyment of religion important in Sikhism?
ii. Name two ceremonies that start with heading of enjoyment.
iii. List some of the salient points of Anand Sahib (Enjoyment with peace of mind).
iv. List some of the salient points of each of the Four Lavaans in Anand Karaj (Marriage to enjoy).
v. How many times does the word "enjoyment" occur in the Guru Granth Sahib?
vi. What are different types of enjoyment and explain the importance of some of them.
vii. What should one do in life to enjoy the Universality of the Sikh Religion?

UNIVERSALITY OF THE SIKH RELIGION

CHAPTER 13

HOW TO END CONFLICTS AND FIGHTING

Peace is universal and the whole world needs it. There are eleven rules as prescribed in the Guru Granth Sahib that can be carried out by all people to resolve any conflict. Conflicts and disagreements are present to a varying degree in all human beings. This happens at all levels, between families, friends, religious places, businesses, work places and countries. Such conflict leads to ill will and destruction. Most of the problems of the world can be resolved if people sit together and discuss with an open mind and in a conciliatory way. The solution lies within us and requires control of mind and body, to overcome the conflicts.

Confrontation, in life, is easy but to compromise and live in peace and harmony is very difficult.

Conflicts and fights, if not prevented or checked, can lead to problems among families, people, religions and countries all over the world. Peace and prosperity throughout the world is very important. Above all the most important thing is peace of mind. If all problems are discussed and compromised on a reasonable basis, then all will have peace of mind and misery will end.

If all people are equal and everyone respects all religions there will be no need to fight based upon religion and superiority. Another reason for fighting is economic disparities among people as well as among nations. The solution to this problem is education. There is no quick fix. It takes long time to educate a nation. Similarly, it takes long time for industrial progress in any country.

Even if we fight eventually it has to end.

1. FAMILY CONFLICTS

Every family has disputes, disagreements and sometimes even fighting. It would be useful to eliminate bickering or at least reduce it to a minimum. Do not look for perfection in your spouse. Learn how to compromise and bend a little rather than break. In case of conflict each spouse should pause and think, "What are we fighting for? Is it worth fighting about? Why not compromise and live peacefully. Healthy criticism is a very welcome sign that should lead to a reasonable compromise in order to resolve conflict.

FAMILY LIFE AND MATHEMATICS

Mathematically 1 and 1 leads to three different answers. Similary when two people marry it could lead to three family situations.

i. ONE PLUS ONE EQUAL TWO

When husband and wife live together ***they end up as two people with one spirit.*** They resolve their differences amicably. Their children will learn how amicably their parents are living and will try to emulate them. As one plus one become two with more power similarly two people have more strength in dealing with day-to-day life situations.

Guru Granth Sahib, The Universal Holy Book, has described clearly how husband and wife should live together.

The third Guru, Amar Das, said:

PUNJABI AND ROMAN	**ENGLISH**
ਧਨ ਪਿਰੁ ਏਹਿ ਨ ਆਖੀਅਨਿ Dhan Pir Ayhi Na Aakhee-an	They are not husband and wife
ਬਹਨਿ ਇਕਠੇ ਹੋਇ ॥ Bahan Ikthay Ho-ay	who just live together.
ਏਕ ਜੋਤਿ ਦੁਇ ਮੂਰਤੀ Ayk Jot Du-ay Moortee	When they have one spirit and two bodies
ਧਨ ਪਿਰੁ ਕਹੀਐ ਸੋਇ ॥ Dhan Pir Kahee-ai So-ay	then they are truly husband and wife.

Guru Granth Sahib (p. 788, line12)

ii. ONE NEXT TO ONE EQUAL ELEVEN

If a 1 is put next to another 1, the mathematical answer is 11. Eleven is much more powerful than one. Similarly when two families along with the husband and wife stand together, their power to resolve daily problems increases tremendously (simile as one becoming eleven).

Years ago, when marriages were arranged, the closeness of the families was paramount. It helped resolve many of the problems that are faced by the newly married young couples. This situation applies equally well for the families of the young couple who select their own partners. If the families get together and show compassion for each other, the newly married couple will emulate the family togetherness. As they say, "Lead by example." The young couple learns more from the honest and hard work performed daily by the elders of the two families. This brings the families together. The new couple learns the strength of the families that leads to the welfare of the community and, eventually, to the prosperity of the whole world.

iii. ONE DIVIDED BY ONE EQUALS ONE

One divided by one, the answer is 1. This is exactly the situation ***when husband and wife are fighting with each other and then end up divided.*** They are separated and become single again. This is the worst situation. This can be avoided if we follow the Guru Granth Sahib, that children are the binding forces in a successful marriage.

The first Guru, Nanak, said:

PUNJABI AND ROMAN	**ENGLISH**
ਗੋਰੀ ਸੇਤੀ ਤੁਟੈ ਭਤਾਰੁ II Goree Saytee Tutai Bhataar	If husband and wife break off,
ਪੁਤੀਂ ਗੰਢੁ ਪਵੈ ਸੰਸਾਰਿ II PuteeN Gandh Pavai Sansaar	the birth of a child keeps them united.

Guru Granth Sahib (p.143, line10)

2. PERSONAL INCIDENTS

Everyone has experienced incidents that create friction, but it can be easily avoided. I will just give two such incidents that happened to me.

i. IN THE GURDWARA

While attending the services at Glen Cove Gurdwara of the Sikhs in Long Island, New York in December 1999, I was observing the model of the future additions and renovations to the Gurdwara. It was a very impressive and I was pleased with the changes . Another family with two teenage children came over and began looking at it. There is a provision for tennis courts and I asked their son if he played tennis. He replied that he did. I then turned to his father and said all this can be accomplished if we do not fight amongst ourselves. To my utter surprise, he said fighting is a part of us. Without any comment I just went inside the Gurdwara hall. ***How can any organization succeed and achieve its objectives if fighting is ingrained in our minds?*** People that have this type of thinking are present in all communities and religions. Problems arise when such people become part of the management. Normal peace-loving people, generally, do not get involved when force is used in the religious places. The Gurdwara is a place for obtaining peace of mind and not for politics or infighting. It sets a very poor example for the coming generations.

ii. AT A WEDDING CEREMONY

A few years ago we went to a Jewish wedding of a close friend's son. While the festivities were going on, a gentleman (father of the bridegroom) seeing my turban came to me. He started asking questions about the Sikh religion. He asked how much the Shiromani Gurdwara Parbhandak Committee of Amritsar, Punjab (the religious organization that controls all historic Gurudwaras in Punjab, Himachel Pardesh and Haryana in India) is involved in running the Sikh Gurdwaras in the USA and Canada. First I was very surprised by his question. I told him that they have no legal control over any Gurdwara in America or Canada. He then told me that he was an attorney and that he represented one party of a Virginia Gurdwara currently in litigation. He mentioned a list of many Gurdwaras in the USA and Canada that were also involved in litigation. I was amazed how much he knew about infighting among the Sikh Gurdwaras. ***It is a shame that Sikhs want their religious disputes to be decided by the courts.***

3. ROLE OF SILENT MAJORITY

It is also true that good, honest, God fearing people do not want to get involved in religious organizations. They are so busy in their work and family that they want to stay away from these organizations. But on the other hand it affects their family as well and also the coming generations. There will be chaos if good people do not come forward in large numbers (sometimes called silent majority) and take an active part in the religious organization to which they belong. If the organizations are left in incompetent people, they will not preach the religion but will become involved in petty fighting.

If people do not fight, there will be Universal Prosperity.

4. ELEVEN RULES TO END CONFLICTS

We should not go to courts to resolve our petty jealousies and differences. Guru Nanak addressed the problems of conflicts and disagreements. We all can stop conflicts and fighting if we follow the eleven rules as prescribed in the Guru Granth Sahib.

In order to resolve the conflicts, Guru Granth Sahib emphasized one word called Mandaa that has many meanings depending the context in which it is used. Some of the ways to express Mandaa in English are ill, hate, humble, bad, inferior, ignorant, evil and wicked. This illustrates the beauty of the Punjabi language: one word is described eight different ways. Eight out of eleven rules use the word Mandaa.

Let us discuss the eleven rules one by one in order to end conflict.

RULE NUMBER 1

DO NOT SAY ILL OF ANY ONE

The question of fighting will not cross the mind

The first Guru, Nanak, said:

PUNJABI AND ROMAN	**ENGLISH**
ਮੰਦਾ ਕਿਸੈ ਨ ਆਖਿ	Do not speak ill of anyone as it
Mandaa Kisai Na Aakh	
ਝਗੜਾ ਪਾਵਣਾ ॥	leads to arguments and conflicts.
Jhagrhaa Paavnaa	
Guru Granth Sahib (p. 566, line 6)	

In just six words Guru Nanak showed how the problems of the whole world could be solved. Do not speak ill of anyone. If we follow that doctrine, there would no longer be conflict or fighting. We should respect each other's views and always find a compromise in order to live in peace and harmony.

People who are respected, admired and held in esteem have one thing in common: a positive attitude. They do not criticize, ridicule or tear others down. They are quick to compliment people but do not use flattery.

People with a positive attitude always find solutions to problems and bad thoughts never enter their minds.

RULE NUMBER 2

CONSIDER ENEMY AS FRIEND

Friends do not fight

The fifth Guru, Arjan Dev, said:

PUNJABI AND ROMAN	ENGLISH
ਏਹ ਵੈਰੀ ਮਿਤ੍ਰ ਸਭਿ ਕੀਤਿਆ	I consider all my enemies as friends
Ayh Vairee Mitar Sabh Keeti-aa	
ਨਹ ਮੰਗਹਿ ਮੰਦਾ ॥	and I do not hate anyone.
Nah Mangeh Mandaa	
Guru Granth Sahib (p.1096, line 17)	

It is not easy to treat an enemy as your friend. It is said time is the best healer. If you have a disagreement with someone, take a break and then eventually all will be forgotten. Later you will be ready to talk to that person in a very conciliatory tone and the matter will be resolved amicably. The animosity will change to friendship, which will, in turn, bring peace of mind.

Below, the qualities of a good friend are enumerated.

1. A good friend is honest enough to tell the truth when others are simply flattering.

2. A good friend is one who believes in me after I have earned his/her trust.

3. A good friend is one who encourages me to dream the impossible and tells me that I can do it.

4. A good friend is one who helps me when I am in trouble.

5. A good friend is one who forgives me and tells me when I have made a mistake.

Appreciate the good qualities of a person and be a good friend.

RULE NUMBER 3

CONSIDER YOURSELF VERY HUMBLE

With no superiority complex, the desire to quarrel is gone

The first Guru, Nanak, said:

PUNJABI AND ROMAN	ENGLISH
ਮੰਦਾ ਜਾਣੈ ਆਪ ਕਉ	Consider yourself as very humble
Mandaa Jaanai Aap Ka-o	
ਅਵਰੁ ਭਲਾ ਸੰਸਾਰੁ ॥	while all others are full of virtues.
Avar Bhalaa Sansaar	
Guru Granth Sahib (p. 991, line 10)	

We always say that the other person is at fault. This is done just to preserve our ego. However, if one admits the fault and apologizes, then the whole matter is finished. (No one is perfect, except God.) The person admitting the fault will have peace of mind and will remove any aggravation that may have ensued. One will be contented if one practices humility, while believing in the virtuousness of others. When one genuinely dislikes something it can be discussed in a very constructive and polite way to convey one's point of view.

Being humble will remove any superiority complex and the desire to quarrel will vanish.

RULE NUMBER 4

DO NOT CALL ANY ONE BAD

Helping people truthfully with no animosity will destroy any desire to fight.

The first Guru, Nanak, said:

PUNJABI AND ROMAN	ENGLISH
ਕਿਸ ਹੀ ਮੰਦਾ ਆਖਿ ਨ ਛਲੈ	Do not call any one else bad
Kis Hee Mandaa Aakh Na Chalai	and make this your way of life,
ਸਚਿ ਖਰਾ ਸਚਿਆਰਾ ਹੇ ॥	and speaking truth will lead one to
Sach Kharaa Sachi-aaraa Hay	truthful living.
Guru Granth Sahib (p. 1027, line 11)	

How many times we call people bad especially if they are not present at that time. Many people start feeling superior by calling others bad. It is better to express your view to the person directly, in a kind and conciliatory way, in order to help him/her. This way you will be doing something good that will be very constructive, and, in turn, it will be appreciated.

If the same God made us all, then I cannot judge who is good or bad.

RULE NUMBER 5

DO NOT CONSIDER ANY-ONE AS INFERIOR

This will lead one to peaceful life.

The first Guru, Nanak, said:

PUNJABI AND ROMAN	**ENGLISH**
ਮੰਦਾ ਕਿਸੈ ਨ ਆਖੀਐ	No one should be considered as inferior
Mandaa Kisai Na Aakhee-ai	
ਪੜਿ ਅਖਰੁ ਏਹੋ ਬੁਝੀਐ ॥	and comprehend this by reading these
Parh Akhar Ayho Bujhee-ai	words.
ਮੂਰਖੈ ਨਾਲਿ ਨ ਲੁਝੀਐ ॥	Do not argue with a prejudiced person.
Moorkhai Naal Na Lujhee-ai	
Guru Granth Sahib (p. 473, line 13)	

Many times we start feeling superior because we have lot of money or lot of power or we begin to believe that we belong to a higher status in life. Sometimes we even start condemning the people we think are inferior. All human beings are equal. There is no superior or inferior. The more one is learned, the more humble one should be. We should try to emulate like the tree: the more fruit it bears, the more it bends, but it still maintains its majestic look.

One should not get tangled with one who is not willing to understand others points of view. There is an old proverb, "You can awaken a person who is sleeping but you can not awaken one who is pretending to be asleep". When confronted with a person, who is not rational and not willing to reason, it is better to leave.

Do not argue with an idiot. People watching from a distance may have rough time distinguishing who is who.

RULE NUMBER 6
NO ONE IS BORN EVIL

Do not associate with evil society and there will be no fighting.

The first Guru, Nanak, said:

PUNJABI AND ROMAN	ENGLISH
ਨਾ ਕੋ ਮੂਰਖੁ ਮੰਦਾ II Naa Ko Moorakh Mandaa Guru Granth Sahib (p. 359, line 16)	No one is born an ignorant or evil person.

No one is born evil. Sometimes, however, the bad influence of society can lead one to perform evil things. Some of the societal evils include murder, adultery, theft, false witness and slander. Five others evils are excessive lust, excessive anger, excessive greed, excessive ego and excessive pride. It may not be possible to eliminate evil, but can be controlled. The formula for controlling evil is explained below:.

Tuning mind, body and soul to praising the bounties provided by God, will definitely make a better human being, devoid of evil thoughts.

RULE NUMBER 7

PERFORM GOOD DEEDS

Good deeds will lead to a peaceful mind and will thus eliminate fighting.

The fifth Guru, Arjan Dev, said:

PUNJABI AND ROMAN	ENGLISH
ਮੰਦਾ ਮੂਲਿ ਨ ਉਪਜਿਓ Mandaa Mool Na Upji-o	Evil never originates in me
ਤਰੇ ਸਚੀ ਕਾਰੈ ਲਾਗਿ ਜੀਉ II Taray Sachee Kaarai Laag Jee-o Guru Granth Sahib (p. 132, line12)	and performing truthful deed is my way of life.

Many times we think of evil only in relation to others. Perhaps it is due to jealousy or just thinking negatively. The mind needs to be reminded that it needs to perform good deeds. This will lift your spirit. Your mind will be calm and your body will generate good chemicals. This will bring glow in your face and you will feel satisfied that you have accomplished something worthwhile.

Without good deeds there will be chaos in this world.

RULE NUMBER 8

KEEP YOUR MIND FREE OF WICKED PEOPLE

This will always keep one from fighting.

The fifth Guru, Arjan Dev said:

PUNJABI AND ROMAN

ਨਾ ਕੋ ਦੁਸਮਨੁ ਦੋਖੀਆ
Naa Ko Dusman Dokhee-aa
ਨਾਹੀ ਕੋ ਮੰਦਾ ॥
Naahee Ko Mandaa
Guru Granth Sahib (p. 400, line 17)

ENGLISH

I have no enemy or known an
evil-minded person
nor is any one wicked to me.

If one keeps away from people who are evil-minded or wicked, then there is no one to fight. It may not be easy but in the long run it will bring peace of mind. Always be in the company of God fearing, people-loving individuals. It will bring contentment and compassion. Life will then be worth living.

Why to commit evil when we have to suffer the consequences.

RULE NUMBER 9

CONSIDER NO ONE AS STRANGER

Without an enemy, there is no one to fight.

The fifth Guru, Arjan Dev, said:

PUNJABI AND ROMAN	**ENGLISH**
ਨਾ ਕੋ ਬੈਰੀ ਨਹੀ ਬਿਗਾਨਾ Naa Ko Bairee Nahee Bigaanaa ਸਗਲ ਸੰਗਿ ਹਮ ਕਉ ਬਨਿ ਆਈ ॥ Sagal Sang Ham Ka-o Ban Aa-ee Guru Granth Sahib (p.1299, line15)	No one is my enemy and none is a stranger and I am a friend of all.

When one considers no one as an enemy and treats all people as friends then peace is achieved. Life is too short to hold grudges against anyone. You may not like a person and may have a difference of opinion, but still there is no need to be bitter about it. Bitterness leads to stress, which cause anxiety, which is the root cause of many diseases.

In order to be a friend of all, one needs to have self-esteem and to show respect (izzat in Punjabi) toward one's community.

To earn respect, a person must have the following qualities.

1. **Is honest in day-to-day dealings.**

2. **Gives constructive suggestions to resolve disputes.**

3. **Is sincere when complimenting others.**

4. **Is dependable in time of need.**

5. **Is well motivated to achieve worthwhile results.**

6. **Is loyal in protecting people when they are being unfairly criticized.**

7. **Is dependable so that their word is better than a legal document.**

Self-esteem has to be earned and cannot be bought.

RULE NUMBER 10

UNIVERSAL BROTHERHOOD

If all are brothers, there is no need for fighting.

The first Guru, Nanak, said:

PUNJABI AND ROMAN	ENGLISH
ਆਈ ਪੰਥੀ	Let universal brotherhood be
Aa-ee Panthee	
ਸਗਲ ਜਮਾਤੀ ॥	your highest aspiration in life.
Sagal Jamaatee	
Guru Granth Sahib (p. 6, line 17)	

Guru Nanak preached universal brotherhood wherever he went. This is one of the most important tenants of the Universality of the Sikh Religion. If one can control oneself by exercising the powers of the mind then it is akin to capturing the whole world. The prayer of the Sikh Religion ends as below.

LET THERE BE UNIVERSAL PROSPERITY.

RULE NUMBER 11

GOD IS IN EVERYBODY

This will eliminate the desire to fight.

The first Guru, Nanak, said:

PUNJABI AND ROMAN	ENGLISH
ਬੁਰਾ ਭਲਾ ਕਹੁ ਕਿਸ ਨੋ ਕਹੀਐ ॥	Whom shall I call bad or good,
Buraa Bhalaa Kaho Kis No Kahee-ai	
ਦੀਸੈ ਬ੍ਰਹਮੁ ॥	when the same God is present
Deesai Barahm	in all.
Guru Granth Sahib (p. 353, line10)	

Guru Nanak reiterated many times that when people really believe that God is in every human being there would be no prejudice, discord or enmity in our outlook. Prejudices and discord come into our consciousness because of our ignorance of not knowing that the same God is the creator of us all. If God is present in all and we all are equal—we cannot judge others as good or bad. Those who love God will always consider equality as truth and truth will lead to truthful living.

There is no high or low. All human beings are equal.

The same God having different names is present in all human beings and in the universe.

5. SUMMARY

Conflicts and fighting cannot be eliminated but can be reduced. The best way to end conflict is to come a compromise in a peaceful way. Remember always that fighting eventually has to end, so try to end it quickly. Every family has disputes and fights. If the families live in harmony then everyone benefits. If the couple quarrels, this leads to divorce and everyone loses. Fighting especially in a religious place brings disgrace to the whole community. Universal prosperity is bound to occur if people stop fighting. It has been observed that good and honest people do not want to get involved in religious organizations. This is true in those organizations that use force to settle the disputes. There will be chaos if good people do nothing.

The Sikh Religion laid down 11 rules to end conflicts and fighting. These are all spelled out in the Guru Granth Sahib. They are

1. Do not speak ill of anyone.
2. Consider enemy as friend.
3. Consider yourself very humble.
4. Do not label anyone as bad.
5. Do not consider others as inferior.
6. No one is born evil.
7. Perform good deeds.
8. Keep your mind free of wicked people.
9. Consider no one as stranger.
10. Universal brotherhood should be the goal.
11. God is in every body, so we cannot judge others as good or bad.

6. EXERCISES

i. Discuss while reading mathematics of one and one and the corresponding three family situations which situation relates to your life and why.

ii. Can you explain why people have an inner desire toward conflict and not compromise?

iii. Arrange the eleven rules to end conflicts as prescribed in the Guru Granth Sahib, according to your way of thinking, putting the most important on top. Give reasons why you arranged the rules in that particular way.

UNIVERSALITY OF THE SIKH RELIGION

CHAPTER 14

HAUME AND FIVE PASSIONS
(No English equivalent word for Haume)

Everyone has Haume but excessive Haume is bad

1. HAUME

Haume is the equivalent to the sum of the five passions or any one of them or any combination of them. The five passions are lust, anger, greed, ego and pride. In Punjabi they are called Kaam, Karood, Lobh, Moo and Hankar, respectively.

Since there is no English equivalent for it, the Punjabi word Haume will be used exclusively. ***Haume is part and parcel of every human being. It is not bad if kept under control.*** This chapter will provide ways in which to reduce it.

The five passions associated with Haume are described below.

KAAM is excessive LUST is a strong desire for sex without feelings of love and affection. It is also a strong desire for power, money, or for any other *thing*.

KAROOD is excessive ANGER, fury, and resentment accompanied by the desire to punish without due process.

LOBH is excessive GREED in order to have more than one's share.

MOO is excessive EGO—the "me, me and me" focus.

HANKAR is excessive PRIDE—always having very high opinion of oneself.

It should, however, be made clear that the five passions, if controlled properly, are beneficial to the individual and the society at large. ***Haume cannot be eliminated in practical life but can be harnessed.***

A person excessively attached to Haume considers only "Me, Me and Me." Every human being has Haume and the five passions. God gave us the five passions for some definite purpose. As long as Haume (five passions of Kaam, Karood, Lobh, Moo, and Hankar) is under control, then all is well. The trouble starts when Haume becomes excessive in everyday life. A question that is often asked, "How do I know when Haume is excessive?" There are no set rules for that. Only one's conscience can tell when Haume is in excess. Guru Nanak made it very clear that Haume, when controlled, can produce good things and that excessive Haume produces bad things. Guru Nanak also gave us ways to control Haume.

Dr. I. J. Singh [1] has described that the passion and feelings that underlie lust, anger, greed, ego and pride are universal in nature. They are not evil but are the driving force of life. Dr. Singh further says that in Gurdwaras one hears endless sermons to destroy these five evils from one's life. ***If these five passions were destroyed completely, one would become a person with no feeling, no wishes, no passion, no pain, and no pleasure.*** There was a reason why that God gave everyone these five passions. It is the excess of these passions that is detrimental. However, one has to tame them and use them wisely for one's betterment and the good of the society.

i. HAUME AS PART OF OUR LIFE

Guru Nanak clearly said that Haume is part of our life and these passions start when we are born and end when we die. Haume plays a part in every aspect of our life. If Haume is under your control then all your deeds bear good fruit. On the other hand too much attachment to Haume can ruin one's life, which leads to others losing respect for that person.

The first Guru, Nanak, used Ha-o as short word for Haume and said

PUNJABI AND ROMAN	**ENGLISH**
ਹਉ ਵਿਚਿ ਆਇਆ ਹਉ ਵਿਚਿ ਗਇਆ ॥	With Haume we come and
Ha-o Vich Aa-i-aa Ha-o Vich Ga-i-aa	with Haume we depart.
ਹਉ ਵਿਚਿ ਜੰਮਿਆ ਹਉ ਵਿਚਿ ਮੁਆ ॥	With Haume we are born
Ha-o Vich Jammi-aa Ha-o Vich Mu-aa	and with Haume we die.
ਹਉ ਵਿਚਿ ਦਿਤਾ ਹਉ ਵਿਚਿ ਲਇਆ ॥	With Haume we give
Ha-o Vich Ditaa Ha-o Vich La-i-aa	and with Haume we get.

ਹਉ ਵਿਚਿ ਖਟਿਆ ਹਉ ਵਿਚਿ ਗਇਆ II Ha-o Vich Khati-aa Ha-o Vich Ga-i-aa	With Haume we earn and with Haume we lose.
ਹਉ ਵਿਚਿ ਸਚਿਆਰੁ ਕੂੜਿਆਰੁ II Ha-o Vich Sachiaar Koori-aar	With Haume we become true or false.
ਹਉ ਵਿਚਿ ਪਾਪ ਪੁੰਨ ਵੀਚਾਰੁ II Ha-o Vich Paap Punn Veechaar	With Haume we reflect on vice or virtue.
ਹਉ ਵਿਚਿ ਨਰਕਿ ਸੁਰਗਿ ਅਵਤਾਰੁ II Ha-o Vich Narak Surag Avtaar	With Haume we go to heaven or hell.
ਹਉ ਵਿਚਿ ਹਸੈ ਹਉ ਵਿਚਿ ਰੋਵੈ II Ha-o Vich Hasai Ha-o Vich Rovai	With Haume we laugh or we weep.
ਹਉ ਵਿਚਿ ਮੂਰਖੁ ਹਉ ਵਿਚਿ ਸਿਆਣਾ II Ha-0 Vich Moorakh Ha-o Vich Si-aanaa	With Haume we become foolish and with Haume we become wise.
ਹਉਮੈ ਕਰਿ ਕਰਿ ਜੰਤ ਉਪਾਇਆ II Haume Kar Kar Jant Upaa-i-aa	With Haume all human beings are created.
ਹਉਮੈ ਬੂਝੈ ਤਾ ਦਰੁ ਸੂਝੈ II Haume Boojhai Taa Dar Soojhai Guru Granth Sahib (p.466, line10)	When we understand & control Haume, then God is revealed.

ii. CURE FOR HAUME

Second Guru Angad explained very clearly that we live with Haume all the time. Excessive ***Haume can be considered a disease but within Haume is the medicine to cure it.*** The medicine is to remember God's Name and then excessive Haume will be controlled.

The second Guru, Angad Dev, said:

PUNJABI AND ROMAN	ENGLISH
ਹਉਮੈ ਏਹਾ ਜਾਤਿ ਹੈ Haume Ayhaa Jaat Hai	It is the nature of Haume
ਹਉਮੈ ਕਰਮ ਕਮਾਹਿ II Haume Karam Kamaahi	that with Haume we do everything.
ਹਉਮੈ ਏਈ ਬੰਧਨਾ Haume Ayee BanDhanaa	When one is excessively attached to Haume

ਫਿਰਿ ਫਿਰਿ ਜੋਨੀ ਪਾਹਿ ॥ Fir Fir Jonee Paahi	then one enters the transmigration of soul.
ਹਉਮੈ ਕਿਥਹੁ ਊਪਜੈ Haume Kithhu Oopjai	From where did Haume come?
ਕਿਤੁ ਸੰਜਮਿ ਇਹ ਜਾਇ ॥ Kit Sanjam Ih Jaa-ay	and how it can be removed?
ਹਉਮੈ ਏਹੋ ਹੁਕਮੁ ਹੈ Haume Ayho Hukam Hai	It is God's command that due to excessive Haume
ਪਇਐ ਕਿਰਤਿ ਫਿਰਾਹਿ ॥ Pa-i-ai Kirat Firaahi	one wanders according to their past actions.
ਹਉਮੈ ਦੀਰਘ ਰੋਗੁ ਹੈ Haume Deeragh Rog Hai	Excessive Haume is like a chronic disease and
ਦਾਰੂ ਭੀ ਇਸੁ ਮਾਹਿ ॥ Daaroo Bhee Is Maahi	within Haume also lies the medicine that cures.
ਕਿਰਪਾ ਕਰੇ ਜੇ ਆਪਣੀ Kirpaa Karay Jay Aapnee	Medicine comes through God's mercy and that
ਤਾ ਗੁਰ ਕਾ ਸਬਦੁ ਕਮਾਹਿ ॥ Taa Gur Kaa Sabad Kamaahi	medicine is to keep God's name in your mind.
ਨਾਨਕੁ ਕਹੈ ਸੁਣਹੁ ਜਨਹੁ Naanak Kahai Sunhu Janhu	Nanak says that you listen carefully and that
ਇਤੁ ਸੰਜਮਿ ਦੁਖ ਜਾਹਿ ॥ It Sanjam Dukh Jaahi	is the way the malady of Haume departs.

Guru Granth Sahib (p. 466, line 16)

iii. HAUME AND SIMPLE ANALOGIES

Guru Nanak used everyday analogies to set people on the right path. His real life examples included: ***an excessively greedy person is like a stray dog, falsehood is like filth, cheating is like eating a dead body, slander is like eating filth and anger is like a fire that burns.***

The first Guru, Nanak, said:

PUNJABI AND ROMAN	ENGLISH
ਲਬੁ ਕੁਤਾ Lab Kutaa	An excessively greedy person is like a stray dog (who wanders every where) while
ਕੂੜੁ ਚੂਹੜਾ Koorh Choohrhaa	falsehood is like a filth which must be swept just as a street-sweeper cleans the dirt

ਠਗਿ ਖਾਧਾ ਮੁਰਦਾਰੁ ॥	cheating is like eating a rotten dead
Thag KhaaDhaa Murdaar	body (carcass).
ਪਰ ਨਿੰਦਾ ਪਰ ਮਲੁ ਮੁਖਿ ਸੁਧੀ	Slandering others is putting the filth of
Par Nindaa Par Mal Mukh SuDhee	others into your own mouth and
ਅਗਨਿ ਕ੍ਰੋਧੁ ਚੰਡਾਲੁ ॥	excessive anger is like a fire, that burns
Agan KroDh Chandaal	the body just like in a crematorium.
Guru Granth Sahib (p.15, line 9)	

iv. HOW TO CONTROL EXCESSIVE HAUME

There are several ways a person can control excessive Haume. Some of the ways given below can be integrated into one's day-to-day life.

A. BY SINGING HYMNS

The first Guru, Nanak, said:

PUNJABI AND ROMAN	ENGLISH
ਅਨਹਦ ਬਾਣੀ ਪਾਈਐ	By singing hymns in praise of God
Anhad Banee Paa-ee-ai	
ਤਹ ਹਉਮੈ ਹੋਇ ਬਿਨਾਸੁ ॥	then excessive Haume can be
Tah Haume Hoay Binaas	controlled.
Guru Granth Sahib (p. 21, line 3)	

B. BY KEEPING GOD'S NAME IN YOUR MIND

Always keep God's name in your mind. That does not mean that one should stop working or stop carrying out family and social responsibilities. Keeping God with you will give peace of mind.

The third Guru, Amar Das, said:

PUNJABI AND ROMAN	ENGLISH
ਹਰਿ ਕਾ ਨਾਮੁ ਮਨਿ ਵਸੈ	By preserving God's name in your
Har Kaa Naam Man Vasai	mind then
ਹਉਮੈ ਕ੍ਰੋਧੁ ਨਿਵਾਰਿ ॥	excessive Haume and excessive anger
Haume KroDh Nivaar	can be controlled.
Guru Granth Sahib (p. 33, line 17)	

C. BY REDUCING DESIRE FOR PASSIONS

Guru Nanak explained how to attain God. It can be done by reducing the desire for excessive power, the desire for excessive sex, and the desire for other women or men. One should also eliminate lying and backbiting, they should reduce his/her love for money, and should decrease excessive pride**. *It should, however, be clear that it is always the excessive passions that are bad. Passions under control are normal.*** We cannot completely eliminate them, but we can always control them.

The fourth Guru, Ram Das, said:

PUNJABI AND ROMAN	ENGLISH
ਪਰਹਰਿ ਕਾਮ ਕ੍ਰੋਧੁ ਝੂਠੁ ਨਿੰਦਾ	Reduce the strong desire for power,
Parhar Kaam KaroDh Jhooth Nindaa	money,fighting and the excessive desire for sex, excessive anger, renounce telling lies, backbiting and
ਤਜਿ ਮਾਇਆ ਅਹੰਕਾਰੁ ਚੁਕਾਵੈ ॥	reduce love for money and eliminate
Taj Maa-i-aa AhaNkaar Chukaavai	excessive pride.
ਤਜਿ ਕਾਮੁ ਕਾਮਿਨੀ ਮੋਹੁ ਤਜੈ	Eliminate your desire for other women,
Taj Kaam Kaaminee Moh Tajai	reduce love for worldly things
ਤਾ ਅੰਜਨ ਮਾਹਿ ਨਿਰੰਜਨੁ ਪਾਵੈ ॥	only then you shall obtain the bright light
Taa Anjan Maahi Niranjan Paavai	of God amidst the darkness of the world.
Guru Granth Sahib (p.141, line 13)	

D. BY TUNING YOUR MIND, BODY AND SOUL TO GOD

Sincerely believing in God and keeping your mind, body and soul tuned to God can reduce the excessive influence of passions.

The first Guru, Nanak, said:

PUNJABI AND ROMAN	ENGLISH
ਕਾਮੁ ਕ੍ਰੋਧੁ ਅਹੰਕਾਰੁ ਬਿਨਸੈ	Excessive Lust, Excessive anger and
Kaam Karood Hankar Binsee	excessive pride can be reduced
ਮਿਲੈ ਸਤਿਗੁਰ ਦੇਵ ॥	when you are in tune with True God
Milai Satgur Dayv	(with mind, body and soul).
Guru Granth Sahib (page 405, line 10)	

2. PASSION # 1—KAAM THE EXCESSIVE LUST

Kaam (or lust) is the excessive desire for sex without feeling for love and affection. ***Lust also includes the excessive desire for power, money and for fighting.*** Human nature is such that we are prone toward lust. As long as lust is not excessive, it could be used for the benefit of the society. Everyone wants to have some sex, some power, some money and to fight for what is right and just. God gave us this passion of lust, but we need to use it properly. However, if we go overboard, then Kaam (excessive lust) takes over and brings misery and destruction. Four types of lust are described below.

i. TYPES OF LUST

A. SEX

Sex is a normal desire and has to be fulfilled by the spouse. Without sex the whole world will come to an end. However, if sex is used indiscriminately with all sorts of people without any love, it is then called KAAM (Excessive Lust) and this leads to all sorts of problems for the person and for society as a whole.

B. POWER

Everyone has some sort of power in order to live in this world. In fact it is required in order to accomplish something worthwhile for society. If this power is achieved by trampling the rights of the other people then it is KAAM (Excessive Lust). KAAM can ruin a society.

C. MONEY

Earning money is the right thing to do. It is required for daily life. You cannot take money with you, but you cannot live without it either. There is nothing wrong with money. It is only the excessive love for money—obtained by improper means—that leads to KAAM (Excessive Lust) and takes away peace of mind.

D. FIGHTING

All human beings have a desire to fight. ***If fighting is done for the right cause and the betterment of the society, it is beneficial.*** Fighting does not only refer to the use of force. Persuasion and using logic can be used to achieve the objective. However, if fighting is carried out indiscriminately, without regard for innocent lives then it leads to KAAM (Excessive Lust), which can destroy civilization.

ii. HOW TO CONTROL EXCESSIVE LUST

A. BY KEEPING GOD'S NAME

Guru Nanak said that we are so much involved in worldly pleasures that there is no time or place for the Naam (name) of God. In order to reduce excessive lust one has to control oneself. That is possible only when God's Name is imbedded in one's heart and mind.

The first Guru, Nanak, said:

PUNJABI AND ROMAN	**ENGLISH**
ਰਸੁ ਸੁਇਨਾ ਰਸੁ ਰੁਪਾ ਕਾਮਣਿ ਰਸੁ	The pleasure of gold and silver, the
Ras Su-inaa Ras Rupaa Kaaman Ras	pleasure of women,
ਪਰਮਲ ਕੀ ਵਾਸੁ II	the pleasure of the fragrance of
Parmal Kee Vaas.	Sandalwood.
ਰਸੁ ਘੋੜੇ ਰਸੁ ਸੇਜਾ ਮੰਦਰ ਰਸੁ	The pleasure of horses, the pleasure
Ras Ghorhay Ras Sayjaa Mandar Ras	of a soft bed in a palace,
ਮੀਠਾ ਰਸੁ ਮਾਸੁ II	the pleasure of sweet treats
Meethaa Ras Maas.	and the pleasure of hearty meals.
ਏਤੇ ਰਸ ਸਰੀਰ ਕੇ	These pleasures of the human body
Aytay Ras Sareer Kay	are so numerous
ਕੈ ਘਟਿ ਨਾਮ ਨਿਵਾਸੁ II	How can the Naam, the Name of God
Kai Ghat Naam Nivaas.	find its dwelling in the heart?
Guru Granth Sahib (p.15, line 12)	

B. BY KEEPING FAITH IN GOD

We cannot eliminate lust, but it certainly can be reduced. Guru Arjan, has shown clearly how ***to subdue Kaam (excessive lust) by having complete faith in God.***

The fifth Guru, Arjan Dev, said:

PUNJABI AND ROMAN	**ENGLISH**
ਹੇ ਕਾਮੰ ਨਰਕ ਬਿਸ੍ਰਾਮੰ	Kaam (excessive lust) lands one in hell
Hay KaamaN Narak BisraamaN	

ਬਹੁ ਜੋਨੀ ਭ੍ਰਮਾਵਣਹ ॥ Baho Jonee Bharmaavneh	and makes the soul wander into innumerable species.
ਚਿਤ ਹਰਣੰ ਤ੍ਰੈ ਲੋਕ ਗੰਮ੍ਯ੍ਯੰ Chit HarnaN Tarai Lok Gam-yaN	Lust pervades throughout the three worlds (on this earth, underneath and above the earth), it controls our thinking and excessive lust
ਜਪ ਤਪ ਸੀਲ ਬਿਦਾਰਣਹ ॥ Jap Tap Seel Bidaarneh	destroys meditation, tuning of the mind to God and good qualities.
ਅਲਪ ਸੁਖ ਅਵਿਤ ਚੰਚਲ Alap Sukh Avit Chanchal	Excessive lust gives one little pleasure of very short duration, makes one's thinking bad, is of unsteady nature and
ਊਚ ਨੀਚ ਸਮਾਵਣਹ ॥ Ooch Neech Samaavneh	is present in all people high as well as low.
ਤਵ ਭੈ ਬਿਮੁੰਚਿਤ Tav Bhai BimuNchit	Excessive lust can be subdued by
ਸਾਧ ਸੰਗਮ ਓਟ ਨਾਨਕ ਨਾਰਾਇਣਹ ॥ SaaDh Sangam Ot Naanak Naaraa-ineh	associating with God's devotees, having complete faith in God who is present everywhere, says Nanak.

Guru Granth Sahib (p.1358, line 5)

3. PASSION # 2—KAROOD THE EXCESSIVE ANGER AND STRESS

Karood is not simple anger that may at times be beneficial. Karood is excessive anger gone out of control and leads to destruction of the society. Anger is an emotion, one of many, which is part of all human beings [2]. ***When anger is harnessed properly it can lead to healthy growth of the body and mind.*** Excessive anger and stress are the cause and affect of each other. Anger can easily lead to stress or the stress can provoke anger. Anger is a normal reaction to many things in life. For example, terrorists destroyed the World Trade Center in New York, USA on September 11, 2001. It was an unprovoked act of killing about three thousand innocent people belonging to 60 different countries. Surely all human beings would be justifiably angry. To counteract this menacing, cowardly act a concerted organized effort by the USA is a very normal way to win this war against terrorists. However, if ordinary human beings take the law into their own hands and start killing other innocent people who just by appearance may look different, then anger becomes Karood (excessive anger). This leads to more misery. Instead of solving problems, Karood creates more.

i. KAROOD (EXCESSIVE ANGER) IS LIKE A FIRE

Guru Nanak explained that excessive anger is like a fire that destroys everything.

The first Guru, Nanak, said:

PUNJABI AND ROMAN	**ENGLISH**
ਅਗਨਿ ਕ੍ਰੋਧੁ ਚੰਡਾਲੁ ॥ Agan Karood Chandaal Guru Granth Sahib (p.15, line 10)	Excessive anger is like fire that burns the body as in a crematorium.

ii. HOW EXCESSIVE ANGER MANIFESTS ITSELF

Excessive anger is a hidden killer of the life within us. All people consider excessive anger to be dangerous and destructive. ***Excessive anger causes many illnesses, depression, and violent crimes, including suicides.*** Excessive anger is a leading killer of love, joy, health, happiness, loving relationships, family harmony, success and prosperity. Excessive anger is a killer of everything that is good, lovely, and fair [3].

iii. STRESS AND ANGER (KAROOD)

When a person is unable to cope with the worldly challenges in life, stress takes over. Metabolism, blood pressure, heart and breathing rates increase. There are two ways to handle this—either control it yourself or seek some help. But in practical life we do neither and that is when we run into trouble [4].

Every one of us has felt stress in life at one time or the other. If unchecked it can lead to many diseases, both physical and mental. If it is under control life becomes very meaningful and peace of mind can be maintained.

iv. WHO IS RESPONSIBLE FOR STRESS

In practice, it is not easy to completely get rid of stress in life. However it can be reduced to a manageable level. Excessive anger can be controlled to lead productive and healthy life. ***The choice lies within ourself.*** Excessive anger can be easily triggered by incidents that occurred recently or long time ago. This leads to stress, suffering, sickness, restlessness and loneliness. This is like living in hell.

One can choose love, joy, happiness, health and contentment, which is like living in heaven. Each and every individual has to decide how to reduce his or her excessive anger.

Excessive anger can be self-inflicted by not forgiving or forgetting the incidents that caused it. We know more about our excessive anger, fears and beliefs than anybody else. We need to pay attention to ourselves. Many people have had repressed, excessive anger for long periods, even from childhood. Often they are not even aware of it and consider it normal.

v. HOW TO REDUCE KAROOD (EXCESSIVE ANGER) AND STRESS

As bad news triggers excessive anger, stress takes over. Fifth Guru Arjan Dev (Guru Granth Sahib Page 1357, line 10) said if we consider pain and pleasure the same way, then our mind, body and soul will be at peace and we will have no grudge against any one. Stress will then take a back seat. This is an ideal situation. In life bad things do happen that can cause stress. We also know that everything happens according to God's will and God has a very good purpose for it. Sometimes we may not understand God's way of doing things.

Another way to reduce stress is ***to eat healthy food to boost energy, immunity and mood. Exercising regularly increases endorphins*** (naturally produced chemical substances that alter sensory perception and reaction) and burns calories, which also help to reduce stress [3].

When things are bad one has to learn from the bad and good experiences. It is better to get actively involved and control the situation by dedicating more energy toward solving the problem, rather than sitting passively.

Meditation and praying to God bring in peace of mind, which eliminates stress. Sometimes solitude and reduced stimulation restore your ability to think clearly, be creative, and maintain emotional calm.

Some of the ways to control excessive anger and stress are given below.

A. BY CONTROLLING THE FIGHTING SPIRIT

Guru Arjan explained that excessive anger leads to fighting and many bad habits. God really protects us from Karood, the excessive anger.

The fifth Guru, Arjan Dev, said:

PUNJABI AND ROMAN	ENGLISH
ਹੇ ਕਲਿ ਮੂਲ ਕ੍ਰੋਧੰ Hay Kal Mool KroDha-N ਕਦੰਚ ਕਰੁਣਾ ਨ ਉਪਰਜਤੇ ॥ Kadanch Karunaa Na Uparjatay	Excessive anger is the root cause of fighting and excessive anger has no compassion ever for any one.
ਬਿਖਯੰਤ ਜੀਵੰ ਵਸੵੰ ਕਰੋਤਿ Bikh-yant JeevaN Vas-yaN Karot ਨਿਰਤੵੰ ਕਰੋਤਿ ਜਥਾ ਮਰਕਟਹ ॥ Nirt-yaN Karot Jathaa Marakteh	The sinful people are under the power of excessive anger and they start behaving (dance) like monkeys.
ਅਨਿਕ ਸਾਸਨ ਤਾੜੰਤਿ ਜਮਦੂਤਹ Anik Saasan Taarhant Jamdooteh ਤਵ ਸੰਗੇ ਅਧਮੰ ਨਰਹ ॥ Tav Sangay ADhamaN Narah	Death's courier chastises with all sorts of punishments to people associated with excessive anger and that also lowers their value in society.
ਦੀਨ ਦੁਖ ਭੰਜਨ ਦਯਾਲ ਪ੍ਰਭੁ Deen Dukh Bhanjan Da-yaal Parabh ਨਾਨਕ ਸਰਬ ਜੀਅ ਰਖੵਾ ਕਰੋਤਿ ॥ Naanak Sarab Jee-a Rakh-yaa Karot	God the destroyer of the sorrows and merciful to all Nanak prays to that God for protection from excessive anger for all human beings.

Guru Granth Sahib (p.1358, line 7)

B. BY CONTROLLING BAD BEHAVIOR

Guru Nanak explained that excessive anger makes one do bad things.

The first Guru, Nanak, said:

PUNJABI AND ROMAN	ENGLISH
ਭੰਉਕੈ ਕੋਪੁ ਖੁਆਰੁ ਹੋਇ BhaNukai Kop Khu-aar Ho-ay ਫਕੜੁ ਪਿਟੇ ਅੰਧੁ ॥ Fakarh Pitay AnDh	An excessively angry person barks like a stray dog, brings ruin on self and blindly pursues bad things.

Guru Granth Sahib (p.1288, line 13)

C. BY NOT ASSOCIATING WITH PEOPLE WHO HAVE EXCESSIVE ANGER

Guru Ramdas cautioned people ***not to associate with people who have anger that is always out of control.*** It is not the ordinary anger that everybody has at times. He meant those who are angry all the time. It is better to stay away from them as much as possible.

The fourth Guru, Ram Das, said:

PUNJABI AND ROMAN	ENGLISH
ਓਨਾ ਪਾਸਿ ਦੁਆਸਿ ਨ ਭਿਟੀਐ	Do not meet or even approach
Onaa Paas Du-aas Na Bhitee-ai	those people
ਜਿਨ ਅੰਤਰਿ ਕ੍ਰੋਧੁ ਚੰਡਾਲ ॥	whose heart is filled with excessive
Jin Antar KaroDh Chandaal	anger that is always out of control as a devil.

Guru Granth Sahib (p. 40, line 9)

D. BY NOT HARBORING ILL WILL AGAINST ANYONE

Farid said that by ***keeping ill will in your mind is not beneficial for anyone. It will create enmity and thus creates more problems.***

Sheikh Farid said:

PUNJABI AND ROMAN	ENGLISH
ਫਰੀਦਾ ਬੁਰੇ ਦਾ ਭਲਾ ਕਰਿ	Farid says do good for those who do evil
Fareedaa Buray Daa Bhalaa Kar	
ਗੁਸਾ ਮਨਿ ਨ ਹਢਾਇ ॥	and harbor no anger in your mind,
Gussa Man Na Hadhaa-ay	
ਦੇਹੀ ਰੋਗੁ ਨ ਲਗਈ	then your body shall not suffer
Dayhee Rog Na Laga-ee	from any disease (mental anguish)
ਪਲੈ ਸਭੁ ਕਿਛੁ ਪਾਇ ॥	and you shall obtain every thing
Palai Sabh Kichh Paa-e	(peace of mind).

Guru Granth Sahib (p. 1381, line 19)

E. BY REMEMBRING GOD AND PERFORMING GOOD DEEDS

People who have ***excessive anger, excessive lust, and are deceitful and dubious in their dealings will go to hell.***

Kabir said:

PUNJABI AND ROMAN	**ENGLISH**
ਆਪਸ ਕਉ ਦੀਰਘੁ ਕਰਿ ਜਾਨੈ	Those who believe themselves
Aapas Ka-o Deeragh Kar Jaanai	to be great
ਅਉਰਨ ਕਉ ਲਗ ਮਾਤ II	and consider others as small,
A-uran Ka-o Lag Maat	
ਮਨਸਾ ਬਾਚਾ ਕਰਮਨਾ ਮੈ	those who are false, in thinking,
Mansaa Baachaa Karmanaa Mai	in speaking and in deeds,
ਦੇਖੇ ਦੋਜਕ ਜਾਤ II	they all go to hell and are punished.
Daykhay Dojak Jaat	
ਕਾਮੀ ਕ੍ਰੋਧੀ ਚਾਤੁਰੀ	People having excessive lust, excessive
Kaamee KroDhee Chaaturee	anger are very clever in a dubious way,
ਬਾਜੀਗਰ ਬੇਕਾਮ II	are deceitful and hate to work (lazy),
Baajeegar Baykaam	
ਨਿੰਦਾ ਕਰਤੇ ਜਨਮੁ ਸਿਰਾਨੋ	waste their whole life in slandering
Nindaa Kartay Janam Siraano	others,
ਕਬਹੂ ਨ ਸਿਮਰਿਓ ਰਾਮੁ II	and they never meditate on God's
Kabahoo Na Simri-o Raam	name.
ਕਹਿ ਕਬੀਰ ਚੇਤੈ ਨਹੀ	Says Kabir those who do not
Kahi Kabeer Chaytai Nahee	remember God
ਮੂਰਖ ਮੁਗਧੁ ਗਵਾਰੁ II	are fools (lack of common sense and
Moorakh MugaDh Gavaar	judgment), idiots (less mental capacity) and brutes (like an animal with no power to reason).

Guru Granth Sahib (p. 1105, line 17)

4. PASSION # 3—LOBH THE EXCESSIVE GREED

Lobh is excessive greed. It is excessive desire to have more than one's share. Every person has some sort of greed and this is part of our living. However, when greed becomes excessive and the person does not care for the rights of others it leads to Lobh (excessive greed), which create all sorts of problems. ***Excessive greed destroys peace and happiness.***

i. WHAT EXCESSIVELY GREEDY PEOPLE DO

Excessively greedy people do not give anything away not even to the most needy people. ***We should develop a habit of helping others by offering whatever one can afford.*** Friends, relatives and God's devotees should stay away from the excessively greedy person. Their dealings with people are not honest.

The fifth Guru, Arjan Dev, said:

PUNJABI AND ROMAN	ENGLISH
ਹੇ ਲੋਭਾ ਲੰਪਟ ਸੰਗ ਸਿਰਮੋਰਹ Hay Lobhaa Lampat Sang Sirmohreh ਅਨਿਕ ਲਹਰੀ ਕਲੋਲਤੇ ॥ Anik Lahree Kalolatay	Excessive greed, you cling even to the great people and they play games in many different ways.
ਧਾਵੰਤ ਜੀਆ ਬਹੁ ਪ੍ਰਕਾਰੰ Dhaavant Jee-aa Baho ParkaaraN ਅਨਿਕ ਭਾਂਤਿ ਬਹੁ ਡੋਲਤੇ ॥ Anik BhaaNt Baho Doltay	Excessive greed makes people deceitful and these people run in different directions, wobble and waver in their dealings.
ਨਚ ਮਿਤ੍ਰੰ ਨਚ ਇਸਟੰ ਨਚ ਬਾਧਵ Nach MitraN Nach IstaN Nach BaaDhav ਨਚ ਮਾਤ ਪਿਤਾ ਤਵ ਲਜਯਾ ॥ Nach Maat Pitaa Tav Lajyaa	Excessively greedy people have no respect for friends, God's devotees, relatives, mother and father.
ਅਕਰਣੰ ਕਰੋਤਿ ਅਖਾਦ੍ਯਿ ਖਾਦ੍ਯੰ AkarnaN Karot Akhaad-ya Khaad-yaN ਅਸਾਜ੍ਯੰ ਸਾਜਿ ਸਮਜਯਾ ॥ Asaaja-yaN Saaj Samajyaa	Excessive greed makes people do, what they should not be doing, makes people eat, what they should not be eating and makes people perform certain tasks that they should not be doing, greed has such a bad reputation.

ਤ੍ਰਾਹਿ ਤ੍ਰਾਹਿ ਸਰਣਿ ਸੁਆਮੀ Traahi Traahi Saran Su-aamee	God save me, save me from excessive greed
ਬਿਗ੍ਯਾਪਿ ਨਾਨਕ ਹਰਿ ਨਰਹਰਹ ॥ Big-yaapati Naanak Har Narhareh	Nanak prays to the powerful God for protection from excessive greed.
Guru Granth Sahib (p. 1358, line 9)	

ii. EXCESSIVELY GREEDY PEOPLE ARE NOT TRUSTWORTHY

An excessively greedy person cannot be trusted. It is better to avoid them. They do not help others. They live and die with excessive greed.

The third Guru, Amar Das, said:

PUNJABI AND ROMAN	ENGLISH
ਲੋਭੀ ਕਾ ਵੇਸਾਹੁ ਨ ਕੀਜੈ Lobhee Kaa Vaysaahu Na Keejai	Do not trust an excessively greedy person
ਜੇ ਕਾ ਪਾਰਿ ਵਸਾਇ ॥ Jay Kaa Paar Vasaa-ay	and one should avoid them.
ਅੰਤਿ ਕਾਲਿ ਤਿਥੈ ਧੁਹੈ Ant Kaal Tithai Dhuhai	At the last moment they will deceive you
ਜਿਥੈ ਹਥੁ ਨ ਪਾਇ ॥ Jithai Hath Na Paa-ay	and will not lend you a helping hand.
Guru Granth Sahib (p. 1417, line 12)	

iii. HOW DO EXCESSIVELY GREEDY PEOPLE BEHAVE?

Excessive greed makes one behave like a mad person who is in search of every thing for himself at all costs. This leads to destruction of one's character.

The fourth Guru, Ram Das, said:

PUNJABI AND ROMAN	ENGLISH
ਲੋਭ ਲਹਰਿ ਸਭੁ ਸੁਆਨੁ ਹਲਕੁ ਹੈ Lobh Lahar Sabh Su-aan Halak Hai	An excessively greedy person behaves like a mad dog with rabies
ਹਲਕਿਓ ਸਭਹਿ ਬਿਗਾਰੇ ॥ Halki-0 Sabheh Bigaaray	and this madness destroys everything.
Guru Granth Sahib (p. 983, line 17)	

5. PASSION # 4—MOO AS EXCESSIVE EGO

Moo is excessive ego. Each one of us is attached to worldly things and we cannot escape from it. However, if we have control over it we can lead a very peaceful life. A person having excessive ego is unduly attached to worldly things. ***Egotistic persons are self-centered and are only concerned for their own welfare.*** They use "I, me and myself" for everything. Ego is a natural instinct. It is part of life. However, excessive ego evokes the picture of a pompous, self-important person. Such a person is self-centered, insensitive and has a complete disregard for the interests of other people.

i. WHO HAS EXCESSIVE EGO?

Almost every body has ego. Excessive ego is also found in almost all types of people, even the most religious and powerful. We should pray to God for protection from excessive ego.

The fifth Guru, Arjan Dev, said:

PUNJABI AND ROMAN	ENGLISH
ਹੇ ਅਜਿਤ ਸੁਰ ਸੰਗ੍ਰਾਮੰ	Undue attachment to worldly things
Hay Ajit Soor SangraamaN	(excessive ego) is so mighty and
ਅਤਿ ਬਲਨਾ ਬਹੁ ਮਰਦਨਹ ॥	ruthless that it destroys even the
At Balnaa Baho Maradaneh	most powerful people.
ਗਣ ਗੰਧਰਬ ਦੇਵ ਮਾਨੁਖੵੰ	Worldly attachment even entices &
Gan GanDharab Dayv Maanukh-yaN	fascinates the learned religious people,
ਪਸੁ ਪੰਖੀ ਬਿਮੋਹਨਹ ॥	musicians who sing God's praises,
Pasu Pankhee Bimohneh	God's devotees, human beings,
	animals & birds.
ਹਰਿ ਕਰਣਹਾਰੰ ਨਮਸਕਾਰੰ	Nanak prays and bows to God who has
Har KarnhaaraN NamaskaaraN	created everything and takes care of
ਸਰਣਿ ਨਾਨਕ ਜਗਦੀਸੑਰਹ ॥	the whole universe for protection from
Sarn Nanak Jagdeesvareh	excessive ego.

Guru Granth Sahib (p. 1358, line 3)

ii. EXCESSIVE EGO CAUSE PROBLEMS

A few of the problems caused by excessive ego are outlined below.

A. If we do anything with personal, excessive ego in mind, it will lead to more troubles and problems in life.

The first Guru, Nanak, said:

PUNJABI AND ROMAN	**ENGLISH**
ਬੰਧਨ ਕਰਮ ਧਰਮ	All relgious rituals and ceremonies are
BanDhan Karam Dharam	entanglements when
ਹਉ ਕੀਆ ॥	performed with excessive ego.
Ha-o Kee-aa	
Guru Granth Sahib (p. 416, line 15)	

B. No matter what one's religion, if excessive ego is practiced in life, they will never know God.

The first Guru, Nanak, said:

PUNJABI AND ROMAN	**ENGLISH**
ਹਉਮੈ ਕਰਤ ਭੇਖੀ	Immersed in excessive ego in any
Haume Karat Bhaykhee	religious garb
ਨਹੀ ਜਾਨਿਆ ॥	one cannot know God.
Nahee Jaani-aa	
Guru Granth Sahib (p. 226, line 14)	

iii. WHAT IS ACHIEVED WHEN EXCESSIVE EGO IS CONTROLLED?

A. What happens when excessive ego is under control? ***Peace of mind and body is obtained.*** This reduces the stress created by day-to-day problems.

The fifth Guru, Arjan Dev, said:

PUNJABI AND ROMAN	**ENGLISH**
ਖੁਦੀ ਮਿਟੀ ਤਬ ਸੁਖ ਭਏ	When excessive ego is controlled then
Khudee Mitee Tab Sukh Bha-ay	happiness follows
ਮਨ ਤਨ ਭਏ ਅਰੋਗ ॥	along with peace of mind and body.
Man Tan Bha-ay Arog	
Guru Granth Sahib (p. 260, line 9)	

B. In order to be with God one has to get rid of excessive ego. The two of them do not coexist.

The first Guru, Nanak, said:

PUNJABI AND ROMAN

ਹਉਮੈ ਕਰੀ ਤਾਂ ਤੂ ਨਾਹੀ
Haume Karee TaaN Too Naahee
ਤੂ ਹੋਵਹਿ ਹਉ ਨਾਹਿ ॥
Too Hoveh Ha-o Naahi
Guru Granth Sahib (p. 1092, line 19)

ENGLISH

Where there is excessive ego
there is no God,
where there is God there is no
excessive ego.

6. PASSION # 5—HANKAR AS EXCESSIVE PRIDE

Hankar is excessive pride. Every person has some pride in achieving something worthwhile. It is good as long as it is under control. ***It is also better to be humble about your accomplishments.***

People with excessive pride have very high opinions of themselves. They always speak very highly of their abilities and accomplishments. They also exhibit an assertive behavior that is very unpleasant.

i. CHARACTERISTICS OF A PERSON WITH EXCESSIVE PRIDE

Guru Arjan Dev said that ***people with excessive pride forget about God who is the creator of all and healer of ills.*** People with excessive pride do not care for their friends and are concerned only for themselves.

The fifth Guru, Arjan Dev, said:

PUNJABI AND ROMAN

ਹੇ ਜਨਮ ਮਰਣ ਮੂਲੰ
Hay Janam Maran MoolaN
ਅਹੰਕਾਰੰ ਪਾਪਾਤਮਾ ॥
AhaNkaaraN Paapaatmaa

ENGLISH

Excessive pride leads to
reincarnation (cycles of birth and death)
and is also the soul of sins.

ਮਿਤ੍ਰੰ ਤਜੰਤਿ ਸਤ੍ਰੰ ਦ੍ਰਿੜੰਤਿ	People with excessive pride forsake
MitraN Tajant SatraN Darirh-aaNt	friends, hold tight to enemies and
ਅਨਿਕ ਮਾਯਾ ਬਿਸ੍ਤੀਰਨਹ ॥	live with countless illusions.
Anik Maa-yaa BisteerniH	
ਆਵੰਤ ਜਾਵੰਤ ਥਕੰਤ ਜੀਆ	Excessive pride cause the living beings
Aavant Jaavant Thakant Jee-aa	to come and go until their soul is
ਦੁਖ ਸੁਖ ਬਹੁ ਭੋਗਣਹ ॥	exhausted, and they experience pain
Dukh Sukh Baho Bhognah	and pleasure with great stress.
ਭ੍ਰਮ ਭਯਾਨ ਉਦਿਆਨ ਰਮਣੰ	Excessive pride makes people unsure
Bharam Bha-yaan Udi-aan RamnaN	and they become lost in a terrible wilderness of doubt,
ਮਹਾ ਬਿਕਟ ਅਸਾਧ ਰੋਗਣਹ ॥	and they contract the most horrible,
Mahaa Bikat AsaaDh Rognah	incurable diseases.
ਬੈਦ੍ਯੰ ਪਾਰਬ੍ਰਹਮ ਪਰਮੇਸ੍ਵਰ	Says Nanak, the only physician is the
Baida-yaN Paarbarahm Parmaysvar	great and supreme God
ਆਰਾਧਿ ਨਾਨਕ ਹਰਿ ਹਰਿ ਹਰੇ ॥	and so meditate on God's Name.
AaraaDh Nanak Har Har Haray	
Guru Granth Sahib (p.1358, line 12)	

ii. HUMBLE PEOPLE GET PEACE OF MIND

People with excessive pride live in hell while those who are humble shall be liberated and have peace of mind.

The fifth Guru, Arjan Dev, said:

PUNJABI AND ROMAN	**ENGLISH**
ਜਿਸ ਕੈ ਅੰਤਰ ਰਾਜ ਅਭਿਮਾਨੁ ॥	Those who believe in the power of
Jis Kai Antar Raaj Abhimaan	excessive pride, they shall
ਸੋ ਨਰਕਪਾਤੀ ਹੋਵਤ ਸੁਆਨੁ ॥	end up in hell and live like a stray dog.
So Narakpaatee Hovat Su-aan	
ਜੋ ਜਾਨੈ ਮੈ ਜੋਬਨਵੰਤੁ ॥	Those who have excessive pride
Jo Jaanai Mai Jobanvant	in their youth
ਸੋ ਹੋਵਤ ਬਿਸਟਾ ਕਾ ਜੰਤੁ ॥	shall become a worm in the manure.
So Hovat Bistaa Kkaa Jant	

ਧਨ ਭੂਮਿ ਕਾ ਜੋ ਕਰੈ ਗੁਮਾਨੁ II
Dhan Bhoom Kaa Jo Karai Gumaan
Those who take excessive pride in wealth and the land they own,

ਸੋ ਮੂਰਖੁ ਅੰਧਾ ਅਗਿਆਨੁ II
So Moorakh AnDhaa Agi-aan
are fools (not intelligent), blind (unable to perceive) and ignorant (not knowledgeable).

ਕਰਿ ਕਿਰਪਾ ਜਿਸ ਕੈ ਹਿਰਦੈ
Kar Kirpaa Jis Kai Hirdai
By the grace of God some people are

ਗਰੀਬੀ ਬਸਾਵੈ II
Gareebee Basaavai
blessed with humility,

ਨਾਨਕ ਈਹਾ ਮੁਕਤੁ
Naanak Eehaa Mukat
says Nanak they shall be liberated from this world

ਆਗੈ ਸੁਖੁ ਪਾਵੈ II
Aagai Sukh Paavai
and will obtain peace hereafter.

Guru Granth Sahib (p. 278, line 6)

7. SUMMARY

There is no English word for Haume. Haume is the equivalent of the five passions or any one of them or any combination of them. Imagine a person living in this world who has no lust, no anger, no greed, no ego and no pride. It is not possible. God created the five passions with some purpose. We all have to live with them. It is the excessive lust, excessive anger, excessive greed, excessive ego and excessive pride that are detrimental. The dividing line between normal and excessive passion is decided by one's conscience. There are no set rules. The general guidelines are: always keep God and the welfare of society in one's mind while performing any deed.

Lust is excessive desire for sex without feeling for love. Lust is also excessive desire for power, money and fighting. Excessive anger and stress are the cause and effect of each other. Anger is sometimes a normal reaction but excessive anger, especially when taking the law into one's own hands leads to destruction of the society. By praying to God, performing good deeds, eating healthy food and exercising properly will reduce anger and stress. An excessively greedy person does not care for the rights of others and is concerned only with one's own desires. People that have excessive egos use "I, me and myself" for everything and are unduly attached to worldly things. People with excessive pride have very high opinions of themselves and do not care for God or for their friends.

8. EXCERCISES

1. What is Haume?
2. How is Haume part of our life?
3. What is the cure for excessive Haume?
4. What are some common analogies for Haume?
5. What are the four ways to control excessive Haume?
6. What is Kaam?
7. In what four different ways is excessive lust manifested?
8. How can we control our excessive lust?
9. What is Karood?
10. When can anger be justified?
11. What causes stress and who is responsible for it?
12. What are the five ways to reduce stress and excessive anger?
13. What is Lobh?
14. What do excessively greedy people do and why they are not trustworthy?
15. What is Moo?
16. Who has excessive ego?
17. What does one achieve by controlling excessive ego?
18. What is Hankar?
19. What are the characteristics of a person with excessive pride?
20. What do humble people get?

9. REFERENCES

[1] Dr. I.J Singh. "The Sikh Bulletin" Vol. 3 No. 12 December 2001 page 12, Roseville, California derived from book *The Sikh Way: A Pilgrim's Progress* by Dr. I. J. Singh.

[2] Go to yahoo.com and search angerproject.com, click Anger Project click for book "The Anger Advantage"

[3] Go to yahoo.com and search for "Anger the Hidden Killer" by Nichols Dwight, click for yahoo ! Directory Personal Home Pages, click Nichols, Dwight- Anger the Hidden Killer.

[4] "Handle Stress Like an Expert" by Megan Othersen Gorman, *Reader's Digest*, May 1999, page 98 to 102.

UNIVERSALITY OF THE SIKH RELIGION

CHAPTER 15

MIRACLES AND SUPERSTITIONS

Miracles and Superstitions are events that cannot be explained by the laws of nature. Miracles are supernatural in origin and only God can perform them. Superstitions are beliefs, practices or rites irrationally maintained by ignorance or by faith in magic or chance. It is like believing that some numbers and certain days are not lucky. ***Miracles and superstitions are unusual beliefs that cannot be explained logically, scientifically, or by common sense.***

1. MIRACLES

A. ONLY GOD CAN PERFORM MIRACLES

Only God can perform miracles. ***Creation of the universe by God is a miracle in itself.*** Whatever God does is righteous and just. Everyone is made to come and then depart and that, too, is God's miracle.

The fifth Guru, Arjan Dev, said:

PUNJABI AND ROMAN	ENGLISH
ਹਰਿ ਕਾ ਏਕੁ ਅਚੰਭਉ ਦੇਖਿਆ Har Kaa Ayk Achambha-o Daykhi-aa	I have seen one miracle of God
ਮੇਰੇ ਲਾਲ ਜੀਉ Mayray Laal Jee-o	O' my dear friends and that is
ਜੋ ਕਰੇ ਸੁ ਧਰਮ ਨਿਆਏ ਰਾਮ ॥ Jo Karay So Dharam Ni-aa-ay Raam.	whatever God does is righteous and just.
ਹਰਿ ਰੰਗੁ ਅਖਾੜਾ ਪਾਇਓਨੁ Har Rang Akhaarhaa Paa-i-on	God has made this beautiful world
ਮੇਰੇ ਲਾਲ ਜੀਉ Mayray Laal Jee-o	O' my dear friends
ਆਵਣੁ ਜਾਣੁ ਸਬਾਏ ਰਾਮ ॥ Aavan Jaan Sabaa-ay Raam.	where everyone comes and goes.

Guru Granth Sahib (p. 541, line 19)

No human being has the power to perform miracles and that includes all ten Sikh Gurus and religious people of all other religions. How can God give that power of miracles to human beings as God is neither born nor dies? Guru Nanak made it very clear as shown below.

The first Guru, Nanak, said:

PUNJABI AND ROMAN	**ENGLISH**
ਸਿਧਾ ਪੁਰਖਾ ਕੀਆ ਵਡਿਆਈਆ ॥	Some people claim to have a
SiDhaa Purkhaa Kee-aa Vadi-aa-ee-aa	great power to perform miracles.
ਤੁਧੁ ਵਿਣੁ ਸਿਧੀ ਕਿਨੈ ਨ ਪਾਈਆ ॥	Only God has the power to
TuDh Vin SiDhee Kinai Na Paa-ee-aa	perform miracles.
Guru Granth Sahib (p. 9, line 13)	

Some people like Sidhs (Yogis) claim to have miraculous powers. Guru Nanak discussed with them and said it in very plain words that He (Guru Nanak) did not perform any miracles. It is recorded by Bhai Gurdas [1] as shown below.

Bhai Gurdas said:

PUNJABI AND ROMAN	**ENGLISH**
ਬਾਬਾ ਬੋਲੈ ਨਾਥ ਜੀ ਸਬਦੁ	Guru Nanak told Sidh named Nath
Bhabha Bholle Nath Jee Shabad	
ਸੁਨਹੁ ਸਚੁ ਮੁਖਹੁ ਅਲਾਈ ॥	listen carefully as I am telling the truth.
Sunoo Sach Mukhoo Alahee	
ਬਾਝੋ ਸਚੇ ਨਾਮ ਦੇ	I believe in the True Naam of God and
Bhajoo Sachee Naam Daay	
ਹੋਰੁ ਕਰਾਮਤਿ ਅਸਾਂ ਤੇ ਨਾਹੀ ॥	I have no other miracles to exhibit.
Hooroo Karamat Assaa Tey Naahe	
Vaars of Bhai Gurdas, Vaar 1 Pauri 43	

Bhai Gurdas, Figure 29 [1] was heavily involved with Sikh Gurus and the Guru Granth Sahib. ***Bhai Gurdas hand scribed the first rendition of the Guru Granth Sahib,*** as dictated by Guru Arjan Dev. During his life Bhai Gurdas was associated with the third Guru Amar Das, the fourth Guru Ram Das, the fifth Guru Arjan Dev and the sixth Guru Hargobind. The Fifth Guru Arjan Dev installed the same rendition of the Guru Granth Sahib for the first time in 1604, in the Golden Temple in Amritsar. Bhai Gurdas was born in 1551 and passed away in 1636 [1]. Bhai Gurdas obtained the works of Guru Nanak through his personal resources and compiled a book called *Vaars*. **Vaars *is considered to be a key to the Sikh scriptures.***

FIGURE 29

BHAI GURDAS (1551 to 1636)

The first rendition of the Guru Granth Sahib was hand scribed by Bhai Gurdas.

Bhai Gurdas's verses shed light on the Sikh moral conduct and the Sikh doctrines. He was an eminent personality in the history of the Sikh religion. He was a brilliant scholar and poet, an able missionary, and an accomplished theologian. Being well versed in Indian religious thought, he was able to elaborate, profoundly, the tenants of Sikhism.

Ninth Guru Tej Bahadur also made it very clear that the Sikh Religion does not believe in miracles. Muslim rulers, before beheading Guru Tej Bahadur (because he refused to accept the Muslim religion), demanded that the Guru show them a miracle to prove that he was a man of God [2]. Guru Tej Bahadur replied that miracles were not of his belief nor of his religion—everything was in God's hands.

B. LOGIC AND MIRACLES

The Sikh Religion is very logical. Relying on miracles for explanation negates logic. The scientific approach can be easily applied to explain the basic principles of the Sikh Religion. ***Science and religion supplement each other.*** Science promotes intellectual curiosity through its search and exact knowledge. This also serves the cause of religion when it is promoted logically and truthfully.

There are several questions that come to mind. Some of them are:

a. Are there two types of people —those with miraculous powers and others without?
b. Are people meditating on God rewarded with the power to perform miracles?
c. There are so many religions. Does every religion has their own way to reward followers with the power to perform miracles?

The answer to all the above questions is no as far as Sikh religion is concerned.

No human being has ever performed a miracle. Those who try are mere tricksters. Some tricks are based upon the ability of the hand to move faster than the eye. Some use magnetic force when performing magical tricks.

Animation [3] is a process whereby still pictures look like moving objects. Greater the number of images, the smoother the animation. In general films use 24 frames (still images) per second while most cartoons use 12 cells (individual drawings) per second. This is how science is used for the benefit of human beings. Such technologies may appear to be miracles, but they are not.

Sidhs (Yogis) who used to live in caves sometimes claimed that they could change into other animals and then return to human form. They used to imitate the sounds of many animals (lions and others) in the caves while claiming that they had actually changed into them. That was simply an illusion, not a miracle.

There are many studies that have proven, without any doubt, that smoke detectors save lives. There are also many other safety devices that save lives everyday. Dialing 911 (in the USA) also save lives by bringing in emergency services in minutes. Are these miracles? The answer is no.

One can think of many things that one may call a miracle like winning the lottery, but this can be explained by theory of probability. Think what computers and animations can do in making films. They are not miracles. Any one with knowledge and experience can create those illusions.

Let us assume some people do have miraculous powers. We are also told that if some one has the power to perform miracles acquired through meditation or other religious means are not supposed to use them. There is a contradiction in this statement.

Presently there are about six billion people on this earth. Let us say 1000 people or about 0.000017%, have the miraculous powers. Some one will use them. So far no one has ever proved conclusively that a miracle has occurred. ***People claiming to have the power to perform miracles can very easily coerce others into believing that they are superior.***

C. EPISODES OF LOGIC AND NOT MIRACLES

There are many accounts in the lives of the Gurus that are discussed by Sikh religious people. Sometimes, when relating the story, it appears that a miracle has been performed by the Guru, which is untrue.. ***If those episodes are presented using logic and common sense, they will have more influence over the young and other followers.***

I will explain this with few examples.

a. EPISODE OF GURU NANAK WITH MALIK BHAGO AND BHAI LALO

Guru Nanak visited a small town called Saidpur, now Eminabad, 15 kilometers southeast of Gujranwala [4] in West Punjab, Pakistan. Guru Nanak stayed with Bhai Lalo, a carpenter instead of Mr. Malik Bhago, the chief of the town. At first Guru Nanak did not go to the feast of Malik Bhago to which all holy men were invited.

Bhago was furious and asked Guru Nanak to meet him. Later Guru Nanak went to his house where all sorts of food were being served. Guru Nanak said that he enjoyed the simple food of Bhai Lalo compared to Malik Bhago's food. ***The reason that Guru Nanak gave was that food prepared by Bhai Lalo was earned by honest hard work. The food prepared in Malik Bhago's house was acquired by exploiting the poor.*** Guru Nanak told Malik Bhago that helping the poor is like being in the company of God. Malik Bhago was so convinced that he devoted rest of his life to the service of his fellow beings. People who recount the episode say that Guru Nanak squeezed both the meals with his hands. Milk came out of the meal of Bhai Lalo while blood came out of the meal of Malik Bhago [5]. The retelling the account in this manner sounds as if a miracle has occurred, but Gurus never perform miracles. They used logic and reasoning to bring people closer to God.

b. EPISODE OF GURU NANAK WITH WALI QUANDHARI AT PUNJA SAHIB

Guru Nanak accompanied by Mardana reached Hasan Abdal, 48 Kilometers from Rawalpindi in present day Pakistan [6]. The Punja Sahib Gurdwara is located in that city (see Figure 30). They stayed below a hill. A Muslim Fakir named Wali Quandhari had built a compound on top of the hill. It was surrounded by natural spring water that fed a well. There was no other source of water for many miles around. Mardana felt very thirsty. Guru Nanak told Mardana to go up the hill for water. Mardana was refused water by the Fakir not once but twice. Guru Nanak then pushed a small rock and water started to flow. Mardana dug deeper and water gushed out. As more water flowed after a month or so, the spring at the top of the hill stopped. That enraged the Fakir.

The Fakir came down and met Guru Nanak. During their discussion Guru Nanak told Fakir Wali Quandhari [6]

" O' friend, those who live so high, should not be dry as rock".

Fakir understood the logic and reasoning of Guru Nanak and was very much impressed. He started praising Guru Nanak and they all shared the water. Later the stone was engraved according to the size of Guru Nanak's palm, (see Figure 31). Thus this place is called Punja Sahib (the Sikh Gurdwara, Palm of Guru Nanak). Some people present this in a different way. They say that Fakir hurled a big stone from the top of the hill and Guru Nanak stopped it with his bare hands [7]. The impression of Guru Nanak's palm was thus printed on the stone. Logically and scientifically, it was not possible.

FIGURE 30

PUNJA SAHIB GURDWARA IN PAKISTAN

FIGURE 31

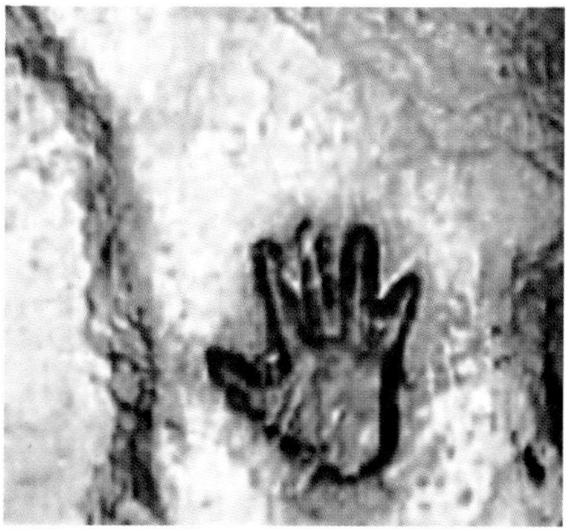

PUNJA (PALM) OF GURU NANAK
ENGRAVED
AT PUNJA SAHIB GURDWARA

I do not understand why people need to resort to miracles in order to illustrate the point of the story. It may be dramatic but is not the truth. People, especially the younger generation, are very smart and will lose confidence in the credibility of the person who is recounting the story. Guru Nanak always used logic and understanding to convince people, not miracles.

For the truly faithful in God, no miracle is necessary
But for those who doubt, no miracle is sufficient.

D. WHY DO PEOPLE BELIEVE IN MIRACLES

There could be many reasons for why people believe in miracles. It could be religious, hopeful (as in curing a deadly disease), just a way of thinking. The human mind is a very delicate thing. It has almost an unlimited capacity to think in all possible ways—it can even believe in things that are impossible. For example one can even conceive that life can be given to a dead person, but it is not possible. No one has ever done it. Sometimes it is possible that a doctor has pronounced a person dead, but he or she may still be alive. Science is not perfect: it is possible that the doctor might have misinterpreted the situation. One also may be brain dead but doctors can now keep such a person alive by tube feeding and other devices.

Dr. J.S. Chandan of New York [8] has mentioned that a cancer patient can survive, even when doctors give up all hope. Sometimes even doctors call such a situation a miracle. The result, however, could be due to prayer or mediating on God (reading or listening to hymns), which is still within the realm of science.

Let us look ***the power of prayer*** from another point of view. Let us say there are 100 people having for example cancer. It is generally believed that 50 people will be cured by their own immune system. Doctors will cure another 30 people using medicine, surgery etc. The next 10 people may or may not be cured. The final 10 people will not survive. The last 20 people may use prayer, meditation, yoga, hypnotism or any such procedure. In some cases it may be possible that their immune system is so energized that they go into remission. However, it may happen in very few cases.

If the effect of prayer can be interpreted by some scientific testing, that may help a good number of people. Therefore, science and religion can be complementary. It appears that in future more progress will be made in using existing or new scientific techniques along with the meditation. This may help people having cancer and other diseases that are not easy to cure.

Science may one day be able to cure cancer through Deoxyribonucleic Acid (DNA) modifying drugs as the Human Genetic Code has been deciphered. Some of the latest techniques that are being tested are [9]:

a. STEM CELLS
Stem Cells can repair a badly damaged heart or other organs as they can transform themselves into any type of tissue cells.
b. VACCINE
Some of the possible diseases in this category that might be alleviated include prostate, cancer, and many other diseases.
c. GENETIC CODE
Small Ribonucleic acids (RNAs), which are short stretches of RNA, function as a kind of natural "off" switch for genes that are responsible for diseases like Human Immunodeficiency Virus (HIV), Hepatitis C, certain types of cancer and other diseases.
d. STATINS DRUGS
They block the enzyme that the liver uses to make cholesterol, such as Lipitor™. They are also being tested for Alzheimer's disease, diabetes and cancer.

E. METAPHORS, SIMILES, AND ALLEGORIES

The Guru Granth Sahib refers many times to metaphors, similes and allegories. It does not mean that they are part of the Sikh Religion. Since most of the people who became Sikhs were Hindus, these stories were ingrained in their minds. Guru Nanak made it very clear, however, that Naam (Divine name of God) is much higher than any other perceived conceptions.

Some of the metaphors, similes and allegories as mentioned in the Guru Granth Sahib are as below.

	Ref. [10]
1. Nine treasures.	Page 4742
2. Eighteen Miracle Powers.	Page 4727 and 4728
3. Eighty-four Men of Miracles.	Page 4735
4. Eighteen Castes.	Page 4729
5. Sixty-eight Pilgrim Stations.	Page 4727
6. Eighteen Hindu Mythological Books.	Page 4729
7. Twenty-seven Hindu Ceremonial Books.	Page 4729

The Sikh Religion does not believe in them. Those interested in details of each one can read the specified page(s) in the Guru Granth Sahib's English translation as given in reference [10].

Let us discuss the categories of nine treasures and eighteen miracle powers. Some people believe that by meditation (Naam Simran) one can get physical possession of gold and diamonds (two of the 9 treasures) and the power to reduce oneself to a single cell and then come back to original form (one of the18 miracles). This is not true. Sikh Gurus made it very clear that these are just metaphors while the real power is in the Naam of God.

The third Guru, Amar Das, said:

PUNJABI AND ROMAN	**ENGLISH**
ਨਵ ਨਿਧੀ ਅਠਾਰਹ ਸਿਧੀ	Nine treasures and eighteen miracle
Nav NiDhee Athaarah SiDhee	
ਪਿਛੈ ਲਗੀਆ ਫਿਰਹਿ	powers of Sidhs are way behind
Pichhai Lagee-aa Fireh	
ਜੋ ਹਰਿ ਹਿਰਦੈ ਸਦਾ ਵਸਾਇ ॥	for those who keep Naam of God
Jo Har Hirdai Sadaa Vasaa-ay. Guru Granth Sahib (p. 649, line 16)	always in their heart and mind.

Metaphors are used in order to bring people closer to God, not to promote belief in miracles and treasures.

F. MIRACLES AND THE SIKH RELIGION

The philosophy of the Sikh Religion is very simple and practical. It is to perform honest work, share with less privileged people, believe in universal prosperity, treat everyone as equal in all respects, and above all pray to God.

Ten living Gurus of Sikhs were human beings at an extraordinary level. They were devoted to social reforms and spiritual enlightenment. By associating Sikh Gurus with miraculous powers, we are undermining their sacrifices. Sikh Gurus never performed any miracles.

Naam is the Divine name of God. Naam Japanaa means pray to God and Naam Simrin is meditation on God. All of the above are given great importance in the Sikh Religion. However, it should be made clear that no one can obtain physical possession of treasures and miracles by praying or meditating on God.

Guru Nanak showed us convincingly that miracles and occult powers have nothing in common with the meditation of God's Name.

The first Guru, Nanak, said:

PUNJABI AND ROMAN

ਸਿਧੁ ਹੋਵਾ ਸਿਧਿ ਲਾਈ
SiDh Hovaa SiDh Laa-ee
ਰਿਧਿ ਆਖਾ ਆਉ ॥
RiDh Aakhaa Aa-o
ਗੁਪਤੁ ਪਰਗਟੁ ਹੋਇ
Gupat Pargat Ho-ay
ਬੈਸਾ ਲੋਕੁ ਰਾਖੈ ਭਾਉ ॥
Baisaa Lok Raakhai Bhaa-o
ਮਤੁ ਦੇਖਿ ਭੂਲਾ ਵੀਸਰੈ
Mat Daykh Bhoolaa Veesrai
ਤੇਰਾ ਚਿਤਿ ਨ ਆਵੈ ਨਾਉ ॥
Tayraa Chit Na Aavai Naa-o
Guru Granth Sahib (p.14, line 6)

ENGLISH

Let us say I become a man of occult powers, performed miracles and obtained great wealth.

Through miracles I become invisible and visible at will
people will then hold me in great awe.

Having all that through miracles I will go astray and forget God
and my mind will never be able to meditate on God's Name.

Praying and meditating on God has extremely good benefits. A person who is truly engulfed in the Naam of God gets his/her own reward in terms of ***peace of mind, faith in one God, a positive approach in daily life, and good health and happiness even in adversity.*** With Naam Simran (meditation on God) one becomes closer to God and then merges with God after death, thus avoiding the birth and death cycles forever.

2. SUPERSTITIONS

Superstitions have no place in the Sikh Religion. All days and all numbers are equally important. Some people consider the number 13 to be a bad omen. There is no such thing. Guru Nanak made it absolutely clear that only people having no knowledge of God's great powers believe in such things.

The first Guru, Nanak, said:

PUNJABI AND ROMAN

ਥਿਤੀ ਵਾਰ ਸੇਵਹਿ ਮੁਗਧ ਗਵਾਰ ॥
Thitee Vaar Sayveh MugaDh Gavaar.
ਨਾਨਕ ਗੁਰਮੁਖਿ ਬੁਝੈ
Naanak Gurmukh Boojhai
ਸੋਝੀ ਪਾਇ ॥
Sojhee Paa-ay.
Guru Granth Sahib (p. 843, line 3)

ENGLISH

Only idiots and fools worry about certain days and numbers as bad omens
Nanak says a God-oriented person understands this and
realizes this as a fact.

The above reference leaves no ambiguity and states clearly that all days as created by God have equal status. However, that does not mean that one cannot celebrate any day that one wants.

Everyone should pray every day of the year. It could be at anytime and the duration will vary from person to person. Days of prayer should not be eliminated due to superstitions.

This should not be construed that certain days should not be celebrated as special. There are many Sikh holidays based upon the birth and passing away of our ten Gurus. There are many other holidays for celebration. While I was studying in Khalsa College, Amritsar, Punjab, India during 1947 to 1949, we had about 35 to 40 holidays per year. While this time really cuts down on education, the holidays were enjoyable.

3. SUMMARY

Miracles and superstitions are against the laws of nature. Only God has the power to perform miracles. No human being has ever performed a miracle. Those who appear to perform them are simply performing tricks. The episodes of Guru Nanak with Malik Bhago and Wali Quandhari are not miracles, as are presented by some people. Guru Nanak used logic and understanding to explain the truth. Science in due course of time will be able to cure many diseases that some people say can be cured by miracles. Metaphors, similes and allegories are mentioned in the Guru Granth Sahib in order to bring people closer to God. They were imbedded in people's mind for centuries but are not part of the Sikh Religion. Worldly possessions are obtained by working honestly, achieving contentment in life by helping less fortunate people, believing in equality for all, attaining peace of mind by praying to God, and living a truthful life. Superstitions have no place in the Sikh Religion. All days and all numbers have equal status.

4. EXERCISES

i. If human beings cannot perform miracles, who can?
ii. Give two examples of episodes of Guru Nanak where logic and not miracles were used.
iii. Explain why metaphors, similes and allegories are used in the Guru Granth Sahib.
iv. How can one acquire worldly possessions, contentment and peace of mind?
v. Why do people believe in miracles?
vi. Explain why superstitions are not allowed in the Sikh Religion?

5. REFRENCES

[1] *Vaars* by Bhai Gurdas. Vaar 1 Pauri 43, Sayings of Guru Nanak, Dr. Harnam Singh Shan, Shiromani Gurdwara Parbhandhak Committee, Amritsar. India 1969 page 173.
Yahoo Search for Bhai Gurdas Click Historical Facts in the Vaars of Bhai Gurdas by Dr. Kuldip Singh Ex-President Institute of Sikh Studies Chandigarh, India.
Bhai GURDAS (1551-1636) *The encyclopedia of Sikhism. Vol III.* By Harbans Singh
http://www.sikh-history.com/sikhhist/gurus/gurdas.html

[2] K.S.Duggal. 1989, *Sikh Gurus*, The Himalayan International Institute, Honesdale, Pennsylvania, USA Page 184.

[3] Yahoo. Search for "Flipbook Movies Activity 2 Unit 1". Click unit 1
http://www.cmp.ucr.edu/exhibitions/education/vidkids/flipbook.html

[4] Yahoo. Search for "Invasion of Babar 1525" Click for "Historical Sikh Events at Gateway to Sikhism: The Invasion of Babar 1525 AD"
http://allaboutsikhs.com/events/babar.htm
Excerpts taken from *The Encyclopedia of Sikhism* Edited by Harbans Singh. Published by Punjabi University, Patiala

[5] K.S.Duggal. 1989, *Sikh Gurus*, The Himalayan International Institute, Honesdale, Pennsylvania, USA. Page 16.

[6] Yahoo. Search for "Punja Sahib Sikh Guru Family Tree"
Click "Sikh Guru Family Tree"
http://www.info-sikh.com/BhagPage1.html

[7] K.S.Duggal. 1989, *Sikh Gurus*, The Himalayan International Institute, Honesdale, Pennsylvania, USA Page 26-27.

[8] Dr. J.S. Chandan. E-mail, Nov 8,2003 on Sikh Diaspora @yahoogroups.com Under the heading Miracles and Sikhism.

[9] *Reader's Digest,* Pleasantville, New York, January 2004 page 156, "Medical Breakthroughs from Cancer Vaccines to Self-healing Hearts."

[10] Manmohan Singh. *Sri Guru Granth Sahib*, English and Punjabi Translation, Distributed by Shiromani Gurdwara Parbandhak Committee, Amritsar, India, second edition, 1983 Volume 8 pages 4727, 4728, 4729, 4735 and 4742.

UNIVERSALITY OF THE SIKH RELIGION

CHAPTER 16

PHILOSOPHY OF THE SIKH RELIGION
GURU NANAK'S ANSWERS TO 89 QUESTIONS

The discussion between Guru Nanak and the Sidhs (Yogis) applies to all people. The purpose of this chapter is to encourage people to ask questions in order to understand the philosophy of the Sikh Religion. Discussion plays a very important role in understanding the Sikh Religion. Guru Nanak had a very frank and detailed discussion with the Sidhs. This occurred at Lake Man-Sarowar, Figure 32, in the mountains of Sumeru, located north east of Kailash in Tibet. The discussion took place some time between the years 1499 and 1539. The Sidhs regarded themselves as very learned people of the Hindu religion. Sidhs took refuge in these mountains to escape the political and social turmoil in India during the reign of the Mughals and other conquerors. During this discussion Guru Nanak answered a total of 89 questions.

The discussion of Guru Nanak and the Sidhs is recorded in detail in Guru Granth Sahib, pages 938 to 946. One can download from the Internet the entire Guru Granth Sahib free of charge using www.srigranth.org in Gurmukhi, Hindi or English. The best way to read is it, in Gurmukhi, the language in which Guru Granth Sahib was written. However, it may not be possible, as many people have migrated to different parts of the world and do not know Gurmukhi language.

1. START OF DISCUSSION

The Sidhs, while sitting in their exalted seats, before starting the discussion, told Guru Nanak to pay reverence and to bow before them. ***Guru Nanak answered in three words "Sacchaa Apar Aparo"*** or "***I bow before God who is True, Limitless and most Admirable.***"

Let us examine the three words.

i. GOD IS TRUE (Saachaa)

Just as 6+4=10, it is a fact that ***God is True; this has been verified over the centuries. God created the whole universe very systematically and methodically.*** Science is the most precise, proven, and documented means that studies Nature and the Universe created by God.

FIGURE 32

LAKE MAN-SAROWAR, KAILASH MOUNTAIN IN TIBET

ii. GOD IS LIMITLESS (Apar)

The scientific community considers space to be limitless. However, our vision is very limited. Our mind has lot of thinking power but it is still very restricted. We know mathematically there is infinity, but it cannot be ascertained. ***God, according to Guru Nanak, is limitless and cannot be comprehended.***

iii. GOD IS MOST ADMIRABLE (Aparo)

God is wonderful, exquisite, and excellent; but such word cannot fully describe his true qualities.

Guru Nanak closed his opening remarks as follows:
I am a sacrifice to my God and will dedicate my body and mind to that God. Truth is obtained by meeting God-loving people and then one is blessed with God's glory. There is no use wandering in the mountains as purity is obtained through Truth. Without the True word of Shabad (hymn) no one is liberated.

2. GURU NANAK'S ANSWERS TO FIRST NINE QUESTIONS

Getting such a response from Guru Nanak to the opening remarks, the Sidhs were taken aback. They began asking the first nine questions. The Sidhs said, "We pray that you answer the questions truthfully. We sacrifice ourselves to the humble saints. We, the detached Sidhs, want to hear your reply. "

QUESTIONS BY SIDHS	ANSWERS BY GURU NANAK
1. Who are you?	I am the one who is forever under the command of God.
2. What is your name?	My name is Nanak.
3. What is your sect?	I belong to a group of people who always abide by True God's wishes.
4. What is the object of your life?	The object of my life is to know myself, and through God-loving people be merged in God who is Truest of the True.
5. Where is your seat?	As God is within all the hearts and so there is my seat and home.
6. Where do you live O' boy?	I live in a place where God resides and God is everywhere.
7. Where have you come?	I have come to this world as per the wishes of God.

QUESTIONS BY SIDHS	ANSWERS BY GURU NANAK
8. Where are you going?	I shall go wherever God's command takes me.
9. What is your way?	To get absorbed in a meditative mood and to ponder over my everlasting God is my way.

3. GURU NANAK'S ANSWER TO THE TENTH QUESTION

A Yogi named Charpat asked Guru Nanak to take some to time before giving his true reply to the following question.

QUESTION BY SIDHS	ANSWER BY GURU NANAK
10. How can one cross over the world ocean (referring to life) that is treacherous and impassable?	For example, a Lotus flower floats on the surface untouched by water and the duck swims against the stream's current and does not get wet. Similarly, one can cross over the world ocean (life) among the worldly temptations by tuning his mind to God and uttering God's Naam, hymns (Shabads).

Guru Nanak also remarked, "What answer I can give to someone who claims to know the answer to the question. I tell the Truth. If you have already crossed the world ocean then how can I argue with you?"

Guru Nanak also said that I am subservient to a person who has the following qualities:

i. One God is enshrined in their mind and is self-contented.
ii. Lives in this world among temptations without excessive desires.
iii. Who understands and make others believe in the inaccessible and Limit-less God.

4. GURU NANAK'S ANSWERS TO QUESTION 11

The Sidhs said "O' learned person, listen to our prayer and we want your true opinion. Do not take it ill and give a suitable reply to the following question."

QUESTION BY SIDHS	ANSWER BY GURU NANAK
11. How can one be united with God (arrive at Great God's door)?	This fickle mind (Man) is united with the True home of God by reciting and tuning his/her mind, body and soul to God's Naam, Hymns (Shabads). The Creator makes this union and inspires us to love the Truth.

Guru Nanak first answered in a very concise way, as shown above, but this question had a very lengthy response.

There is no English translation of Punjabi word Man [1]. Man includes mind, heart and soul. There is nothing in English word that combines the ***ability of the mind, the emotions of the heart and the indestructible quality of the soul.*** It is a seat of collective thought and feeling. Man is the power with which one thinks, decides and feels the source of all human good and evil. An indestructible attribute from Man can be released from the body and then merge with God. ***By controlling Man one can seek union with God.***

Upon hearing Guru Nanak's response of union with God, a Sidh named Luhaareepaa, the disciple of Gorakh, explained his way of union with God as follows:

i. We live away from the business world and the hustle and bustle of the cities.
ii. We live in the woods among the trees and the plants.
iii. For food we eat fruits and roots.
iv. By bathing at holy places we obtain peace of mind and not even an iota of filth attaches to us.

Above is the spiritual wisdom spoken by the Sidhs.

Guru Nanak replied that in order to be united with God one should observe the following:

i. Keep your mind alert both at and away from home.
ii. Have no evil intentions for others.
iii. Without the Naam (meditation of God), Man (mind, body and soul) is not united with God and the hunger for God does not depart.
iv. The shop and the city are in my body (home) where one carries out the true business.
v. Living in the woods is not the way to be united with God.
vi. Sleep little and eat little.

Guru Nanak said this is the essence of real wisdom.

The Yogis continued the discussion and said that by instructing your mind in the following way, you will never suffer again.

i. Wear the garb of the Yogis as required by Gorakh (the Lord of the Yogis).
ii. Put on earrings.
iii. Have a bowl and start begging.
iv. Put on a patched coat.

Among the twelve schools of Yoga ours is Ai Panth. For the other eleven see reference [2]. Among the six schools of Hindu Philosophy [3] ours is the Yoga.

Six schools of philosophy are :

i.	Yoga	Practical ways for center of consciousness.
ii.	Sankhya	Manifestation.
iii.	Vedanta	Contemplative self-inquiry.
iv.	Vaisheshika	Physical sciences.
v.	Nyaya	Elements and states of matter.
vi.	Mimasa	Reasoning process.

Guru Nanak replied:
God-loving people understand that the real Yoga is obtained by following the steps that follow:.

i. Let earrings be constant absorption of Naam (meditation of God), in the mind and eradicate excessive ego and excessive worldly attachment.
ii. By discarding excessive lust, excessive anger, excessive ego and through the word of the God's Hymn (Shabad) one attains True understanding.
iii. Let patched coat and begging bowl be the realization that God pervades everywhere. This way God will carry you across the world ocean of life.

Guru Nanak further continued:

i. God is True and True is God's Name. Analyze it. One will find the word of God to be True.
ii. Turning away from excessive worldly things is your beggar's bowl.
iii. The five elements (air, water, fire, earth and space) should be considered your head cover (cap).
iv. Let your body be your meditation mat.
v. Controlling your mind should be your loin-cloth.
vi. ***Let truth, contentment and self-discipline be the principles in your life.***

Finally, a God-loving person dwells on God's Naam.

5. GURU NANAK'S ANSWERS TO QUESTIONS 12 to 22

The Sidhs said that if one understands the essence of reality to the following questions, then that person is our religious preceptor.

QUESTIONS BY SIDHS	ANSWERS BY GURU NANAK
12. Who is hidden?	God is hidden in each and every heart.

Here is some scientific justification for why God cannot be seen: God made the whole universe in a very methodic way. Why should God be present only on earth for us to see as God permeates everything in the whole universe and beyond. The visible range of our eyes is very small 400 to 700 nanometers in the Electromagnetic Spectrum. Why should God reside in this tiny range and deprive the rest of the universe of God's existence. For details see Chapter 10 Fourth Principle-Pray to God Daily, under the heading, Why We Cannot See God.

13. Who is liberated (referring to life)?	A God-oriented person who meditates on God is liberated.
14. Who is the person that is united with God from within and without?	One who comprehends the God's Naam, hymns (Shabads) is united with God within and without.
15. Who comes? 16. Who goes?	Self-centered person comes and perishes (goes). A God-oriented person merges in Truth.
17. Who is permeating and pervading the three worlds (earth, water and space)?	True God is pervading the three worlds of earth, water and sky and a God-oriented person knows that.
18. How is one bound and consumed by the serpent of Maya, the worldly things?	A person with evil intellect is bound and eaten by Maya, the worldly things, the Serpent.
19. How does one lose?	A self-centered person loses.
20. How does one gain?	A God oriented person gains.
21. How does one become immaculate and pure?	By controlling excessive ego, one becomes pure and merges with God
22. How is the darkness of ignorance removed?	One's darkness of ignorance is removed by meeting True God.

Guru Nanak further explained that if one's inner self is immersed with God then one's mind remains in peace and the physical body does not fall prey to bad temptations. One can then consider the cave of equipoise, where everything is in perfect equilibrium, as one's True Home. ***Guru Nanak also said that True God loves the truthful people.***

6. GURU NANAK'S ANSWERS TO QUESTIONS 23 TO 38

The Sidhs asked Guru Nanak for his true opinion about the following questions.

QUESTIONS BY SIDHS	ANSWERS BY GURU NANAK
23. What is the reason that forsaking your home you have started living alone?	I left my home in order to search for God-oriented people.
24. Why have you adopted this religious garb?	I have worn this dress in order to have inner vision of God.
25. What is your merchandise if you are a trader?	I trade in the merchandise of Truth.
26. How will you obtain salvation for your followers?	The God-oriented people will obtain salvation with the grace of God.
27. By which way you have changed your course of life?	By being attached to True God I have changed my life and my wandering is over (referring to reincarnation).
28. With what have you attached your mind?	I have attached and immersed my mind to the heavenly Hymns.
29. How have you subdued your hopes and desires?	I have controlled my hopes and desires by chanting True God's Naam (Shabads).
30. How have you obtained God's supreme light within you?	By being God centered and with the grace of God I have found God's supreme light within me.
31. How can one eat iron without teeth? (do anything)	By controlling the three temptations [4] of, excessive ego, excessive optimism and excessive pessimism, one can then eat iron without teeth (can do anything).

Guru Nanak further said that God the Liberator, frees people from the transmigration of soul.

QUESTIONS BY SIDHS	ANSWERS BY GURU NANAK
32. What view you have regarding the beginning?	No one knows the beginning. One can only think and talk about it in terms of wonder.
33. Where did God abide in the beginning?	In the beginning the profound God dwelt within self.
34. What is your opinion regarding the earrings of spiritual knowledge?	Desirelessness is considered to be the earrings of God's spiritual knowledge.
35. Who abides in all living beings?	True God lives in all living beings.
36. How can death's stroke be eliminated?	If one realize God, the creator of the whole universe, then one is not affected by death's stroke. Nanak then becomes a slave of such person.
37. How can one enter the home of fearlessness?	By comprehending God's hymns (Shabads), one can get rid of excessive ego and corruption, then can one abide in one's own home of fearlessness.
38. How can one obtain contentment and conquer adversaries of anger, greed and worldly attachments?	By serving one God and none else, one can obtain contentment and conquer adversaries of anger, greed and worldly attachments.

7. GURU NANAK'S ANSWERS TO QUESTIONS 39 TO 48

Sidhs said any person who can explain these questions will be called Guru and will not have even one iota of greed.

QUESTIONS BY SIDHS	ANSWERS BY GURU NANAK
39. From where has the human being come?	It was from God's command that brought the human beings.

QUESTIONS BY SIDHS	ANSWERS BY GURU NANAK
40. Where do they go?	God's will takes them back.
41. How do they get merged?	They get merged according to God's will.
42. How can human beings obtain the formless reality of God?	By listening to God's words, hymns (Shabads) one can easily merge in the pure formless reality of God.
43. How can a God-oriented person enshrine love for God?	By practicing truth and realizing God's dignity and worth, one is then blessed with God's love.
44. God is the listener and God is the Creator, Nanak share with us your wisdom?	Wondrous is the will of God who is the listener and Creator. God gives the Command and knows the True way of life of all the creatures.
45. When does life start?	Taking of breath is the beginning of life.
46. At present what type of teaching is to be practiced?	Faith in True God is controlling at this time.
47. Who is your Guru and of whom are you a disciple?	God's Naam (Shabad) is my Guru. I am God's disciple and love to meditate on God.
48. What type of religious uttering do you perform that keeps you detached?	I remain detached by being absorbed in God who cannot be described in words.

Guru Nanak emphasized that God is my Guru who takes care of all and is true through all ages.

8. GURU NANAK'S ANSWERS TO QUESTIONS 49 THROUGH 56

The Sidhs then said "O boy Nanak, listen and answer questions."

QUESTIONS BY SIDHS	ANSWERS BY GURU NANAK
49. How can Hymns (Shabads) ferry human beings across the terrible ocean?	By meditating on God's divine discourse human beings can cross the terrible ocean (referring to life and salvation).

Guru Nanak also said that a God-oriented person can reduce the desire for ego.

QUESTIONS BY SIDHS	ANSWERS BY GURU NANAK
50. How can one chew iron with "teeth of wax" (colloquialism)?	Iron can be chewed by the power of God's divine hymns (Shabads). However, a self centered person will find this world very difficult.
51. What is that food that takes away pride?	Pride can be conquered by keeping absorbed in the True Fear of God. Believing also in one God and pondering over God's Name (Shabads). That is the food.
52. How can one live in the mansion, house of snow (colloquialism)?	One can live in the mansion, house of snow by enshrining the True Name of God in one's mind and by keeping mind and body immersed and dyed with the color of God's Love.
53. How can one wear robes of fire in the above house (colloquialism)?	The fire of excessive lust, excessive anger and corruption is quenched with the mercy of the Beloved God.
54. Where is that cave where The mind remains calm?	By eradicating excessive ego, excessive individualism from within, believing in one God and none other, one becomes closer to God. This is the cave where mind remains calm.
55. Who is the one that pervades here and there? (meaning: everywhere)	There is only one God that pervades here and there, within and without.
56. What is the realization that makes the mind merge with the mind itself?	When the fire of bad desires, excessive anger, excessive greed, excessive worldly love and excessive ego are quenched then the mind merges with itself (becomes one with God). This realization is obtained through the grace of God.

9. GURU NANAK'S ANSWERS TO QUESTIONS 57 TO 61

QUESTIONS BY SIDHS	ANSWERS BY GURU NANAK

The Sidhs asked Guru Nanak to give thoughtful replies to the following five questions.

57. How can the mind that is Like the moon, dark and cold, get illuminated?	By uttering God's Naam, hymns (Shabads) the mind is illuminated infinitely.
58. How does the sun blaze so brilliantly?	When the sun dwells in the house of the moon, the darkness is gone.
59. How can the constant watchful gaze of Death be turned away?	Abiding by God's Name in the mind, death ceases then happiness and sadness appear to be the same.
60. By which intellectual way God save the honor of the God-oriented person?	God himself saves and redeems the honor of the God-oriented person.
61. Who is that powerful person that conquers death?	With faith in God the mind merges in the Truth, and with God's grace one is not concerned with death.

Guru Nanak further explained his responses.

i. There is power in God's Name. God is known to be the most exalted one.
ii. Without God's Name human beings suffer from pain of death.
iii. Complete peace of mind is obtained by merging one's soul with God.
iv. When one believes in only one God then one enters God's home.
v. When the breath blows across the sky of the Tenth Gate* [5] and vibrates then one intuitively meets the eternal, unchanging God.

*The Nine Gates refer to the 9 apertures of the body. They include two ears, two nostrils, two eyes, one mouth, one anus, and one for urine.
Tenth Gate is for union with God.

vi. God is within us, without us and God is permeated in the three worlds.

vii. Vice and virtue look the same to the person who realizes God in the fourth state* [6],

* Four stages of mind are i) Awake ii) Sleeping iii) Deep Sleep iv) Absorption of mind with God.

viii. He who knows the mystery of God (that is pervading in all hearts) is the manifestation of the Primal, the Pure and Divine God.

ix. One who is absorbed in Pure God's Name is like God who is creator of all.

10. GURU NANAK'S ANSWERS TO QUESTIONS 62 TO 70

QUESTIONS BY SIDHS	ANSWERS BY GURU NANAK

The Sidhs said everyone speaks of the Immortal God.

62. How is Immortal God obtained?	God-oriented people obtain the Immortal God by controlling their mind, body, and soul.
63. What type of people are embedded with the imperishable God?	People when embedded with God become God like from whom they are originated. For them there is no transmigration of soul and they do not come and go.
64. What is that place where evil thoughts are destroyed?	Evil thoughts are destroyed, by comprehending God's Naam, hymns (Shabads).
65. One who do not understand the Reality of God why do they suffer in pain?	The self-centered person does not understand the reality of God's Naam, hymns (Shabads). Those people having evil intellect are separated from God and thus suffer in pain.

Guru Nanak further explained:

i. Submitting to God's will, one is blessed with all virtues and divine knowledge and thus obtain honor at God's place.

ii. One who possesses merchandise and wealth of True God's Name, hymns (Shabads) saves him/herself and induces others to save themselves as well.

iii. One who intuitively understands and is tuned to God obtains honor. No one can evaluate the worth of that person.

iv. **Whereever I look I see God pervading everywhere.** Through God's True love, one crosses the world ocean (transmigration of soul).

QUESTIONS BY SIDHS	ANSWERS BY GURU NANAK
66. How can one obtain divine knowledge to swim across this worldly ocean?	Understanding the True God's Naam, hymns (Shabads) one obtains divine knowledge, then swims across and reaches the door of salvation.
67. What is the name of that place where God lives?	The Invisible God lives within all of us and wherever I look God is there.

Further Guru Nanak explained:

i. ***As air is all-pervading so is God all-pervading. God has no qualities and God has all qualities. God is all-inclusive.***
ii. **When God bestows mercy then God's Naam, hymns (Shabads) abide in one's mind and doubt is dispelled from within.**
iii. Body and mind become pure through the Pure God's Naam, hymns (Shabads). God's Name is then enshrined in one's mind.

68. By what way can one cross the terrible world ocean?	With the understanding of God's Naam hymns (Shabads) the terrible world ocean can be crossed. One then knows one God here and thereafter.
69. The breath when exhaled extends out ten finger lengths from the nostrils. What is the support of that breath?	O' Yogi, the True God is the support of the exhaled breath that extends out ten finger lengths from the nostrils.

Further Guru Nanak explained:

The God-oriented person utters and comprehends the Reality of God and realizes that God is infinite and cannot be perceived.

70. While speaking and playing how can one be stable and steady?	When one effaces the three temperaments [7] (excessive optimism, excessive pessimism and excessive egotism) and enshrines God's Naam, hymns (Shabads) within the mind, then ego is gone and the mind becomes steady.

Further Guru Nanak explained:

i. When one knows God within and without then one professes love for God's Naam, hymns (Shabads).
ii. When God that cannot be perceived reveals to one then that person is blessed with divine knowledge while the Sidhs (Yogis) think they perceive God through breath control using the central, left and right bronchi.
iii. The True God is above the three devices of breath control. By True God's Naam, hymns (Shabads) one merges with God.

11. GURU NANAK'S ANSWERS TO QUESTIONS 71 TO 79

QUESTIONS BY SIDHS	ANSWERS BY GURU NANAK
71. How can the invisible God be seen?	God has no form, no color, and is free from darkness and worldliness. God is recognized and seen through the God's Naam hymns (Shabads).

Guru Nanak further explained:

Hear dear Yogis, Nanak says truthfully, instruct your mind that the God-oriented person is tuned to the True God and by God's grace one is united with God. God is all-wise and sees all. ***Through perfect destiny, one merges with God.***

72. Yogi's said air is the life of the mind. What is the food that air eats?	Air gets its food form God and nowhere else. However, thrust for ego never goes away.
73. How should Yogis having spiritual knowledge live?	The Yogis having spiritual knowledge shall obtain immortality by imbruing in God's Naam, hymns (Shabads).
74. What is the job of a Yogi expert in religious matters?	The job of the Yogi is to remain fully satisfied with True God.
75. With what knowledge does one remain steadfast?	By feeling happiness and pain alike one remains steadfast in mind.
76. With what type of food one remains fully satisfied?	With the True God's Naam, hymns (Shabads) as food,one remains fully satisfied and is not afraid of death.

Guru Nanak further explained:
For a person who is not imbrued with God's love, is not absorbed in God's Nectar, and is not aware of God's word. That person

A. That person remains distressed.
B. That person is consumed by one's inner fire.
C. That person's seed is not preserved (regarding the propagation of the next generation as God-oriented people).
D. That person does not utter God's Naam, hymns (Shabads).
E. That person does not reform one's life.
F. That person does not meditate on the True God.

For a person who speaks the unutterable discourses of God,

A. That person, remains balanced in life (treats happiness and agony alike)
B. That person, attains God who is present everywhere.
C. That person is imbrued with God's love by the grace of God.
D. That person, by obtaining Nectar, is absorbed in Truth.
E. That person ponders over God and his/her inner fire is quenched.
F. That person's soul finds peace by drinking God's Nectar
G. That God-oriented person crosses the world ocean, contemplating the True God with God's grace.
H. That rare person understands this wisdom and this is attuned to God through deep meditation.

QUESTIONS BY SIDHS	**ANSWERS BY GURU NANAK**
77. Where does the mind like an elephant reside?	When God shows mercy and leads one to the True God, then the mind like an elephant resides in its own home within. When one control the excessive ego the wandering mind is restrained and becomes pure.
78. Where does the breath reside?	The breath resides in the navel region of the body.
79. Where should God's Naam reside (O' detached Nanak) wandering so that the wandering of the mind may cease?	God's Naam resides within all of us, and deep in our body and mind. When the of our mind ceases, the mind then receives the light of God that is pervading in the three worlds.

Guru Nanak further explained:

i. Sorrows are gone when one's appetite is for True God and one is then fully satisfied with truthful living.
ii. A God-oriented person knows the unsung sound of the God's Naam, hymns (Shabads) through God and only rare people understand this.
iii. One who tells the truth and is imbrued with truth; It is the dye (color) of True God that never fades.

12. GURU NANAK'S ANSWERS TO QUESTIONS 80 TO 89

QUESTIONS BY SIDHS	ANSWERS BY GURU NANAK
80. How can the root source of all (God) be known?	When the mind becomes stable and steady within our body, then God-oriented person realizes the root source of all (God).
81. How can one realize one's own soul (real self)?	One can realize soul (real self) by searching and this occurs through God' grace.
82. How can the sun enter into the house of the moon?	When God-oriented person removes excessive ego from within, then the sun easily enters into the house of the moon (this relates to our body).
83. When there was no heart and body where did the mind reside?	When there was no heart and body then the mind abided in the Detached God.
84. When there was no support of the navel-lotus, then in which home did the breath reside?	When there was no support for the navel-lotus the breath stayed in its own home tuned to the God's Love.
85. When there was no form or shape how could one lovingly focus on God's Naam (Shabad)?	When there was no form or shape or social class then God's Naam (Shabad) resided in God who cannot be seen or traced.
86. When there was no body, fashioned from ovum and sperm, how could one measure God's value and vastness?	When there was no body, no world and no sky then the light of the Formless God pervaded the three worlds.

QUESTIONS BY SIDHS	ANSWERS BY GURU NANAK
87. When God's color, garb and form were not seen, how could then the True God be known?	When the color, garb and the form of one God were not seen then every thing resided in the wonderful God.

Guru Nanak further explained:

Without the True God's Name no one can become pure, as these are the unspoken True Words.

88. How and in what way did the world came into being?	We all came into this world with Haume of excessive lust.
89. By what disaster will it end?	By forgetting the God's Naam, hymns (Shabads) the world will suffer and then perish.

13. SUMMARY

Guru Nanak explained the philosophy of the Sikh Religion through 89 answers to the questions posed by Sidhs (Yogis). Guru Nanak stated that there is one God that is True, Limitless and most Admirable. One must live in this world with people and not lead a secluded life. One has to live honorably with all the temptations of the world.

The word Man in Punjabi has no English equivalent. Man is a combination of mind, body and soul used together or individually as required by the Shabad (hymn). Union with God is obtained by meditation on God's Naam, hymns (Shabads) and by renunciation of excessive lust, excessive anger, excessive greed, excessive ego and excessive pride. The Sidhs (Yogis) way to union with God is what one wears, how one eats, where one lives l(in the woods away from people) and believing in Ai section of Yogis. Guru Nanak disagreed with that system.

Guru Nanak emphasized that modesty, contentment and self-discipline are the principles of life. God cannot be seen as God permeates the whole Universe and it is not scientifically possible for our eyes to see God.

If one's inner self is immersed in God then one's mind is at peace. God also loves truthful people.

Hopes and desires can be controlled by chanting True God's Naam, hymns (Shabads). One can be liberated (from transmigration of soul) by the grace of God who is the Liberator. True God lives in all living beings.

Human beings come according to God's command and they merge according to God' s will. Guru is God and God is Guru. God's love is obtained by practicing truth and realizing God's dignity and worth. Life begins by taking breath. God is our Guru who takes care of all and is True through all ages.

By controlling bad desires of excessive anger, excessive greed, excessive worldly love and excessive ego the mind merges with itself (becomes one with God).

Mind can be illuminated, by uttering God's Naam, hymns (Shabads). God saves God-oriented people. Complete peace of mind is obtained by merging one's soul with God. By absorbing in Pure God's Naam one is like God, the creator of all.

The Tenth gate (the other nine are apertures in our body) is where one meets True God. Those who follow God's path get tuned to truth. The evil thoughts are destroyed by contemplating God's Naam, hymns (Shabads). As air pervades everywhere so God is all-pervading. God is infinite and cannot be perceived. By chanting God's hymns (Shabads), one merges with God.

By keeping happiness and pain alike, one remains steadfast in mind. Some rare people understand this wisdom. By God's grace and contemplating on True God, one can cross the world ocean of life. Sorrows are gone when one's appetite is for True God. The God-oriented person is fully satisfied with truthful living.

When there was no body, no world and no sky then the light of the Formless God pervaded the three worlds. By forgetting the God's Name world will suffer pain and will perish.

14. EXERCISES

i. Explain why the discussion is very important to the Universal Religion of Sikhism.
ii. Explain what Guru Nanak said to the Sidhs when they asked him to bow before them.
iii. What is the meaning of the Punjabi word Man and what is its importance?
iv. What is the basic difference between Guru Nanak's way of union with God and that of the Sidhs?

v. What are the three things that Guru Nanak mentioned should be the principles of our day-to-day lives?
vi. Explain why God cannot be seen with our eyes.
vii. What type of people are united with God?
viii. What type of people come and go (referring to transmigration of soul)?
ix. How can one control excessive hopes and excessive desires?
x. When was the world created?
xi. How can one control, excessive anger, excessive greed, excessive ego, excessive pride and excessive worldly attachments?
xii. Where did human beings come from?
xiii. Where do human beings get merged?
xiv. How can one have love for God?
xv. When does life begin?
xvi. How does the mind merge with self?
xvii. How can mind be illuminated?
xviii. Who has the power to conquer death?
xix. How can one get complete peace of mind?
xx. Explain the importance of the Tenth Gate?
xxi. How can one save him/herself and others as well?
xxii. How can evil thoughts be destroyed?
xxiii. What does one obtain by keeping happiness and pain alike?
xxiv. What type of people live truthful lives?
xxv. Who was there when there was no body, no world, and no sky?
xxvi. When will the world perish?

15. REFERENCES

[1] W. H. McLeod. *Guru Nanak and the Sikh Religion*, 1988 3rd Impression, Page 178, Oxford University Press, New Delhi, India
[2] Manmohan Singh. *Sri Guru Granth Sahib*, English and Punjabi Translations, 1983 Vol 8 Page 4746, Shirimoni Gurdwara Parbhandak Committee, Amritsar, Punjab, India.
[3] http://www.swamij.com/six-schools-indian-philosophy.htm "Six Schools of Indian Philosophy" by Swami Jnaneshvara Bharati.
[4] Manmohan Singh. *Sri Guru Granth Sahib*, English and Punjabi Translations, 1983 Vol 8 Page 4739, Shirimoni Gurdwara Parbhandak Committee, Amritsar, Punjab, India.
[5] Reference [4] page 4742.
[6] Reference [4] page 4733.
[7] Reference [4] page 4739.

UNIVERSALITY OF THE SIKH RELIGION

CHAPTER 17

EDUCATION, KNOWLEDGE, WISDOM

The Sikh Religion approves of all types of education for the betterment of society. ***Education is development of knowledge, wisdom, skill and character acquired from teaching, training, study or experience.*** All these qualities are extremely important not only for surviving in this world but also for being a good citizen of the world. Knowledge, wisdom, skill and character, even if not acquired in a formal institution, are part and parcel of education.

An educated person is generally free of prejudices, ignorance and tries to reason and understand before accepting any idea.

Education can be classified into three categories. All of them are very important. Education for girls as well as boys is equally important. It is said that if a boy gets education, only one person is educated. If a girl gets education, the whole family gets educated. The three categories for education, knowledge and wisdom are:

FORMAL EDUCATION TO BE A BETTER PROFESSIONAL
RELIGIOUS EDUCATION TO BE A BETTER PERSON
DAY-TO-DAY EDUCATION TO BE A BETTER WORLD CITIZEN

The above three categories are discussed below.

1. FORMAL EDUCATION TO BE A BETTER PROFESSIONAL

Such an education is generally acquired at formal schools and colleges. The higher the education, the better it is for the profession. It is almost becoming universal to get an education at a formal educational institution. They produce professional people in almost all fields, including science, medicine, religion, psychology, economics, finance, business, art and history. Almost all countries are making it compulsory that all people should have some sort of formal education. ***Formal education is the cornerstone for our success in the competitive world in which we live in.*** One has to be a professional in their particular field. It does not make much difference what field of education one wants to pursue. It is very advantageous to get as much education as one can from the schools. Every educational field makes a positive contribution to the advancement of society. One must enjoy the work and do one's best in whatever type of profession one chooses in one's life.

In general three professions are considered noble because of their special importance in life. One is teaching, as it imparts knowledge to the students; the second is medicine, as it saves lives; and the third is agriculture, as it gives food to live. However, it should be emphasized that all other professions are essential for our day-to-day living.

It is very important for people belonging to the Sikh Religion not only to get as much education as possible but also to help others who can least afford it. The question is, How does one help? The easiest way is to sponsor a scholarship for a needy student after one is well established in their profession. Select any school of your choice. It could be the school from where one has graduated. A small endowment fund can be established where only the interest is used for awarding the scholarship. Thus the scholarship can go on forever. One can think of many other ways to help in the education of needy people.

2. RELIGIOUS EDUCATION TO BE A BETTER PERSON

This can be acquired at religious place of worship but more so by reading the Holy Books. For people belonging to the Sikh Religion learning of Punjabi in Gurmukhi script is very essential. One has to read the words written in the Guru Granth Sahib in order to understand the real meaning. English translation or in any other language do help considerably but sometimes it does not convey the real meaning. ***Religious education, in true sense, makes one a better person.***

i. RELIGIOUS EDUCATION IN SCHOOLS

Educational institutions paid by governments do not allow religious teachings as part of their curriculum. Since there are so many religions it is not possible to teach all of them. It is also the policy of democracies that religion is not the responsibility of the government; it should be left to individuals and the private sector. Education without religious teaching is not complete. The question is, How does one get religious education? It is not easy. Not many people attend their place of worship, for many reasons, and are thus devoid of religious teaching.

Educational institutions paid by religious organizations do have religious teaching. However, it is restricted to the religion to which that organization belongs. Sometimes these religious organizations become very fanatic and thus cause unrest in the community. As long as peace and harmony with other religions is preached and practiced, no problems will be created.

The Sikh Religion emphasizes the importance of education, knowledge and wisdom. ***It clearly states that one must understand and comprehend before believing any part of the religious or any other teaching*** [1] and [2].

Second Guru, Angad, paid special attention to the proper education of all people. He insisted that children should be taught in their mother tongue, and to that end he simplified and codified the Gurmukhi script and popularized its use among the people. This was the most important contribution of Guru Angad [3]. Later, the Guru Granth Sahib was written in Gurmukhi script of the Punjabi language.

The spiritual part of our life is even more important than the education received from our schools and colleges. ***Spiritual knowledge leads to contentment and peace of mind. It makes a better person to serve humanity.***

ii. TRANSLATION OF THE GURU GRANTH SAHIB IN DIFFERENT LANGUAGES

For those who do not know the Punjabi language, the Guru Granth Sahib has been translated into many different languages. ***It is very easy to get English, Roman and Hindi translations on the Internet.***

Several individuals have translated the Guru Granth Sahib into English. This is required especially for those who do not know Punjabi in Gurmukhi script. They have tried their best to translate it into English and must be commended for their efforts. However, there is no standardized English translation that is universally accepted. It would be very nice if a group of highly intellectual people would translate it into very simple English. Literal translation into English does not covey the real meanings of Shabads (Hymns) as the Guru Granth Sahib is written in poetry in Gurmukhi language. It should be translated in a way that explains the real meaning of the Shabads (Hymns) that can be easily comprehended by a person who has no knowledge of Punjabi. It would also help people who do not belong to the Sikh religion.

The English translation of the Bible [4], [5] is not free from controversy. There have been many English translations of the Bible starting from the fourteenth century and people are still adding English translations today. The Old Testament was originally written in Hebrew and the New Testament was translated from Greek. The most popular of all English translations is the New International Version (NIV). This is the translation of choice for the majority of Protestants. It is highly meaning-based. The Catholics use their own version, which is more literal.

I hope some day, sooner rather than later, the Guru Granth Sahib will be translated into English language that is universally accepted all over the world.

iii. RELIGIOUS EDUCATION FROM THE GURU GRANTH SAHIB

Guru Granth Sahib stressed very heavily that religious education is of utmost importance for the development of the human mind and its relation to God and society.

A. EDUCATION AS A PREREQUISITE TO SERVE HUMANITY

Serving humanity is one of the fundamental teachings of the Sikh Religion. To help others is good for the individual, community, country and the world at large. It is therefore necessary to have some instructions on how to best serve humanity. The world is changing rapidly, and today everyone has to deal with the following conditions.

a. ***Finding ways to live peacefully with racially diverse societies.***
b. ***Being tolerant and respecting all other religions.***
c. ***Using international cooperation and collaboration to solve world problems.***
d. ***Being ready to adjust to new technological advancements in every field.***

It is thus imperative that one must be appropriately educated to render service to humanity. According to the Sikh Religion the purpose of religious teaching (education) is to prepare one to help others.

The Guru Granth Sahib puts great stress on *comprehending* religious teaching rather than following it blindly.

The first Guru, Nanak, said:

PUNJABI AND ROMAN	**ENGLISH**
ਵਿਦਿਆ ਵੀਚਾਰੀ	First deliberate and understand the religious
Vidi-aa Veechaaree	teaching (education)
ਤਾਂ ਪਰਉਪਕਾਰੀ ॥	Only then one can help others.
TaaN Par-upkaaree.	
Guru Granth Sahib (p. 356, line 14)	

B. NO EMANCIPATION WITHOUT KNOWLEDGE (EDUCATION)

The Sikh Religion says that salvation or liberation cannot be achieved without knowledge and education. Understanding of religious teachings is very important for emancipation.

The first Guru, Nanak, said:

PUNJABI AND ROMAN	ENGLISH
ਮੁਕਤਿ ਨਹੀ	One cannot be emancipated without
Mukat Nahee	
ਬਿਦਿਆ ਬਿਗਿਆਨਿ II	education and knowledge.
Bidi-aa Bigi-aan	
Guru Granth Sahib (p. 903, line 14)	

C. IMPORTANCE OF UNDERSTANDING THE SHABADS (HYMNS)

A person belonging to the Sikh Religion must understand the words written in the Shabads (Hymns) in the Guru Granth Sahib. The following two verses make very clear the importance given to the understanding of the written words.

The first Guru, Nanak, said:

PUNJABI AND ROMAN	ENGLISH
ਸਿਖੀ ਸਿਖਿਆ	Person belonging to Sikhism is the
Sikhee Sikhi-aa	one who contemplates on the
ਗੁਰ ਵੀਚਾਰਿ II	religious teachings.
Gur Veechaar	
Guru Granth Sahib (p. 465, line 10)	

The first Guru, Nanak, said;

PUNJABI AND ROMAN	ENGLISH
ਸਭਸੈ ਊਪਰਿ	Highest importance is given to the
Sabhsai Oopar	discussion and understanding
ਗੁਰ ਸਬਦੁ ਬੀਚਾਰੁ II	of the Shabads (Hymns).
Gur Sabad Beechaar	
Guru Granth Sahib (p. 904, line 13)	

D. EVALUATION OF SHABADS (HYMNS)

Evaluation of Shabads (Hymns) should take into account present day living, especially relating to the country of adoption, but it has to be a two-way discussion: listening and asking questions. There is complete freedom of expression in the Sikh Religion. Any discussion can be carried out if one listens and expresses one's view to others in an intelligent way.

The first Guru, Nanak, said:

PUNJABI AND ROMAN	ENGLISH
ਜਬ ਲਗੁ ਦੁਨੀਆ ਰਹੀਐ	As long as one lives in this world
Jab Lag Dunee-aa Rahee-ai	
ਨਾਨਕ ਕਿਛੁ ਸੁਣੀਐ ਕਿਛੁ ਕਹੀਐ ॥	Nanak says, one must listen and
Naanak Kichh Sunee-ai Kichh Kahee-ai. Guru Granth Sahib (p. 661, line 1)	express to others (about Truth).

E. DO NOT FOLLOW BLINDLY

Do not follow blindly what religious preachers are saying. ***Evaluate the words and be sure that they are logical and are following the teachings as written in the Guru Granth Sahib.*** It is made clear in the following two verses.

The first Guru, Nanak, said:

PUNJABI AND ROMAN	ENGLISH
ਪਹਿਲਾ ਵਸਤੁ ਸਿਞਾਣਿ ਕੈ	First evaluate the things (religious
Pahilaa Vasat Sinjaan Kai	teaching)
ਤਾਂ ਕੀਚੈ ਵਾਪਾਰੁ ॥	then make a deal (adopt them).
TaaN Keechai Vaapaar Guru Granth Sahib (p. 1410, line 5)	

The fifth Guru, Arjan Dev, said:

PUNJABI AND ROMAN	ENGLISH
ਬੂਝੈ ਬੂਝਨਹਾਰੁ ਬਿਬੇਕ ॥	Those who use acute intellectual knowledge
Boojhai Boojhanhaar Bibayk Guru Granth Sahib (p.285, line 12)	understand the Shabads (Hymns).

F. IMPORTANCE OF RESEARCH

Research is very important for interpreting the Shabads (Hymns). ***One must use logic in today's highly technological society.*** It will thus become very easy to convince the younger generation about the teachings of the Guru Granth Sahib.

The first Guru, Nanak, said:

PUNJABI AND ROMAN	ENGLISH
ਖੋਜੀ ਉਪਜੈ ਬਾਦੀ ਬਿਨਸੈ ॥	One who searches for God is successful
Khojee Upjai Baadee Binsai Guru Granth Sahib (p. 1255, line 7)	and the one who quarrels perishes.

G. SERVE GOD WISELY

Even when the grace of God is upon you to serve God, emphasis is on the use of wisdom in doing so. Wise people also get respect and honor from the community and society in general.

The first Guru, Nanak, said:

PUNJABI AND ROMAN	ENGLISH
ਅਕਲੀ ਸਾਹਿਬੁ ਸੇਵੀਐ	Serve God wisely and
Aklee Saahib Sayvee-ai	
ਅਕਲੀ ਪਾਈਐ ਮਾਨੁ ॥	through wisdom honor is obtained.
Aklee Paa-ee-ai Maan. Guru Granth Sahib (p.1245, line 3)	

H. READING WITHOUT UNDERSTANDING IS NOT EDUCATION

The Sikh Religion says that reading alone is not educational. ***One has to comprehend the real meaning of the Shabads (Hymns).*** It has been clearly explained in the following two quotations from Guru Granth Sahib.

The first Guru, Nanak, said:

PUNJABI AND ROMAN	ENGLISH
ਪਾਠ ਪੜੈ	By merely reciting Holy Books
Paath Parhai	
ਨਹੀ ਕੀਮਤਿ ਪਾਇ ॥	one does not comprehend the real worth.
Nahee Keemat Paa-ay. Guru Granth Sahib (p.355, line 8)	

The third Guru, Amar Das, said:

PUNJABI AND ROMAN	ENGLISH
ਪੜਿ ਪੜਿ ਥਾਕੇ	One can be exhausted by continuously reading
Parh Parh Thaakay	
ਸਾਂਤਿ ਨ ਆਈ ll	and still does not find peace of mind.
SaaNt Na Aa-ee.	
Guru Granth Sahib (p.120, line 6)	

I. MIND AND KNOWLEDGE

Education is very important for guiding the mind toward the right direction. One has to study the Shabads (Hymns) to acquire knowledge and use in day-to-day living.

Kabir said:

PUNJABI AND ROMAN	ENGLISH
ਮਨ ਸਮਝਾਵਨ ਕਾਰਨੇ	In order to enlighten one's mind
Man Samjhaavan Kaarnay	
ਕਛੂਅਕ ਪੜੀਐ ਗਿਆਨ ll	one must study and acquire
Kachhoo-ak Parhee-ai Gi-aan	knowledge.
Guru Granth Sahib (p. 340, line 8)	

J. PRAY FOR ENLIGHTENED MIND

People belonging to the Sikh Religion pray and ask for the gift of proper educational enlightenment.

The fifth Guru, Arjan Dev, said:

PUNJABI AND ROMAN	ENGLISH
ਦਾਸ ਤੇਰੇ ਕੀ ਬੇਨਤੀ	This is my (one who believes in God)
Daas Tayray Kee Bayntee	prayer
ਰਿਦ ਕਰਿ ਪਰਗਾਸੁ ll	that I be blessed with an enlightened
Rid Kar Pargaas	mind.
Guru Granth Sahib (p. 818, line 9)	

iv. RELIGION AND POLITICS (GOVERNMENT)

Most of the democratic countries in this world are secular. ***Religion and politics are kept separate.*** Generally, religion is the responsibility of the individual and there is no government involvement. This is an ideal situation. However, some countries involve religion either directly or indirectly in politics. This occurs in those countries where vast majority of the people, belong to only one religion. Thus it becomes very difficult for minorities to exercise their religious rights.

In most of the countries in this world people of different religions live together often as neighbors. This trend is increasing considerably due to the fast movement of people from one country to another. In many cases people are migrating and acquiring citizenship in other countries. ***So it appears that religions that have universal appeal will find more receptive people and will flourish.***

People have been fighting with each other from the very beginning of time. Many times religion is the bone of contention. They may be Christians, Muslims, Jews, Hindus, Sikhs or members of any other religion. Thus, religion enters into politics and starts dictating how the country is run, according to their religion. Some countries are mixing religion and politics officially in their constitutions. This varies from country to country. ***Some countries treat all people as equals while others do not.***

v. SIKH RELIGION AND POLITICS

This is a very controversial issue in the Sikh Religion. It is discussed below.

A. PERIOD FROM 1469 TO 1849

During the period of the ten Sikh Gurus, Muslims were the rulers. They were committing atrocities among all types of people. The persecution of innocent people in India was going on for thousands of years before and after Christ. The local Hindu people were so weak that there was no opposition to the Muslim invaders. It was essentially a religious war. Someone had to unite the Hindus (make them soldiers) in order to protect their religion from the aggressors. Sikhs were the only force and so lot of Hindus joined the Sikh religion to fight the invaders.

A very novel concept of MIRI-PIRI (soldier as well as a devoted religious person), was started by 6th Guru Hargobind in 1606. This was created to stop the brutal killing by Muslim invaders and to create a just society. Fifth Guru Arjan

Dev, father of the sixth Guru, was brutally tortured to death by the Muslim rulers. The only reason was that he belonged to the Sikh religion.

MIRI (Soldier) represents strength, courage, power and bravery. PIRI (Religion) represents compassion, humility, love and service to the needy. This was a unique concept in order to free people from the foreign invaders. No innocent people were ever killed. The involvement of religion was absolutely essential as there was no legitimate government. The MIRI-PIRI concept was the right thing to do and religion was the driving force to unite people for the common cause of defeating the invaders.

Muslim invaders continued their atrocities unabated. The Muslim rulers in Delhi beheaded ninth Guru Tegh Bahadur as he was protecting the Hindu religion and refused to change from Sikh religion to a Muslim religion. His son, the tenth Guru Gobind Singh gave rise to the Khalsa Sikh concept in 1675 by giving a distinct physical appearance to Sikhs—long hair and a turban. The concept of MIRI-PIRI, was then put into practice, on a large scale by Guru Gobind Singh. This was extremely successful in curbing the Muslim invaders. However, it took about 91 years after the death of Guru Gobind Singh (1708) to establish the Sikh Kingdom. ***It was Maharaja Ranjit Singh who defeated the Muslim invaders in 1799. The Sikh kingdom was a secular government and not a Sikh religious government.*** Maharaja Ranjit Singh recruited people from all religions for very important positions in the government as well as in the army. Thus every body was considered equal regardless of religion, color, caste or creed. The period of the Sikh Kingdom ended in 1849 when the British conquered India.

B. PRESENT SITUATION

At present the Golden Temple in Amritsar, Punjab, India is the main religious center for the Sikhs. Akal Takht, built by sixth Guru Hargobind, is a part of Golden Temple complex. The organization that runs the temple makes decisions affecting the Sikh community. Here religion and politics intermix to a great extent, even now. ***Theoretically political organizations are separate from the Sikh religion, but in practice there is not much difference. Political leaders in Punjab directly or indirectly appoint religious leaders.***

There is another complication—the government of India is also involved in the Sikh Religion. India is a secular country and the government should not be involved with any religion. However, government of India approved the Sikh Gurdwara Act of 1925. . Although it was passed during the British regime, it is still controlled by the present government of India. There is no Hindu Act, Muslim Act, Christian Act, Buddhist Act or Jain Act. There is no reason why the government (laden with bureaucracy) should be involved in the Sikh religion.

Sikhs must control their own religious affairs without Government involvement. Governments of all other democratic countries do not control any religion. Let learned Sikhs draft their own constitution or procedures as they see fit. Later amendments should be incorporated depending upon new circumstances but they should not change the basic concepts mentioned in the Guru Granth Sahib. Some of the procedures could accommodate the general customs of the adopted country (for example sitting on the chairs instead on the floor). While other amendments should outline that Sikhs of all types need to be treated as equals, in all respects.

C. FUTURE SUGGESTIONS

Does every Sikh have to be a soldier and a religious person? I have to be a professional to earn my living in order to take care of my family's needs. I also have to be a religious person. There is no problem with that, but do I have to be a soldier? At the present time being a soldier is a profession. Wars are fought by scientific techniques. And winners are those having the latest technology. ***I see no need for myself to be a soldier along with my profession.*** I could become a soldier if that is what I want as my profession. The function of a soldier is to defend the country of its adoption.

SECULAR DEMOCRACY

Almost all Sikhs in India or outside India are living in secular democratic countries. The combination of religion and politics is not desirable. People use indirect means to mix politics and religion, that must be discouraged.

SIKHS IN A MAJORITY

Let us take the case where Sikhs are in a majority, as in the state of Punjab in India. Elections are held as per the constitution of the country. Since independence was acquired in 1947, there has almost always been a Sikh Chief Minister. ***So there is no need to mix religion and politics. Sikhs are part of the government at all levels.***

SIKHS IN A MINORITY

Let us take the case where Sikhs are in a minority, such as in Vancouver, British Columbia, Canada. In the year 2000 a Sikh named Ujjal Singh Dosanjh, who was born in Punjab, India, was elected Premier of British Columbia, Canada.

This is only possible in a democracy where rights of all are protected. His election was due to hard work and community service, regardless of his religion, caste, gender, color or ethnicity.

Ironically just 91 years ago Sikhs were not allowed to stay in Canada. Gurdit Singh a Sikh charted Komagata Maru, a Japanese steamliner in 1914. The ship brought 376 people (mostly Sikhs) from Punjab, India to the Vancouver harbor. Canadian authorities did not allow the ship to dock and was turned back.

In democracies things change. It may take time, but a qualified person who is willing to work hard can be elected to very high positions***. In Canada there are many Sikhs who have elected to the Canadian Parliament. Thus there is no need to mix religion and politics.***

MIRI-PIRI IN TODAY'S LIFE

Sikhs hold many high positions in the governments of their adopted countries. There is no need to intermix religion and politics: MIRI (Soldier) power should rest with the government (politics) and PIRI (Religion) is the jurisdiction of the religious people and should not be involved in politics.

Guru Gobind, the tenth Guru, when speaking with Nand Lal, said there is no need to wear a sword. "I need the service of your pen."[6]. ***In the present society let us use pen and not sword to solve all our problems in a peaceful way.***

Let us assume that people belonging to the Sikh Religion have a legitimate grievance. It can be achieved by peaceful means instead of resorting to force. In a democracy pen is mightier than the sword. No one loses their life and by fighting with a pen legitimate objective can be achieved. There is no need to use force. Peaceful means are the most persuasive ways to achieve the objective in democratic countries.

3. DAY-TO-DAY EDUCATION AND BEING A BETTER WORLD CITIZEN

This education is acquired on a daily basis for the rest of our lives. It involves dealing with people and can be learned anywhere, at work, home, or any other place. One also has to be current with the world developments There is no need for any formal training. The main objective of this education is to work for the good of humanity regardless of religion, color, ethnicity, or any other division of the human race.

How can one acquire such knowledge on a daily basis? One has to be current not only with the adopted country but also with the whole world. The following are some of the ways to be current with world affairs.

i. USE OF MODERN TECHNOLOGY

All countries of the world have become intertwined not only for business but also for social and cultural exchanges through the Internet. ***Knowledge is power and it is very important to use this technology to be a better world citizen.*** For instance, the whole Guru Granth Sahib can be downloaded free by using **www.srigranth.org** [7]. Information on all other religions can be obtained in a similar manner.

ii. WORLD WIDE ORGANIZATIONS

There are many organizations that one could join in order to learn more about a particular subject. ***These organizations could be in one's profession, or could be social, cultural or religious.*** One such group is Sikh Diaspora@yahoogroups.com. One can get answers to the questions that are not discussed in Gurdwaras. Just to name a few topics like premarital sex, dating, homosexuality, abortion, five symbols of Sikhs, status of women, rituals, miracles, definition of a Sikh and so on. For a good discussion group the members have to maintain laws of decency and the moderators have to check that no personal remarks by any member get into the discussion. One can choose a specific Internet group according to the requirements of the individual. This way one can get deeper knowledge of the subject of interest.

iii. TELEVISION, AUDIO VISUAL, TRAVEL

Use of television and other audio-visual techniques can enhance our knowledge about societies living in different parts of the world. Many people also visit different countries, which brings people in close contact with each other. They, in turn, can learn many things (business related, socially, culturally or, religiously related) that can be incorporated in their own country.

4. BHAI VIR SINGH AN IDEAL PERSON

Bhai Vir Singh, Figure 33 is an example of an ideal person. No body can equal him in education, knowledge and wisdom. He was born in 1872 when the Sikhs were in complete disarray, due to the end of Maharaja Ranjit Singh's rule and (later) the British takeover of India. The Sikh religion was under attack from the Hindus and the Christians. The Punjabi language also was in great trouble. ***It was the writings of Bhai Vir Singh that elevated the spirit of the Sikhs.***

FIGURE 33

BHAI VIR SINGH
1872 to 1957
IDEAL PERSON

Bhai Vir Singh used pen and not the sword to accomlplish the great objective. Thus the Punjabi language was revived [8],[9],[10].

i. BHAI VIR SINGH AS EDUCATIONALIST

Bhai Vir Singh graduated from Church Mission School (high school) in Amritsar with distinction, receiving the Gold Medal. Bhai Vir Singh was an eminent scholar, poet, and great author. He was the founding member of Khalsa College, Amritsar. He also founded the Sikh Educational Committee to promote education on a large scale. He founded Khalsa Tract Society, in 1894, for propagating the Sikh religion and culture. In 1899 Vir Singh started the publication of *Khalsa Samachar*, a weekly paper of the Sikhs that is still being published in Amritsar, India today. He also established Wazir-I-Hind Press.

Vir Singh was a poetic genius with religious bent of mind. He is the most prolific writer in Indian history. He wrote 6 to 8 hours a day for 60 years and his writings are considered classics. Bhai Vir Singh is acknowledged as the creator of modern Punjabi literature.

In Punjabi language Bhai Vir Singh occupies the same place as Rabinder Nath Tagore (Noble Laureate) in Bengali and Wordsworth in English.

Khuswant Singh [8] sums up Bhai Vir Singh's contributions:

"Wherever the Punjabi language is spoken there will also be Vir Singh's name. Whenever the Sikhs begin to doubt their faith, there will be Vir Singh's spirit to inspire them and beckon them to the fold."

ii. SIMPLICITY OF BHAI VIR SINGH

Bhai Vir Singh was a very humble person. He never appeared at public functions. He never made a speech. He spoke softly. The dominant quality that he left with the visitors was gentleness. He never sought publicity. ***Vir Singh was truly modest and genuinely shy by nature.*** I met him in 1947 when I was 18 years old. My aunt used to live in Amritsar, very close to the house of Bhai Vir Singh; she was also related to him. She, too, was also a writer and asked me to deliver some material to Bhai Vir Singh. I went by bicycle, papers in one hand, hockey stick in the other. When I arrived, I saw a small man with white turban. I said "This is for Bhai Vir Singh Ji." I gave the papers to him and left. When my aunt asked if I delivered the papers, I described the person I saw and she confirmed that it was, in fact, Bhai Vir Singh. I was struck by his wonderful simplicity.

iii. BHAI VIR SINGH AS SOCIAL REFORMER AND HUMANITARIAN

a. At the age of 20 Bhai Vir Singh joined Singh Sabha (Sikh Reform) Movement. The main purpose was to counteract the attacks on Sikh principles at the intellectual level while bringing awareness to the masses.
b. He established an institute for widows called Vidhya Ashram, Amritsar.
c. He started the Blind Asylum in Amritsar.
d. He founded free a Homoeopathic Hospital in Amritsar for the medical needs of the poor people.
e. Bhai Vir Singh also was instrumental in starting Punjab and Sind Bank for the Sikhs to manage their own finances.

Bhai Vir Singh received many awards including Padma Bhushan from the Government of India in 1956. He died in Amritsar in 1957 at the age of 85.

5. FIRST SIKH COLLEGE OF HIGHER LEARNING

The Sikhs recognized the importance of education about 53 years after the death of Maharaja Ranjit Singh. Sir (a title given by the British) Sunder Singh Majithia [11] founded Khalsa College, Figure 34.

The first four principals from 1898 to 1924 were British. They were Dr Johan Campbell Oman (1898 to 1899), M.G.V. Cole (1900 to 1910), R.G.Wright (1910 to 1915) and G.A.Wathen (1915 to 1924). Sardar Bahadur (another title given by the British) Bishan Singh became the first Sikh principal in 1928. This was followed by Bhai Jodh Singh in 1936 who will always be remembered for his professional achievements.

I was a student at Khalsa College, Amritsar, from 1947 to 1950 where I completed my B.S. (Honors) in Chemistry. At that time the chemistry department was very well recognized both inside and outside of India. Bhai Jodh Singh was the principal during that period. He was very well respected and accomplished a great deal, not only for the college but also for the Sikhs in general.

The main building is a masterpiece of Sikh architecture. The college building, a unique architectural monument, is a tourists' delight.

FIGURE 34

KHALSA COLLEGE AMRITSAR, PUNJAB, INDIA
Master Piece of Sikh architecture 1892

6. SUMMARY

Three types of education are very important in order to be a world citizen. Education in a formal school makes one a better professional. Religious education makes one a better person. Day-to-day education is meant to make one a better citizen of the world. Having acquired three types of education (formal, religious and day-to-day) will give peace of mind to the individual and will lead to peace throughout the world. Many examples from the Guru Granth Sahib that explain clearly that it is very important to comprehend the words rather than just read them. It is better to really understand, rather than follow blindly, the teachings of the Sikh Religion.

Politics and religion is very controversial in the Sikh Religion. Years ago all religions were intertwined with politics. The same was true in the case of the Sikh Religion. Even now a days the Sikh Religion and politics are indirectly connected. In the secular democracies of today there is absolutely no need to intermix religion and politics. Peaceful means are the best ways to achieve the objective in a democracy. The pen is mightier than the sword in the present day society.

Minorities can achieve meaningful results to their satisfaction if they are persistent and work hard for their objective. A Sikh born in Punjab became the Premier of British Columbia, Canada. That same province refused Sikhs and others from Punjab entrance into Canada in 1914. Using modern technology is a good way to become a better world citizen. A typical example of a Sikh as an ideal educationalist is Bhai Vir Singh. No one can equal him in education, knowledge and wisdom. Khalsa College, Amritsar, was the first institution of higher learning. It was built in 1892 and is a marvel of Sikh architecture.

7. EXERCISES

i. In order to be a good citizen name three types of education.
ii. What is formal education and how can it be justified?
iii. Give reasons why religious education is important.
iv. Give several quotations showing the importance of education so as to comprehend the meaning of the words written in the Guru Granth Sahib.
v. Should religion and politics be kept separate or not? Give reasons to justify your convictions
vi. Explain the MIRI-PIRI (Soldier-Saint) concept. Why it was very successful 400 years ago? Explain how at present it is better to use pen rather than sword to solve the world problems.

vii. Give examples of how one acquires day-to-day education in order to be a better citizen?

viii. Give an example of an ideal educationalist with regard to education, knowledge and wisdom. Give reasons to support your views.

8. REFERENCES

[1] Dr. (Bhai) Harbans Lal. 1996. "Guru Granth Sahib on Education". *The Sikh Courier International*, Vol. 36. No. 81. Middlesex, Greater London. p. 3-9.

[2] Prof. Devinder Singh Chahal. 2002. "Philosophy of Guru Nanak." The *Sikh Bulletin*, Vol.4. No. 4. Roseville, California USA p. 7-13.

[3] K. S. Duggal. 1989. *Sikh Gurus Their Lives and Teachings*. The Himalayan International Institute, Honesdale, Pennsylvania, USA. p.63.

[4] http://www.friktech.com/rel/canon/english.htm
"The Bible in English, Early Translations."

[5] http://www.geocities.com/bible_translation/compare.htm
"Recent English Bible Versions Compared" by Wayne Leman.

[6] Dr. Teja Singh, Guru Nanak Shrine Fellowship, E-mail Sikh-Diaspora@yahoogroups.com date November 7, 2002.

[7] Go to 'Yahoo.com'. Search for 'Sikhnet.com/s/gurugranthsahib'.
Or www.srigranth.org for translations of *Guru Granth Sahib*.

[8] Khuswant Singh. 1995. "Bhai Vir Singh." *The Sikh Courier International*, Vol. 35. No. 79. Middlesex, Greater London. p. 24-25.

[9] J.S. Guleria Late. 2003. "Bhai Vir Singh—As I Knew Him." *The Sikh Courier International,* Vol. 45. No. 95. Middlesex, Greater London. p. 11-17.

[10] Gurbachan Singh Talib. "Bhai Vir Singh: Life, Times and Works," *Encyclopaedia of Sikhism*, edited by Dr. Harbans Singh
www.sikhpoint.com/religion/ind_BhaiVeerSinghji.asp

[11] *Tribune India*. Feb 10, 2006 by Varinder Walia,
"Khalsa College: A beacon of light"
http://www.tribuneindia.com/2006/20060209/aplus.htm#2

UNIVERSALITY OF THE SIKH RELIGION

CHAPTER 18

EATING AND EXERCISE

Proper eating and exercise are essential for a healthy life. What does the Sikh Religion state with regard to eating and exercise? Guru Granth Sahib and our Gurus have made themselves very clear about eating and exercise: Our aim is to have long and happy life. Scientists and religious people have spent countless hours and endless energy trying to find ways to attain the goal of a long and happy life. The answer lies within ourself. We should know ***that long and happier life is a by-product of healthy nutrition, physical exercise, and mental peace (by being a religious person).*** If we take care of ourselves and perform good deeds then the whole body will prosper and our goal for long and happier life will be met.

Guru Nanak said eating and drinking are essential for survival.

The first Guru, Nanak, said:

PUNJABI AND ROMAN	**ENGLISH**
ਖਾਣਾ ਪੀਣਾ ਪਵਿਤ੍ਰੁ ਹੈ	Eating and drinking are essential
Khaanaa Peenaa Pavitar Hai	
ਦਿਤੋਨੁ ਰਿਜਕੁ ਸੰਬਾਹਿ ॥	for the survival of every body.
Diton Rijak Sambaahi	
Guru Granth Sahib (p. 472, line 19)	

1. GOLDEN RULES FOR EATING

The question is: What does one eat? Is there a general guideline? Guru Nanak clearly laid down the rules for all human beings to follow.

Guru Nanak said
to avoid foods that pain the body and produce evil thoughts.

The first Guru, Nanak, said:

PUNJABI AND ROMAN	**ENGLISH**
ਬਾਬਾ ਹੋਰੁ ਖਾਣਾ ਖੁਸੀ ਖੁਆਰੁ ॥	Addressing all: Do not eat food
Baabaa Hor Khaanaa Khusee Khuaar	that is not pleasing to the body,
ਜਿਤੁ ਖਾਧੈ ਤਨੁ ਪੀੜੀਐ	causes pain to the body, and
Jit Khaadai Tan Peereeai	
ਮਨ ਮਹਿ ਚਲਹਿ ਵਿਕਾਰ ॥	produces evil thoughts in the
Man Mah Chalah Vikaar	mind.
Guru Granth Sahib (p.16, line 13)	

Everytime we want to put something into our body one must first ask, Is it good for me or not? Then check with the three rules laid down by Guru Nanak as shown in the above hymn and explained below.

i. ***Do not eat food that is not pleasing to the body. Some examples are foods that cause allergic reactions or the food that is not nutritious.***
ii. ***Do not eat food that gives pain to the body—that is, food that leads to disease.***
iii. ***Do not eat food or drink beverages that produce evil in the mind. Some examples are drinking alcohol, smoking, and taking drugs not prescribed by doctors.***

The above directive is good for people all over the world now and for all times to come. Everyday new and modified food items are being produced. Thus we have to make decisions about what is good to eat. The above rules by Guru Nanak are scientifically very sound and will lead to a healthy life.

Another directive is not to eat too much; Guru Nanak expresses strong disapproval of doing so.

The first Guru, Nanak, said:

PUNJABI AND ROMAN	**ENGLISH**
ਫਿਟੁ ਇਵੇਹਾ ਜੀਵਿਆ	A person leads a cursed life if one
Phit Ivehaa Jeeviaa	
ਜਿਤੁ ਖਾਇ ਵਧਾਇਆ ਪੇਟੁ ॥	swells their belly by excessive eating.
Jit Khaae Wadhaa-i-aa Pet	
Guru Granth Sahib (p.790, line 18)	

2. SCIENTIFIC REASONS WHY OUR BODY NEEDS PROPER NUTRITION

The mind influences every cell in the body. Mind and body are inseparable. The mind-body machine has *a* ***simple theory "whenever a thought is created, chemicals go with it".*** This insight has allowed us to understand why the ***chronically depressed person is four times more likely to get sick.*** The distressed mental state of a person gets converted into certain biochemicals in the body, which create illness. If a person is depressed, sadness is felt in every part of the body. The brain's output of neurotransmitters become depleted, hormone levels drop, the sleep cycle is interrupted, neuropeptide receptors on the outer surface of skin cells become distorted, platelet cells in the blood become stickier and even the tears become chemically different.

There are three things that we have to deal with. Body and mind are under our control while the soul is the property of God. Our food habits and exercise keep our body in good shape. Our mind needs something other than food. Our mind has to be in tune with God and that is why religion is very important.

Our physical body faces constant challenges in life. There are stresses—both mental and physical—associated with ever-changing world. Every change affects us, whether it occurs inside or outside our body. Adjusting to these changes is crucial. If the body loses its balance for a long period of time, illness or death may even result. The aging process is a built-in mechanism. The body is aging beyond our control because it has been programmed to live that way.

We are victims of stress, sickness and aging. We have to be aware and be knowledgeable about controlling them in order to lead a happy and normal life. To lose awareness is to lose intelligence, to lose intelligence is to lose control over our body and mind. New knowledge, new skills, and new ways of looking at the ever-changing world, keep the mind and body growing and occupied; and we are better able to deal with the daily stresses of life.

Eating healthy food is very important to keep our body fit and trim. The proper type of food can lead to fewer diseases. It is very tempting to eat food having synthetic chemicals. They are tasty on the tongue and are readily available, however, they may not be good for the body.

3. MEAT EATING

If we follow the above golden rules (section 1), then ***eating meat should not be forbidden.*** If one is a vegetarian, then it is their choice and is perfectly acceptable.

Some people do not want to eat meat as it involves killing an animal. However, it should be made very clear that vegetables also have life.

Either way, vegetarian or non-vegetarian, one must eat food that is good for one's body. At present about six billion people are living in this earth. No two people are alike. Thus the food needs for each one is different. One has to decide the type of food they should eat by taking into account one's nutritional and medical needs, as well as religious beliefs.

Guru Nanak and Mardana were in Kurukshetra (Ambala, Haryana, India) at a fair due to solar eclipse [1]. Guru Nanak asked Mardana to cook deer that has been presented to them. Finding a pilgrim cooking meat in the holy premises caused a big uproar and people started shouting. Guru Nanak patiently listened to the disapproval. When Guru Nanak sung the following hymns the crowd became silent. Guru Nanak said that meat eating is not bad.

i. USE OF MEAT FOR ALL TIMES

The first Guru, Nanak, said:

PUNJABI AND ROMAN	**ENGLISH**
ਮਾਸੁ ਪੁਰਾਣੀ ਮਾਸੁ ਕਤੇਬੀਂ Maas Puraanee Maas KaytaabeeN	Meat is allowed in Hindu Holy Books (Puraanas) and Muslim Holy Book (Koran)
ਚਹੁ ਜੁਗਿ ਮਾਸੁ ਕਮਾਣਾ ॥ Chahu Jug Maas Kamaanaa	Throughout the four ages, meat has been used.
ਜਜਿ ਕਾਜਿ ਵੀਆਹਿ ਸੁਹਾ Jaj Kaaj Vee-aahi Suhaavai	In sacred feasts and marriage festivities
ਓਥੈ ਮਾਸੁ ਸਮਾਣਾ ॥ Othai Maas Samaanaa Guru Granth Sahib (p. 1290, line 4)	meat is served.

However, there is no need to specify what type of meat (chicken, fish, cow, pig, etc) is good or not. Just follow the three golden rules mentioned in section 1. One will then come up with the right answer.

ii. WE ALL ARE MADE OF FLESH

Guru Nanak made it perfectly clear that ***we all are made of flesh and flesh is produced from flesh.***

The first Guru, Nanak, said:

PUNJABI AND ROMAN	**ENGLISH**
ਪਹਿਲਾਂ ਮਾਸਹੁ ਨਿੰਮਿਆ PahilaaN Maasahu Nimmi-aa	First, the mortal is conceived in the flesh
ਮਾਸੈ ਅੰਦਰਿ ਵਾਸ ॥ Maasai Andar Vaas	and then he dwells in the flesh.
ਜੀਉ ਪਾਇ ਮਾਸੁ ਮੁਹਿ ਮਿਲਿਆ Jee-o Paa-ay Maas Muhi Mili-aa	When coming alive one's mouth takes flesh
ਹਡੁ ਚੰਮੁ ਤਨੁ ਮਾਸੁ ॥ Had Chamm Tan Maas.	One's bone, skin and body are flesh.
ਮਾਸਹੁ ਬਾਹਰਿ ਕਢਿਆ Maasahu Baahar Kadhi-aa	When one comes out of the womb of flesh
ਮੰਮਾ ਮਾਸੁ ਗਿਰਾਸੁ ॥ Mammaa Maas Giraas	One gets milk from the flesh of breast.
ਮੁਹੁ ਮਾਸੈ ਕਾ Muhu Maasai Kaa	One's mouth is flesh
ਜੀਭ ਮਾਸੈ ਕੀ Jeebh Maasai Kee	One's tongue is flesh
ਮਾਸੈ ਅਮਦਰਿ ਸਾਸੁ ॥ Maasai Andar Saas	Ones breath comes from the flesh.
ਵਡਾ ਹੋਆ ਵੀਆਹਿਆ Vadaa Ho-aa Vee-aahi-aa	When one grows up and gets married
ਘਰਿ ਲੈ ਆਇਆ ਮਾਸੁ ॥ Ghar Lai Aa-i-aa Maas	then one brings home a spouse of flesh.
ਮਾਸਹੁ ਹੀ ਮਾਸੁ ਊਪਜੈ Maasahu Hee Maas Oopjai	Flesh is produced from flesh
ਮਾਸਹੁ ਸਭੋ ਸਾਕੁ ॥ Maasahu Sabho Saak	all relatives are made of flesh.

Guru Granth Sahib (p. 1289, line 11)

iii. NO NEED TO QUARREL OVER MEAT

Guru Nanak explained further that there is ***no need to quarrel over meat***. However, one should always remember and meditate on God's hymns (Shabads).

The first Guru, Nanak, said:

PUNJABI AND ROMAN	**ENGLISH**
ਮਾਸੁ ਮਾਸੁ ਕਰਿ ਮੂਰਖੁ ਝਗੜੇ	The fools argue about flesh and meat
Maas Maas Kar Moorakh Jhagrhay	
ਗਿਆਨੁ ਧਿਆਨੁ ਨਹੀ ਜਾਣੈ ॥	as they do not know spiritual wisdom
Gi-aan Dhi-aan Nahee Jaanai	and meditation.
ਕਉਣੁ ਮਾਸੁ ਕਉਣੁ ਸਾਗੁ ਕਹਾਵੈ	No body knows the difference between
Ka-un Maas Ka-un Saag Kahaavai	flesh and greenery
ਕਿਸੁ ਮਹਿ ਪਾਪ ਸਮਾਣੇ ॥	thus who is committing a sin.
Kis Meh Paap Samaanay	
Guru Granth Sahib (p. 1289, line 15)	

Tenth Guru Gobind Singh also allowed meat eating. However he said that the animal should be killed with one stroke [2], called Jhatka. Most of the animals now are being killed by one stroke since it is more efficient and the pain to the animal is reduced. Muslims and Jews kill slowly while reciting religious hymns. Meats from those ceremonies are called Halal and Kosher, respectively.

4. PHYSICAL EXERCISE

Physical exercise is exceedingly important for keeping the body fit and healthy. The type of exercise varies from individual to individual as well as with age. One should get involved in some sort of group sport. It is said if you perform physical activity in a group then it lasts for a long time. By getting involved with other people, ***sport not only becomes a physical exercise but also a social activity.***

i. ADVANTAGES OF DAILY PHYSICAL ACTIVITY

The American Heart Association [3] has explained the advantages of daily physical activity as below:

A. Reduces the risk of heart disease by improving blood circulation throughout the body

B. Keeps weight under control.

C. Improves blood cholesterol levels.

D. Prevents and reduces high blood pressure.

E. Prevents bone loss.

F. Boosts energy level.

G. Helps manage stress.

H. Releases tension.

I. Improves the ability to fall asleep quickly and sleep well.

J. Improves self-image.

K. Counters anxiety and depression and increases enthusiasm and optimism.

L. Increases muscle strength, giving greater capacity for other physical activities.

M. Provides a way to share an activity with family and friends.

ii. PHYSICAL ACTIVITY AND SIKH GURUS

Second Guru, Angad Dev [4] used to organize games and sports for the children. This was done to ***maintain healthy bodies and to foster a sense of discipline.***

Sixth Guru Hargobind, during 1595 to 1644, started promoting sports, in a real sense, for the people belonging to the Sikh Religion. Mainly it was horseback riding and sword training. During that time Mughal rulers were slaughtering innocent people. There was no end in sight. Only way to stop the invaders was to organize an effective army. The martyrdom of the fifth Guru Arjan by the Mughal rulers caused a strong movement in the country to conquer the brutal rulers. This training incorporated not only physical exercise but also discipline among the soldiers. Henceforth Sikhs were to carry arms and ride horses. This was the real starting point for the army. Guru Hargobind maintained a regular army with forts and armaments needed for the battles. ***During morning and evenings Guru Hargobind would perform prayers and devotional services. In between, time was spent horse racing, hunting, and marching in parades and carrying out maneuvers.***

Tenth Guru Gobind Singh had a very large army. ***Training with a sword, riding horses and all other army maneuvers not only trained the soldiers, but also served as physical activities.*** This was done on a very large scale and almost all Sikhs were involved in this struggle. With time, physical activity became part of the regular army.

Today anyone can perform any type of exercise. It could be yoga, walking, swimming, tennis, soccer, cricket, football or any other physical activity. The main point is that it must be on a regular basis in order to be effective for the health and overall well being of the body.

iii. SIKHS AND SPORTS

Sikhs, in general, are very active in sports at all levels and have earned great eminence by wining many medals. Although they are only 2% of the population of India, they excel in many different sports.

Thus sport is an integral part of the lives of Sikhs. Every Sikh is supposed to take part in and excel in sports. It not only keeps the body healthy, it keeps the person from engaging in bad habits or behaviors. As it is said, an idle person's brain is the devil's workshop. It is better to be busy and get involved in sports. Sport not only builds healthy body but also inculcates sense of discipline.

iv. SPORTS AT ALL AGES

Exercise and sports can be performed at any age. The nature of exercise can vary with age. ***Walking is a very good exercise at any age.***

There is an example of Mr. Fauja Singh of Ilford, England originally from Punjab, India who started running marathon (26 miles) when he was 89 years old. Fauja Singh, Figure 35, [5] shattered his own world record for people over 90 by one hour to 5 hours, 40 minutes on September 30, 2003 in Toronto, Canada. He was 92 years old at that time. He has 4 children, 13 grandchildren and 5 great-grandchildren.

In 2004, Adidas, the sports footwear manufacturer, signed Fauja Singh to appear in its advertisement campaign of ***"Impossible is Nothing"*** n Britain [6]. He shares the money received with many charities including those for premature babies. ***Fauja is described as the "oldest running for the youngest".***

FIGURE 35

"IMPOSSIBLE IS NOTHING"

FAUJA SINGH 92
WORLD MARATHON RECORD HOLDER FOR PEOPLE OVER 90
5 HOURS AND 40 MINUTES IN 2003

Fauja attributes his success to a healthy diet including his favorite ginger curry, daily relaxation by praying at a Sikh Gurdwara, warm baths and running or walking 10 miles a day. There is no excuse for not exercising. It is for the overall good of the body and leads to a good, healthy, and productive life.

Another example is of Mr. Vijay Singh, Figure 36 [7], of Indian Sikh ancestry [8]. ***On September 6, 2004 Vijay became the number one golf player in the world*** when he won the Deutsche Bank Championship in Boston, USA [9]. Singh has won very prestigious golf championships in many countries. His father Mohan Singh [10] was an aircraft technician and part-time golf instructor. His grandfather came from India and settled in Fiji to work in the cornfields during 1900s [10]. Vijay was born in 1963 in Fiji but now lives with his family in Florida, USA. Singh's success is due to a good work ethic. Singh made $23 million in the last 30 months as of May 2005 [11]. Let us hope more young people get energized and follow in the footsteps of Vijay Singh.

v. MY PERSONAL OBSERVATION OF SPORTS IN THE USA

When I came to USA in 1957, I was awestruck to learn that almost everyone was involved in some kind of sport. The ordinary person as well as the president had an interest in sports. I was really very happy to observe this; I admired it quite a bit. I remember clearly that in one of my chemistry classes the professor was lecturing while listening to the radio (on very low volume) to hear the score of a University of Texas football game (I was studying there for my Ph.D.). There was no objection from any of the student as we all wanted to know the score!

In professional sports in the USA people earn very good salaries. It is an excellent encouragement and is also very good for the country. Involvement in sports gives brings the country together and makes everyone feel proud. The stadiums are generally full of sport spectators, each one rooting for his/her team. Rarely is there a fight in the crowd. ***The whole program is well organized and this reflects the maturity of the nation and the character of its people.***

vi. MY FAMILY AND SPORTS

My father, the late Moti Singh Mayell, was an excellent field hockey player during the early 1920s. We used to live in Choudri Budh Singh Mayell Street, Sialkot City, now part of Pakistan; the street was named after my great-grandfather. One day my father went for an interview for a teaching position at the Scotch Mission High School in Sialkot. His jacket was full of medals that he earned while playing field hockey. All other candidates laughed at him, however, he got the job.

FIGURE 36

VIJAY SINGH

WORLD'S NUMBER 1 GOLF PLAYER IN 2004

**"PAPA TRUST YOUR SWING"
BY VIJAY'S 9 YEAR OLD SON**

The British person in charge of the school recognized the value of sports to the education of the students. Besides teaching mathematics and science he was also in-charge of all sports and scouting activities at the school.

I also used to play field hockey, as did all the male members of the Mayell family. In the USA in early 1960s I practiced with U.S. Olympic field hockey team in Rye, New York. This opportunity was due to Mr. Gurcharan Singh who was an Olympic field hockey player in India as well as in the USA. I now play tennis and I received first place in the Senior Men's Tennis tournament in Stamford, Connecticut, two years in a row (2002 and 2003). My brother, Kultar Singh Mayell, played field hockey and represented Singapore for many years.

5. SUMMARY

One should aim to live a long and happy life. Eating and exercise are both essential to life. Guru Nanak laid down three golden rules for eating. Do not eat food that is not pleasing to the body. Do not eat food that gives pain to the body. Do not eat food or drink beverages that produce evil in the mind. Meat eating and vegetarianism are both allowed in the Sikh Religion. Physical activity is very important for our body. It reduces the risk of heart disease, helps manage stress, improves ability to fall sleep quickly and to sleep well, etc. Second Guru Angad, sixth Guru Hargobind and tenth Guru Gobind Singh encouraged physical activity. Sikhs in general are very good at sports and it a very big asset. Some examples are Fauja Singh who runs marathons at age 92 and Mr. Vijay Singh who is one of the best golfers in the world. Physical activity not only builds a healthy body but also inculcates sense of discipline.

6. EXCERCISES

i. Why is eating and drinking important?
ii. What are the three golden rules for selecting food for our body?
iii. Explain why proper nutrition is important.
iv. Is meat allowed in the Sikh Religion?
v. Why do we need physical activity and what are its advantages?
vi. Explain why Sikh Gurus were involved in physical activity.
vii. Explain the relationship between sport and Sikhs.
viii. Why does sports inculcate discipline ?
ix. Why don't people indulge in sports when it can be done at any age?

7. REFERENCES

[1] Kartar S. Duggal 1989. *Sikh Gurus*. Second printing, Himalayan International Institute, Honesdale, PA, USA. p. 17-18.

[2] Dr. Sukhbir Singh Kapoor, 1988, *The Ideal Man*, Khalsa College London Press, p. 143.

[3] American Heart Association.
http://www.justmove.org/fitnessnews/healthf.cfm?Target=dailybene.html
Yahoo. Search for "Benefits of Daily Physical Activity" Click for "The Benefits of Daily Physical Activity"
http://www.americanheart.org/presenter.jhtml?identifier=764

[4] Kartar S.Duggal, 1989. *Sikh Gurus*. Second printing, Himalayan International Institute, Honesdale, PA, USA. p. 63.

[5] Yahoo Internet. http://hapepo.de/imag/fauja_singh_5.jpg
fauja_singh_5.jpg185 x 330 pixels
www.realrunner.com/newzealand/2worldrecordspage.htm
Realrunner.com, Realbuzz.co.nz

[6] Fauja Singh in deal with Adidas March 23, 2004
http://inhome.rediff.com/sports/2004/mar/23fauja.htm
Fauja Singh, marathon runner, 92 by
Richard Askwith Sunday April 6, 2003
http://observer.guardian.co.uk/osm/story/0%2C6903%2C929850%2C00.html

[7] The Associated Press Updated: 8:15 p.m. ET Sept. 8, 2004
http://msnbc.msn.com/id/5945451

[8] http://vijay-singh.biography.ms/

[9] By Jerry Potter, *USA TODAY* Posted 9/6/2004 6:02 PM Updated 9/8/2004 12:21 AM
Yahoo Search for "Singh tops Tiger in Boston", Click for USATODAY.com "Singh tops in Boston, claims world No. 1 ranking"

[10] "Fiji's headlines ignore native's win" By Rob Mueller
Posted Sunday, April 9, 2000 at 11:51 p.m. EDT CNN *Sports Illustrated*
http://sportsillustrated.cnn.com/augusta/stories/041000/top_singh3.shtml

[11] *The Advocate*, Stamford, CT USA Wednesday May 11, 2005 page C6, a newspaper.

UNIVERSALITY OF THE SIKH RELIGION

CHAPTER 19

DRINKING, SMOKING AND DRUGS

The Sikh Religion prohibits drinking, smoking, and the use of drugs. These three vices are extremely bad for the health of all those people who consume them. It has been proven so scientifically, as well as from the religious point of view. Logic and reasoning will prove it as well. Those who drink, smoke, and use drugs in large quantities, end up as alcoholics, get cancer, and become junkies. (When I speak of drugs I mean those not prescribed by physicians and those not used according to manufacturers' directions.)

There is no easy solution once people become hooked on these products. Unscrupulous people make tremendous amounts of money by selling these products legally or illegally. With so much money at their disposal lobbyists are hired to influence elected officials. The laws are thus passed that always favor selling the products. Alcohol and smoking products are sold legally while drugs are sold illegally. ***Alcohol and tobacco lobbyisst influence politicians directly while illegal use of drug lobbyists use indirect means to get favors from the elected officials.*** This chapter is very important from a practical point of view especially for the younger generation. ***They are quite often peer pressured into using these products.*** It requires a great deal of conviction in order to say no. Nobody wants to have any of the diseases directly caused by these products. In fact, Just think, it has been reported, that some products if inhaled even just once, in large quantity, can lead to death. One has to select between living a healthy life vs. a few hours of being high and living a miserable life as a result.

Shiromani Gurdwara Parbhandak Committee, Amritsar, India, issued a directive called Sikh Rehit Maryada (Code of Conduct) in 1945. Section four, chapter X, sub section (J) states that

"A Sikh must not take hemp (cannabis), opium, liquor, tobacco, in short any intoxicant "

It is very clear that the use of alcohol, tobacco and drugs in any shape or form is strictly forbidden in the Sikh Religion.

SPECIAL APPEAL TO YOUNG PEOPLE

This is a special appeal to all children including mine to stay away from these products. There will be daily temptations of drinking, smoking and use of drugs but be firm in your beliefs even if your friends belittle you. ***The best way to get away from temptations is to get involved in sports.*** Participating in sports will allow good chemicals to be released in your body and this has been proven scientifically. ***The other way to divert your attention from temptations is to do some thing good for the downtrodden people.*** That will produce great contentment and mental satisfaction.

So far I have discussed collectively the damaging parts of these three vices. Now I will discuss them individually from the scientific, medical and religious points of view

1. DRINKING ALCOHOL

Drinking means use of ethyl alcohol inside one's body. Ethyl alcohol is made by the fermentation of corn, potato mashes, fruit juices, beet and corn sugar molasses. Ethyl alcohol is generally referred to as alcohol.

i. DRINKING ALCOHOL AND SIKH RELIGION

Is drinking allowed by the Sikh Religion? The answer is no. ***Third Guru Amardas made it very clear that by drinking one loses intellect.***

The third Guru, Amar Das, said:

PUNJABI AND ROMAN	**ENGLISH**
ਮਾਣਸੁ ਭਰਿਆ ਆਣਿਆ	One person brings a full bottle,
Maanas Bhari-aa Aani-aa	
ਮਾਣਸੁ ਭਰਿਆ ਆਇ ॥	another person fills the cup.
Maanas Bhari-aa Aa-ay.	
ਜਿਤੁ ਪੀਤੈ ਮਤਿ ਦੂਰਿ ਹੋਇ	By drinking wine, one's intellect
Jit Peetai Mat Door Ho-ay	departs and
ਬਰਲੁ ਪਵੈ ਵਿਚਿ ਆਇ ॥	madness enters one's mind.
Baral Pavai Vich Aa-ay	

ਆਪਣਾ ਪਰਾਇਆ ਨ ਪਛਾਣਈ	one cannot distinguish between his
Aapnaa Paraa-i-aa Na Pachhaan-ee	own and other people
ਖਸਮਹੁ ਧਕੇ ਖਾਇ ॥	and God make them wander aimlessly.
Khasmahu Dhakay Khaa-ay	
ਜਿਤੁ ਪੀਤੈ ਖਸਮੁ ਵਿਸਰੈ	Drinking wine one forgets God
Jit Peetai Khasam Visrai	
ਦਰਗਹ ਮਿਲੈ ਸਜਾਇ ॥	and is punished in God's Court.
Dargeh Milai Sajaa-ay	
ਝੂਠਾ ਮਦੁ ਮੂਲਿ ਨ ਪੀਚਈ	Do not drink this false wine at all
Jhoothaa Mad Mool Na Peech-ee	
ਜੇ ਕਾ ਪਾਰਿ ਵਸਾਇ ॥	and it is all in your power.
Jay Kaa Paar Vasaa-ay	
ਨਾਨਕ ਨਦਰੀ ਸਚੁ ਮਦੁ ਪਾਈਐ	Nanak says true wine is obtained by the
Naanak Nadree Sach Mad Paa-ee-ai	grace of God
ਸਤਿਗੁਰੁ ਮਿਲੈ ਜਿਸੁ ਆਇ ॥	and to whom the True God meets.
Satgur Milai Jis Aa-ay	
ਸਦਾ ਸਾਹਿਬ ਕੈ ਰੰਗਿ ਰਹੈ	Those people are absorbed forever in
Sadaa Saahib Kai Rang Rahai	the love of God and
ਮਹਲੀ ਪਾਵੈ ਥਾਉ ॥	they will get a seat in God' place.
Mahlee Paavai Thaa-o	
Guru Granth Sahib (p. 554, line 13)	

Drinking serves no good purpose; it makes one intoxicated and in turn one loses thinking power.

The fifth Guru, Arjan Dev, said:

PUNJABI AND ROMAN	**ENGLISH**
ਹੋਛਾ ਮਦੁ ਚਾਖਿ ਹੋਏ ਤੁਮ ਬਾਵਰ	Drinking worthless wine
Hochhaa Mad Chaakh Ho-ay Tum Baavar	makes one intoxicated and
ਦੁਲਭ ਜਨਮੁ ਅਕਾਰਥ ॥	in this way one wastes the
Dulabh Janam Akaarath	precious human life.
Guru Granth Sahib (p. 1001, line 8)	

The River Ganges is a very holy place in the Hindu religion. Ravidas who was a Hindu said that even if wine were made with holy water it would still not be good.

Ravi Das said:

PUNJABI AND ROMAN	ENGLISH
ਸੁਰਸਰੀ ਸਲਲ ਕ੍ਰਿਤ ਬਾਰੁਨੀ ਰੇ	Even if wine is made from the water
Sursaree Salal Kirat Baarunee Ray	of the Ganges (Holy river) even then
ਸੰਤ ਜਨ ਕਰਤ ਨਹੀ ਪਾਨੰ ॥	God loving people, do not drink it.
Sant Jan Karat Nahee PaanaN	
Guru Granth Sahib (p. 1293, line 4)	

Let us discuss how religions perceive the drinking of alcohol. Muslims, Hindus, Sikhs, Buddhists and Jains do not permit alcohol. Christians and Jews allow the drinking of wine. **It is ironic that most Sikhs drink, although drinking is not permitted in the Sikh Religion.** I hope after reading some Sikhs may stop or at least reduce their drinking habit. By not drinking alcohol one will lead a productive and healthy life.

ii. ALCOHOL AND SCIENCE

A. HOW ALCOHOL WORKS IN OUR BODY [1]

When a person drinks alcohol, 20 percent of it passes through the stomach wall directly into the bloodstream. The rest passes to the small intestines where it also moves to the blood stream. When the alcohol reaches the brain it causes intoxication, which impairs the ability to think clearly. The blood with the alcohol then circulates to the liver, which breaks down the alcohol and removes it from the body. ***The alcohol is metabolized to acetaldehyde*** and then finally to carbon dioxide and water. In alcoholics acetaldehyde gets accumulated. Acetaldehyde is highly toxic. It causes nausea, rapid heartbeat, dizziness, and headache. It creates depression, anxiety, and confusion. ***Alcoholics do not have a problem with alcohol, they have a problem with acetaldehyde build-up, which is toxic to the body.***

It should not be confused with the alcohol produced from food ingested in our body. Alcohol thus produced is immediately used by the body and thus has no chance to produce toxic chemicals.

B. IS ALCOHOL GOOD FOR HEART?

It is very questionable that alcohol is good for the heart. Some doctors, based certain medical studies, are saying that moderate drinking may be good for the heart. One to two drinks a day are permitted, though a moderate amount for a young person may be much different than for a senior citizen. In general, a 12-ounce bottle of beer, a 4-ounce glass of wine, and a 1½-ounce shot of 80-proof spirits all contain the same amount of alcohol (one-half ounce). Each of these is considered a "drink equivalent" [2]. ***The bad effects of alcohol far outweigh the little good it produces.*** This is made very clear in the discussion that follows.

Recently I read an article [3] in our local newspaper under the heading:

BOOZE LOBBY VS. AMERICA'S YOUTH

American Congress authorized $500,000 to the National Academy of Sciences to study underage drinking. It was supposed to define a national policy for reducing the No. 1 health and safety threat to teens. The National Academy of Sciences is a very highly respected scientific organization. A panel of respected researchers, academics and prevention experts was chosen. Study is under final review (as of July 2003).

Meanwhile alcohol industry and its supporters in Congress and the administration have conducted a campaign of intimidation against National Academy of Sciences. One hundred and thirty eight (138) members of Congress have sent to the President of the National Academy of Sciences warning him that the $500,000 appropriation was not intended to produce policy changes that would adversely affect the alcohol industry.

The American Medical Association in the February issue has said that underage drinking accounts for 20% of all alcohol consumed. The alcohol industry's political connection has reached a remarkable level. They have hired Robert Koch (married to President Bush's sister, Dorothy Bush Koch) to be president of the Wine Institute, a lobby for 600 American wineries.

Even if the alcohol lobby cannot bury the National Institute of Science's report they will make it sure it finds little support on Capitol Hill or in the administration. The American Medical Association has said that teenage drinking is an epidemic in all communities. ***The alcohol industry will make it sure that the report of the National Institute of Sciences will die quietly, as will the young teens, due to excessive alcohol consumption.***

The article further states, that, by all accounts, alcohol is the most dangerous drug to young people—far more than any illegal drug. ***Alcohol is linked to three main causes of teen deaths: accidents, murder and suicide. It kills 6½ times as many American youth as all illegal drugs combined.***

The question is: Why there is no national anti-underage drinking campaign in the USA? The answer is very simple (as mentioned above): the alcohol lobby. Remember when cigarette manufactures showed studies that smoking was good for people? The sponsor of the study dictates the nature of the conclusions, as is clearly shown by the above Booze Lobby.

C. EFFECTS OF ALCOHOL ON HUMAN BODY [4]

The body organs that are mostly affected by alcohol are the liver, digestive system, brain and heart.

a. EFFECT OF ALCOHOL ON LIVER

Liver breaks down alcohol in the body and therefore is the chief site of alcohol damage. It enlarges the liver (fatty liver). Liver cells swell, become inflamed and die causing blockage (Alcoholic Hepatitis). Flow of blood through the liver is obstructed when fibrous scar tissue (Cirrhosis) is formed in place of healthy cells. Alcohol in the liver also alters the production of digestive enzymes, causing accumulation of acetaldehyde, a toxic substance. ***Ten to thirty percent of people in the United States die because of liver failure due to excessive use of alcohol.***

A diseased liver cannot convert stored glycogen into glucose, thus lowering blood sugar and producing hypoglycemia. A diseased liver cannot detoxify bloodstream (A healthy liver normally eliminates some of the dead red blood cells.) Also, it cannot manufacture bile (for fat digestion), prothrombin (for blood clotting and bruise prevention), and albumin (for maintaining healthy cells).

b. EFFECTS OF ALCOHOL ON DIGESTIVE SYSTEM

Large amounts of alcohol may inflame the mouth, esophagus, and stomach, possibly causing cancer in these locations, especially with people who also smoke. Alcohol increases the stomach's digestive enzymes, which can irritate the stomach wall, producing heartburn, nausea, gastritis, and ulcers. Alcohol may also inflame the small and large intestines.

c. EFFECTS OF ALCOHOL ON THE BRAIN

Within moments of ingestion, alcohol reaches the brain where it stimulates, depresses and induces a hypnotic state and sleep. Some members of Alcoholic Anonymous say that the first drink of the day sets up craving for more**. *Sooner or later the first drink will lead to overindulgence.*** Consumption of two strong drinks before dinner leads to three to five drinks a day. People who drink claim they do it for relieving fatigue, anxiety and depression, but in fact heavy drinking increases such feelings.

Alcohol affects the central nervous system of the brain by disrupting its ability to retrieve and consolidate information. Even moderate alcohol consumption affects cognitive abilities, while larger amounts interfere with the oxygen supply to the brain, a possible cause of blackout or temporary amnesia during drunkenness. Alcohol abuse destroys brain cells. Other effects include mental disorder such as increased aggression, antisocial behavior, depression and anxiety.

d. EFFECTS OF ALCOHOL ON HEART

Moderate daily drinking may be good for the heart, but for many the risks outweigh the benefits. Even one binge (about five drinks) may produce irregular heartbeats, and alcohol abusers experience increased risk of high blood pressure, heart attacks, heart arrhythmia, and heart disease. Alcohol may cause cardiomyopathy (a disease of the heart muscle). Cessation of drinking aids in recovery from this condition.

e. OVERALL PROBLEMS WITH ALCOHOL

in short alcohol can lead to the following problems [5]: liver disease, pancreatic disease, cardiovascular disease, gastrointestinal problems, neurological disorders, reproductive system disorders, cancers, psychiartic comorbidities, legal problems, employment problems, family problems and can have negative effects on children.

iii. TREATMENT OF ALCOHOLICS [4]

It is well known that first drink leads to second and third and so on until one becomes alcoholic. Without hospitalization or residency in a therapeutic community, the late-stage alcoholic usually succumbs to insanity and death. *Alcoholics enjoy a good recovery rate once they stop drinking.* For a small number of alcoholics, a brief stay of 3 to 10 days in a detoxification center may be necessary.

For long-term care, the alcoholic can recover at a rehabilitation center or in the inpatient treatment unit of a hospital. These centers provide alcohol-free environments; continued medical care; group, individual, and family therapy; classes about alcoholism; and regular Alcoholics Anonymous meetings

iv. LIVING SOBER [4]

Quitting drinking is only the first step in recovering from alcoholism. ***Walking, jogging, sports, or a regular schedule of exercise promotes good health, self-esteem and provides a healthy outlet for energy.*** Research indicates that exercise releases brain chemicals that simulate a natural high. Even a walk after dinner is very helpful.

v. SHOULD A PERSON DRINK OR NOT?

The choice to drink or not is individual's decision. There are some who say moderate drinking is good for the heart. On the other, hard drinking can lead to a host of problems that can lead to debilitating diseases. There are very few people who can control their drinking habits. It is better not to drink, as the risks to one's health outweigh the benefits of alcohol. ***If elimination of alcohol is not possible then reducing the consumption of alcohol is an important step.*** Think carefully and decide for your own body. It is all up to the individual: live a healthy life or one with bad liver and host of other possible diseases.

vi. ANTIBACTERIAL EFFECT OF ETHYL ALCOHOL

The antibacterial effect of alcohol used outside the body should not be confused with drinking alcohol routinely inside the body. ***There are some very good antibacterial properties of alcohol.*** Many medicinal products contain alcohol varying from 1% to 25% [6]. If required for medicinal use one has to take it. Listerine mouthwash contains 16% alcohol. Some cough syrups contain considerable amount of alcohol. There is another product called Purell which contains 62% alcohol. It is used for washing hands to kill bacteria. Doctors and medical professionals wash their hands with products containing 60% alcohol [7] instead of water and soap The alcohol does not penetrate the hands; it simply vanishes after killing the bacteria.

2. SMOKING TOBACCO

Smoking in this case is inhaling from cigarettes. Cigarettes are made from the leaves of tobacco plants after proper curing. Tobacco is also used for chewing, snuffing, cigar and pipe smoking, etc..

i. SMOKING AND SIKH RELIGION

Smoking and the use of tobacco are prohibited in the Sikh Religion. ***Tenth Guru Gobind Singh strictly forbade Sikhs to take tobacco in any form.*** That included smoking or chewing of tobacco. According to Sikh Rehit Maryada (Code of Conduct) as discussed in page 1 of this chapter, tobacco (smoking) is not allowed. During Amrit initiation ceremony, a Sikh has to give clear and categorical pledge not to use tobacco in any form.

It is also very heartening to know that Sikhs do not smoke even today.

ii. SMOKING AND SCIENCE [8]

Smoking and the use of tobacco are very dangerous. ***Smoking causes cancer of the lung, mouth, throat, bladder, colon, rectum, pancreas and cervix.*** Smoking increases the risk of heart attack. It slows wound healing. It jeopardizes the life and health of unborn babies. It also places families of smokers at risk for lung disease due to second-hand smoking. All these diseases can be prevented by just not smoking.

Simply put, smoking kills, Figure 37 [9]. It is better to quit smoking in order to lead a healthy life.

iii. CHEMICALS IN TABACCO [8]

There are more than 4000 chemicals in tobacco. Sixty of those are known to be cancer causing. The most damaging to health are explained below.

FIGURE 37
SMOKING KILLS PEOPLE

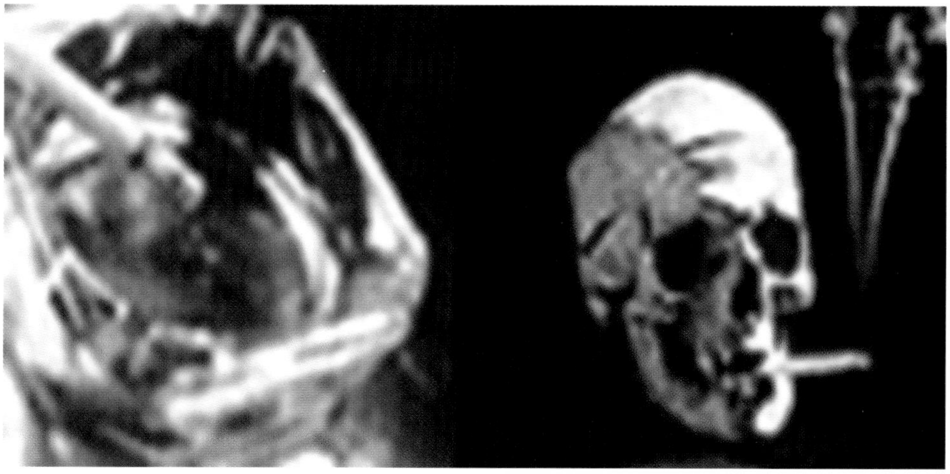

DO NOT WAIT UNTIL IT IS TOO LATE TO QUIT

SMOKING CAUSES CANCER AND MANY OTHER DISEASES

A. NICOTINE

Nicotine is a toxic, powerfully addictive drug that affects the brain and body. It raises blood pressure that causes hardening of the arteries. Nicotine is so toxic that it is being used as an insecticide for plants. ***About 0.6 gram of nicotine is lethal to humans.***

B. TAR

Tar is an oily brown substance that is found in tobacco leaves. This is inhaled while smoking and collects in the lungs. ***Tar causes cancer.***

C. CARBON MONOXIDE

This is poisonous colorless gas that is released by the burning of tobacco. When it is inhaled it enters the bloodstream and interferes with the working of the heart and the blood vessels. ***Up to 15% of a smoker's blood may be carrying carbon monoxide instead of oxygen.*** Car exhaust fumes also contain carbon monoxide.

D. OTHER CHEMICALS

Some of the other chemicals found in cigarettes include the following products:

Arsenic	Rat poison
Ammonia	Cleaning products
Cyanide	Deadly poison
Acetone	Nail polish remover
Butane	Cigarette lighter fluid
DDT	Insecticide
Formaldehyde	Medical preservative
Sulfuric Acid	Car batteries
Cadmium	Toxic metal in batteries
Freon	Gas in refrigerators
Metoprene	Pesticide

iv. TYPES OF CANCER CAUSED BY SMOKING [10]

The following types of cancer have been observed with people who smoke.

A. Lung Cancer
B. Cancers of the mouth and throat
C. Esophageal cancer
D. Bladder and kidney cancer
E. Pancreatic cancer
F. Stomach cancer
G. Liver cancer
H. Colorectal cancer
I. Cervical cancer
J. Leukemia
K. Breast cancer

v. SECOND HAND SMOKING (PASSIVE SMOKING) [11]

The US Environmental Protection Agency (EPA) has published a major assessment of the respiratory risks of passive smoking. The report concludes that exposure to environmental tobacco smoke (ETS), commonly known as ***second hand smoke, is responsible for approximately 3000 lung cancer deaths each year.*** This occurs in nonsmoking adults and impairs the respiratory health of hundreds of thousands of children.

Smoking is really very devastating to human beings. If tobacco were discovered today it would be banned for good. Tobacco industry is surviving for two reasons:. first, the powerful lobby of the tobacco manufactures and second, the inability of people who are addicted to smoking and cannot quit.

vi. TREATMENT OF SMOKERS [12]

There are methods available to help people quit smoking. Some of them are described below.

A. COLD TURKEY METHOD

Best way is to quit smoking called the cold turkey method. It depends solely on the willpower of the individual to quit smoking forever.

B. NICOTINE REPLACEMENT METHODS

Another method is nicotine replacement therapy. Instead of inhaling, nicotine is dispensed under controlled conditions through a nicotine patch on the skin, through the nose via a nicotine nasal spray or through mouth by way of nicotine chewing gum.

C. BEHAVIOR METHODS

Such methods include using smoke free zones and socializing with friends who do not smoke.

D. OTHER METHODS

Some of the others methods are acupuncture, hypnosis, meditation and so on.

vii. BENEFITS OF NOT SMOKING [13]

The following are some of the benefits of not smoking.

A. HEALTH

Health benefits are major and immediate, at ALL ages.

B. REDUCED DEATH RATE

Quitting smoking decreases the overall risk of death (all causes combined) by 50% in 15 years as compared to those who still smoke.

C. REDUCED RISK OF HEART DISEASE

The risk of heart attack is decreased by 50% within 24 hours of quitting.

D. REDUCED RISK OF STROKE

The risk of having a stroke or a brain aneurysm (bleeding in the brain) goes down by 30%-50% in those who quit.

E. REDUCED RISK OF LUNG CANCER

The risk of lung cancer is decreased by 80%-90% after 15+ years of abstinence.

F. REDUCED RISK OF SMOKER'S COUGH

Within three months of quitting, smokers' cough disappears in most people.

G. QUALITY OF LIFE

a. ***Smell and taste improve within days.***
b. ***Decreases harm to others from second-hand smoke exposure.***
c. ***Fire prevention.***
d. ***Increased work productivity.***
e. ***Improvement in self-esteem.***
f. ***Cost savings.***

The expenditure for smoking one pack per day for thirty years is approximate to the price of a Porsche car.

3. DRUG ABUSE

This is explained in little detail in order to discourage people to use drugs. Drug abuse refers to the experimental and recreational use of illegal drugs (those not prescribed by a doctor.) Drug abuse occurs in all socioeconomic groups. It may involve highly educated and professional people as well as those who are uneducated and unemployed. Drugs are bad for one's health and they lead to premature death as well [14] (see Figure 38).

Drugs encompass many different types of products, unlike drinking, which is confined to alcohol and smoking, which includes only tobacco. Drugs vary considerably not only in chemistry, but their effects differ from person to person. Generally, however, most of drugs, when used illegally, can be harmful.

People who are addicted often have low self-esteem, are immature, are easily frustrated, and have difficulty solving personal problems and relating to people of the opposite sex. They are often withdrawn and depressed.

Eight types of drugs that are used illegally are:

A. Narcotics
B. Antianxiety drugs and Sleep aids
C. Marijuana
D. Amphetamines
E. Cocaine
F. Hallucinogens
G. Phencyclidines
H. Inhalants

How drugs cause death is shown by the very tragic case of ***Elvis Presley*** [15]. He was under the influence of drugs. Being very famous he could get drugs through his doctor. Dr. George Nichopoulos, the primary physician of Elvis prescribed many drugs, including testosterone (sex hormone), amphetamines (stimulant), Dilaudid (narcotic pain reliever), Dexedrine (stimulant), Demerol (narcotic pain reliever), Quaaludes (sedative) and Amytal (sedative) [15]. His physical problems included blood clots, hypoglycemia and an enlarged heart. His liver was more than twice the normal size and his colon was distended. His weight on a diet of junk food and downers had zoomed from 175 pounds to 245 pounds in three years. ***Elvis Presley died at the age of 42 in 1977 due to drug abuse.***

FIGURE 38

DRUGS MAKE JUNKIES

i. DRUGS AND THE SIKH RELIGION

Sikh Rehit Marayada (Code of Conduct) as discussed in page 1 of this chapter shows clearly that Sikhs must not take hemp (cannabis), opium or any other intoxicant. ***Drugs of any kind, not prescribed by doctors, are forbidden in the Sikh Religion.***

Guru Nanak likened drug addicts to fish—they need drugs like a fish need water. ***A drug addict will lead a ruinous life while God-loving people will have a contented, healthy and peaceful life.***

The first Guru, Nanak, said:

PUNJABI AND ROMAN	ENGLISH
ਅਮਲੀ ਅਮਲੁ ਨ ਅੰਬੜੈ Amlee Amal Na Ambrhai	A drug addict can not live without drugs
ਮਛੀ ਨੀਰੁ ਨ ਹੋਇ ॥ Machhee Neer Na Ho-ay.	Just as fish cannot live without water.
ਜੋ ਰਤੇ ਸਹਿ ਆਪਣੈ Jo Ratay Seh Aapnai	Those who are tuned to God
ਤਿਨ ਭਾਵੈ ਸਭੁ ਕੋਇ ॥ Tin Bhaavai Sabh Ko-ay.	They love everyone in this world.

Guru Granth Sahib (p. 557, line 4)

ii. DRUGS AND SCIENCE [16]

The eight types of drugs, as mentioned above, which are used by drug addicts, will be discussed individually.

A. NARCOTICS (TYPE 1)

a. WHAT ARE NARCOTICS

Doctors use narcotics as powerful pain relievers. They are called opioids as they are derived from opium plant. They include codeine, morphine, oxycodone, hydromorphone, and meperidine. Heroin, which is one of the strongest narcotics, is illegal to use in United States.

b. PROBLEMS

Narcotic addiction leads to a strong psychological and physical dependence.

Narcotic users develop the following lung problems:
Lung irritation Pneumonia Abscesses Pulmonary Emboli

When people use shared or non-sterilized needles they develop:
Viral hepatitisLiver damage Bone infection AIDS

Drug overdose can be very serious:
It may cause coma
It can lead to death by suppressing respiration and the lungs can fill up with fluid.

c. TREATMENT

People who are overdosed on narcotics need immediate medical treatment in a hospital or Drug Addiction Treatment Centers.

B. ADDICTION TO ANTIANXIETY DRUGS AND SLEEP AIDS (TYPE 2)

a. WHAT ARE ANTIANXIETY DRUGS AND SLEEP AIDS?

These drugs are
Benzodiazepines Barbiturates Glutethinides Chloral Hydrates
Meprobamate

b. PROBLEMS

Drugs used to treat anxiety and induce sleep can cause both psychological and physical dependence.

When used in large quantities they cause:
Decrease alertness Slurred speech Poor coordination Confusion
Slow breathing Cause depression and anxious cycles
Memory loss Faulty judgment

Older people also have the following problems
Speaking slowly Difficulty in thinking and understanding
Falling, leading to hip fractures

c. TREATMENT

The best way is to stop using them but it is not easy. Symptoms of withdrawal are listed below:

First 12 to 20 hours:
Nervous, restless and weak Hands and legs may shake
2nd Day: Tremors may be severe and cause weakness.
2nd and 3rd day: If a person takes 8 times or more than the prescribed daily dose, they can have severe seizures.
(It can be fatal in case of Barbiturates and Glutethimide.)

Even 1 to 3 weeks after withdrawal seizures may occur.
Other effects are:
Dehydration Delirium Insomnia Confusion Visual and auditory hallucinations

It may take a month or more to return to normal with proper medical care

C. MARIJUANA ABUSE (TYPE 3)

a. WHAT IS MARIJUNA

Marijuana is the dried buds and leaves of the plant called Cannabis sativa. Marijuana abuse is widespread in schools. Marijuana is generally smoked in the form of cigarettes or as hashish. This plant contains more than 400 chemicals.

b. PROBLEMS

The following problems are associated with the use of Marijuana:

Depresses brain activity
Puts one in dreamy state—ideas are disconnected and uncontrollable.
Time, color and spatial perceptions may be distorted
Color seems brighter
Sounds seem louder
Appetite may increase
Communicative and motor abilities decrease (so one should not drive).

Large quantity users of marijuana may also:
Be confused and disoriented
Have toxic psychosis—Not knowing who they are
Not knowing where they are
Or what time it is
Have panic attacks
Have increased heart rate
Have blood shot eyes
Have dry mouth

Prolonged use in men reduces testosterone, reduce the size of the testes and sperm count.
Prolonged use in women causes irregular menstrual cycles.

Heavy smoking of marijuana has the same effects as cigarette smoking on the lungs: bronchitis and lung cancer.

c. TREATMENT

The best treatment is to stop smoking marijuana. (It should be done under the care of doctor and medical professionals.)

Withdrawal symptoms are increased muscle activity (jerkiness) and insomnia.

D. AMPHETAMINE ABUSE (TYPE 4)

These come under the category of stimulants.

a. WHAT ARE AMPHETAMINES?

Amphetamine drugs include:
Amphetamine
Methamphetamine (Speed)
Methylenedioxymethamphetamine (Ecstasy, MDMA or Adam)

b. PROBLEMS

Dependence on amphetamines is both psychological and physical.
Amphetamines were originally used for weight loss, but no longer; people are now using them illegally.

Speed is the most commonly abused drug in United States. Ecstasy was widespread in Europe; it also has become popular in the United States.

Many amphetamine abusers are depressed and use these drugs to elevate their mood. In addition to stimulation, amphetamines increase the blood pressure and heart rate. Fatal heart attacks have occurred in healthy young athletes. ***Death is more likely to occur with Ecstasy,*** especially when it is used in warm rooms with no ventilation and when the user is very physically active (such as when they are dancing). Ecstasy is also toxic to the nervous system.

Heavy users of Amphetamines become psychotic, as it causes:
Anxiety, paranoia and a distorted sense of reality.
Psychotic reactions also include visual and auditory hallucinations (seeing and hearing things that do not exist).

c. TREATMENT

Discontinuation of amphetamines causes tiredness or sleepiness that may last for 2 to 3 days. Thus chronic users should be hospitalized during withdrawal and be under the care of a medical professional.

E. COCAINE ABUSE (TYPE 5)

This comes under the category of stimulants.

a. WHAT IS COCAINE?

Cocaine is a white powder that comes from the leaves of the coco plant, which is grown in South America. It may be taken orally, inhaled through the nose, or injected.

b. PROBLEMS

The effects of cocaine are similar to those of amphetamines. However, cocaine is much more powerful stimulant.
Cocaine:
Increases the blood pressure and the heart rate even in healthy young athletes.
CausesIntestinal damage

- Extreme nervousness
- Nerve damage (feeling that something is moving under the skin)
- Seizures
- Hallucinations
- Sleeplessness
- Paranoid delusions
- Violent behavior (The abuser may be dangerous to him/herself or others)
- Miscarriage and side-effects on the fetus

c. WITHDRAWAL SYMPTOMS

Extreme fatigue and depression
Suicidal urges

After several days when mental and physical strength have returned the abuser may attempt suicide.

d. TREATMENT

Due to the suicidal nature immediate treatment in a hospital or a drug treatment center is necessary. The most effective methods for treating cocaine abusers are counseling and psychotherapy.

F. HALLUCINOGEN ABUSE (TYPE 6)

a. WHAT ARE HALLUCINOGENS?

Hallucinogens are

LSD (Lysergic acid diethylamide)
Magic mushrooms (Psilocybin)
Peyote (mescaline)
STP, DOM (2,5-dimethoxy-4-methyl-amphetamine), a derivative of amphetamine

b. PROBLEMS

These drugs produce false hallucinogens.
They distort auditory and visual sensations.
Sensations may cross over. Listening to music may cause colors to appear and move in time with the rhythm.

Psychological effects are

Impaired judgment. The abuser might think he/she can fly and may even jump out of a window resulting in severe injury or death.
Hallucinogens stimulate the brain.
They develop extreme anxiety and panic especially with LSD, resulting in bad trips.

c. WITHDRAWAL

Chronic users, especially with LSD, suffer flashbacks. Generally flashbacks disappear after a 6-to-12 month period but can recur as long as five years after the last use of LSD.

G. PHENCYCLIDINE ABUSE (TYPE 7)

a. WHAT IS PHENCYCLIDINE?

Phencyclidine is ***Angel Dust***, a PCP developed in 1950 as anesthetic. The legitimate medical use of PCP was stopped in 1962 as patients developed severe anxiety and delusions. It is now synthesized illegally. PCP is most often smoked after it is sprinkled on plants as parsley, mint leaves, tobacco or marijuana. PCP is also taken orally or injected.

b. PROBLEMS

PCP depresses the brain
People become confused and disoriented
They do not know where they are, how they are, or what time or day it is.
They go into trance as if they are hypnotized.
Salivation and sweating may increase
PCP abusers may be combative. They do not feel pain so they continue fighting.
Blood pressure and heart rate increase
Muscle tremors (shaking) are common

Very high dosages of PCP cause:
High blood pressure, which can result in stoke; auditory hallucinations (hearing voices); seizures; a life-threatening high fever,;coma and possible death.
It also can damage the brain, kidneys and muscles.

c. TREATMENT

Doctors and medical professionals are the only ones who can help. Soothing talk does not help; it may even make them more agitated. They may be given tranquilizers and other drugs to calm them.

H. INHALANT ABUSE (TYPE 8)

a. WHAT ARE INHALANTS?

Inhalants are used more frequently among teenagers. They are found in many household products. When the product's fumes are directly inhaled the effects are stronger. Some of the products are: ***Airplane glue, rubber cement, spray paint, hair spray, nail polish remover, gasoline, dry-cleaning fluid, spot remover and paint remover or thinner.***

b. PROBLEMS

Intoxication Dizziness Drowsiness Confusion Slurred speech Reduced ability to stand and walk.

Death can occur even the first time when one of these products is directly inhaled either due to breathing problems (as the lung is coated with the product, which prevents oxygen from entering the blood stream) or an irregular heartbeat.

Chronic use can cause
Damage to the brain, heart, kidney, liver and lungs.
Bone marrow can be damaged causing anemia

c. TREATMENT

Evaluate and treat any organ damage.
Education and counseling for psychological and sociological problems.
Parent's involvement even before the problem starts.

4. SUMMARY

None of the three vices—drinking, smoking or drugs—is permitted by the Sikh Religion. For medical reasons it is best to avoid them. Drinking leads one to become an alcoholic. The liver, digestive system, brain and heart are badly affected by drinking in large quantities. Those who say that drinking is good, completely ignore the damage to the body caused by it. For those who cannot quit, it is advisable to decrease consumption

Smoking is a very dangerous addiction. Smoking causes cancer of the lungs, mouth, throat, bladder, colon, rectum, pancreas and cervix. Just quitting smoking can prevent all these diseases. It may not be easy. There are several ways to stop smoking. The best way is to stop altogether through your own will power. Others are by nicotine patch, nicotine nasal spray, or nicotine chewing gum. Another treatment deals with changing the behavior pattern of the smoker. The benefits of not smoking are: good health, better quality of life, reduced risk of lung cancer, decrease in the incidence of heart attack, disappearance of smoker's cough, cost savings, and reduced risk of bleeding in the brain.

Drugs come in many different types and cause much more damage to human bodies than alcohol and smoking. Drug abuse occurs in all socioeconomic groups. There are essentially eight different types of drugs that are abused most often. They are 1. Narcotics (Pain relievers) 2. Anti-anxiety drugs and sleep aids

3. Marijuana (depresses brain activity) 4. Amphetamines (stimulant) 5. Cocaine (stimulant) 6. Hallucinogens (distort auditory and visual sensations) 7. Phencyclinidines (brain depressors) 8. Inhalants (drowsiness, confusion). All of these drugs when abused cause serious problems affecting the brain, heart, lung, distortion, confusion, hallucinations, stimulation, depression and death. Drugs seriously affect the body. People on drugs must seek immediate medical treatment if they want to lead normal, healthy lives.

5. EXERCISES

1. Why are drinking, smoking and drugs are not permitted in the Sikh religion?
ii. How does alcohol become toxic to the body?
iii. What do you think of the power of the booze lobby?
iv. Explain the effect of alcohol on the liver, digestive system, brain and heart?
v. How should one treat alcoholics ? What are the benefits of exercise to recovering alcoholics?
vi. Explain why smoking is forbidden in the Sikh Religion Sikhism and Sikhs do not smoke?
vii. List the types of cancer caused by smoking?
viii. How can the smoking habit be avoided?
ix. List the benefits of not smoking?
x. How many different categories of drugs are abused?
xi. Why are drugs more dangerous than drinking and smoking?
xii. List 12 types of problems generally associated with abuse of the eight different categories of drugs?
xiii. What is the most preferred way to stop the misuse of drugs?
xiv. How can inhalants lead to death, even if they are used just once in large quantity?

6. REFERENCES

[1] www.iwr.com/ezine/issue111.htm "Scientific Explanation of Alcoholism," Dr. Lendon Smith, edited by Dorothy Q. McDonald.

[2] Yahoo Search for "Thomas A. Pearson, MD, PhD; From the Nutrition Committee of the American Heart Association Alcohol and Heart Disease" Click for "Alcohol and Heart Disease- -Pearson 94 (11): 3023— Circulation" http://circ.ahajournals.org/cgi/content/full/94/11/3023

[3] Mr. Jim Gogek, a journalist and a Robert Wood Johnson Foundation Fellow. *Stamford Advocate* dated July 16, 2003 under the Topic "Booze Lobby Vs. America's Youth".

[4] Yahoo Search for
"Columbia University College of P & S Complete Home Guide Alcohol"
Click for "Overview of Alcohol-Related Problems"
[5] http://www.aafp.org/afp/990115ap/361.html
Sandra K. Burge, Ph.D., and F. David Schneider, M.D., M.S.P.H.
University of Texas Health Science Center, San Antonio, Texas
[6] www.addictionend.com/bookonline/34.htm
Click # 34 Alcohol Content in Common Preperations
[7] www.health.gov.on.ca/english/public/pub/pubhealth/handwash.html
Click "Ontario Ministry of Health and Long-Term Care—Public".
[8] Go to Yahoo.com. Search for "smoking and cancer" Search for "Cancer and Smoking"
www.cancer.ie/smoking/
[9] Google.com Images "SMOKING KILLS PEOPLE".
http://www.salaam.co.uk/lifestyle/images/smoke.gif
[10] Yahoo Search for "Smoking and Cancer Fact Sheet no. 4—ASH"
http://www.ash.org.uk/html/factsheets/html/fact04.html
[11] Yahoo Search for "Smoking and Cancer Secondhand Smoke Publications EPA/600/6-90/006F" Click for
"Secondhand Smoke Publications Fact Sheet: Respiratory Health Effects of Passive Smoking"
http://www.epa.gov/smokefree/pubs/etsfs.html
[12] unr.edu/homepage/shubinsk/smoke.html
Dr. Bob's (Dr. Robert Shubinski) Quit Smoking Page
Click for "Various methods of how to stop smoking".
[13] unr.edu/homepage/shubinsk/smoke.html
Dr. Bob's (Dr. Robert Shubinski) Quit Smoking Page
Click for "Benefits of Quitting."
[14] Yahoo Images "DRUG ADDICTS" Click "204_mkaymackey.JPG".
www.esse.ou.edu/~cwaller/discussion.html
[15] Alanna Nash, *Reader's Digest*, Pleasantville, New York, July 2003, pages 150 to 172. "The Colonel & The King".
[16] *The Merck Manual* 1997, Second Printing, Merck Research Laboratories, New Jersey, USA, Pages 440 to 454

UNIVERSALITY OF THE SIKH RELIGION

CHAPTER 20

LEARN PUNJABI THE EASY WAY

This chapter is written for people who want to learn Punjabi on their own. It is not, however, a replacement for courses offered by professional teachers of Punjabi. ***My basic reason for learning Punjabi in Gurmukhi script was to read and understand the Guru Granth Sahib.***

I had always wanted to learn Punjabi, however, time passed, and I became busy, with family and work obligations. I could speak Punjabi but could not read or write it. I studied Urdu and Persian along with English—but not Punjabi—at Scotch Mission High School in Sialkot City, now in Pakistan. I came to the USA in 1957. There was no need for me to learn Punjabi after I emigrated, so my desire to learn it got further delayed. I graduated from the University of Texas, Austin, Texas with a PhD degree in chemistry in the year 1962. Thereafter I came to Stamford, Connecticut, about 40 miles from New York City and have been living there for the last 44 years. In 1964, a few of us started the Sikh Cultural Society and later on started the Gurdwara in Richmond Hill, Queens, New York. We used to listen the Kirtan—singing of hymns—from the Guru Granth Sahib in classical Ragas. My understanding of the words was not great, although the music was soothing. I understood some words, but the real meaning evaded me.

During 1980s a very learned person came from India to New York and explained some aspects of the Sikh Religion to the congregation. He was very impressive. After the program was over I met him individually. I asked one question and I was impressed by his very logical reply. My question was, are people with and without long hair equal in all respects, especially when Guru Nanak who started the Sikh Religion said, "there is no high and no low?". I asked him if he would present his explanation to the congregation, but he declined. I was disappointed in his refusal. ***From there onward, my curiosity to know and understand what is actually written in the Guru Granth Sahib increased considerably. This prompted me to learn Punjabi in Gurmukhi script.***

The big question was how to learn Gurmukhi. I came upon a book "Learn Punjabi through English" written by Mr. Ganathe [1] who is not a Sikh. He comes from from the southern part of India. Most people who speak Punjabi come from the northern part of India. My main objective was to understand the meaning of the hymns as written in the Guru Granth Sahib. Since my knowledge of Punjabi was not proficient, I had to use the English translation to grasp the meaning of the hymns. I consulted the English translations by two prominent writers. The writers are Manmohan Singh's 8 volumes [2] and Mr. Pritam S. Chahal's 4 volumes [3]. The English translation was very helpful to me.

I developed my own simple way of learning Punjabi, while working toward my objective of reading the Guru Granth Sahib. ***This is a self-teaching process.*** This approach is meant for those who have no access to a regular teacher and have a great desire to learn Punjabi, on their own. ***This is especially beneficial for the younger generation of the Sikh Religion who are either born or brought up in the USA, Canada, UK or other countries.***

Learning Punjabi as second language is must for all people belonging to the Sikh Religion. However, it may not be possible for many people to learn Punjabi. Thus this little course may help some people to read Guru Granth Sahib. English translations are very helpful, but the true meaning of the teachings of the Guru Granth Sahib is best discovered by reading it in its original language in Gurmukhi Script.

1. ORIGIN AND HISTORY OF THE PUNJABI LANGUAGE

Punjabi at present is the language of the northern part of India and also Punjab province of Pakistan. Excavations at Mohenjo-daro in Sind (Pakistan), Harappa in Punjab (Pakistan), and Ropar in Punjab (India) have shown a glorious civilization that existed in that region, at least five thousand years ago [4]. People lived there in well-built brick houses with good floors and bathrooms. The city had a drainage system and its roads and streets were straight and wide. A sanitation system was organized. There was a great public bath (swimming pool) 180 feet long by 108 feet wide surrounded by galleries. ***Thus the civilization of the Indus Valley, which includes Punjab, is older than the civilization of the Aryan invaders.***

According to *The Encyclopedia of Sikhism* [5] the following is a chronology of the language of the Indus Valley.

i. ***VEDIC language*** 1500 to 500 BC (before Christ)

ii. ***SANSKRIT*** was the next language. Extensive literature was produced in Sanskrit up to the 11th and 12th centuries BC..

Panini [6], a well known Sanskrit grammarian, is credited with writing 4000 grammatical rules—a remarkable achievement. Panini was born about 520 BC in Shalatula near Attock on the Indus River (now part of present day Pakistan) [6]. Panini lived in the present day Punjab where Sanskrit was developed. Sanskrit and Vedic were languages of the religious sacred books. Sanskrit ceased to be the spoken language of the masses by the 6th century BC. In fact the normal language of communication among the masses was an entirely different language.

iii. ***PALI*** was the spoken language of the northern part of India from about 500 BC to the beginning of the Christian era.

iv. Then there were several languages given a common label: ***PRAKRIT***. Prakrit was used from the beginning of the Christian era to about 500 AD.

v. The next phase of several languages also had a common label: ***APABHRANSHA***.

vi. It was from Apabhransha that ***PUNJABI*** developed some time around 11th century.

While Panani was working on Sanskrit, he mentioned that the common language of the people was different. Some people like Professor Darshan Singh [4] and Professor Devinder S. Chahal [7] are of the view that the present day Punjabi is a somewhat modified form of that language. The Persians (year 1000) gave the name Punjab (land of five rivers) to that region of northern part of India. ***Thus Pali, Prakrit or Apabhransha may be some sort of ancient Punjabi in modified forms [7].*** The common people used Punjabi in its ancient form before Sanskrit was developed for religious texts.

Dr. Kuldip Singh [8] says there is a ***close resemblance between present day Punjabi and Sanskrit.*** To prove that he has quoted Dr. Om Parkash Kahol "Of all Indian languages, Punjabi is the most closely related to Sanskrit in its essentials—verbs, phonology, as well as syntax". Bengali, Marathi and Hindi show transition from Sanskrit in stages, i.e., from Sanskrit to Prakrit to Apabhramsha and then to the present form. Punjabi, on the other hand, existed along with Sanskrit. It can be said that Punjabi was the language of the common people and Sanskrit of the Hindu religious people called Brahmins.

To prove the above hypothesis the following words (Figure 39) bear a very close resemblance to each other.

FIGURE 39
Sanskrit and Punjabi

Sanskrit	Punjabi	Meaning
Rakta	**Rakat, RATT**	**Blood**
Sapta	**Satt**	**Seven**
Dughda	**Duddh**	**Milk**
Lakshmi	**Lachhmi**	**Wealth**
Pakshi	**Panchhi**	**Bird**
Vriksha	**Brichh**	**Tree**
Lakshan	**Lachhan**	**Symptom**
Loka	**Kok, Log**	**People**
Shoka	**Shok, Sog**	**Grief**
Charma	**Chamm**	**Leather**
Putra	**Puttar**	**Son**
Grama	**Gram**	**Village**
Mutra	**Mootar**	**Urine**
Bharata	**Bhra**	**Brother**
Sarva	**Sabb**	**All**
Krita	**Keeta**	**Done**
Jehba	**Jeebh**	**Tongue**

However, more work needs to be done in order to prove beyond any doubt the hypothesis that Punjabi is older or as old as Sanskrit.

It was Guru Nanak (1469 to1539) who devised the way to write the 35 alphabets of the Punjabi language in Gurmukhi script. The 35 alphabets (poem of the alphabets) have been very clearly written in the Guru Granth Sahib from pages 432 to 434. They are under the heading "Patee Likhee." This language can be called as Nanaki script [9] (same as Gurmukhi). Dr. Lightener the first Director of Education in Punjab said in 1879 that Gurmukhi is the name of the language that flowed from the mouth of Guru Nanak [9]. Guru Nanak explained the basic tenants of the Sikh Religion in the spoken language of the people called Punjabi. People thus flocked to Guru Nanak, as they could understand the teachings very clearly.

Second Guru Angad (1539 to 1552) accepted the configuration of each alphabet as devised by Guru Nanak but rearranged the order of the alphabets. This modification has been accepted and is good today and for all times to come. This script has been used to write all of the Guru Granth Sahib. This rearrangement is the equivalent to the Punjabi of today, which is used in the northern part of India and also in the Punjab region of Pakistan (they use different script but same Punjabi language).

2. CONCEPTION OF GOD AS STARTING POINT

The very first lines of Guru Granth Sahib are my starting point. Almost all people belonging to the Sikh Religion know these lines by heart. It is the conception of God as enunciated by Guru Nanak:

CONCEPTION OF GOD

PUNJABI	ROMAN	ENGLISH
੧ਓਂ	Ik-oNkar	***There is only one God.***
ਸਤਿ ਨਾਮੁ	Sat Naam	God's name is Truth.
ਕਰਤਾ ਪੁਰਖੁ	Kartaa Purakh	God created every thing
ਨਿਰਭਉ	Nirbha-o	God is without fear.
ਨਿਰਵੈਰੁ	Nirvair	God is not against any body.
ਅਕਾਲ ਮੂਰਤਿ	Akaal Moorat	God's shape never changes.
ਅਜੂਨੀ	Ajoonee	***God is neither born nor dies.***
ਸੈਭੰ	SaibhaN	***God is everywhere.***
ਗੁਰ ਪ੍ਰਸਾਦਿ॥	Gur Parsaad	By God's grace
॥ ਜਪੁ ॥	Jap	Worship.

Guru Granth Sahib. p.1 line1

3. DETAILS OF LEARNING PUNJABI

In order to understand any language one has to learn the alphabets, vowels, semi-vowels and conjunctions. The following four Tables show 35 Alphabets, 10 Vowels, 3 Semi-Vowels and 4 Conjuncts. They are explained in Gurmukhi, Roman and English. Table 5 will aid one in teaching him or herself the Gurmukhi script, for one of the most important statements, in the Guru Granth Sahib: the Conception of God.

TABLE 1

ALPHABETS AND HOW TO WRITE THEM

There are thirty-five alphabets in Gurmukhi. The first three are also vowels.

When writing, start with number 1 as shown inside each alphabet, then proceed to 2, 3, 4, and 5 ,as the case may be. This procedure shows clearly how to write from the beginning to the end of each and every Alphabet.

TABLE 2

VOWELS

There are ten vowels in Gurmukhi.
By using the first three alphabets with signs, ten vowels are created.

GURMUKHI			ROMAN	ENGLISH
No	Vowel	Example		Example
1.	ਓ	ਓ	O (O long)	Go
2.	ੁ	ਉ	U (U short)	Full
3.	ੂ	ਊ	OU (U long)	Pool
4.	ਅ	ਅ	A (A short)	At
5.	ਾ	ਆ	AA (A long)	All
6.	ੈ	ਐ	AI (Diphthong)	Dine
7.	ੌ	ਔ	AU, OU, AU Diphthong	House
8.	ਿ	ਇ	I (I short)	India
9.	ੀ	ਈ	EE (I short)	Feet
10.	ੇ	ਏ	E, AY (E long)	Pay

Examples are given in English

TABLE 3

SEMI-VOWELS

There are three Semi-Vowels in Gurmukhi.

1. BINDI* (Example of mother)

GURMUKHI Bindi	GURMUKHI Example	ROMAN	ENGLISH
ਾਂ	ਮਾਂ	Maa'n	Mother

*Bindi is a short nasal sound pronounced like 'n or 'm.
It is used only with the long vowels.

2. TIPPI (Example of color)**

GURMUKHI Tippi	GURMUKHI Example	ROMAN	ENGLISH
ੰ	ਰੰਗ	Rang	Color

**Tippi is a long nasal, used only with the short vowels. When tippi is used, it makes the letter next to it a double sound.

3. ADDHAK* (Example of Delhi)**

GURMUKHI Addhak	GURMUKHI Example	ROMAN	ENGLISH
ੱ	id`ll	**Dillee**	**Delhi**

***Addhak is not a semi-vowel, but it gives a double sound without a nasal sound and is thus used as a semi-vowel.

Examples are given in English

TABLE 4

CONJUNCTS

There are 4 conjuncts in Gurmukhi

A conjunct is a combination of consonants, first is half pronounced, while the other is pronounced fully.

	CONJUNCTS		EXAMPLE	
No.	**Gurmukhi**	**Roman**	**Roman**	**English**
1.	੍ਹ	**HA**	**Kilhaa**	**Fort**
2.	Î	**YA**	**Gyaan**	**Knowledge**
3.	੍ਰ	**RA**	**Prem**	**Love**
4.	੍ਵ	**VA**	**Dvaar**	**Wall**

Examples are given in English

TABLE 5

SELF-TEACHING OF PUNJABI (GURMUKHI) OF THE CONCEPTION OF GOD IN THE GURU GRANTH SAHIB

Conception of God			Gurmukhi Alphabets and Vowels			
Gurmukhi	**Roman**	**English**	**Gurmukhi**	**Roman**		**English**
ੴ	ik-oNkar	There is only one God	ੳ	oorra	1st	alphabet & 1st vowel
ਸਤਿ ਨਾਮੁ	Sat Naam	God's name is Truth	ਸ	sassa	4th	alphabet
			ਿ	i	8th	vowel
			ਤ	tatta	21st	alphabet
			ਨ	naanaa	25th	alphabet
			ਾ	aa	5th	vowel
			ਮ	mamaa	30th	alphabet
			ੁ	u	2nd	vowel

TABLE 5A

SELF-TEACHING OF PUNJABI (GURMUKHI) OF THE CONCEPTION OF GOD IN THE GURU GRANTH SAHIB

Conception of God			Gurmukhi Alphabets and Vowels		
Gurmukhi	**Roman**	**English**	**Gurmukhi**	**Roman**	**English**
ਕਰਤਾ ਪੁਰਖੁ	Kartaa Purakh	God created everything	ਕ	kakaa	6th alphabet
			ਰ	raaraa	32nd alphabet
			ਤ	tatta	21st alphabet
			ਾ	aa	5th vowel
			ਪ	papaa	26th alphabet
			ੁ	u	2nd vowel
			ਰ	raaraa	32nd alphabet
			ਖ	khakhaa	7th alphabet
			ੁ	u	2nd vowel

TABLE 5B

SELF-TEACHING OF PUNJABI (GURMUKHI) OF THE CONCEPTION OF GOD IN THE GURU GRANTH SAHIB

Conception of God			Gurmukhi Alphabets and Vowels		
Gurmukhi	**Roman**	**English**	**Gurmukhi**	**Roman**	**English**
ਨਿਰਭਉ	Nirbha-o	God is	ਿ	i	8th vowel
		without	ਨ	naanaa	25th alphabet
		fear	ਰ	raaraa	32nd alphabet
			ਭ	bhabhaa	29th alphabet
			ਉ	oorra	1st alphabet
			ੁ	u	2nd vowel
ਨਿਰਵੈਰੁ	Nirvair	God is not	ਿ	i	8th vowel
		against any	ਨ	naanaa	25th alphabet
		body	ਰ	raaraa	32nd alphabet
			ਵ	vavaa	34th alphabet
			ੈ	ai	6th vowel
			ਰ	raaraa	32nd alphabet
			ੁ	u	2nd vowel

TABLE 5C

SELF-TEACHING OF PUNJABI (GURMUKHI) OF THE CONCEPTION OF GOD IN THE GURU GRANTH SAHIB

Conception of God			Gurmukhi Alphabets and Vowels		
Gurmukhi	**Roman**	**English**	**Gurmukhi**	**Roman**	**English**
ਅਕਾਲ ਮੂਰਤਿ	Akal Moorat	God's shape	ਅ	airaa	2nd alphabet & 4th vowel
		never	ਕ	kakaa	6th alphabet
		changes	ਾ	aa	5th vowel
			ਲ	lalaa	33rd alphabet
			ਮ	mamaa	30th alphabet
			=	ou	3rd vowel
			ਰ	raaraa	32nd alphabet
			ਿ	i	8th vowel
			ਤ	tatta	21st alphabet
ਅਜੂਨੀ	Ajoonee	God is	ਅ	airaa	2nd alphabet
		Neither born	ਜ	jajaa	13th alphabet
		nor dies	=	ou	3rd vowel
			ਨ	naanaa	25th alphabet
			ੀ	ee	9th vowel

TABLE 5D

SELF-TEACHING OF PUNJABI (GURMUKHI) OF THE CONCEPTION OF GOD IN GURU GRANTH SAHIB

Conception of God			Gurmukhi Alphabets and Vowels		
Gurmukhi	**Roman**	**English**	**Gurmukhi**	**Roman**	**English**
ਸੈਭੰ	SaibhaN	God is	ਸ	sassa	4th alphabet
		Everywhere	ੈ	ai	6th vowel
			ਭ	bhabhaa	29th alphabet
			ੰ	n	2nd semi vowel
ਗੁਰ ਪ੍ਰਸਾਦਿ	Gur Parsaad	By God's	ਗ	gaga	8th alphabet
		grace	ੁ	u	2nd vowel
			ਰ	raaraa	32nd alphabet
			ਪ	papaa	26th alphabet
			੍ਰ	ra	3rd conjunct
			ਸ	sassa	4th alphabet
			ਾ	aa	5th vowel
			ਿ	i	8th vowel
			ਦ	dadaa	23rd alphabet
ਜਪੁ	Jap	Worship	ਜ	jajaa	13th alphabet
			ਪ	papaa	26th alphabet
			ੁ	u	2nd vowel

The very first lesson teaches not only Punjabi (Gurmukhi) but also the Conception of God according to the Sikh Religion. This is very clearly shown in Table 5. One has to study this very diligently. This inspires one to read the Guru Granth Sahib, which is the main objective of this chapter. Each and every alphabet, vowel, semi-vowel and conjuncts used in the Conception of God is explained in Gurmukhi, Roman and English. This chapter, however, is not a replacement for learning through formal lessons from a teacher fluent in both Punjabi (Gurmukhi) and English.

I have given a very simple approach for not only learning Gurmukhi but also for reading the Guru Granth Sahibl. By going through Table 5 and the Conception of God, the following is achieved:

ALPHABETS	
16 out of 35 Alphabets	***(45%)***
VOWELS	
8 out of 10 Vowels	***(80%)***
SEMI-VOWELS	
1 out of 3	***(33%)***
CONJUNCTS	
1 out of 4	***(25%)***

This lesson will help in reading the Guru Granth Sahib, which is a good beginning. One has to learn rest of Gurmukhi from a teacher and has to pay good attention in order to understand the meaning of the hymns written in the Guru Granth Sahib. Alternatively, one can read the English translation side by side with the Gurmukhi to understand the meaning of the hymn. One can easily download the Guru Granth Sahib in Gurmukhi, English, Roman and Hindi along with searchable features. Use www.srigranth.org for downloading and searching [10]. I would like to thank Dr. Kulbir Singh Thind and his son Jasjeet Singh Thind for making this available to all people without any cost. One can also use sikhnet.com/s/gurugranthsahib.

4. SUMMARY

The origin of Punjabi language bears a close resemblance to Sanskrit, as many words are similar. In fact, Punjabi may be as old or even older than Sanskrit, however, it has not been proved conclusively. Four Tables given in this chapter allows one to learn Gurmukhi's (Punjabi's) 35 Alphabets, 10 Vowels, 3 Semi-Vowels and 4 Conjuncts. By studying Table 5 one can learn considerable portion of the Gurmukhi language. The main objective of reading the Guru Granth Sahib is thus made possible, especially for those who do speak Punjabi but never learnt the Gurmukhi script. For all others who do not know Punjabi, this could be a first lesson for learning Punjabi in Gurmukhi Script.

5. EXCERCISES

i. There are 16 Alphabets in the Conception of God in Tables 5 to 5D, find them and write them in the appropriately numbered column.

ALPHABETS

1	2		4		6	7
8					13	
						21
	23		25	26		
29	30		32	33	34	

ii. There are 8 Vowels in the Conception of God in Tables 5 to 5D, find them and write them in the appropriately numbered column.

VOWELS

1	2	3	4	5	6		8	9	

iii. There is 1 Semi-Vowel in the Conception of God in Tables 5 to 5D, find it and write it in the appropriately numbered column.

SEMI-VOWELS

	2	

iv. There is 1 Conjunct in the Conception of God in Tables 5 to 5D, find it and write it in the appropriately numbered column.

CONJUNCTS

		3	

v. Explain how this approach of learning Punjabi in Gurmukhi Script was helpful to you as a first step in achieving your final objective of understanding the Guru Granth Sahib.
vi. What are pros and cons of the hypothesis that Punjabi language is older or as old as Sanskrit?

6. REFERENCES

[1] N.S.R. Ganathe,1981. *Learn Punjabi in 30 Days*, Balaji Publications, Madras, India, 2nd edition.

[2] Manmohan Singh, 1981, *Siri Guru Granth Sahib* (Gurmukhi, English and Punjabi translations), Shiromani Gurdwara Parbandhak Committee, Amritsar, Punjab, India, 2nd edition, 8 volumes.

[3] Pritam Singh Chahil, 1993, *Siri Guru Granth Sahib* (Gurmukhi, Roman and English translation), Pritam Singh Chahil, New Delhi, India, 4 volumes.

[4] Darshan Singh, Professor of Punjab University, India, 2000, *The Sikh Courier International*, Great Britain, Vol. 40, No 89, p. 36-40. "Language and Culture of Punjab".

[5] Harkirat Singh in *Encyclopedia of Sikhism* editor Harbans Singh, Punjabi University, India, Vol. 3, p. 385 By E-mail from Joginder S. Ahluwalia of Richmond, California, USA through Sikh-Diaspora@yahoogroups.com

[6] Go to yahoo.com. Search for "Biography of Panini" Click for "Panini". Written by O'Connor, J.J and Robertson Nov. 2000, School of Mathematics and Statistics, University of St. Andrews, Scotland. http://www-groups.dcs.st-and.ac.uk/~history/Mathematicians/Panini.html also http://www.worldhistory.com/wiki/P/Panini-(scholar).htm

[7] Devinder Singh Chahal, Professor, "Understanding Sikhism," *The Research Journal*, Laval, Canada, Vol 3 number 2, 2001 pages 24 to 29.

[8] Yahoo.com Search for "Sikh Review Punjabi Language Kuldip Singh" Click Sikh Review
Kuldip Singh Dr. F.R.C.S. Punjabi Language and the Gurmukhi Script - Origin & Development.
http://www.maboli.com/seva/sikh_review/1996/august_96/sajjeCulture.htm

[9] E- mail by Dr. Kuldip Singh through Sikh-Diaspora@yahoogroups.com dated May 4, 2004 Reference to Lightener R. W. Dr. First Director of Education in Punjab, 1879, History of Indigenous Education in Punjab, pages 31 to 32.

[10] Use http://www.srigranth.org or sikhnet.com/s/gurugranthsahib. Courtesy of Dr. Kulbir Singh Thind and his son Jasjeet Singh Thind.

UNIVERSALITY OF THE SIKH RELIGION

CHAPTER 21

PROPAGATION OF SIKH RELIGION IN THE ADOPTED COUNTRY

I am going to concentrate mostly on why propagation of the Sikh Religion is important in the adopted country. It may apply also in India, but they may have different requirements.

The main reason to propagate the religion is to spread the teachings of Guru Nanak throughout the whole world—to all six billion people. The important aspects of the Sikh Religion are:

1. Perform good deeds for the benefit of humanity.
2. To love human beings is to love God.
3. Do not speak ill of any other religion.
4. Treat everyone, including women, as equals in all respects.
5. Have a good work ethic.
6. Share one's blessing with less fortunate people.
7. Pray daily to God who created the whole universe.
8. God is neither born nor dies and is present everywhere.
9. Truth is higher than everything but higher still is truthful living.
10. To obtain peace of mind keep mind, body, and soul in tune with God.

Are Sikhs following the above practices in spreading the Sikh Religion? The fact is that young Sikhs born or brought up in their new, adopted country do not think so. Sikhs teachings must be brought to the attention of those who follow other religions. When spreading the Sikh religion, Sikhs should try to make the following changes:

1. Use of the language of the adopted country.
2. Promote education among the Sikh religious preachers.
3. Promote Equality of Sikhs with and without long hair as well as women.
4. Use chairs and tables in the Gurdwara.
5. Eliminate Rituals.
6. Eliminate fighting in Gurdwaras.
7. Eliminate politics in religion.
8. Provide Hygienic conditions.
9. Provide access for handicapped people.
10. Be punctual.

The changes suggested in propagating the Sikh Religion in the adopted country are in agreement with the teachings as written in the Guru Granth Sahib.

Since the inception of the Sikh Religion and up to 1947 the Universality of the Sikh Religion was maintained not only in theory but also in practice. The first period was during the ten Gurus from 1469 to 1708. Second period was during the Maharaja Ranjit Singh from 1780 to 1839. The third period was from 1849 to 1947, during the British control of India. During the above three periods Universality of the Sikh religion was in tact. However, after the Independence of India in 1947 universality has not been practiced. ***The teachings as written in the Guru Granth Sahib make it very clear that Sikh Religion is universal. Sikh Religion also respects all other religions.*** Hymns not only of Sikhs but also of Hindus and Muslims are recorded in the Guru Granth Sahib. In order to revitalize the Universality of the Sikh Religion, especially for the Sikhs living in their new adopted countries, several suggestions are explained in detail in this chapter.

I will be discussing—from my own experience of living in the USA for more than 49 years—how the Universality of the Sikh Religion can be propagated. Gurudwara is a place where people belonging to the Sikh Religion congregate and worship. I remember the day in 1965 or so, when a small number of Sikhs (including me) started the first Gurudwara in the eastern part of USA, in Richmond Hills, Queens, New York. People from all religions, Sikhs, Hindus and even some Muslims used to come. ***Universal appeal of the Sikh religion was preserved. It is sad to say that it is not so today.*** In order to spread the Universality of the Sikh Religion all of the changes suggested are in conformity with the teachings of the Guru Granth Sahib.

Since rituals are not part of the Sikh Religion, then why we are still practicing them? If Equality is the cornerstone of the Sikh Religion, then why it is not being carried out? ***As more people are becoming educated they ask questions and want logical answers that should relate to their day-to-day life. Years ago nobody asked such questions about religion.***

Sikhs who came from India and settled in their new, adopted country deserve lot of credit. They put in lot of effort and money to buy or built the Gurdwaras. They are running the Gurdwaras on a regular basis. It is a good beginning. However, for the coming generations who are born or brought up in their adopted countries—like the USA, Canada and Britain—changes have to be made. These changes are required to keep pace with the technological advances and to adjust to the day-to-day living of the adopted country.

I am going to discuss the above changes that need to be made in order to spread the Universality of the Sikh religion. As time goes by there will be a need for more changes. ***Changes have to be handled very tactfully and should be in accordance with the teachings as written in the Guru Granth Sahib.*** These changes are especially important for the Sikhs living in western countries like the USA, Canada, Britain and other countries as well.

1. USE LANGUAGE OF THE ADOPTED COUNTRY

This is one of the most important requirements. ***Even the best message, if not conveyed in the language that people understand, has no meaning.*** In fact it may be counterproductive. Guru Nanak also used the language of the common people of Punjab to convey his message.

Most of the Sikhs who were born or lived most of their life outside India do not know Punjabi in Gurmukhi script. It is easier to say that they should learn it. However, it is not the practical solution for the majority of Sikhs. Some may learn Punjabi and that is good but their numbers are extremely small.

Language of the adopted country (like English for USA, Canada and Britain) must be used along with Punjabi to explain the teachings of the Sikh Religion. . ***English must be used in the main hall where the religious services are being performed.*** Many Sikhs do not know Punjabi. It is the duty of the organizers of the Gurdwara to see that Punjabi along with the language of the adopted country is used. This is for the benefit of all who are attending the services. It is very important for all to grasp the real meaning of the words written in the Guru Granth Sahib. They have come from far and near and have spent many hours to attend the services. There may be some problems in translating Punjabi into English. It is due to the colloquiums of the Punjabi language and the cultural at the time it was written. ***Thus simple English must be used to convey the real meaning of the hymns.***

When an native-born American comes to a Gurdwara he/she does not understand anything. On the other hand if I go to a Christian church I understand everything. It is because the service is performed in English—the language spoken by the people.

Let us examine the language of the Bible. In the United States it is written in English. However the original Bible was written in Hebrew (Old Testament) and Greek (New Testament). The Christian Religion has spread all over the world. In almost all countries they use the local, common language of the people to spread the message of Christ through the Bible.

We have failed to recognize that our next generation brought up in USA is American and not Indian. They have Indian ancestry. ***The young are rebelling. The elder Sikhs know that but are not willing to believe or do any thing to counteract it.*** The young people say it in open words that a change is required in propagating the Sikh religion in our Gurdwaras. The management in charge is not willing to change. The young Sikhs do not understand Punjabi, however, very little attempt is made to use English language in the Gurdwara. Consequently, these young Sikhs lose interest. They feel that they do not miss much by not going to the Gurdwara. They would prefer to watch a football game instead.

The Guru Granth Sahib is written in eleven languages while the script is Gurmukhi. English language would have been incorporated if it was in use at that time. Thus it is clear that the use of other languages is not prohibited in spreading the teachings of the Sikh Religion.

It should also be made very clear that learning of Punjabi by every Sikh is also very important. Punjabi could be a second language. The main objective is to read the Guru Granth Sahib in order to grasp the real meaning. For the beginners, Chapter 20 may help in learning Punjabi at the beginning level. Some may be able to read the Guru Granth Sahib as I did. On the other hand, not all people can learn Punjabi. ***Therefore, teaching in the language of the adopted country along with Punjabi is very important.***

In the future I think more Gurdwaras will start using English along with Punjabi, however, it will take some time. It also depends upon how second or third generation Sikhs want to propagate the Universality of the Sikh Religion, assuming they are still part of the Sikh Religion by that time.

2. EDUCATION OF SIKH RELIGIOUS PREACHERS

The Sikh religious preachers in the Gurdwaras are called Ragis (who sing hymns) and Granthis (who explain religion). They come from India, do not have formal education, and cannot give sermons in English. Their presentation is not geared to the problems that the congregation is facing in their adopted countries on a day-to-day basis. Ragis and Granthis are more interested in either keeping their immigration status in tact or in making money. Some who are knowledgeable in the Sikh religion cannot relay the message to the highly educated congregations in the USA, Canada, UK and other countries.

Thus changes are required in order to spread the Universality of the Sikh Religion in the new, adopted countries. Other than the use of English language the most important criteria is that the preachers must be educated.

Preachers should have at least Bachelor's degree from a reputable university of the country where the Gurdwara is located. The major subject should be theology with special emphasis on Sikh Religion and minor in sociology and/or psychology. In cases of the USA, Canada and UK, the preachers must be fluent in English as well as Punjabi.

During Guru Nanak's time many Hindu preachers were unmarried and often led a very secluded life. ***Guru Nanak said humanity is served better by being married and living within the community.*** Preachers not marrying had become a ritual in the Hindu religion. Guru Nanak said this ritual must go.

In the new, adopted countries religious preachers are required to perform many duties. The congregation looks upon the preacher in times of need. Congregants may consult a preacher with spiritual questions, day-to-day family problems, emotional stress, mental depression, and etc. Currently, preachers so not fill this role as advisor in the Gurdwaras. The religious preacher has to be a dedicated family person.

The preachers should relate the Sikh teachings and history to the day-to-day problems that the congregation is facing in their adopted country***. Appropriate quotations from the Guru Granth Sahib should be used to justify the sermon.***

To perform the above duties ***the preacher has to be paid well so he or she can maintain their family and educate their children, according to the standards of the adopted country.***

Some of the requirements of a preacher are explained above, but the question remains: who is responsible for making these changes? Obviously it is the management of the Gurdwaras that hires the preachers. The management of the Gurdwaras in the USA, Canada and Britain are mostly concerned with their own importance in the society. They are not well versed in the Sikh religious philosophy and are not much concerned in propagating the Sikh Religion in the adopted country.

If the present management is not going to make any change then it is left to the next generation of the Sikhs. The young Sikhs educated in the adopted country may take over the management. They may institute services as required by the congregation including spiritual counseling or may advise congregants when they are under great emotional stress or have family problems.

Unless the educated people both young and old take an active part in the Sikh religious philosophy, changes will not take place. ***Thus the decision to change lies with the silent majority.*** In the meantime propagation of the Sikh religion will suffer significantly. As the congregation is highly educated and sees no meaningful change in the presentation of the Sikh Religion in the Gurdwaras, they rarely attend or get involved in the Gurdwara. They are so busy in earning a living, taking care of their family needs, and adjusting to the newly adopted country that religion is left to the preachers (Ragis and Granthis). Whatever the preacher in charge says or does is carried out. It is not the fault of the preacher since this is what they have learned from their religious instructors in India. ***At present there is no room for discussion in an intelligent way even outside the services.***

3. EQUALITY OF SIKHS WITH AND WITHOUT LONG HAIR

The lack of equality among people belonging to the Sikh religion is a very serious problem. ***Although equality is the motto of Sikh religion, but it is not being practiced among Sikhs.***

First let us explain the basic concepts of the Sikh Religion. Besides believing in one God and Truth, Guru Nanak made it very clear that all people are equal in all respects. Guru Nanak said that there is no high and no low.

People interpret equality in their own way. Some say that equality is by allowing all people to attend Gurdwara. Others say that Sikhs who are Khalsa (Amritdhari, the baptized Sikhs) be given special rights as regards the election or selection of the management of Gurdwaras. Others may have their own versions of equality.

According to me equality is when all people are equal in all respects irrespective of their appearance, caste, sex, color, creed, nationality, religion or any other way people want to divide each other. ***Equality at present is not being followed.*** The main bone of contention is between Sikhs with and without long hair. Of course Sikh men with long hair wear turbans and thus are different in appearance. This is a very emotional and divisive issue among the Sikhs. ***The solution lies within the Sikhs.*** If not solved it will be more dangerous than any external threat from other religions. Let us evaluate this and come up with a good solution.

The question is: Can Sikhs with and without long hair live on an equal basis in all respects with each other?

There is no clear-cut solution at present that is acceptable to all.

BACKGROUND HISTORY OF THIS ISSUE

Tenth Guru Gobind Singh made it mandatory for Khalsa Sikhs to have long hair. However, there were many Sikhs during the period of Guru Gobind Singh who did not have long hair. Along with the Amrit ceremony (Baptism), Khalsa Sikhs should have five K's. Five K's are Kachha (short pant), Kara (steel bangle), Kirpan (sword), Kangha (comb) and Kesh (long hair).

Guru Gobind Singh raised the army of Khalsa to stop the Muslim invaders who were plundering India for centuries. However in his army there were also Sikhs without long hair along with Hindus and Muslims.

During British rule (1849 to 1947) many Gurdwaras, before the Gurdwara Act of 1925, were under the control of people who were not Sikhs. After suffering many casualties during peaceful demonstrations, the British Government allowed Sikhs to control Gurdwaras. In 1925 Sikh Gurdwara Act was passed and a representative body Sikhs called Shrimoni Gurdwara Parbhandak Committee in Amritsar, India, took control of the Gurdwaras. ***Later in 1945 the Sikh Reht Maryada or the Sikh Code of Conduct vested all religious power with the Khalsa Sikhs.*** Even today Khalsa Sikhs are controlling most of the Gurdwaras, although they are in very small minority among the whole Sikh population.

PRESENT SITUATION

At present about 80 % of the Sikhs do not have long hair.

Mr. Tarlochan Singh, [1] Chairman of National Commission for Minorities in India said ***that in Punjab, 80 percent of Sikh school students do not keep long hair.*** Mr. Singh also said that 90 percent of Punjab's sportsmen are Sikhs but none wore a turban. Dr. Sangat Singh writer of many books and award winner wrote [2] that ***in several regions of Punjab (Malva, Doaba and Majha) 80 percent of the Sikhs do not have long hair.*** Outside of India the percent of Sikhs without long hair is even much higher than 80 percent.

Dr. Kharak Singh Mann, a religious leader, admitted in one of the conferences of the Institute of Sikh Studies in Chandigarh, that 80 % of the Sikhs in Punjab villages are non-keshadhari (without long hair). That was inspite of them working for about five years (special program called Chetana Lehar) in villages to have long hair and turban [2A].

Recently a Sikh returned to USA from Punjab and found that 100% of the children in village school that he visited do not have long hair [3]. This trend is reaching an alarming proportion. He was completely disappointed when he took his five-year-old son with him to show the Sikhs in Punjab with long hair.

I will give an example of our Mayell family. When I was young (born in 1929) almost all (about 50 male Sikhs) of our family living in Choudhi Budh Singh Mayell Street in Sialkot, Pakistan, wore turban and had long hair. Within a short span of about 70 years things have changed drastically. Now only 10% of the male members have long hair. The same trend is happening in large number of Sikh families in India as well as outside India.

It is easy to blame somebody else as to why this is happening. But these are the facts of life. We have to live with it and find a solution where all Sikhs with and without long hair can live together as equals. We also have to think what will happen in 50 or 100 years from now.

There would be no problem if all people belonging to the Sikh Religion had long hair or all had short hair. The other four K's required for Khalsa Sikhs are not controversial and most of the Sikhs can easily adjust to them or make some compromise. ***It is basically a question of appearance, as male Sikhs with long hair and turbans look very different. This leads to a lack of unity among the Sikhs in the community.***

Both sides claim to have valid reasons, but there is a big rift between the two sides. It is a fact that the number of Sikhs not having long hair is increasing considerably and that cannot be stopped. Sometimes this rift runs deep, not only among different families but also within the same family. ***It happens quite often that one member of the family has long hair while the other does not.***

The very basic thing, that is common between people with or without long hair, is they all belong to the same Sikh Religion. The mode of prayer is the same, all believe in the Guru Granth Sahib and there is no difference in almost everything that is social and cultural. These are the real binding forces. The solution is not easy but is possible.

Before going further let us discuss the pros and cons of people with and without long hair. There are many advantages of having long hair and at the same time there are also many negatives.

REASONS FOR HAVING LONG HAIR

The following are some of the reasons for having long hair. I am sure people can think of many other reasons.

a. FUNDAMENTAL REASON

The fundamental and most important reason is that the tenth and last living Guru Gobind Singh made it mandatory to have long hair in order to be called a Khalsa. ***It is thus a religious symbol for a Khalsa.***

b. CODE OF CONDUCT

The Sikh code of conduct issued by the Shiromani Gurdawara Parbhandak Committee in Amritsar Punjab in 1945, defined that a Sikh should have long hair and also should have taken Amrit. However, Delhi Sikh Gurdwara Management Committee in 1971 defined that a Sikh should have unshorn (long) hair. They omitted taking of Amrit as requirement to be called a Sikh. By contrast The Sikh Gurdwara Act of 1925 defined that a Sikh means a person who professes the Sikh religion. They do not mention long hair and Amrit as requirements to be called a Sikh. The 1925 definition includes all types of Sikhs through the world. ***Thus there are three definitions of a Sikh. Two of them specify long hair while the third does not.***

c. APPEARANCE

The men, especially those with long hair and turban, look significantly different in appearance than those without a turban. They can be spotted very easily from a distance. They are of the view that ***all Sikhs especially male, must have long hair and a turban and that they are the only ones who should be treated equally in all respects.*** Some people say ***long hair and a turban is like a uniform***.

d. GOD'S GIFT

Human beings came to this world with God's gift of hair. We should not cut it.

REASONS FOR NOT HAVING LONG HAIR

The following are some of the reasons for not having long hair. I am sure people can think of many other reasons. It is not easy to convince the young Sikhs about having long hair. They want answers that are logical and acceptable in modern and technologically advanced societies.

a. DIFFICULT TO KEEP

It is not easy to maintain a beard, long hair and a turban. This is evident as the number of Sikhs having long hair is diminishing considerably, both inside and outside India.

b. RELIGIOUS INTERPRETATION

Many people give reasons—based upon the Sikh religion—that keeping long hair is not essential to be called a Sikh. They include the following:

b1. Guru Gobind Singh never made it mandatory for all Sikhs to have long hair but he did so for Khalsa. ***Thus one could be a Sikh without having long hair.*** **All Khalsa are Sikhs but all Sikhs are not Khalsa** unless they take Amrit (baptized) as explained by Dr. McLeod [4] (Tiwana's Review), and Dr. Dhillon [5].

b2. ***The first nine Gurus were not Khalsa but they were Sikhs.***

b3. If Guru Nanak refused to put sacred thread (Hindus use for baptism as Guru Nanak was born in a Hindu family) under his shirt that is not conspicuous, then why are the five K's essential—especially the long hair?

b4. The main objective of the Sikh Religion is ***to lead truthful living and to strive for salvation.*** Those objectives can be achieved without having long hair.

b5. ***Guru Nanak said there is no high and no low.*** We all are equal. Thus there is no need to differentiate among people with and without long hair.

c. EQUALITY BY GURU GOBIND SINGH

Guru Gobind Singh was a strict believer in equality. He said

"Recognize all human beings as one
The same God is the Creator and Sustainer of us all
Perceive no distinction among them." [6]

Guru Gobind Singh accepted people who do not have long hair as Sikhs. Guru Gobind Singh's army had Sikhs (Khalsa), Sikhs without long hair, Hindus and Muslims. They were all fighting side by side for the same cause to get rid of the foreign invaders and to control their own destiny politically and religiously. They all fought together on an equal basis. They gave their lives, the ultimate sacrifice, for the right cause as enunciated by Guru Gobind Singh.

d. MEETING PEOPLE OF OPPOSITE SEX

Young people complain that ***long hair is a hindrance to dating and meeting people of the opposite sex.*** This may be the most important reason why the young do not have long hair.

e. JOB SITUATION

It is not easy to get a job in western countries when one has long hair, a beard and a turban.

f. INFLUENCE OF MOVIES AND TELEVISION

The actors create lasting impressions on viewers through film and television. ***Most of the time it is the indirect perception, as almost all actors are not having long hair.*** This is particularly so for those who are born and brought up in their adopted country (i.e., USA, Canada, Britain, and so on).

SOLUTIONS TO THIS PROBLEM

Having explained the differences between the two types of Sikhs with and without long hair, let us see if unity is possible. We all know unity is strength. Thus in order to spread the Universality of the Sikh Religion it is extremely important for all Sikhs to be united. In ***social, cultural and day-to-day situations Sikhs with and without long hair have no problems.*** This division is noticeable only at a religious gathering. This problem will vanish if the same social atmosphere is also carried out in a religious gathering.

Some possible solutions are given below. Only time will tell how Sikhs inside and outside India will unite to solve this problem.

SOLUTION BASED UPON COMPROMISE

Let this problem take its own course. With time, solutions will come that take into account the requirements of the community. What it means is that when Sikhs without long hair are in the majority, some of them will be elected to the management positions of the religious organizations. The executive committee will have both types of Sikhs and thus equality will prevail. This process has already started in many Gurdwaras in Canada and the USA. However, it will take a long time. Many significant changes are required in the Gurdwaras that are discussed in this chapter. During this timeframe a lot of Sikhs will stay away from Gurdwara services. Later, they may even join some other religion, especially if they are married to a person of different faith. ***Thus many people may leave Sikh religion forever.*** These people will be devoid of the teachings as written in the Guru Granth Sahib. However, they have another option of reading the Guru Granth Sahib without going to Gurdwara. It is through the Internet that the Guru Granth Sahib is available in Punjabi, English, Hindi and Roman, without spending any money. Nevertheless, such numbers will be very small. Religious and social gathering is very important in any community to convey the message of Guru Nanak.

SOLUTION BASED UPON DIVISION

If the Gurdwara Management is determined that Sikhs without long hair can never become part of the management, then Sikhs without long hair may start their own Gurdwara. This will lead to two types of Gurdwaras. ***There will be one type of Gurdwara for those Sikhs who believe strictly that long hair is essential to be called a Sikh and there will be other type of Gurdwara where Sikhs with or without long hair are treated equal in all respects.*** This creates a rift between the Sikhs. However, if both sides agree to this solution then it may not be bad. In due course, people may start attending either of the Gurdwaras depending upon their choice and without any hard feelings.

COMPARISON WITH THE JEWISH RELIGION

Since the Jewish religion faced a similar problem, let us examine how it was solved. Jews represent about 2% of the U.S. population, or about 5.5 million persons. Sikhs, likewise, compose about 2% of India's population. According to a 1990 survey conducted by the Council of Jewish Federation [7], 6.8% of the total U.S. Jewish population was Orthodox. Also, some of the very religious Jewish sects do not allow male members to cut their hair. In a few years, Sikhs with long hair may represent the same percentage in the U.S.

Orthodox Jews strive to maintain the original elements of their laws with very few or no changes. Similarly a very small percentage of Sikhs feel that cutting of long hair is not allowed and no change can be made.

Within the Jewish religion, the Modern Orthodox, Conservative and Reform branches have made modifications in keeping with today's society. Similarly Sikhs should make changes to cope with the highly educated Sikh congregation.

Jews are free to worship where services and practices meet their beliefs and needs. Men in the very Orthodox communities wear black suits and hats and grow beards. The women wear long dresses and cover their hair. These groups may express the feeling that they are the true observers. This for long has been a subject of debate. Men in other congregations generally do not have beards(unless they choose to do so) and their are no restrictions on female clothing.

Solutions to these problems rest with Sikhs themselves. To my way of thinking, it is better to unite through compromise because we are all part of the same family. ***If we can unite socially on equal basis, the same can be done at religious gatherings. It means equality for all Sikhs, including women of course, in all respects.***

4. USE OF CHAIRS AND TABLES IN GURDWARAS

About 500 years ago when Sikh religion was started there were no chairs or tables either in the houses where people lived or in the Gurdwaras. Thus it was customary to sit on the floor. With modern day changes in technology things have changed. Now almost everybody has chairs and tables at home. On the other hand Gurdwara managements still want people to sit on the floor.

As we grow older it is very difficult to sit on the floor for long hours. The religious program generally lasts for 3 to 4 hours, far more than the mind can really comprehend. Most of the senior citizens have knee, back and many other problems and thus need special attention. We should not forget that we all have to go through the same process of aging. ***Chairs must be provided in the main hall and they should be set up near the Guru Granth Sahib*** so they can easily see and hear the religious ceremonies. We must honor and respect the older generation.

As long as the Guru Granth Sahib is installed at a higher elevation, in order to provide proper respect, then the chairs should cause no problem.

Chairs and tables must be provided in the Langar hall (eating place) as well. The easiest way to serve food for large numbers of people is a buffet system. In this system food is put on the tables. People select what they want. Most of the people eat while standing while others sit on the chairs. The real purpose of the Sikh Religion is that all people should eat together on an equal basis. Sitting on the chairs or eating while standing does not violates that purpose. It is far more comfortable to sit in the chair than to sit on the floor.

Our forefathers understood this problem especially for the western countries. They allowed the use of chairs. ***A very important resolution [8] regarding chairs in religious places was passed on April 25,1935.*** It happened during the meeting of the Dharmik Sulaakaar Committee of very prominent Sikhs in Punjab, India. The resolution is as follows.

"In Europe or America, where it is a standard practice to sit on chairs in *Religious places—there is no harm in sitting on chairs in Gurdwaras, provided that the Guru Granth Sahib is placed at a higher elevation".*

It was due to the farsightedness of the following highly educated and respected Sikhs that the above resolution was passed in 1935.

1. S. Kahan Singh Nabha
2. Professor Jodh Singh
3. Professor Teja Singh
4. Professor Ganga Singh
5. Jathedar Mohan Singh

It should also be mentioned that Professor Teja Singh, Professor Ganga Singh and Jathedar Mohan Singh also signed the Sikh Reht Maryada, the Sikh Code of Conduct. ***Thus it is more than acceptable to use chairs and tables in the Gurdwaras.***

Guru Nanak Gurdwara in Surrey, Canada was using chairs in the Langar hall, a place for eating. Mr. Ranjit Singh, in charge of the highest Sikh Religious authority called ***Akal Takht in Amritsar, India, issued Hukamnama (order) declaring six Canadian Sikhs as guilty of religious misconduct on April 20, 1998*** [9]. This in fact was an order to stop using chairs and to sit on the floor. Refusal to renounce the use of tables and chairs means removal from the Sikh religion.

The six Canadian Sikhs are as follows.

1. Mr. Giani Harkirat Singh, a former Head Granthi (religious preacher).
2. Mr. Balwant Singh Gill, President, Guru Nanak Gurdwara, Surrey, Canada.
3. Mr. Tara Singh Hayer, Editor, *Indo-Canadian Times* (weekly).
4. Mr. Jarnail Singh Bhandal, Senior Vice-President, Khalsa Dewan.
5. Mr. Rattan Singh, President, Akali Sikh Society, Vancouver.
6. Mr. Kashmir Singh, Record Secretary, Khalsa Dewan.

All of the above six Sikhs defied the ban and refused to appear before the Akal Tahkt in charge, in Amritsar, Punjab, India. Akal Takht issued **"tankhaiya"** which excommunicated the six Canadian Sikhs effective July 25, 1998. However, this edict had absolutely no effect on the six Canadian Sikhs. The chairs are still being used in the same Gurdwara in Canada. ***Members of the same Gurdwara overwhelmingly elected the "excommunicated" Sikhs [10]. This edict not only failed but also backfired.***

In fact more Gurdwaras in the USA and Canada have started using chairs not only in the Langar hall but also in the main hall where the Guru Granth Sahib is installed. ***It only proves Akal Takht edicts issued in Amritsar, India, has no effect on the Sikhs living outside India.***

People in charge of Sikh Religious institutions must learn to move with the modern amenities that have nothing to do with the basic teachings of Sikh religion, as written in the Guru Granth Sahib. Sikh Religion is a very logical and progressive. There is absolutely no harm in using the new techniques in preaching. Sitting on the floor will not bring better understanding of the teachings or the hymns.

Sitting on the floor has become a ritual. It takes long time for the people to change to chairs. Some times a compromise may be the best solution. Both options of sitting on the floor as well as on the chairs should be given to all. This way all will be satisfied. There is, however, one advantage to sitting on the floor—in a limited space, many more people can be accommodated.

The main purpose is to understand and put into practice the words written in the Guru Granth Sahib.

5. RITUALS AND PROCEDURES

Ritual is performing an act without ever understanding its meaning. Many times rituals are followed blindly and may have lost significance with regard to the teachings of the Sikh Religion.

Procedure is a certain way that is required and understood by all. Without procedures there will be chaos. In practical life some times rituals and procedures overlap. One has to be very careful in drawing a line between a procedure and a ritual. An established procedure can become a ritual. Some times it is difficult to see where one ends and the other begins.

A. HOW PROCEDURES BECOME RITUALS

Procedures that can be explained logically are acceptable. Some procedures are necessary as long as everybody understands its meaning. Sometimes ritual and procedure can be intermingled, especially if the ritual has been used for a long time and nobody has objected.

Procedures are essential and may vary from country to country while the basic principles of the Sikh Religion as written in the Guru Granth Sahib, do not change. It is amazing how rituals evolve. Sometimes unintentionally the rituals creep in from other religions. This is particularly so if the people belonging to the religion are in very small minority. This has happened in India where Sikhs are only two percent of the population. ***Many rituals of Hindu religion have become part of the Sikh Religion.*** This will go on unless concerted effort is made by the Sikhs to stop the rituals. This, however, does not mean to show any animosity to people of other religions. All efforts must be made by the Sikhs to live in close cooperation with people of all other religions.

I am going to show some examples how procedures change to rituals. One can think of many other procedures that have become rituals.

i. READING OF THE GURU GRANTH SAHIB (AKHAND PAATH)

Reading of Guru Granth is the best thing one can do provided people understand the hymns and put them into practice in day to day life. ***However reading the Guru Granth Sahib without undersatnding becomes a ritual.***

Let us discuss reading of the Guru Granth Sahib in 48 hours. It is called Akhand Paath in Punjabi. The Guru Granth Sahib's 1430 pages are read in 48 hours, approximately two pages per minute, by many people, usually in two hour shifts. Most of the time nobody is listening except for the person who is reading (also is paid to do so) at a very fast speed. This is a typical case where the procedure has turned into a ritual. The person who gave the money for reading believes, blindly, that all the wishes will be fulfilled. The readers consider this as a profession in order to make money. People start coming about two hours before the ending. There is a large gathering of relatives and friends at that time. Finally Langar is served in a very lavish manner and they all enjoy that.

The only redeeming part of Akhand Paath is that at least some people hear hymns from the Guru Granth Sahib for two hours or more out of 48 hours. They still do not understand the real meaning but do so as a ritual. May be it gives mental satisfaction to the person who is paying for this Akhand Path. The young generation find it very repugnant that so much time and money is spent but no one really comes away with any real meaning of the Sikh Religion.

ii. COVERING OF THE HEAD IN THE GURDWARA

Everybody in the Gurdwara Hall in the presence of the Guru Granth Sahib must cover their head. ***Covering of head is considered a mark of respect according to the Eastern culture. It must be followed.***

It becomes a ritual when people are forced to cover their head when the Guru Granth Sahib is not present. This rule is generally forced by the Sikhs who have a turban, as their head is covered all the time. It is not easy for those who do not wear a turban and for the ladies to cover their heads while eating in the Langar or in other parts of the Gurdwara. ***This shows how a good procedure of covering the head becomes a bad ritual.***

Culture of the country also plays a significant role. People in the western world consider covering the head in a religious place as disrespectful.

iii. REMOVING SHOES

It is very hygienic if shoes are removed before entering Gurdwara. It is a good practice and requires less cleaning of the house of worship. Removing of shoes should also be encouraged when entering any home. In order for people to be comfortable in removing shoes the management must see that the place is neat and clean. It must be properly heated in winter and cooled in summer.
If people are forced to remove their socks also then it becomes a ritual especially when the place is not clean, not heated in winter or cooled in summer.

iv. WHERE SHOULD PEOPLE SIT IN THE CONGREGATION HALL

Generally men sit on one side of the congregation hall in the Gurdwara, while ladies sit on the others side. Children are generally playing or running from mother to father and vice versa. This has become a ritual. It is much better when the family sit together along with their children so all can benefit without causing any disturbance.

v. OBSERVENCE OF TIME SCHEDULE FOR RELIGIOUS SERVICES

Timing for the services must be specified and adhered to strictly. It is advisable that the total time for services ***should not be more than one and a half hour*** (not including the Langar). This is strictly an administrative problem and can be very easily resolved.

vi. NAMING OF NEWBORN CHILD

After a child is born and when the mother has recovered physically, the family goes to the Gurdwara for the naming ceremony. The Guru Granth Sahib is opened at random and the first alphabet of the hymn is selected. The initial name of the newborn child shall start with that alphabet. The middle and the last name are generally fixed. The middle name for men is Singh and for women is Kaur. The last name is that of the family that goes from generation to generation. Some Sikhs have only two names and they do not use the last or family name.

This procedure has some merit. ***However some say that all alphabets are equally important.*** Using only one alphabet, selected at random, is very limited in selecting the name.

B. WHY RITUALS ARE NOT GOOD

Definition of a ritual can make a big difference in its interpretation. Irving Hexman [11] defines ritual as sacred custom or any form of repetitive behavior that is fixed by tradition. The question is who sets the tradition? Can it ever be changed or is it fixed forever? Can we ask for a logical reason for the particular ritual? Years ago no one asked any questions about the rituals. They accepted them without any reservation. It was taken for granted. Now people are educated. They read the Guru Granth Sahib. Some who are not proficient in Punjabi read the English translation that is easily available on the Internet. ***They find what is written in the Guru Granth Sahib is not being followed by the religious preachers.*** Rituals that are forbidden have crept into the Sikh Religion. The above definition as ritual being tradition is not applicable to the Sikh Religion and will be explained below.

Dr. Doris Jakobsh [12] writes why Sikh writers see rituals as negative. ***It is not that Sikh writers have negative connotations about rituals; there is just no place for ritual in the Sikh Religion.*** We are discussing those rituals (traditions) that cannot be explained by logic and reasoning.

Guru Nanak throughout his life used logic and reasoning to propagate the Sikh religious philosophy. Logic and reasoning starts with the first page of the Guru Granth Sahib and continues to the last 1430th page. Guru Nanak made it very clear that old traditions and rituals that are not good for the society must go.

If one follows rituals without understanding, it is like closing one's mind. It then leads to blind faith.

The first Guru, Nanak, said:

PUNJABI AND ROMAN	**ENGLISH**
ਕਰਮ ਧਰਮ ਬੰਧਕਾਰੀ ॥ Karam Dharam BanDhkaaree Guru Granth Sahib (p. 635, line 9)	Religious rituals and ceremonies leads to blind faith (without thinking power).

Believing and understanding one's religion is more important, especially in the present, highly technologically advanced society. There is no need for those customs that keep one away from God.

The first Guru, Nanak, said:

PUNJABI AND ROMAN	**ENGLISH**
ਜਾਲਉ ਐਸੀ ਰੀਤਿ Jaala-o Aisee Reet	Get rid of those rituals
ਜਿਤੁ ਮੈ ਪਿਆਰਾ ਵੀਸਰੈ ॥ Jit Mai Pi-aaraa Veesrai Guru Granth Sahib (p. 590, line 2)	that lead one to forget the loving God.

The Sikh Religion is very simple and is categorically against rituals. If nothing is done to eliminate the rituals, the people belonging to the Sikh Religion will not be following the teachings of Guru Nanak or what is written in the Guru Granth Sahib.

Most of the time the rituals are a carryover and nobody questions their utility. There are many other reasons why rituals take control. It is one thing to read the Guru Granth Sahib but entirely different to comprehend the words and then to put them in practice. Guru Granth was written in Punjabi the common language of the people. The authenticity of every hymn in the Guru Granth Sahib by Sikh Gurus, Hindu and Muslim saints, is clearly mentioned at the beginning of every hymn. For comparison the original holy books of Hindus were written in Sanskrit, of Muslims in Arabic, of Christians in Greek and Jews in Hebrew. People do not speak those languages on a daily basis. Also the authenticity of the people who wrote and the time frame work cannot be traced.

The question is then why rituals and miracles have crept into the Sikh Religion. Guru Nanak opposed rituals but they are still being practiced. Let us study the reason in a logical way.

Whole of the Guru Granth Sahib is written in a poetic form. It is true of any poetry that a complete story is compressed into few words. To understand one has to know the background history of that particular situation and that particular place and time. Most of the people in the congregation in a Gurdwara enjoy the hymns being sung in very melodious classical music. There are only few who comprehend the words. On the other hand there are many who even do not understand the Punjabi language. This is especially true for people who are born and or brought up in the USA, Canada, England, and other countries. It would be ideal if all people knew the Punjabi language in Gurmukhi script so they can read and understand the teachings as written in the Guru Granth Sahib. This, however, is not so and is not going to change. In fact more people are moving away from the Punjabi language, especially if they are living outside of India.

The next best thing is that each hymn in Punjabi should also be explained in simple English. Although there are many English translations of the Guru Granth Sahib, most of them use literal translation. The colloquial words in Punjabi are very difficult to translate into the English language. Thus many times the real meaning is not conveyed properly. The English translation must take into account the background history of that particular hymn.

When people understand the real meaning then they will start asking why the rituals are still being followed. ***This educational approach will go a long way in eliminating the rituals that are not germane to the real Sikh religious philosophy.***

C. PRESENT STATUS OF RITUALS IN SIKH RELIGION

Guru Nanak advised Muslims that besides reading the Koran they must follow the truth written in the Koran. At the same time Guru Nanak also chastised Hindus for practicing the caste system and believing in idols.

Guru Nanak never condemned any religion but criticized the hypocrisy of its practitioners.

Alice Basarke [13] has described the present status of rituals in the Sikh Religion. She is of the opinion that all these stern warnings issued by Guru Nanak against rituals are not being followed by the people who believe in Sikh Religion [13]. Very few people belonging to the Sikh Religion are willing to admit the malady of rituals, and a very small number of people want to eradicate them.

The Sikh Religion must be presented to the younger generation, in a logical way, especially for those living in the USA, Canada, England and other countries. Ways and means should be devised to eliminate the rituals. By preaching traditional values, with no ability to explain reason or necessity, the next generation is not going to follow the Sikh Religion. Sikh children want to be included but feel isolated and rejected by a community that refuses to recognize the reality of the modern world, where we all live. ***The irony of the situation is that the community that lives in the past, and is unable to change and adapt to the modern world is a community in danger of self-annihilation.*** If we are unable to keep our children, in the fold of the Sikh Religion, then who will propagate the teachings of Guru Nanak? [13]

Let me give some examples to illustrate why rituals are no good.

D. CASTE SYSTEM AS A RITUAL

Traditionally Indian society was divided into four castes according to the Hindu Religion. This practice was so immersed in the society that most people followed it as a ritual. The caste system's fundamental assumption is that all human beings are not equal and that is decided the moment they are born into that particular family.

The four castes in the Hindu religion are: the Brahmans (the elite—all political power was given to the Brahman priesthood), the warriors (fighting force), the traders (business people) and the untouchables (those who perform all menial work).

Many Sikhs are still following the caste system as a carry over from the Hindu Religion. This is strictly against the fundamental belief of the Sikh Religion that states unequivocally that all people are equal in all respects. The profession of a person is not determined by being born in a certain designated family. Guru Nanak said this ritual of caste system must go.

Even today Sikhs are divided into many sects. Some of them are Jatt , Saini, Bhaapaa, Rorha, Tarkhaan, Raamgarheeaa, Mazhabee, Khatree, Labaanaa and many more. There are separate Gurdwaras for people belonging to different castes in Sikh Religion. This is true both inside and outside India.

The Gurdwaras are also based upon people belonging to urban or rural areas, different regions of the state, and different villages. This is absolutely against the basic principles of the Sikh Religion. Guru Nanak ridiculed caste system while people belonging to the Sikh Religion are still practicing it.

How can one explain the caste system to the present young generation who are very highly educated, intelligent and well versed in modern world problems? They question why we are practicing the caste system when it is forbidden?

There is no satisfactory answer other than it is totally against the basic principles of the Sikh Religion as written in the Guru Granth Sahib.

Guru Nanak made it absolutely clear that good deeds in life are more important than caste system.

The first Guru, Nanak, said:

PUNJABI AND ROMAN	**ENGLISH**
ਜਾਤਿ ਜਨਮੁ ਨਹ ਪੁਛੀਐ	God never set the caste system at birth
Jaat Janam Nah Poochhee-ai	
ਸਚ ਘਰੁ ਲੇਹੁ ਬਤਾਇ II	It is the truthful living that counts.
Sach Ghar Layho Bataa-ay	
ਸਾ ਜਾਤਿ ਸਾ ਪਤਿ ਹੈ	One's respect and status in society
Saa Jaat Saa Pat Hai	
ਜੇਹੇ ਕਰਮ ਕਮਾਇ II	is determined by the deeds performed
Jayhay Karam Kamaa-ay	in your lifetime.
Guru Granth Sahib (p. 1330, line 8)	

Guru Nanak further explained that the caste system is neither required in this world nor it can be carried into the next world. It is futile to divide people based upon the caste system.

The first Guru, Nanak, said:

PUNJABI AND ROMAN	**ENGLISH**
ਜਾਣਹੁ ਜੋਤਿ ਨ ਪੁਛਹੁ ਜਾਤੀ	God's light is within all of us,
Jaanhu Jot Na Poochhahu Jaatee	God does not ask for your social status or caste,
ਆਗੈ ਜਾਤਿ ਨ ਹੇ II	and there is no caste or status
Aagai Jaat Na Hay	in the next world.
Guru Granth Sahib (p. 349, line 13)	

E. IDOL WORSHIP AS A RITUAL

Hindus believe in worshipping idols and stones. Sikhs believe in one Formless God, with innumerable names. This concept is similar to Islam whose followers believe in one God who has 99 names. Some Sikhs may still be doing some sort of idol worship but it is wrong. There is no need to worship idols, as God is present everywhere within and without. ***Guru Nanak made it absolutely clear, in very strong words that there is no use in worshipping idols and stones and this ritual must go.***

The first Guru, Nanak, said:

PUNJABI AND ROMAN	**ENGLISH**
ਹਿੰਦੂ ਮੂਲੇ ਭੂਲੇ ਅਖੁਟੀ ਜਾਂਹੀ ॥	Hindus have forgotten one God
Hindoo Moolay Bhoolay Akhutee JaaNhee	and are on the wrong path.
ਨਾਰਦਿ ਕਹਿਆ ਸਿ ਪੂਜ ਕਰਾਂਹੀ ॥	They worship the idols as
Naarad Kahi-aa Se Pooj KaraaNhee.	Instructed by Narad.
ਅੰਧੇ ਗੁੰਗੇ ਅੰਧ ਅੰਧਾਰੁ ॥	As if they are like blind, dumb
AanDhay Gungay AnDh AnDhaar	and devoid of knowledge.
ਪਾਥਰੁ ਲੇ ਪੂਜਹਿ ਮੁਗਧ ਗਵਾਰ ॥	By worshipping stones they
Paathar Lay Poojeh MugaDh Gavaar	behave like ignorant fools.
Guru Granth Sahib (p. 556, line 9)	

Is worshipping the Guru Granth Sahib a ritual? There is a difference between paying respect and worshipping. Sikhs always pay respect to the Guru Granth Sahib but worship one God. If one does not comprehend the words written in the Guru Granth Sahib then it can become a ritual.

Namdev explained in a very logical and an easy way to explain that ***it is no good to worship stone but instead one should worship God.***

Nam Dev said:

PUNJABI AND ROMAN	**ENGLISH**
ਏਕੈ ਪਾਥਰ ਕੀਜੈ ਭਾਉ ॥	One stone is lovingly decorated.
Aykai Paathar Keejai Bhaa-o.	
ਦੂਜੈ ਪਾਥਰ ਧਰੀਐ ਪਾਉ ॥	While other stone is walked upon.
Doojai Paathar Dharee-ai Paa-o.	
ਜੇ ਓਹੁ ਦੇਉ ਤ ਓਹੁ ਭੀ ਦੇਵਾ ॥	If one stone is God then other
Jay Oh Day-o Ta Oh Bhee Dayvaa.	stone must be God.
ਕਹਿ ਨਾਮਦੇਉ ਹਮ ਹਰਿ ਕੀ ਸੇਵਾ ॥	Says Nam Dev I worship only
Kahi Naamday-o Ham Har Kee Sayvaa.	God.
Guru Granth Sahib (p. 525, line 5)	

F. PRIESTLY CLASS AS A RITUAL

Dr. Dilgeer [14] has summarized the position of priests in the Sikh Religion.

There is no priestly class in Sikhism. Any Sikh, male or female, can perform services in a Gurdwara. Similarly there are no missionaries (as a class) in Sikhism. Some people serve as preachers called Bhai (literally brother) or Granthi (one who can read the Guru Granth) or Ragi (one who can sing Hymns and some others who interpret the Hymns). In fact anyone can do the job of a Ragi or Granthi. However, people are generally busy with their lives and leave these lower paying jobs to others. The preachers in Sikh religion have no special status like Christian Priests or the Muslim Mullah or the Hindu Pujari.

Similarly, there is no class of SANT or Saint as well. In the twentieth century several such people have emerged who calls themselves (or love to be called) "Sant" but it is not Sikh-like. In the Sikh Scriptures, term Sant has been used for the Almighty God only. In Sikhism there is no agent in between man and the Almighty God. This Sant-dom is copy of Hinduism and it has harmed the Sikhs a lot [14].

Let me give one quote from the Guru Granth Sahib to show that only God can be a Saint or Sant.

The fifth Guru, Arjan Dev, said:

PUNJABI AND ROMAN	**ENGLISH**
ਨਾਨਕ ਦਾਸੁ ਇਹੈ ਸੁਖੁ ਮਾਗੈ	Nanak the devotee of God asks for
Nanak Daas Ihai Sukh Maagai	happiness,
ਮੋ ਕਉ ਕਰਿ ਸੰਤਨ ਕੀ ਧੂਰੇ ॥	and humility as shown by the dust
Mo Ka-o Kar Santan Kee Dhooray	(earth) created by God that we trample with every step.
Guru Granth Sahib (p. 13, line 19)	

Some people think it is the dust of the Sants like on which we walk. That is not correct. There are certain idioms associated with Punjabi language that cannot be translated literally into English. The word slave does not mean that one is a real slave. It means that Nanak believes in God just like a slave believes in his/her master. The word Saint or Sant means God and nobody else. Similarly the word dust refers to being very humble like dust that we trample with every step. Thus let me be as humble as dust that is created by God. The word dust is used so ordinary person can understand the humility.

To use word Saint or Sant before a name is against the Sikh Religion. No Sikh religious organization has ever issued the designation Saint or Sant. It is a self-selected designation by the individual. The present day Saints or Sants consider themselves above the ordinary people. Quite often they have their own place of worship where followers come to them. They provide personal leadership and may become focus of devotion. These Saints or Sants many times assume lot of power over their congregation and start behaving as semi-Gurus. The congregation donates a considerable amount of money that gives Saints or Sants power, both politically and religiously. They encourage strict regimes. They start pressing for vegetarianism, celibacy, and may have a healing ministry. ***This power some times leads to a cult system.***

This ritual of Saint or Sant is strictly from the Brahman caste system of the Hindu religion. Somehow it has crept into the Sikh Religion. This is contrary to the teachings of the Guru Granth Sahib. Thus this practice of using Saint or Sant before the name must be condemned.

On the other hand, real dedicated religious preachers of the Sikh Religion consider themselves as very humble and down to earth. They serve humanity with real teachings of Guru Nanak. They not only preach but also follow the five principles of the Sikh Religion. They are honest living, share one's blessings, treat everybody equal in all respects, lead truthful life and pray to God.

Guru Nanak laid down some of the requirements of a religious person. He was addressing the Hindu Brahman priest, in order to explain what a religious person should do in his/her life.

The first Guru, Nanak, said:

PUNJABI AND ROMAN	**ENGLISH**
ਸੋ ਬ੍ਰਹਮਣੁ ਜੋ ਬਿੰਦੈ ਬ੍ਰਹਮੁ ॥	The real religious person is one who
So Barahman Jo Bindai Barahm	knows God,
ਜਪੁ ਤਪੁ ਸੰਜਮੁ ਕਮਾਵੈ ਕਰਮੁ ॥	and practices meditation, discipline,
Jap Tap Sanjam Kamaavai Karam	self control and performs good deeds,
ਸੀਲ ਸੰਤੋਖ ਕਾ ਰਖੈ ਧਰਮੁ ॥	and religiously believes in
Seel Santokh Kaa Rakhai Dharam	humility and contentment.
Guru Granth Sahib (p. 1411, line 16)	

Although there is no priest system in the Sikh Religion, the so-called religious preachers have assumed those powers especially in Amritsar, India. They use it to excommunicate Sikhs rather than bring more people into the Sikh Religion. The best way to handle excommunication is just ignore it completely. For example, the six Canadian Sikhs ignored the edict and still used the chairs. This has been explained early in this chapter under the heading Use of Chairs and Tables in Gurdwaras, section 4.

G. "SACRED" THREAD AS A RITUAL

Hindus have a religious custom of putting on "sacred" cotton thread, signifying the spiritual rebirth of a Hindu. It is like baptism among Christians. Guru Nanak's parents who were Hindus arranged a lavish function to put "sacred" thread on Nanak. Young Nanak refused to wear the "sacred" thread, as he had no faith in the rituals. They argued with the child, Nanak, but no one succeeded in persuading him [15]. Guru Nanak later sang the following hymn as to why he was against the ritual of putting on the "sacred" thread. ***Nanak stressed that sympathy for others, contentment, self control and moral excellence are more important than just putting on a thread.***

The first Guru, Nanak, said:

PUNJABI AND ROMAN	**ENGLISH**
ਦਇਆ ਕਪਾਹ Da-i-aa Kapaah	Let sympathy for others be your cotton
ਸੰਤੋਖੁ ਸੂਤੁ Santokh Soot	Let contentment be your thread
ਜਤੁ ਗੰਢੀ Jat Gandhee	Let self-control be your knot
ਸਤੁ ਵਟੁ ॥ Sat Vat	Let truth be your twist.
ਏਹੁ ਜਨੇਊ ਜੀਅ ਕਾ ਹਈ Eyhu Janay-oo Jee-a Kaa Ha-ee	If you have such a "sacred" thread
ਤ ਪਾਡੇ ਘਤੁ ॥ Ta Paaday Ghat	Then put it on.
ਨਾ ਏਹੁ ਤੁਟੈ Naa Ayhu Tutai	Such a thread should not break
ਨਾ ਮਲੁ ਲਗੈ Na Mal Lagai	Nor it should get dirty
ਨਾ ਏਹੁ ਜਲੈ ਨ ਜਾਇ ॥ Naa Ayhu Jalai Na Jaa-ay	Nor it should burn or get lost.
ਧੰਨੁ ਸੁ ਮਾਣਸ ਨਾਨਕਾ Dhan Su Maanas Naanakaa	Nanak says blessed are those
ਜੋ ਗਲਿ ਚਲੇ ਪਾਇ ॥ Jo Gal Chalay Paa-ay	who wear such a thread around their neck.

Guru Granth Sahib (p. 471, line 2)

Guru Nanak was trying to tell Hindus to be good Hindus. It is no use to perform ceremonies just for show and appearance.

At present lot of young Sikhs say if putting on a thread is a ritual then having long uncut hair for Sikhs is also a ritual. They have a very legitimate question. Tenth Guru Gobind Singh initiated Khalsa by baptizing them. That was the need at that time. So in order to be a Khalsa one has to have long uncut hair. However a person with or without long hair is a Sikh. This, I believe, should answer the question raised by the young Sikhs.

Guru Nanak said in very simple words that doing good things is better than putting on "sacred" thread. Guru Nanak condemned the rituals which are just for show.

The first Guru, Nanak, said:

PUNJABI AND ROMAN	**ENGLISH**
ਹਿੰਦੂ ਕੈ ਘਰਿ ਹਿੰਦੂ ਆਵੈ ॥	A Hindu goes to the house of
Hindoo Kai Ghar Hindoo Aaavai	another Hindu.
ਸੂਤੁ ਜਨੇਊ ਪੜਿ ਗਲਿ ਪਾਵੈ ॥	Chanting the sermon, he puts the
Soot Janay-oo Parh Gal Paavai	"sacred" thread round his neck.
ਸੂਤੁ ਪਾਇ ਕਰੇ ਬੁਰਿਆਈ ॥	If the person wearing the "sacred"
Soot Paa-ay Karay Buri-aa-ee	thread commits sins and performs bad
ਨਾਤਾ ਧੋਤਾ ਥਾਇ ਨ ਪਾਈ ॥	deeds even though his body is neat and
Naata Dhotaa Thaa-ay Na Paa-ee	clean, it is still not accepted by God.
Guru Granth Sahib (p. 951, line 18)	

The same thing applies to Sikhs that simple appearance is of no value if one does not perform good deeds.

H. FIVE PRAYERS OF MUSLIMS AS RITUAL

Guru Nanak did not tell anyone to adopt the Sikh Religion but persuaded people to follow the universal path in helping humanity. Guru Nanak was not against praying but was not in favor of performing five prayers in a day as a ritual. ***If one performs five prayers keeping in mind the five good characteristics of life then one will be called a good Muslim. The five things are to be truthful, live honestly, give to charity, be good to all and pray to God.***

The first Guru, Nanak, said:

PUNJABI AND ROMAN	ENGLISH
ਪੰਜਿ ਨਿਵਾਜਾ Panj Nivaajaa	Muslims have five prayers
ਵਖਤ ਪੰਜਿ Vakhat Panj	They pray five times a day
ਪੰਜਾ ਪੰਜੇ ਨਾਉ ll Panjaa Panjay Naa-o	They have five names for those prayers.
ਪਹਿਲਾ ਸਚੁ Pahilaa Sach	Let the first prayer be truthfulness
ਹਲਾਲ ਦੁਇ Halaal Du-ay	Second prayer be honest living
ਤੀਜਾ ਖੈਰ ਖੁਦਾਇ ll Teejaa Khair Khudaa-ay	Third prayer be charity.
ਚਉਥੀ ਨੀਅਤਿ ਰਾਸਿ ਮਨੁ Cha-uthee Nee-at Raas Man	Fourth prayer be good to all
ਪੰਜਵੀ ਸਿਫਤਿ ਸਨਾਇ ll Panjvee Sifat Sanaa-ay	Fifth prayer be for the praise of God.
ਕਰਣੀ ਕਲਮਾ ਆਖਿ ਕੈ Karnee Kalmaa Aakh Kai	By performing good deeds as prayer
ਤਾ ਮੁਸਲਮਾਣੁ ਸਦਾਇ ll Taa Musalmaan Sadaa-ay	then you may call yourself a Muslim.
ਨਾਨਕ ਜੇਤੇ ਕੂੜਿਆਰ Naanak Jaytay Koorhi-aar	Nanak says false people obtain falsehood
ਕੂੜੈ ਕੂੜੀ ਪਾਇ ll Koorhee Koorhee Paa-ay	and nothing else but falsehood.

Guru Granth Sahib (p. 141, line 3)

During Guru Nanak's period, Muslims were the rulers and they were committing many atrocities and were also engaged in rituals. They were not following the tenants of the Muslim religion. Guru Nanak explained very clearly that ***a good Muslim should be merciful, have faith in one God, live an honest life, be modest and have good conduct.*** There is no room for mere rituals.

The first Guru, Nanak, said:

PUNJABI AND ROMAN	ENGLISH
ਮਿਹਰ ਮਸੀਤਿ Mihar Maseet	Let mercy be your mosque
ਸਿਦਕੁ ਮੁਸਲਾ Sidak Muslaa	Faith in God your prayer-mat
ਹਕੁ ਹਲਾਲੁ ਕੁਰਾਣੁ II Hak Halaal Kuraan	Honest living your holy book (Koran)
ਸਰਮ ਸੁੰਨਤਿ Saram Sunat	Modesty your circumcision
ਸੀਲੁ ਰੋਜਾ Seel Rojaa	Good conduct your fasting
ਹੋਹੁ ਮੁਸਲਮਾਣੁ II Hohu Musalmaan	Then you shall be a true Muslim.
ਕਰਣੀ ਕਾਬਾ Karnee Kaabaa	Let good acts be your holy place (Kaaba)
ਸਚੁ ਪੀਰੁ Sach Peer	Truth your spiritual guide
ਕਲਮਾ ਕਰਮ ਨਿਵਾਜ II Kalmaa Karam Nivaaj	Good deeds your creed and prayer.
ਤਸਬੀ ਸਾ ਤਿਸੁ ਭਾਵਸੀ Tasbee Saa Tis Bhaavsee	Rosary (not just counting beads) but prayer that is pleasing to God
ਨਾਨਕ ਰਖੈ ਲਾਜ II Naanak Rakhai Laaj	Nanak says then God will preserve your honor.

Guru Granth Sahib (p.140, line 18)

Although Guru Nanak was addressing Muslims, but this in fact applies to all irrespective of their religion, be it Sikh, Christian, Hindu, Jew, Buddhist or any other religion. How many people are merciful, have faith in one God, live an honest life, are modest, perform good deeds and have good conduct? We all have to learn great lessons from the real teachings of Guru Nanak. Guru Nanak's philosophy is universal and applies to all humanity. Guru Nanak has great power in convincing people to perform good deeds by using logic and persuasion to put them on the right path.

6. GOOD DEEDS

Guru Nanak made it absolutely clear that good deeds are much more important than rituals. This applies to all people, irrespective of their religion. It also includes even those who do not believe in God. Most of the time Guru Nanak refers to two religions Hinduism and Islam. These were the only religions during Guru Nanak's time. Hindus were the original people in India while Muslims were the outsiders who ruled India at that time.

However the importance of good deeds applies to all whether they are Sikhs, Hindus, Muslims, Christians, Buddhist, Jews or any other religion. Guru Nanak wrote the following to emphasize good deeds.

The first Guru, Nanak, said:

PUNJABI AND ROMAN	**ENGLISH**
ਮੁਸਲਮਾਨੁ ਕਰੇ ਵਡਿਆਈ ॥ Musalmaan Karay Vadi-aa-ee	Muslims glorify their own faith.
ਵਿਣੁ ਗੁਰ ਪੀਰੈ ਕੋ ਥਾਇ ਨ ਪਾਈ ॥ Vin Gur Peerai Ko Thaa-ay Na Paa-ee	No one is accepted by God if spiritual teachings are not followed.
ਰਾਹੁ ਦਸਾਇ ਓਥੈ ਕੋ ਜਾਇ ॥ Raahu Dasaa-ay Othai Ko Jaa-ay	Even if they are shown the way, only a few follow that path.
ਕਰਣੀ ਬਾਝਹੁ ਭਿਸਤਿ ਨ ਪਾਇ ॥ Kaarnee Baajhahu Bhisat Na Paa-ay	Without good deeds no one is admitted to Heaven.

Guru Granth Sahib (p 951, line 19)

Guru Nanak said that good deeds are important in this world. People performing good deeds will be recognized in the next world as well.

The first Guru, Nanak, said:

PUNJABI AND ROMAN	**ENGLISH**
ਏਥੈ ਜਾਣੈ ਸੁ ਜਾਇ ਸਿਞਾਣੈ ॥ Aythai Jaanai So Jaa-ay Sinjaanai	Those who know God in this world will also be recognised by God in the next world.
ਹੋਰੁ ਫਕੜੁ ਹਿੰਦੂ ਮੁਸਲਮਾਣੈ ॥ Hor Fakarh Hindoo Musalmaanai	The rest whether Hindus or Muslims are fooling themselves.

ਸਭਨਾ ਕਾ ਦਰਿ ਲੇਖਾ ਹੋਇ ॥ Every one is answerable to God.
Sabhnaa Kaa Dar Laykhaa Ho-ay
ਕਰਣੀ ਬਾਝਹੁ ਤਰੈ ਨ ਕੋਇ ॥ Without good deeds no one is saved.
Karnee Baajhah Tarai Na Ko-ay
Guru Granth Sahib (p. 952, line 3)

Guru Nanak went to Mecca, the holy city of the Muslims in Saudi Arabia. Guru Nanak was asked many questions during discussions with people who were visiting Mecca. They asked Guru Nanak, are you a Hindu or Muslim? Guru Nanak's reply to this vexed question was I am neither a Hindu nor a Muslim. I believe in one God, who is the master of all creation, who pervades everywhere and who is beyond birth and death. People were bent upon establishing the religion of this man of God and asked him which religion was the superior of the two, the Hindu or Muslim? Guru Nanak replied [16] as below:

WITHOUT GOOD DEEDS THEY ALL REPENT.

7. OTHER IMPORTANT CHANGES

I will discuss some of the important items that need changes or adjustments. These changes can be easily resolved by mutual understanding. In fact these are required to be in conformity with the common practices of the adopted country.

i. HYGIENIC CONDITIONS IN GURDWARAS

Many Gurudwaras, at present, are not following the hygienic conditions of the adopted country. This relates especially to the bathrooms, kitchen and the place where food is served. Kitchens should be kept clean and not smelly by installing exhaust fans and any other suitable improvements. As for cleaning bathrooms, a volunteer system does not work. It should be done by professional cleaning services.

There is very good possibility that in future hygienic conditions will become better. It depends upon the management of the Gurdwara. ***This however must be done in order to comply with the laws and regulations of the health departments of the adopted country.*** There may be some legal implications if someone gets sick or may die due to bad hygienic conditions in the Gurdwara.

ii. SOCIAL FUNCTIONS IN GURDWARAS

Both religious and social functions are important for the community and should be held in the Gurdwaras. Members of the organization donated a great deal of money to construct the Gurdwaras. Alcohol may be forbidden in the Gurdwara. The young people will stay more often within the Gurdwara if wedding parties and dance functions are allowed. One solution could be to build a social hall next to Gurdwara as a separate building. Christian Churches and Jewish Synagogues in the USA allow all sorts of social functions on such premises.

Some religions put quite a bit of emphasis in celebrating their religious function as social events. Examples are Diwali of the Hindus and Christmas of the Christians. Thus people belonging to other religions join them. The reason is they make it comfortable for others to join. Sikhs should emulate these religions, in this respect. ***The birthday of Guru Nanak, the founder of the Sikh Religion, should be celebrated by holding social functions by inviting people of other religions to participate.*** This needs to be done in addition to the religious congregations performed by the people in the Gurdwara. It will help considerably if some function of the Sikhs is held near Christmas in the western countries. There is an atmosphere of festivity created in the month of December due to Christmas, especially in the USA, Canada, Britain and other countries. Our young people feel left out during that time. This way they will feel better that we celebrate Guru Nanak's birthday socially as well as religiously.

iii. INTERNAL QUARRELS IN GURDWARAS

In any society or organization there is always difference of opinion. As long as the discussion is healthy there is no problem. People generally compromise and do not take them personally. The problem arises when both sides think they are right and nobody wants to compromise. This situation has happened in many Gurdwaras in many cities in USA.

The main reason for internal quarrels is that the management of the Gurdwaras have no depth of the teachings of the Sikh Religion. They are interested in their power and position in society. ***Often the quarrels and fighting, end up in the courts.*** How can a judge having no knowledge of the Sikh Religion solve the problem? Most of the times they are personal rivalries, either between families or friends. They are then brought in a very dubious way into the religious affairs of the Gurdwara. This leads to friction among the members of the Gurdwara. Some of the other reasons include use of the Gurdwara money for their personal expenditures, or sponsoring their relatives or friends for immigration on religious grounds.

Sikhs who take their differences into the court for a legal solution have no knowledge of the real teachings of Guru Nanak, succeeding nine Gurus and Guru Granth Sahib. They have no zeal for the propagation of the Sikh Religion. This leads to bad publicity and affects the reputation of the Sikhs.

One way to stop the internal quarrels is for the management to realize that the purpose of the Sikh Religion is to serve humanity. ***When the management realizes that helping the needy is the main objective then the idea of infighting will never occur.***

It is my opinion that in the future Sikhs will listen to logical explanations and there will be a big decrease in fighting. Everybody has a right to disagree in a respectful way. If the opinions are discussed in a rational way, compromise is always possible. The main objective in any religious place is to get peace of mind. If the management and the preachers pursue the above objective there will be no fighting in the Gurdwaras.

Young Sikhs born or brought up in USA, Canada, Britain and other countries do not understand the fighting in the Gurdwaras. They get turned off from the religion and thus stop attending the Gurdwaras. They all believe that ***Gurdwaras are for peace of mind and to help create overall peace in the world—they are definitely not a place to fight.***

iv. PROVISION FOR HANDICAPPED PEOPLE IN GURDWARAS

Most of the Gurdwaras have no provisions for access for handicapped people. This is against the laws of most of the countries like USA, Canada, UK and many others. There is no excuse for that. The laws of the adopted country must be followed. Gurdwaras must go overboard to accommodate handicapped people. I think with time this will improve. Proper ramps must be installed. Wheelchairs should be allowed inside the main hall, close to the place where the Guru Granth Sahib is installed. ***If handicapped access is not installed it can lead to legal problems.***

v. PUNCTUALITY OF TIME

There should be a time limit for the length of the service and ***the allocated time must be strictly observed.*** At present the duration of program in the main hall is about four hours. People also drive between 30 minutes and to sometimes up to two hours to reach the Gurdwara. It is very difficult to sit on the floor for four hours. The human mind cannot comprehend what is being said for such a long time. ***The total time should not be more than one and a half hour*** (not including Langar and social time). Time must be adhered to strictly.

vi. MEMBERSHIP FEES

Membership fees must be substantial in order to cover the expenses of the building, the Granthi, and the Ragis (preachers). Members must realize their responsibility in selecting or electing the right type of people to run the Gurdwara. Preachers have to be paid according to the standard of the adopted country.

8. POLITICS AND SIKH RELIGION

The main question is should religion and politics be separate or both can live side by side. Theoretically it will be nice if they are separate as there are so many religions in this world. It is also fortunate that not too many new religions are springing up. In practical life both religion and politics do interact with each other. In some countries it is direct while in others indirect. ***In almost all countries religion does play a part in running the government.***

Politics is how to run the government and is for all people irrespective of their religion. Religion is essentially for the moral uplift of the society. Government makes money by taxing people. Religion makes money by voluntary contributions. There is one common thread between religion and politics?theoretically both want to help and uplift the people. In practice it is not so. People fight based upon religion and also based upon politics. People in this world should live a peaceful life, be God-fearing and believe in love. For some odd reason they find a way to fight and kill each other. The winner is the one who has the most sophisticated means to kill the other. Thus it can be said that might is right on a practical level. Theoretically it should not be so. The mighty people should be humble and take care of the less fortunate people.

Some countries make it official that the country has to follow the laws as written in their Holy Book. Many democratic countries keep religion and politics separate according to their constitution. ***However, in practice, the religion of the majority does seep into politics***, but it is not always deliberate. For example in USA (where religion and politics are separate), during the initial stages of the selection of the candidate for the president, religion does play a part, indirectly.

In many Muslim countries people are selected for political positions based upon the fact that they follow Islamic law. I have mentioned two extreme cases. Many countries are in between. They may say religion and politics are separate but in many cases they overlap in practical life.

Many years ago, all over the world, there was no distinction between religion and politics. People of one religion used to fight against people of another. People were being converted to other religions either forcefully or by persuasion.

Let us discuss how the Sikh religion perceives religion and politics. It would help considerably to first discuss the history of the Sikhs. India was basically a Hindu/Buddhist country. Then the Muslims invaded and eventually ruled India. In order to resist the Muslim invaders, Guru Gobind Singh created the Khalsa Sikh army.

The question of separation of politics and religion was discussed during the period of Gurus. The Sixth Guru, Har Gobind, constructed Akal Takht in the Golden Temple complex in 1606. ***This Takht was established to discuss the secular political matters and military strategy. On the other hand The Golden Temple is meant purely for worship of God.***

There are five Takhts. They are Gurdwaras of extreme historic importance in the Sikh religion. They are so mentioned in daily prayer. Their location in India is given in Figure 40 [17]. The first Takht is called Akal Takht, Figure 41 [18]. It is the primary seat of Sikh political?cum religious?authority. It was built during The Sixth Guru Hargobind in June 1606 inside the Golden Temple complex in Amritsar, Punjab. The other four Takhts are connected with the life of Guru Gobind Singh (1666 to 1708). The second is Takht Patna Sahib, Figure 42 [19] where Guru Gobind Singh was born in 1666. Third is Takht Keshgarh Sahib Figure 43 [20] where Guru Gobind Singh baptized Sikhs as Khalsa in 1699. Fourth is Takht Damdama Sahib Figure 44 [21] where Guru Gobind Singh prepared the final version of the Guru Granth Sahib. The fifth is Takht Hazur Sahib located on the banks of river Godavari in Nander, Maharashtra, Figure 45 [22]. Guru Gobind Singh was cremated in 1708 in the inner room of the Takht Hazur Sahib, called Angitha Sahib.

Guru Gobind Singh carried out secularism in a practical way with his army of Khalsa Sikhs, Sikhs who were not Khalsa, Hindus, and Muslims. People of all religions joined together as Guru Gobind Singh was fighting against the tyranny of outside invaders as well as those within the country. Later Maharaja Ranjit Singh ruled Punjab right up to Afghanistan. His regime was truly secular. Besides Sikhs he had Muslims and Hindus in very important positions in his regime.

During the British rule from 1847 to 1947 the number of Christians increased considerably. Therefore, the religion of the rulers does play an important part in increasing their numbers.

FIVE SIKH HISTORIC TAKHTS IN INDIA

FIGURE 40

LOCATION OF 5 TAKHTS IN INDIA

FIGURE 41

AKAL TAKHT IN THE GOLDEN TEMPLE COMPLEX AMRITSAR, BUILT 1606

FIGURE 42

TAKHT PATNA SAHIB PATNA, BIHAR

FIGURE 43

TAKHT KESGARH SAHIB ANANDPUR, PUNJAB

FIGURE 44

TAKHT DAMDAMA SAHIB TALWANDI SABO, PUNJAB

FIGURE 45

TAKHT HAZUR SAHIB NANDER, MAHARASHTRA

Initially Hindus, Muslims and Sikhs were united in fighting for freedom against the British rulers. They all worked hard to achieve this freedom. However, the Muslims wanted a separate country and Pakistan was formed in 1947. Sikhs in India are only 2% of the population. Sikhs are mostly concentrated in Punjab, the northern part of India, although they are spread all over the world.

In general India is a secular country but religion does play an important part. It is all done indirectly. In Punjab where Sikhs are the majority, religion and politics do intermingle?sometimes directly and many times indirectly. Many times the government gives grants to semi-religious places run mostly by one religion.

The government of India holds the elections for the management of the Sikh Gurdwaras in Punjab in association with the Sikh Religious organization. ***Thus therefore, the Sikh Religion and politics are not always separate.***

As far as the Sikh Religion is concerned, the Guru Granth Sahib is a Universal Holy Book. Due to this universality people belonging to other religions like Hindus, Christians and Muslims in Punjab are not adversely affected. Sikhs, Hindus and Muslims composed the hymns of the Guru Granth Sahib. This holy book applies to people of all other religions including Christianity, Judaism, and Buddhism. ***Some people believe that since Sikh religion has great respect for all other religions it should make no difference if politics and religion are indirectly related.***

However, according to the law of the democratic countries religion and politics are kept separate according to their constitutions. Sikhs living in their adopted countries have to follow the laws of that country. If the law somehow discriminates against the Sikhs then all efforts should be made peacefully and legally to change that law.

9. MINORITIES IN DEMOCRACY

As long as one belongs to the majority religion it makes no difference. The question is how about the minorities? This is very difficult. ***Minorities have to be vocal and bring out their point of view in a very democratic way.***. The vote of the minority can make a difference in the selection of the candidates. Thus a balanced situation can be maintained.

Minorities can occupy very high positions in democratic countries if they are willing to work hard. I will explain this by giving many examples in several countries.

A. CONGRESSMAN OF THE UNITED STATES OF AMERICA

Dr. Dalip Singh Saund, Figure 46, [23] who made history in November of 1956 by becoming the first native of Asia and a Sikh to be elected to the Congress of the United States of America. It was almost unthinkable for an Asian to become a United States Congressman in those days.

Born in Punjab, India in 1899, he got his BA degree in Mathematics in 1919 from Punjab University. He came to the USA in 1920. In 1924 he had completed his MA and Ph.D. in mathematics. He could not find a job so he started working on a farm. Later he became actively involved in politics. However, he could not hold any office until he was a citizen. That happened in 1949 when Harry Truman signed the Luce-Celler Act in 1946. Clare Booth Luce was a congresswoman from Connecticut and Emanuel Cellar, a congressman from New York. Asians were then considered on par with the Europeans for immigration purposes.

A very interesting incident took place while Dr. Saund was campaigning. Saund describes it this way "Just three days before the election, a prominent citizen who was opposing me bitterly saw me one morning in the town restaurant and said in a loud voice: 'Doc, tell us, if you're elected, will you furnish the turbans or will we have to buy them ourselves in order to come to your court?' 'My friend,' I answered, 'you know me for a tolerant man. I don't care what a man has on top of his head. All I'm interested in is what he's got inside of it.' All the customers had a good laugh at that and the story became the talk of the town during the next few days."[23]

Saund was re-elected in two subsequent elections. It was while seeking a record fourth win that Saund suffered a paralytic stroke and became handicapped for the rest of his life. He breathed his last in 1973. [23]

B. MEMBERS OF PARLIAMENT IN CANADA

At present (2006), there are eight members of the Canadian Parliament whose ancestry is from India and Pakistan. Six out of the eight are Sikhs, one is a Hindu and one a Muslim. They are shown in Figure 47 [24]. ***This illustrates the determination and maturity of the minority community in solving the problems of their newly adopted country.*** They have been elected to very important positions in the government. They can resolve the problems facing the community in a legal and peaceful way. Thus, being a minority in democracy is not a hindrance; it is a sign of progress.

FIGURE 46

DR. DALIP SINGH SAUND
FIRST ASIAN ELECTED TO THE U.S. CONGRESS

FIGURE 47

MEMBERS OF PARLIAMENT IN CANADA

Ujjal Singh Dosanjh
Member of Parliament
Sikh, Born in Punjab, India

Gurbax Singh Malhi
Member of Parliament
Sikh, Born in Punjab, India

Ruby Dhalla
Member of Parliament
Sikh, Born in Canada

Navdeep Singh Bains
Member of Parliament
Sikh, Born in Canada

Nina Grewal
Member of Parliament
Sikh, Born in Japan

Sukh Dhaliwal
Member of Parliament
Sikh, Born in Punjab, India

Deepak Obhrai
Member of Parliament
Hindu, Born in Tanzania

Rahim Jafeer
Member of Parliament
Muslim, Born in Uganda

Some of the achievements of the elected memebers are outlined below.

i. PREMIER OF BRITISH COLUMBIA , UJJAL SINGH DOSANJH

On February 24, 2000, Mr. Ujjal Singh Dosanjh became the first Sikh to be made the Premier of British Columbia. This made him Canada's first non-white and first Indo-Canadian provincial premier.

Ujjal came to Canada in 1968 and worked in the sawmills in Vancouver for many years. He got his law degree in 1979 from British Columbia University. He was first elected in 1991 to the provincial assembly and was made Attorney General in 1995. He was elected in the House of Commons in 2004. Since July 24, 2004 he has been the Minister of Health in the Federal Cabinet [25]. Ujjal's detailed explanation of the Komaghata Maru ship's attempted landing in Canada in 1914 are given in Chapter 4.

As a prominent moderate Sikh, Ujjal used to speak out against the violence by Sikh extremists in India. The extremists in Canada targeted him. In 1985 he was physically attacked in the parking lot of his law office with a lead pipe. He received 80 stitches in his head and a broken hand. Also, his constituency office was firebombed on the morning of December 26, 1999 [25].

ii. MEMBER PARLIAMENT, GURBAX SINGH MALHI

Malhi's achievements are summarized below.

Malhi has been appointed to the following three positions: Parliamentary Secretary to the Minister of Industry, Minister of Human Resources, and Minister of National Revenue.

On Malhi's insistence Canadian law was changed in 1993 to allow Sikhs to wear turbans in Parliament.

Malhi introduced the Akhand Path ceremony (continuous reading of the Guru Granth Sahib in 48 hours) and the Diwali celebration to Parliament Hill. These are held every year.

In 1997, he succeeded in having the Canadian government open a liaison office in Chandigarh, India.

Malhi was also instrumental in having the government of Canada produce a Canadian postage stamp bearing the Khanda Sahib, symbol of the Sikhs.

The Khanda

iii. MEMBER OF PARLIAMENT, RUBY DHALLA

Besides being a beauty queen, actress, and doctor, Ruby Dhalla has accomplished a great deal politically. She initiated a national fundraising concert for people affected by the tsunami disaster. The concert, which raised $4 million was a live telecast organized in collaboration with Canadian artists & performers. Dhalla also organized a relief effort for the victims of the earthquake in Pakistan.

Ruby was appointed to the Standing Committee on Health, is an associate critic for consumer affairs in the Official Opposition, Vice-President for the Canada-India Inter-Parliamentary Friendship Group and Vice Chair for the Canada–U.S. Parliament Group.

iv. MEMBER PARLIAMENT, NAVDEEP SINGH BAINS

Although Mr. Bains is still young, he has accomplished a great deal. He promotes trade policies and he is the chairman of the Foreign Affairs subcommittee on Human Rights and International Development. Mr. Bains was awarded an honorary doctorate from Harvard University for his work on human rights issues across America.

Bains served as the Parliamentary Secretary to the Prime Minister from October 2005 to February 2006.

He has concentrated his efforts on internationally related causes, specifically developing relationships with emerging markets.

Domestically, Navdeep worked tirelessly to draft a National Youth Strategy to highlight the importance of involving youth in the political process.

v. MEMBER PARLIAMENT, NINA GREWAL

Ms. Grewal is interested in immigration and women's issues and is a member of sevral committees. She is working hard to keep streets free from drug and gun crimes.

vi. MEMBER PARLIAMENT, SUKH DHALIWAL

First elected in January 2006, Sukh Dhaliwal is the Associate Critic for the Status of Women, Seniors and Multiculturalism.

He is an active and eloquent spokesman for local small businesses.

Mr. Dhaliwal is a member of the Surrey Memorial Hospital Foundation's Emergency Campaign Cabinet.

vii. MEMBER PARLIAMENT, DEEPAK OBHRAI

Obhrai has been appointed as Parliamentary Secretary to the Minister of Foreign Affairs.

He has served on a variety of committees, such as the Standing Committee on Foreign Affairs and International Trade and the Subcommittee on Human Rights and International Development.

Mr. Obhrai has participated in trade missions to India, China, Japan and the United Arab Emirates.

viii. MEMBER PARLIAMENT, RAHIM JAFEER

Following the 2006 elections, Jaffer was named as Chair of the Conservative Caucus by the Prime Minister of Canada.

C. INDIA

i. PRIME MINISTER OF INDIA, MANMOHAN SINGH

Sikhs although a very small minority in India?about 2% in India occupy many important positions.

Dr. Manmohan Singh (Figure 48) became the Prime Minister of India in 2004. He is widely regarded as the architect of India's economic reform program and a believer in globalization with a human touch. His greatest asset among the ordinary people is that he is the honest and most knowledgeable politician in India. He is the first Sikh to hold the top post in India.

FIGURE 48

Dr. Manmohan Singh Prime Minister of India
ARCHITECT OF INDIA'S ECONOMIC PROGRESS

Singh had many challenging positions both inside and outside India. To his utter surprise he was made the Finance Minister of India in 1991 [26]. The country's economic situation was extremely bad and its foreign exchange reserve was only equal to about two week's of imports. His friends told him that he was going to become a scapegoat and that he might fail within six months. Singh took it as a challenge.

He told Parliament that we must convert this crisis into an opportunity to build a new India. During his speech while presenting the Budget, he quoted Victor Hugo: "No power on earth can stop an idea whose time has come."

Singh slashed red tape, simplified the tax system, removed stifling controls and regulations to create environment conducive to business [26]. It worked extremely well and the country survived.

The result was that productivity in the Indian industry grew like never before. The entire world is viewing India as an emerging power and eagerly watching its economic progress. There are about 300 million middle class Indians that is more than the population of USA.

Manmohan Singh said if the economic momentum continues it is possible to banish poverty in about ten years time [26].

He mentioned that his administration is tackling many more challenges. Some of them are corruption, cleanliness, diplomacy, lack of adequate infrastructure, shortcomings in agriculture growth, lack of electricity, education, health and employment [26].

He was born in 1932 in Gah (now in Pakistan). He graduated from the University of Cambridge in 1957 and got doctorate degree from Oxford University, England in 1962. Both were in economics. He taught in many universities. He was Governor, Reserve Bank of India, then Finance Minister and now Prime Minister since 2004.

India is really fortunate to have Manmohan Singh as Prime Minister. That ensures the progress of India in becoming a world power to reckon with.

ii. CHIEF OF THE INDIAN ARMY, JOGINDER JASWANT SINGH

It is almost a Sikh tradition that one member of almost all Sikh families be a part of the military. This has been going on for generations in India.

General Joginder Jaswant (J.J.) Singh (Figure 49) became Chief of the Indian Army in 2005. Although the Sikhs have been the bulwark of the Indian Army since its inception, he is the first Sikh officer that has been selected to the top post. Hailing from a family of Army people, he is a third generation soldier. His grand father served during the First World War in Mesopotamia (present day Iraq). His father Colonel Jaswant Singh Marwah served during the First World War. General Singh was born in Bahawalpur (now in Pakistan). After partition of Punjab in 1947 his family migrated to Patiala, Punjab, India [27].

General Singh has contributed articles in professional journals and his work on "Sino-Indian Border Dispute" and "Strategy to Boost Defence Exports" have been highly acclaimed. He is a thinking soldier and very professional. He is all for the modernisation of the Army with high technology and revolution in Military Affairs [27].

He was wounded in Kashmir during 1991-1992 and was awarded the War Wound Medal. He performed an admirable service during the 1999 Kargil conflict with Pakistan. He is a recipient of the Param Vishisht Sewa Medal in 2004 that is India's highest peacetime military award [27]. He plays squash, basketball and golf.

D. US ARMY, UDEY SINGH'S RESPONSIBLITY AND SACRIFICE

Lots of Sikhs have now migrated to the USA. They have also joined the U.S. Military. Uday Singh, a Sikh, born in India joined the U.S. Army in August 2000, Figure 50 [28]. Specialist Uday Singh, 21, of Lake Forest, Illinois, was killed on December 1, 2003, in Iraq. Singh was the first Indian casualty of the war. Uday's body was flown from the U.S. to Chandigarh, India for cremation. Lieut. General James Campbell Commander of U.S. Army Pacific Command, Brigadier General Mark O'Neil, and many US soldiers were present at the cremation. The cremated body remains were then brought to the USA for burial at Arlington National Cemetery in Virginia on January 8, 2004, Figure 51 [29].

Brigadier General Mark O'Neill presented Preet Singh, father of Uday, with citations that posthumously awarded Uday Singh the Bronze Star for valor, promoted him to sergeant and made him a citizen of the U.S., for which he gave his life.

U.S. General Camphell playing glowing tributes to "a brother in arms and India's son", said: "Today, two great democratic nations pause and mourn the loss of this courageous young man who chose the life of a soldier."

The 21-year-old trooper hailed from a military family. His father served in the Indian Army, his grandfather fought during the second World War in

FIGURE 49

General J.J. Singh Chief of Indian Army

FIGURE 50

UDAY SINGH

FIGURE 51

ARLINGTON NATIONAL CEMETERY, VIRGINIA

Mesopotamia and his great-grandfather fought during the first World War I in Mesopotamia (now Iraq).

10. ABSORBING POWER OF THE SIKH RELIGION

Sikhs have to put in a lot of effort so that people of other religions understand the basics of the Sikh Religion. This is very important in a global society. When any community is in the minority, they have to exert much more to convey their message.

Sikhism is a Universal Religion if we follow what is written in the Guru Granth Sahib. Almost all people who joined the Sikh Religion during Guru Nanak's time and the succeeding nine Gurus, came from other religions. Maharaja Ranjit Singh maintained the Universality of the Sikh religion, so many more people joined the Sikh Religion during his rule. ***Not many people, including Sikhs, really know the universal aspect of the Sikh Religion in a practical way.***

Several years ago I met a Sindhi gentleman. In general, Sindhis are Hindus who migrated to India in 1947 from the Sindh province, now in Pakistan. They are great devotees of Guru Nanak. He said that all Sikhs are Hindus. He gave many reasons including that Guru Nanak was born to a Hindu family. I listened for a while and then said Sikhs consider all Sindhis to be part of the Sikh Religion. Here was a compromise and on that we shook hands.

There should be a mechanism to incorporate people such as Sindhis into the Sikh Religion. One way is that Sikhs should treat them as equals and accept them with open arms.

Another way to increase the absorbing power of the Sikh Religion is ***to broaden the definition of a Sikh.*** It is not easy to define any religion. However there are three definitions of a Sikh by three different Sikh institutions. At present Sikhs are not unanimous on any of these three definitions.

The three definitions are as below.

i. 1925 DEFINITION OF A SIKH [30]

This definition is written in **The Sikh Gurdwara Act 1925**.
SIKH MEANS A PERSON WHO PROFESSES THE SIKH RELIGION or in the case of a deceased person, who professed the Sikh religion or was known to be Sikh during his lifetime.

If any question arises as to whether any living person is or is not a Sikh, he/she shall be deemed to be a Sikh if they make the declaration below:

"I solemnly affirm that I am a Sikh, that I believe in the Guru Granth Sahib, that I believe in the Ten Gurus, and that I have no other religion."

ii. 1945 DEFINTION OF A SIKH [31]

This definition of a Sikh is according to Sikh Reht Maryada of 1945 by Shiromani Gurdwara Parbandhak Committee (SGPC) of Amritsar, Punjab, India.

Section 1 Chapter 1 Article 1

"Any human being who faithfully believes in One Immortal Being, Ten Gurus, from Guru Nanak Dev to Guru Gobind Singh, The Guru Granth Sahib, the utterances and teachings of the ten Gurus and the baptism bequeathed by the tenth Guru, and who does not owe allegiance to any other religion is a Sikh."

iii. 1971 DEFINITION OF A SIKH [32]

This definition is according to the Delhi Sikh Gurdwara Act of 1971 by Delhi Sikh Gurdwara Management Committee (DSGMC) of Delhi, India.

"A Sikh means a person who professes the Sikh religion, believes and follows the teachings of Sri Guru Granth Sahib and the ten Gurus only and keeps unshorn hair and has no other religion."

The basic difference between the three definitions is as below.

1925 definition includes all types of Sikhs.
1945 definition requires that a baptized person is a Sikh.
1971 definition requires that a person must have unshorn hair.

All other requirements in the three definitions can be very easily compromised.

As Sikhism is a universal religion thus it becomes almost necessary to select the definition that includes all Sikhs. Thus 1925 definition fits very well. However it should be emphasized that anyone has a right to be baptized or have unshorn hair if they so desire.

The definition of a Sikh should be very broad. Another reason is that at least 80% of the Sikhs do not have long hair. The 1945 and 1971 definitions require long hair in order to be called a Sikh. However, there is no such requirement in the 1925 definition of a Sikh. Thus Sikhs of all categories can be accommodated in 1925 definition.

SIKHS WHO DO NOT HAVE LONG HAIR

The following observations prove that 80% of the Sikhs do not have long hair.

The statements by very famous Sikhs Mr. Tarlochan Singh [1] and Mr Sangat Singh [2], Sikhs who have visited Punjab [3], and Sikhs from our own families prove that at least 80% of the Sikhs do not have long hair. This has been discussed in this chapter, section 3 under the heading Present Situation.

POLL ABOUT THE DEFINITION OF A SIKH

A poll was conducted among the members of Sikh Diaspora (SD) Group (*sikh-diaspora@yahoogroups.com*). *The topic was the definition of a Sikh.* There are about 1200 members of this group living mostly in the USA, Canada, UK and few other countries. Almost all of them are educated Sikhs. Discussion regarding the 1925 definition of a Sikh was conducted from October to December of 2002. There were 35 participants with a total of about 150 messages both for and against. I have hard copies of all of the comments.

The overall conclusion of the poll is as follows.

	1925 DEFINITION OF A SIKH
DEFINITE YES	**21 (60%)**
LEANING TO YES	**8 (23%)**
DEFINITE NO	**6 (17%)**

The results are quite clear that 83% of the Sikhs (of SD group) living outside of India approve of the 1925 definition of a Sikh. The 1925 definition of a Sikh will include all 25+ million Sikhs spread all over the world. This is a real poll with practically no error. Names and addresses of all those responded (many with full address and few with e-mail) were recorded and filed. Overall discussion was very productive and was also very emotional. In addition there were 12 more people (with their names and addresses) who said yes to the 1925 Definition of a Sikh but are not members of the SD group.

In my opinion Sikhs have to broaden the classification and accept the 1925 Definition of a Sikh in order for it to be a Universal religion. It includes Sikhs living all over the world. It will create unity among all Sikhs and will make it easy to propagate the Sikh religion.

Will people of other religions join the Sikh Religion at this time? It is possible, theoretically. However, people of other religions are not going to join the Sikh Religion in any significant numbers in the near future.

Some people may start attending the modern or reformed Gurdwaras if they treat everybody equal and spread the philosophy and teachings of the Guru Granth Sahib. It becomes very difficult for others to join when the main criteria of equality of the Sikh religion is not practiced among the Sikhs themselves. Fighting inside the Gurdwaras and not abandoning the rituals are also deterrents for others to join the Sikh religion. The other reasons are not using the language of the adopted country, not using modern means of communications and not using logic and reasoning in explaining religion to the highly educated people. If some people join the Sikh Religion, the numbers are going to be very small, compared to the large number of people who joined the Sikh religion during the period of ten Gurus (1499 to 1708) and Maharaja Ranjit Singh (1799 to 1839).

The world is getting smaller due to the availability of information through technology. People are traveling to different countries in large numbers and are living among different cultures and religions. Marriages between people of different religions are taking place. This cannot be curtailed. ***Marriages between Sikhs and non-Sikhs are going to increase considerably throughout the world.*** This is also happening among all other religions in this world.

Are Sikhs willing to accept the people of other religions into Sikh fold, with open arms? The answer is no as of today. There are two main reasons. First the Universality of the Sikh religion is not practiced, as such, by the Sikhs. Second the requirement of having long hair and a turban is a deterrent to accepting new members..

In this world, logic and reasoning are the only things that will prevail. If a Sikh marries a non-Sikh, conditions should be made so congenial that both become followers of the Sikh Religion. Whether it will really happen is doubtful. The changes suggested should not compromise in the basic teachings as prescribed in the Guru Granth Sahib.

The solution is to revive and increase the absorbing power of the Sikh religion—and this has to begin with the Sikh community itself.

If nothing is done then a Sikh marrying a non-Sikh will get absorbed into other religions, mainly Hinduism and Christianity. This is what is happening today.

Let us assume that in the coming 50 years the Universality of the Sikh Religion is widely accepted and preached from the religious places without emphasizing the requirement for physical appearance. Then there is a good chance that not only Sikhs, but also non-Sikhs may join the Sikh Religion. Even if they do not accept the Sikh Religion, they will be very sympathetic to it.

Let me discuss a personal experience that I have observed in the last 49 years of my living in the USA. Initially there were about 20 Sikh families in New York and the surrounding areas in early 1960s. We all knew each other very well. All of us were married with Sikh families. As the time progressed and people got used to the American system, things began to change. ***Children belonging to the Sikh families started to marry people of other religions.*** The elders did not like it in the beginning. Today parents accept their marriages and do not ask any questions, although they would still prefer that they marry into a Sikh family.

Think of what happened to Buddhism and Jainism, both started in India. In 1951 there were only 181,000 Buddhists in India. Their number has now increased to several millions in India [33], largely due to the influx from Tibet rather than from spreading. Jainism started in the 6th century and has only about 4 million followers [33]. The decline of Buddhism and Jainism is also due to the absorbing power of the Hindu religion.

Will Hinduism in India absorb Sikh religion? The answer is no, provided Sikh Religion is practiced as written in the Guru Granth Sahib. To spread the teachings of Guru Nanak and the succeeding nine Gurus, equality for all is the cornerstone of Sikh Religion.

Sikhism will never be finished no matter what happens. Much depends upon how the next generation propagates the Sikh Religion. If we are not rational and make no changes then more Sikhs will join other religions. The choice of whether the Sikh religion remains restricted or revives the absorbing power in accepting people of other religions with open arms is up to the Sikhs themselves.

Let us just discuss why other religions have more absorbing power. The world's two big religions, Hinduism and Christianity, have very open-end requirements to be a Hindu or a Christian. You have to just believe in Christ to be called a Christian. To be a Hindu one has to follow Hinduism that is essentially a social system. The definitions are so broad that almost any one can become a Hindu or Christian.

These two religions absorb others because Christians use their excellent organization abilities and Hindus accept anyone with practically any view about God.

The Sikh Religion has all the requirements to absorb people of any other religion. Sikhs have to follow, in practice, the Universality of the Sikh Religion as written in the Guru Granth Sahib. Sikh Religion respects people of all other religions.

11. SUMMARY

There are ten reasons given why Sikh Religion should be propagated. There are also ten changes suggested that are required to propagate the Sikh Religion in this global community with its ever-changing advanced technologies. The Universality of the Sikh Religion was maintained from 1469 to 1947. After the independence of India in 1947, the concept of the Universality changed dramatically?in the wrong direction. Although several intellectuals are working to present the Universality of the Sikh Religion (as started by Guru Nanak), however, people, in general, are not accepting it. People have their preconceived notions and are not willing to put into practice the real aspects and teachings of the Sikh Religion. There is a dire need for educated people who can articulate the teaching of Guru Nanak and the succeeding nine Gurus logically and scientifically to the inquisitive minds of the younger generation.

It is of great importance that English the language of the adopted country be used along with Punjabi. Most of the young Sikhs do not know Punjabi. The Guru Granth Sahib is written in eleven languages, thus use of other languages is not prohibited in spreading the teachings of the Sikh Religion. The preachers must be professionally educated in a recognized university of the adopted country. They must be very conversant in English and Punjabi. It is the responsibility of the management to hire a preacher who can fulfill the needs of the congregation settled in the adopted country.

Equality is the cornerstone of Sikh Religion. The real main issue that divides the Sikh community is how equality is interpreted. One group says that only those people who have long hair are to be treated equally. Other group says all people should be treated equally in all respects with or without long hair. Both sides claim to have valid reasons, but there is a big rift between the two sides. It is an enigma and it is not easy to resolve. The two possible solutions are either to compromise by treating all Sikhs with or without long hair as equals or to divide and have two types of Gurdwaras. Obviously compromise is better, but is not acceptable to all. Use of chairs in the main hall as well as in the Langar hall should be encouraged. A very important Sikh religious body in Punjab allowed the use of chairs in 1935 as long as the Guru Granth Sahib is at a higher elevation. Some Sikhs in Canada were excommunicated by Sikh religious organization in Punjab for using chairs. This edict backfired as nobody paid any attention to it. The members of the same Gurdwara elected all excommunicated Sikhs for the management positions.

Many times procedures become rituals. Several examples like reading the Guru Granth Sahib in 48 hours, covering the head all the time, removal of socks and many others are mentioned. Rituals lead to blind faith and lead us away from God. Using logic and reasoning Guru Nanak criticized the caste system, idol worship, the priestly class, use of the sacred thread, and performing five prayers as rituals.

People follow rituals because they do not understand the teachings of the Guru Granth Sahib and the inability of the preachers to use logic in their presentations. Guru Nanak stressed the importance of good deeds instead of believing in rituals. Good deeds are remembered during this life and in the next world as well.

Many improvements can be easily adopted by compromise and common sense. They are better hygienic conditions, allowing social functions in the Gurdwara, elimination of violent clashes in the Gurdwara, provisions for handicapped people, punctuality, increases in membership fees, and elimination of politics from religion.

Minorities can occupy very important positions in democratic countries, including Dr. Dalip Singh Saund the first Asian and a Sikh to be elected to the U.S. Congress and Dr Manmohan Singh, the first Sikh Prime Minister of India. Above all the absorbing power of the Sikh Religion must be increased. Using the 1925 definition of a Sikh will help considerably. That definition states that Sikh is a person who professes the Sikh religion. Creating amicable conditions for people of other religions who marry a Sikh and explaining to them the real teachings of the Sikh Religion. The solution to all these problems can be achieved by education (academic and religious), use of logic and reasoning in solving day-to-day problems of the community and moving forward with changing world conditions.

In conclusion one should adopt the following ten principles in life in order to be a better person.

1. ***Perform good deeds for the benefit of humanity.***
2. ***Loving human beings is like loving God.***
3. ***Do not speak ill of any other religion.***
4. ***Treat every one, including women, as equals in all respects.***
5. ***Have a good work ethic.***
6. ***Share one's blessing with less fortunate people.***
7. ***Pray daily to God who created the whole universe.***
8. ***God is neither born nor dies and is present everywhere.***
9. ***Truth is higher than everything but higher still is truthful living.***
10. ***To obtain peace of mind keep mind, body and soul in tune with God.***

12. EXERCISES

i. Enunciate ten reasons why Sikh Religion should be propagated?

ii. What are the ten changes that should be made to propagate the Sikh Religion with respect to the technological advancements in the world?

iii. How can the Universality of the Sikh Religion can be revived? Give specific examples from this chapter in addition to your own suggestions. Give practical solutions.

iv. Why use of the language of the adopted country is very important to teach the Sikh Religion in the Gurdwara?

v. Why preachers should have a degree from the university of the adopted country?

vi. What is the best solution to unite Sikhs with and without long hair?

vii. Why did the edit of excommunication of Sikhs in Canada for using chairs by the religious leaders in Punjab backfire?

viii. Why are the Sikh youth rebelling and why are their questions being not answered according to their satisfaction?

ix Explain at least five procedures that have become rituals? From your own experience in the Gurdwara give more examples. Explain how to improve and still keep the basic tenants of the Sikh Religion.

x. Give reasons why rituals have crept into the Sikh Religion and how to stop them.

xi. Explain five different rituals not allowed by the Sikh Religion.

xii. Explain clearly what Guru Nanak stressed one should do in life instead of rituals.

xiii. Explain 6 changes that can be easily resolved by compromise and common sense and while maintaining the teachings as written in the Guru Granth Sahib?

xiv. Should politics and religion be separate or can they live side by side?

xv. What are the names of four Sikhs who achieved very important positions in the USA, Canada ,and India for the first time?.
xvi. What is the importance of Akal Takht?
xvii. Why are the five Takhts important in the Sikh religion?
xviii. What are the names of the five Takhts and their locations?
xvix. How can the absorbing power of the Sikh religion be increased?
xx. Write five practical aspects of the Sikh Religion to be done on a daily basis.

13. REFERENCES

[1] Tarlochan Singh. India's National Newspaper *The Hindu*, October 5, 2003. Slams Sikh sportsmen for not sporting turbans.
[2] Sangat Singh. Sikh Bulletin, California Vol. 3 No 11 Nov. 2001 pages 14 to 19.
[2A] Dr. Devinder Singh Chahal, E-mail, Sikh-Diaspora@yahoogroups.com April 23, 2006.
[3] *The Sikh Bulletin* Vol. 7, Number 2, February 2005 Page 3 referred to vis internet learning-zone@yahoogroups.com
Editor Hardev Singh Shergill, Roseville, California
[4] W.H. McLeod. "Sikhs of the Khalsa": *A History of the Khalsa Rahit, Oxford University Press*, New Delhi, 2003.
http://home.istar.ca/~cye/Sikhs%20of%20the%20Khalsa.html
Book Review by Jagpal S. Tiwana issued by The Maritime Sikh Society, Halifax, Canada
[5] Dr. Sukhraj Singh Dhillon. "Universality of the Sikh Philosophy: An Analysis" *The Sikh Review*, Volume 52:5, Number 605, pages 15-20, May 2004.
[6] Dr. Sukhbir Singh Kapoor. 1988, *The Ideal Man,* Khalsa College London Press. p. 108. Referenced to Dasam Granth, Akal Ustat Verses 85-85 Published by Bhai Jawahar Singh Kirpal Singh, Amritsar, India 1966.
[7] Google search for "Orthodox Jews in USA Question 2.21" Click for Question 2.21: How many Jews are there today in the USA?
Council of Jewish Federation, North American Jewish Data Bank
http://www.faqs.org/faqs/judaism/FAQ/02-Who-We-Are/section-22.htm
[8] E-mail, December 30, 2002 by Mr. Jagdish Singh of Sarnia, Canada. Page 14 Panthak Mute, compiled by Dr. Kirpal Singh, published by Dr. Man Singh Nirankari.
[9] Panth Khalsa
http://www.panthkhalsa.org/panth/LangarHukamNama.php
Frontline
http://www.hinduonnet.com/fline/fl1519/15190390.htm

[10] A. P. Kamath "Vancover Sikhs Snub Hard-liners" October 26, 1999. Yahoo.com, Search for Vancover Sikhs Snub Hard-liners, Click On Record http://www.rediff.com/news/1999/oct/26us4.htm
Also E-mail from Major Singh Thind, Secretary Khalsa Dewan Society, Vancouver, Canada. Sikh-Diaspora@yahoogroups.com
December 14, 2002

[11] Yahoo.com Search for 'Irving Hexman *Concise Dictionary of Religion'* Click for 'Princeton Library' Click for '*Concise Dictionary of Religion* (Irving Hexman)' Click for 'R' and find Ritual or
http://www.acs.ucalgary.ca/~nurelweb/concise/WORDS-R.html

[12] Dr. Doris Jakobsh, E-mail in Sikh-Diaspora@yahoogroups.com May 28, 2002.

[13] Alice Basarke, *The Sikh Bulletin*, Vol.3, No.11, pages 10-12, Roseville, California,USA, 2001.

[14] Dr. Harjinder Singh Dilgeer, "Gurdwara, Nishan Sahib, Nagara, Priest"
http://www.dilgeer.com/nishan.htm

[15] K.S. Duggal, 1989, *Sikh Gurus*, The Himalayan International Institute, Honesdale, Pennsylvania, USA Page 9.

[16] Varan Bhai Gurdass, Vaar 1,Pauri 33, 1.3
Reference Dr. Harbans Lal Academy of Guru Granth Studies, " Guru Nanak's Crusade against Ritualism and His Focus on the Essence" Arlington, Texas, USA Page 5 and
K.S. Duggal, 1989, Sikh Gurus, The Himalayan International Institute, Honesdale, Pennsylvania, USA Page 28.

[17] Google.com Search for Takhts
Click takhts.jpg
www.amritsar.com/ takhts.shtml

[18] Yahoo.com search for Akal Takht
Click for akaltakht2.jpg
www.sikh-history.com/sikhhist/events/akaltakht.html

[19] Google.com Search for Takht Patna Sahib
Click patna.jpg
allaboutsikhs.com/gurudwaras/gd-patna.htm

[20] Google.com Search for Takht Keshgarh Sahib
Click for anandpur1.jpg
www.sikhs.org/ gurdwaras/guru10-7a.htm

[21] Google.com Search for Takht Damdma Sahib
Click sridamdamasahib.jpg

[22] Goggle.com Search for Takht Hazur Sahib
Click for Skh.jpg
www.punjabilok.com/faith/gurudwara/sri_hazur.htm

[23] http://www.tribuneindia.com/2002/20020112/windows/main2.htm
Roopinder Singh "Remembering the U.S. Congressman" from India
Saturday, January 12, 2002, *The Tribune*, India

[24] Wikipedia, the free encyclopedia
Wikimedia Foundation Inc.
200 2nd Ave. South #358
St. Petersburg, FL 33701-4313 USA

[25] http://en.wikipedia.org/wiki/Ujjal_Dosanjh
Ujjal Dosanjh - Wikipedia, the free encyclopedia.

[26] http://news.bbc.co.uk/1/hi/world/south_asia/3725357.stm
Manmohan Singh, India's architect of reforms
By Soutik Biswas, BBC News May 22, 2004
Also
Indo-Asian News Service "World is watching India, it's time to make history, says PM" New Delhi, August 15, 2005
http://www.hindustantimes.com/news/181_1462214,0008.htm

[27] "J.J.Singh to be Army Chief" The Tribune, November 28, 2004
Online edition, Tribune News Service.
Also http://www.hindustantimes.com/news/181_1462214,0008.htm

[28] http://www.rememberingudaysingh.com/images/frame_uday.jpg

[29] http://www.arlingtoncemetery.net/uday-singh.htm

[30] Dr. Devinder Singh Chahal. 2000, "Understanding Sikhism," *The Research Journal*, Vol 2, No 1, Pages 41 to 46. Gurdwara Act, Definition of a Sikh.

[31] http://www.sikhs.org/rehit.htm
Sikh Reht Maryada.

[32] Gurcharan Singh Lamba. E-mail, January 24, 2000.
24 Shahedd Udham Singh Nagar, Jalunder City, Punjab, India.
Also by Dr. Devinder Singh Chahal 'Defining a Sikh' Institute for Understanding Sikhism, Lavel, Quebec, Canada

[33] Bradnock, Robert and Roma. 1996. *Buddhism and Jainism*. India Handbook 6th edition, Passport Books, Chicago, Illinois, USA, p. 73-78

INDEX

INDEX (CONTINUED)

INDEX (CONTINUED)

INDEX (CONTINUED)

INDEX (CONTINUED)

INDEX (CONTINUED)

INDEX

INDEX

INDEX